AAI-6/2? 45.00

Please remember that this is a library book,
and that it belongs only temporarily to each
person who uses it. Be considerate. Do
not write in this, or any, library book.

WITHDRAWN

WITHDRAWN

MIRRORS OF MINDS:
Patterns of Experience
in Educational Computing

MIRRORS OF MINDS:
Patterns of Experience
in Educational Computing

Papers from the
Center for Children and Technology, Bank Street College

Edited by

Roy D. Pea
New York University

Karen Sheingold
Bank Street College

WITHDRAWN

Ablex Publishing Corporation
355 Chestnut Street
Norwood, N.J. 07648

Printed in the United States of America.

Library of Congress Cataloging-in-Publication Data

Mirrors of minds.

  "September 1986."
  Bibliography: p.
  Includes index.
  1. LOGO (Computer program language)—Study and teaching.
2. Cognition in children. 3. Education—Data processing.
I. Pea, Roy D. II. Sheingold, Karen.
QA76.73.L63M57 1987 370.15'6 87-1274
ISBN 0-89391-422-3
ISBN 0-89391-423-1 (pbk.)

Cover art is an adaptation of *Sky and Water II* by M. C. Escher.

Ablex Publishing Corporation
355 Chestnut Street
Norwood, New Jersey 07648

CONTENTS

SHAPING THE TECHNOLOGY

LIST OF TABLES AND FIGURES

Figures

Tables

PREFACE

The computer is too often the starting point for contemporary discussions of the roles for technology in education. Treated as the newest delivery machine for teaching and learning, the computer and its kin—software, videodisc, and other information technologies—become the main topics. It is our conviction that a more productive orientation for the uses of technologies in education will result if one begins instead with the processes of education, and with the learner rather than the computer in the spotlight of inquiry. This book of essays is testimony to that conviction, and reveals the plethora of complex basic issues one faces in doing research centered on the learner and the educational process rather than the machine.

We find that the age of information makes new demands on the ways we think about education and on research relating to it. In a fundamental way, the possibilities are far more open-ended than in prior research. The nature of children's cognitive capabilities when knowledge-based tools are made available to support their thinking is a challenging terrain to explore. Moreover, the significance of social contexts and culture to students' learning with new technologies become all the more central to understand as the mutual influences of technology and context become apparent. Finally, basic questions arise about how information-handling tools and the new forms of literacy and skills they require change the very goals of education.

How might the researcher respond who is concerned with improving both our basic understanding of children's learning and thinking and the processes of education that depend on them? One could engage, as we sometimes have, in descriptive studies of what children learn in a particular classroom environment with an already-available software program. But it does not take very long to become dissatisfied with "existing" learning outcomes given the current state of educational computing, and to wish to create new, research-informed software environments, in which it is possible to craft learning contexts and software features for more effective education.

At the entry gate of this delicate bridge between descriptive and pre-scriptive studies, one faces difficult decisions in selecting orienting themes and directions. A few good research questions that can lead work down a productive path may be more important than a vast portfolio of data from studies with a too diffuse or overly specific orientation. For this reason, many chapters in this volume have a reflective character, seek-ing to clarify fundamental issues upon which a research program or de-velopment agenda can be built, or to critically situate particular studies in a broader context, such as mind-media studies, critical inquiry, defini-tions of literacy, conceptions of intelligence, or early symbolic develop-ment.

Given the many possible ways that technologies could be designed for children's learning and thinking, what are the ways in which uses of computers could positively influence the processes and outcomes of education and human development? As educators begin to integrate these powerful tools into educational practices, what contributions are made by unique aspects of this interactive medium, of children's inter-pretations of the machine and their patterns of software use, and of teaching practices and classroom organizational contexts? How might what we know about the history of media and innovation in education, and of the cognitive impacts of technologies such as writing systems in-form the directions we take in creating and testing new electronic learn-ing environments?

As the title to this volume of essays suggests, we have continually found that educational technologies serve as mirrors of minds and the cultures in which they "live." Rather than radically amplifying or trans-forming the processes of teaching and learning, as many predicted, they instead reflect the expectancies represented in classrooms and the knowl-edge and skills of individuals using them. Although one can point to dramatic cases of intellectual or affective development supported by computer environments, the broad-scale changes at even a classroom level, much less a societal one, appear to be slow to emerge and elusive to study. The comparison with studies of changes in thinking one might have carried out shortly after the invention of the printing press is apt. Would the profound societal impact and changes in patterns of thought documented centuries later by Eisenstein, Ong, and others have been observable so early?

This collection presents selected papers addressing aspects of the above questions from staff of Bank Street College's Center for Children and Technology (CCT). Since its inception in 1980, CCT's researchers have worked to define new research inquiries and to document students' and teachers' uses and understandings of educational technologies in an emerging field at the interface of psychology, education, and technology. Like a recent book edited by Norman and Draper (1986) on *User-Centered*

System Design, we find important perspectives in the cognate disciplines of the cognitive sciences—computer science, psychology, anthropology, linguistics, sociology, and artificial intelligence. But with education as the focus, other research is also central—in developmental psychology, and on the processes of education as they take place in classrooms, with their associated organizational constraints and supports. To consider the nature of the child-teacher-instructional environment system that shapes teaching practices and learning outcomes (with or without the new technologies), one must acknowledge these diverse contributions. The chapters of the book thus often straddle traditional academic boundaries in the interdisciplinary nature of the problems they address and in their methodologies of inquiry. We have found these travels invigorating, as well as essential, and the work exciting to do.

CCT research has provided basic and applied cognitive studies (e.g., on children learning computer programming), critical theoretical analyses, and formative analyses of the roles for new software and other information technologies in the cognitive and social growth of the child, in the organization of math and science learning in classrooms, and more broadly, in the restructuring of educational goals and practices in modern times. The studies and essays here rarely offer ''answers'' to the general questions such as those presented above. They more commonly serve to illuminate the inquiry space and to provide central dimensions for programs of research and development. We feel that this is appropriate in the early state of this interdisciplinary field.

The contributions selected for this volume are representative of the wide range of work at CCT, except for new software development and in-process research activities yet to be reported. We hope the collection provides a valuable sourcebook for scholars, students, educators, policy-makers, and designers/developers of educational technologies to learn about seminal issues in the new field emerging at the interface of psychology, education, and technology. Insofar as we have been at all successful in seeking to capture not only the particularities but general issues in child-computer interaction in educational contexts, the book should serve well as a foundational text for graduate studies in the field.

The contributions to the book are organized in three major sections, beginning with the first part of the book, USING TECHNOLOGY IN CONTEXT. In this section, the five chapters consider how cultural tools are shaped and changed by their use in the contexts for which they are made. In this sense, the uses of computer technologies mirror the classrooms, schools, and districts that they serve. They reflect not just minds, but also systems of social interaction and cultural values.

But the human systems that are mirrored in the use of technology are themselves interacting with and reflecting on the technology and its uses. The computer is a tool whose interpretation is central to its use in context. "What is the computer for?" has been a compelling question for those who have sought to incorporate it into the life of the classroom and school. Since the computer can be for many purposes, to ask what the computer is for is to ask, at least in part, what educational goals it best serves. The complex dialogue between the technology and its users (in this case, not only learners, but teachers and other educators, and the educational system itself) is one that we hope will lead to a rethinking of the goals of education, and to the provision of more powerful tools to support their pursuit.

In attempting to understand this dialogue between the technology and its users, we have examined the educational context at several levels —the classroom, the school, the district, the curriculum and its educational assumptions about what, as Alfred North Whitehead put it, is worth knowing. But one cannot look at the use of computers in schools without looking for change. We have both described the kinds of changes that occur (or do not) when computers are used in particular ways in specific settings and have offered analyses of the kinds of changes that we view as beneficial.

The chapters in this section address, both descriptively and analytically, how computer-based technologies may or may not contribute to educational innovations. The first chapter, *Interpretations of Logo in Practice*, by Jan Hawkins, details the experiences and reflections of two teachers involved in a two-year classroom experiment with the computer programming language and educational philosophy known as Logo. The chapter describes and illustrates the changing interpretations teachers make of Logo as they and their students interact with it. It is clear that over the course of that 2-year period the goals of the students and those of the teachers with respect to Logo do not always converge.

Denis Newman discusses and exemplifies the importance of the coordination of student and teacher goals in what he terms *Functional Learning Environments for Microcomputers in Education*. Teachers, students, and software together set up functional learning environments, where students' learning is purposive and the goals of teachers are also served. In the next chapter, Laura Martin examines preliminary findings on the adoption of the multimedia *Voyage of the Mimi* materials for math, science, and technology education by sixteen teachers in four school districts in the greater New York area. At the district level, she finds that aspects of district organization affect the success of the innovation.

Both the chapter by Sheingold, Martin, and Endreweit, *Preparing Urban Teachers for the Technological Future* and Simmons' contribution, *Beyond Basic Skills: Literacy and Technology for Minority Schools*, take urban schools as the context to be studied and analyzed. Sheingold et al. examine computer-related teacher education in urban districts and find reflected a core set of issues concerning both the profession of teaching and the challenges faced by urban schools. Teachers' shaping the use of technology becomes an opportunity, it is argued, for them to help design the school of the future. In Simmons' analysis of literacy in urban schools, he highlights a critical dilemma. The information age has changed the very meaning of literacy to one in which higher order thinking skills are central, yet urban schools continue, through their curriculum and uses of technology predominantly for drill and practice, to emphasize basic skills. He proposes using the power of the technology to help teachers implement new models of literacy in urban schools.

The second part of the book, TECHNOLOGY AND THINKING PROCESSES, is devoted to five chapters on technology and thinking processes. Three chapters focus on the cognitive requirements and outcomes of learning computer programming, in particular the Logo language derived from Lisp (the lingua franca of artificial intelligence) in order to make its powerful functions accessible to young children. As a whole, they make apparent that both learning to program and attaining broader cognitive outcomes from doing so, such as becoming better at planning or reasoning, are more challenging than many educators currently realize. We find that students' current reasoning capabilities are mirrored in programming, serving better as predictors of how well they learn to program rather than as general thinking skills outcomes.

In *Mapping the Cognitive Demands of Learning to Program*, Kurland, Clement, Mawby, and Pea present data from a multivariate research program designed to ascertain what cognitive skills, such as procedural reasoning, might predict students' progress in learning to program.

In their essay, *On the Cognitive Effects of Learning Computer Programming*, Pea and Kurland develop a critical review of existing findings on whether learning to program promotes the development of general higher mental functions. They recommend more of a differentiated and developmental perspective on what it means to "program," which would investigate how specific learning-teaching interactions in particular programming contexts contribute to transformations of a student's programming knowledge and skills and related reasoning abilities.

Logo and the Development of Thinking Skills by Pea, Kurland, and Hawkins offers a reflective and descriptive look at a series of empirical studies on whether elementary and middle-school students become better planners as a result of learning Logo programming. They discuss how their research rationale was adapted as findings from children's difficulties in learning to program emerged, and suggest how more positive outcomes could be engendered by creating a "culture of thinking" by means of any rich symbolic technology, including Logo.

In *Integrating Human and Computer Intelligence*, Pea explores from a Vygotskian perspective the important implications of theoretical and technical advances in artificial intelligence for the psychological study of learning and development, and for enhancing educational processes. He outlines how recent findings on giftedness, cross-cultural studies of cognition, and the development of computer expert systems suggest prospects for human-computer intelligent systems that can work together to solve problems, learn, and develop.

Sheingold discusses various roles for *The Microcomputer as a Symbolic Medium* in early childhood education and, in particular, the relationship between hands-on experiences and experiences with computer-based microworlds. She suggests ways in which computer experience can enhance early symbolic development, promote reflection on creative processes, and engender knowledge of computational devices per se.

In the third part of the book, SHAPING THE TECHNOLOGY, five chapters address important precursors to the design process, sources of ideas for design, and the kinds of research that can both precede and accompany design and development. Each chapter provides a somewhat different route toward the design and development process.

Although work at CCT has put learners and the classroom context at the center of study, the technology itself comprises a critical domain within which to instantiate and test theories. It provides a rapidly changing set of cultural tools to explore, understand, and, ultimately, mold to new educational purposes. The technology offers tools for demonstrating concretely our educational perspectives and aims, mirroring the minds of those who make it.

Three very general approaches are illustrated by the Hawkins chapter on *Computers and Girls*, the Char, Newman, and Tally chapter on *Interactive Videodiscs for Children's Learning*, and by the Hawkins, Mawby, and Ghitman paper on *Practices of Novices and Experts in Critical Inquiry*. Each takes a large problem—a population not well served, a technology ill-understood, an educational process not well implemented in classrooms —and, through research, sets the stage for design and development.

Specifically, Hawkins considers the meaning of computers to girls as we thus far understand it. For the most part, computers are tied to mathematics, science, and business—fields that often do not match girls' images of who they are or should be. Studies show large sex differences in interest and proficiency with computers. Yet, under some conditions, girls find computer-based activities engaging and useful. These conditions raise issues about both the type of software one might design for girls and, more generally, the uses to which computers are legitimately put in schools. For Hawkins, how the machine itself is interpreted is as important as the design of software that girls want to use.

Char, Newman, and Tally take a different tack. They view the interactive videodisc technology as one that has been underutilized for educational purposes. Is it a viable medium for children to make their way around, and for teachers and students to use in classrooms? While most videodiscs present programmed instruction with pictures, a few make good use of the novel features of this educational medium by taking advantage of its many visual and auditory features and giving the learner a great deal of control. Armed with some exemplary discs, for which they had to provide auxiliary software programs as supports for classroom activities, they began to discover the educational potentials of this medium. The research they did will inform future interactive video design.

The third example of very general routes to design and development is the chapter by Hawkins, Mawby, and Ghitman. The authors have identified critical inquiry as a set of higher-order skills they both want to understand and to help support students' learning of in classrooms. They have decided to design and develop a piece of software that scaffolds inquiry processes. In order to do so, however, they need to know much more about how novices and experts carry out inquiry tasks. Thus the research they report is intended to provide the empirical foundation for the development of a software tool for critical inquiry in classrooms. An underlying assumption here is that studies of novices and experts can enable researchers to identify aspects of the inquiry process for which technological support will be particularly useful.

The other two chapters in this section (Char & Hawkins, Hawkins & Kurland) broadly address issues of who contributes to the development of educational technology and how. In all of the development work that has been done by CCT staff, users are given a prominent role in shaping the technology by means of extensive formative research as software is being designed and implemented.

While both papers underscore the central importance of formative research for the development of educational technology, they emphasize different strategies for doing so. Char and Hawkins in, *Involving Teachers in the Formative Research and Design of "The Voyage of the Mimi,"* detail the many roles that teachers can play in the research, design, and development of educational software, drawing on their experience in the development of *The Voyage of the Mimi* materials. Hawkins and Kurland, in *Informing the Design of Software Through Context-Based Research,* highlight the importance of going beyond formative studies to develop viable educational software. They illustrate the importance of understanding the context within which a piece of software will be used. In addition, they show how, under particularly favorable circumstances, basic research can critically inform software design.

These chapters were all written within the last four years at the Bank Street College of Education. Many of them have appeared in print before and we would like gratefully to acknowledge the permission to reprint them that has been granted by our publishers:

Chapter 6: To appear in D.N. Perkins, J. Lochhead, & J. Bishop (Eds.), *Thinking*, Hillsdale, NJ: Erlbaum, 1986.
Chapter 7: In E. Klein (Ed.), *Children and computers: New Directions for Child Development* (Vol. 28), (pp. 75–96), San Francisco: Jossey Bass, 1985.
Chapter 8: *New Ideas in Psychology*, 1984, 2, 137–168. Pergamon Press.
Chapter 9: In M. Chen & W. Paisley (Eds.), *Children and microcomputers: Research on the newest medium* (pp. 193–212). Beverly Hills, CA: Sage, 1985.
Chapter 10: In P.F. Campbell & G.G. Fein (Eds.), *Young children and microcomputers* (pp. 25–34). Englewood Cliffs, NJ: Prentice-Hall, 1986.
Chapter 13: *Sex Roles*, in press. Plenum Press.

In addition, with the exception of Chapters 2, 5, 11, 12, 14 and 15, these reports have been widely distributed at cost as part of the Technical Report Series from the Center for Children and Technology, and subscribed to by many libraries, programs in teacher education, research groups and centers, graduate schools, and individual researchers, developers, and teachers. Terre Weinbel and Laura Bryant deserve special thanks for managing distribution tasks.

We would especially like to express our appreciation for the encouragement and support of the research reported in this book provided by The Carnegie Corporation of New York, CBS Educational and Professional Publishing, The Ford Foundation, National Institute of Education, National Science Foundation, Sony Corporation of America, The Spencer Foundation, U.S. Department of Education, and The Xerox Foundation. More detailed acknowledgements of funding support appear with each chapter.

Throughout our five years of existence as a Center, many people have worked with us on the research and development activities reported in these chapters in the capacity of research assistants and associates or education coordinators. We thank Jeffrey Aron, Nancy Cahir, Barbara Dubitsky, Kathleen Fiess, Carla Freeman, Monica Hamolsky, Margaret Heide, Sally MacKain, Thomas Roberts, William Tally, Kathy Wilson, and Jan Wootten for their contributions. George Burns and Michael Cook deserve special thanks for their active roles in our classroom research. Our secretaries Donna Bernardini, Marla Henriquez, Veronica Herman, Terre Weinbel, and Mei Mei Woo have provided word-processing support at different times throughout this period.

The copy editing of this manuscript was handled with great proficiency by production editor Ruth Kolbe, who has provided continually cheerful and ever-competent service since she began working on our technical report series several years ago. Kristine MacKain deserves special thanks for the excellent subject index.

It is hard to express how special an institution Bank Street College of Education has been, and what a unique context for research and development it fosters. It has housed our center since its beginnings, and provided the supportive environment necessary for our research activities to develop. Our colleagues in this setting have continually served to orient our work to utility in practice. The leadership of its president, Richard R. Ruopp, and his creative ideas for improving children's lives with new technologies, has been instrumental in making a productive home for the Center. Beyond this, of course, we are thankful to the teachers and children of Bank Street's own School for Children. Many other schools throughout the greater New York metropolitan area have helped us in our studies, but to our resident colleagues we offer a special debt of gratitude. Their willingness to participate in joint educational experiments, their forthrightness in questioning our assumptions, and their demonstration in practice of what it means to put children at the center of education, have affected and significantly improved our work.

We find particularly significant the original name of the college when it was founded in 1916—The Bureau of Educational Experiments. It is in that spirit that we have planned and carried out our work. We hope that others can sense our excitement about studying children's thinking and education with and through educational technologies, and that the fruits of our labors might inspire others to advance the education that will empower children to face the challenges of the future.

Roy D. Pea

Karen Sheingold

September 15, 1986

PART I

USING TECHNOLOGY IN CONTEXT

CHAPTER 1

THE INTERPRETATION OF LOGO IN PRACTICE

Jan Hawkins

Innovations in education seldom simply arrive and radically redefine the activity or meaning of learning situations. Rather, educational innovations take hold gradually, affecting certain aspects of the setting, and are interpreted and shaped by the participants. As one aspect of a research program conducted at Bank Street College's Center for Children and Technology, we were concerned with understanding how a particularly promising educational innovation—using computer technology to learn general problem-solving skills through programming in the Logo language—was assimilated into the classroom.

Educational innovations, which are often embodied in radically new materials (e.g., new math), new perspectives on learning (e.g., open education), or new technologies (e.g., language labs, television, and computers), have complex histories in individual classrooms and in American education in general. Like ideas or text materials, such innovations are interpreted in terms of the knowledge, experience, and setting of the teachers and students who encounter them. Thus, they do not change the broad educational landscape by leveling what was already there, but instead offer opportunities for reshaping the existing content in individual settings. One must also expect interpretations of the innovations themselves as they are practiced in the complex systems of classrooms. This is what happened with Logo.

The following is an account, itself an interpretation, of the ways in which two teachers thought about, grappled with, and practiced Logo in their classrooms over the course of two years. One source of information is utilized: the perspectives of the teachers as expressed in interviews throughout the two years, and in journals they kept during the first two months of the experiment. The teachers began with a set of beliefs and expectations that were revised and developed as they attempted to fit their classrooms to Logo, and Logo to their classrooms.

3

The coherence of the teachers' developing views based on what they thought, tried, and observed is important to preserve as an interpretive voice for the experiment. It is but one of several accounts that can be given of our larger experiment. The overall research program was designed to help us understand the cognitive and social effects of children's experiences with Logo and computers in classrooms. We conducted many studies and collected several types of information, including longitudinal case studies of individual learners, experimental studies of planning skills and understanding of programming concepts, assessments of expertise, observational studies of interactions in classrooms, videotaped studies of peer collaboration, and analyses of collaborative skills in group-structured situations. It was essential that all these studies—careful, detailed fragments of the whole—be seen in a single context, that of the classroom experience of Logo. In order to provide this descriptive context, teachers were interviewed, classrooms were regularly observed, lessons were recorded, and records of children's work were collected. The interviews with the teachers were particularly rich and, taken together, provide a coherent picture of what took place.

THE DEVELOPMENT OF LOGO

Logo was developed as a programming language for children by a team at MIT in the late 1960s and the 1970s; Seymour Papert (1980) has become its principal spokesperson. The language was designed to introduce children to programming concepts and, through this experience, to develop powerful higher order thinking skills that could be transferred to other contexts. Logo is accompanied by a particular pedagogy: Children are to learn through self-guided discovery methods, pursuing their own goals and ideas with minimal adult intervention or systematic presentation of concepts or skills. Thus, it has been claimed that children develop general problem-solving skills through self-initiated and self-guided exploration of Logo. Logo has been described as a special and rich environment for the acquisition of high-level logical and reasoning skills (Papert, 1980; Papert, Watt, diSessa, & Weir, 1979).

The availability of Logo also filled a need in the educational community: Computers were rapidly being acquired by schools, but without good software or clear notions for defining their role and use. Logo offered a powerful way of using the machines, a rationale with broad-ranging and highly desirable learning outcomes, accompanied by respect for the child's natural capacities and learning initiatives. Our research program was designed to look closely at the development of children's understanding in the most salient educational environment offered by our culture—the classroom.

At the time of our research (September 1981–February 1984), Logo was a new and relatively untried system for use in education. While the accomplishments of individual students using the language had been documented (see Papert et al., 1979), most material described the powerful potential of Logo. There was no critical analysis of the cognitive concepts or processes required to achieve facility in using Logo, or of its incorporation into classrooms.

THE TEACHERS AND CLASSROOMS

The study was located in two classrooms at an independent school in Manhattan. One classroom included 25 (11 boys, 14 girls) 8- and 9-year-old children (third and fourth graders); the other consisted of 25 (11 boys, 14 girls) 11- and 12-year-old children (fifth and sixth graders). The children encompassed a variety of ethnic and socioeconomic backgrounds and a range of achievement levels. Each classroom had six microcomputers: three Apple II Plus computers and three Texas Instruments (TI) 99/4 computers.

These classrooms were selected because the children met our age requirements, and because the teachers expressed interest in participating in the research. These were experienced and talented teachers. The basic philosophy advocated by the Logo developers was compatible with the teachers' perspectives on education, generally described as a child-centered learning approach.

The teachers (two men), as well as the school math coordinator (a woman), attended a 6-week summer course in Logo conducted by the New York Academy of Sciences, with Dr. Papert as one of the instructors. Skeptical at first, both teachers became engrossed in the topic of programming and completed the course feeling optimistic about Logo's potential as an important learning experience for children. The teachers and the coordinator continued to meet regularly to advance their understanding of Logo and to help one another with their programming work during the first part of the school year.

Over the course of the experiment, the teachers acquired considerable skill in Logo in particular, and programming in general. In addition to the two years of work with the children in their classrooms, the teachers developed and taught courses in Logo and computers in education to master's degree candidates in a graduate program. Together they wrote a book about Logo applications in education, and guides for educational software designed to introduce programming concepts.

In the spring of the pilot year, six microcomputers were placed in each of the two classrooms, and Logo became a part of the classroom activities for the last two months of the school year. Throughout the next two school years, the teachers sought to engage the children's interest in and develop their understanding of Logo. Our research period, therefore, covers three groups of about 50 children each: one 2-month pilot period, and two complete cycles of school years. Thus, the teachers had the opportunity to work out and rework their approach to the innovation, modifying the introductory material and course of instruction for each successive group.

INTERVIEWS

In addition to frequent informal discussions, each teacher was formally interviewed ten times throughout the research period. These interviews constitute the bulk of the material discussed here. Each session lasted between 45 minutes and two hours, and was conducted by one or more members of the research team. The interviews were structured, covering some of the same questions each time and focusing on new issues as they arose. The teachers were invited to reflect and speculate on their experiences, and the interviewer(s) encouraged them to develop their ideas throughout the discussion. In addition to these dialogues, the teachers kept journals of their experiences with computers during the initial 2-month pilot period. This material is cited where appropriate, particularly because it provides some detailed information about what the teachers initially thought about the innovation.

METHOD OF ANALYSIS

The interview sessions were tape-recorded and transcribed for analysis. Qualitative analyses were performed on the material. The transcriptions were read several times by several readers in order to develop a system for categorizing the material. The interviews were divided into segments according to class, date, and overall theme. The themes included definitions and redefinitions of Logo as a classroom element, discussions of cognitive abilities and transfer, evaluations of Logo and problems encountered, strategies for supporting the learning or teaching of Logo, and the social context of the classroom. The interview material was then reorganized by theme and date so that changes in the experience within each of these categories over the two years could be noted.

THE ROLE OF RESEARCH

Computers and Logo were introduced into these classrooms as part of a research project to document and analyze the cognitive and social effects of this technological innovation for education. Rather than imposing a point of view or curriculum, we, as researchers, were interested in how the teachers themselves chose to incorporate this innovation. It was a collaborative venture, and what each of us saw had some influence on what the others thought and did. The children were also aware that they were participating in an "experiment" which was intended to try out computers and Logo in classrooms.

The following account—a description of what the teachers did with Logo and how they thought about its value for the children—is divided chronologically into two sections. First, we describe the pilot period and the first year of the experiment for each classroom. The activity during the second year, which was significantly reorganized, is described in the second section.

Throughout the project, teachers pondered two major questions: "What is Logo and what is its value?" and "How should I organize a learning experience with Logo?" In their interviews, the teachers defined and redefined Logo; they worked to understand how Logo could be used as a learning tool in the classroom, and to define its possible value for children. These definitions and evaluations changed considerably over the course of the two years.

The fact that these interpreters' relationship to Logo was as "teacher" in a particular kind of setting is critical. The development of a perspective is based on the mode of engagement: The teacher's perspective will be quite different from the researcher's, which, in turn, will differ from that of the software developer. These teachers were concerned with roles for Logo as part of a complex, ongoing, and multifaceted program of learning that they had carefully constructed during their previous years of teaching.

SECTION 1. PILOT PERIOD AND FIRST YEAR: WHAT IS LOGO AND WHAT IS ITS VALUE FOR CHILDREN?

The Teachers' Expectations

Before beginning the Logo experiment with their summer training sessions, both teachers (hereafter known as Dan [the younger class] and Jeff [the older class]) were somewhat critical of and skeptical about computers and their role in the larger culture. Both reported that they had had frustrating experiences with the technology prior to their involvement with the experiment. For example, at the culmination of a law suit, Dan had been told that there was no legal basis for his complaint since he had been the victim of a "computer error": "It's in the computer. There's no responsibility." Jeff, on the other hand, recognized that computers were part of our culture, but that there was great potential for misuse. His concern was that use of the technology by children might be trivialized and focus on videogames rather than educational applications. Despite these experiences and reservations, both teachers volunteered for the intensive experiment and enthusiastically looked forward to learning more about the technology and its potential for classroom use. Logo seemed a promising possibility for children in their classrooms because of its claim to engage and develop general problem-solving skills.

Both teachers found the summer seminars engrossing and challenging. One reported that he had had trouble picking up programming concepts, but that he very quickly became immersed. He described the learning process as one of reaching a plateau of knowledge, struggling for a while, and then reaching another plateau—a unique experience for him because he was used to effortless learning and acquiring skills without difficulty. Consequently, he sometimes felt frustrated as he wrestled with Logo. The other teacher found the logic of programming easy to learn, but reported that "it was difficult to orchestrate the commands for a purpose," that it was often hard to figure out how to construct a program to suit a desired goal.

At the end of the training period, both teachers felt that they had made significant progress, but that they had a considerable way to go before they could be fully functional with the language in the classroom setting.

Thus, at the beginning of the experiment, Dan and Jeff were enthusiastic about the educational potential of Logo. They found the claims for the development of general problem-solving skills in the context of a self-discovery pedagogy to be persuasive. Although they had some reservations, they expected that Logo could be a powerful learning tool for children to explore. Two kinds of expectations were expressed. First, that Logo could be a unique type of school task for the practice and development of certain types of *thinking skills:*

It could enhance kids' ability to deal with problems abstractly.

* * * * *

It could help them to structure their thoughts and think about things on an abstract level—maybe make it easier for them to plan out something on paper, communicate at a meeting, draw plans for something to build, understand geometry.

* * * * *

It might help kids doing logical and analytic thinking.

It's real work as opposed to assigned problems to solve. They'll learn to be better thinkers, to discuss questions and mull things over—a sense of self-initiation, setting up tasks and solving them. I hope they'll be able to discuss a process whereby they solve a problem better, how to go about it, and I hope it will generalize to any problem, like scenery for a play. They'll be able to break it down into pieces, to use analytic skills.

With respect to the types of skills engaged, the teachers felt that Logo might be a vehicle for (a) developing analytical skills that could be used to approach and solve many types of problems, and (b) giving kids conceptual tools and language for discussing, presenting, and communicating about the problem-solving process.

However, each teacher also expressed reservations about Logo's possible limitations:

> I'm not sure, though, to what extent working on computers makes kids deal with the most important questions they have to deal with—it's for intellectual, not affective or value, questions. Analytic thinking could be helped by computers, but I'm not sure of its role in life—the breaking down of a situation into components.
>
>   *   *   *   *   *
>
> I still sometimes wonder about its purpose—what really do children learn from it?

It is interesting to note that neither teacher disussed the value of Logo in terms of the importance of learning programming as a skill; it was interpreted primarily as a means for learning general problem-solving skills.

The second major expectation was that Logo could be a learning environment that supported *self-initiated, expressive learning.* The innovation was valued for the claim that children could individually engage in developing their own skills, at their own pace, and in the context of self-selected goals:

> The best scenario as far as I'm concerned is children working on their own creations, not drill and practice or presenting of concepts. I'd like them to feel, "I want to follow my own ideas."
>
>   *   *   *   *   *
>
> You should do whatever you feel like, according to your own imagination. You get immediate results, rather than have to find out all the things necessary to deal with programming—there's a possibility that kids will be working on their own ideas independently.
>
>   *   *   *   *   *
>
> In a classroom, it's a different experience. There are times when you shouldn't be answerable to anyone else, it's completely personal, no other input. It's a piece of work that is theirs and they will talk about.

In terms of the classroom curriculum, both teachers thought that Logo was most similar to creative writing because it offered children a medium for expressing their own ideas. Logo was unique, however, in that the skills and ideas developed in this expressive context were *logical and analytical.*

The Pilot Period: Classroom Work

For the pilot period, Dan, the teacher of the younger group, decided to impose little structure on Logo learning. He was committed to the position that Logo was a self-expressive medium for children, fully supportive of self-discovery learning:

> It's different from most of what goes on except for writing. They can use it in their own way. If it's a powerful tool, they can use it themselves.

The principal structure he felt he needed to provide was the scheduling of work (two 1-hour periods a week for each child, plus lunch and before school; organization of partners), and helping with the complexity of the relative geometry of the turtle movements ("eliminate the geometrical traps"). Dan decided to show the children the basic turtle movement commands (e.g., forward, back, left, right, color commands), and then "have them play with it a lot. But I won't give them ideas. I want to see their own ideas."

Over the course of the six weeks, Dan had only two meetings with the whole class, in which he demonstrated the capability of Logo "sprites" (objects whose shape, color, and movement can be user-defined) and introduced the concept of programming. All other teaching was done individually. Occasionally, Dan wrote commands or small programs on the blackboard for the children to copy and try out. Scheduling presented a problem for him—how to arrange for all kids to work on the computers regularly. But he also reported that the presence of the computers loosened up the classroom space and kept half the class occupied, enabling him to work intensively with small groups on other things.

Contrary to expectations, Dan found he had to supply the children with ideas, which he did on an individual basis. He found the projects some children chose to do disappointing. The children looked to their world of experience with computers to find projects; many of them decided to do videogames, and were disappointed by their inability to reproduce them in Logo.

Additional problems encountered by Dan were: (a) many children didn't know how to "take the next step" in their projects; (b) children found the angle inputs required by turtle geometry to be a problem; (c) many had difficulty with the idea of information storage in computers—they were puzzled by the question: "If the program is stored on a disk and you recall it, where is the information?" (Mawby, Clement, Pea, & Hawkins, 1984).

Like Dan, at the outset of the experiment Jeff decided to provide the children with the basic commands and allow them to follow their own interests and pace as they worked with Logo. He decided to begin with turtle graphics and bring in sprites later in the term. The children were encouraged to develop their own goals, and Jeff supported their learning either individually or in small groups. No large-group meetings were held to teach computer concepts; when the children wanted to know something, they asked either Jeff or an experienced peer. Ideas spread through the class, and Jeff found that children shared programs freely with one another. He anticipated that the children would have trouble with certain concepts (e.g., variables and directionality), but expected them to master these in three to four weeks. The children were scheduled for two periods a week with the computer, and they could elect to do additional work before school or during lunch. However, additional computer work was contingent on having finished all other assignments.

The Pilot Period: Reflections
At the end of the 2-month pilot period, both teachers were excited about the experiment and had observed some children doing sophisticated and interesting things with Logo. Dan commented: "Some kids got involved with computers on an abstract level and thought about computer problems in a way they wouldn't think about other problems." However, both teachers were beginning to express reservations about Logo, which they made explicit in several ways. Contrary to expectations, they had noticed substantial individual differences in children's interest in and learning of Logo. A few children became thoroughly engrossed in the activity, whereas others showed no interest or even hostility. Jeff said: "I wasn't able to figure out how to get the uninvolved kids involved." He was dissatisfied with many of the projects chosen by the children, such as the replication of videogames.

Concern was also expressed about the shallowness of the children's knowledge. The teachers felt that many children's level of engagement and contact with Logo was too low to permit them to make sense of what was going on.

> They simply seemed to accept the logic of the computer on its own grounds rather than struggling to understand it: "If that's the way you do it, that's the way you do it."

*   *   *   *   *

> I thought they would be going home and deciding how to program things, but no. They seemed to work on programming only when they actually worked on the machines.

*   *   *   *   *

> I was not surprised at the direction—games—but I was surprised at how little discussion there was other than "what should we do next."

As Dan became more familiar with the Logo language, it became less clear to him just what depth of understanding was desirable for the children:

> The kids *do* understand it because they can use it. I see that there's a great limitation to *my* understanding—I don't *really* know what it means to "make quotes" or "read character." It's a whole program that I just have to accept,

that I have never bothered to find out just what goes on in that program. So I discovered that I wasn't giving kids the opportunity to use things that they didn't understand....It's led me to present elements in a way that is functional to them. It's possible to go a lot farther this way.

Neither teacher saw evidence of the transfer to other areas of the cognitive abilities gained through programming. Initially, they focused on the Logo language as a potentially powerful environment for developing general thinking skills; after two months, they were beginning to be skeptical of this claim.

I didn't see much cognitive effect. I didn't see them talk about programming, and I didn't see the skills showing up anywhere else.

* * * * *

Transfer? It's hard to say where it shows up. They weren't even thinking that way about the computers a lot of the time.

The First Year: Revisions for Classroom Work

At the beginning of year 1, both teachers decided that more structure was required if the children were to become competent users of Logo. They elected to give further individual support for the discovery and development of Logo project ideas, and to require greater adherence to a work schedule by all the children.

Dan gave the children little preparation other than to introduce the functions of drawing and animation. Since 17 of the children in his class had been in the pilot Logo group, Dan decided to have them help the inexperienced children learn basic concepts. This strategy "ended up hard" because, when the experienced children were paired with the inexperienced, "the experienced ones already had the idea of programming and took over."

To support children's formulation of project ideas, problems and techniques were written on the blackboard by Dan as a source of information. The problems were intended both to challenge the students and to give them ideas about what could be done. He also supplied mimeographed handouts on these topics so that the children could use them at the computers and, if they wished, take them home. Dan continued to work with the children individually or in small groups as the need arose; there were no large-group sessions. He felt that it was too early to begin critical discussions with the students about the technology:

It would be interesting but they're very young, very young to have a critical perspective. I'm going to get a lot of these videogame junkies talking about how wonderful it is. So that puts me in the position of having to do editorializing for them, or having to sit there saying, "uh huh."

Jeff also organized the first year's work of the older students around helping them find and work on their own projects. Teaching took place individually and in small groups, and Jeff encouraged the experienced children to help the inexperienced ones. Meetings were held to talk about the projects under construction, and about computers in the larger cultural context. Computer work was no longer contingent on finishing other work.

The teachers increasingly recognized the complexity of learning Logo. Their attention was beginning to coalesce on the skills and experiences needed to do interesting things with Logo as a programming environment, rather than discussing Logo as a vehicle for learning general cognitive skills. For example, three months into the school year, Jeff expressed his goals for the children in these terms: ''My underlying goal is for them to learn to put together programs of greater and greater complexity, to be able to achieve more and more with programs.''

By November, Jeff reported that many children were having difficulty understanding important programming concepts: Recursion was vague to most, and variables and procedures were not used effectively. The learning was child-centered: Individuals were assigned to work twice a week and during these periods were free to explore the uses of the Logo language. Jeff worked with individuals, occasionally making a suggestion about how to expand the program, but he did not require children to progress to new concepts. He also provided written sheets and cards for the children, which served as mnemonic devices for certain techniques. Occasionally, he gave them a complete program if he felt it was easier for them to use it as an unanalyzed tool. The children sometimes adapted these programs to suit their own purposes. Jeff recognized that the children often chose projects that were too ambitious to complete, and he tried to help them to proceed more gradually.

In February, Jeff offered some programmed games to the children and suggested that they try to make modifications. This strategy for learning did not work well because the children preferred playing the games to playing with the programs. In addition, those children who were sophisticated enough to make interesting modifications in their programs were already involved in other self-development work. At this point, Jeff attempted some group lessons on special topics, such as random numbers, but after a few sessions did not find this format particularly successful for getting kids involved or helping them to develop new skills. Jeff also began teaching to selected individuals the use of more sophisticated Logo topics (e.g., xy coordinates, conditionals, tests, toplevel, and addressing memory locations). He encouraged children to take on certain kinds of programming goals (e.g., animation, guessing games, and word games). He reported that he had no formal class curriculum in computers: The children who were interested kept making new things; the children who lost interest did very little.

By the end of the year, Jeff described his goals for Logo entirely in terms of computers: "My goal is mastery—being able to manipulate and make sense of what to do with computers." Similarly, Dan expressed the value of Logo in a more limited fashion than he had at the outset of the experiment: "It's good for teaching about programming."

As a result of their increasing awareness of the complexity of the language, both teachers struggled throughout the year to understand what the children needed to know as they learned Logo, and the value of devoting significant amounts of time to its practice.

> In teaching subjects, I generally have a clear idea of what kind of skills I expect them to be learning and, in giving them specific work, I have a good sense of what kids are able to do—analyzing and assessing their work. With the computer, it's still an early stage of development in my thinking. It's very difficult to understand what is going on with kids' understanding of computers, and this is true for kids who are very good with it and those who are not very good. I haven't yet built up a way of analyzing what happens when I give them a task, and what it means to succeed. I will think that the next step will be too hard and it won't be, or I'll think that it'll be simple and it turns out to be difficcult. It can be very unnerving because no matter how good the kids' work is, there's a lack of understanding on my part of what really they're doing and where they ought to be going with it. [Dan]

Thus, Dan continued to revise his Logo program throughout the year. Midway, he added the element of "optional lessons" to his learning structure—giving occasional lessons on a special topic to a small group of children who expressed interest (e.g., how to write procedures with variables). The technique was demonstrated, documentation sheets were distributed, and the children who participated could then diffuse the information to other members of the class. Teaching was done individually or in small groups, based on expressed interest. Large-group meetings were considered inappropriate because Dan believed that individual learning styles varied. At this point, like Jeff, Dan began to give children programs in Logo that they could use as tools in their own work:

> One thing that's really changed is my thinking about giving the kids programs. This came about with the "read character" program, which seemed like a very complicated program to just hand to the kids. I didn't know at what point they would understand what was happening until I showed the program to one kid who was not terribly concerned with understanding what the syntax meant. They were very capable of understanding how to type it out and which parts needed to go where, and therefore had their own understanding of how the program worked.

"Computer sharing" was introduced as a method of communicating information: The class began to meet as a group, and individual children presented and explained their work.

In the spring, Dan noticed a loss of interest in Logo on the part of many children, and began to work harder at scheduling time at the computer for all of them. He felt that sequenced presentation of material was not possible because the children were working with a variety of things. His support consisted of helping children solve local problems, and working with them on ideas for moving ahead with their projects. The focus of the small-group sessions switched from demonstration of de-contexted techniques to demonstration of programs embodying specific techniques. As noted earlier, Dan had recognized that a major problem for the children was "putting the pieces together." He therefore decided to show them whole, working programs in order to give them some idea of how the techniques functioned in the achievement of goals. He also began to work with the children to help them connect a series of programs into one "superprogram":

> A major part of what I've been showing them is how to connect a series of programs, how to think about joining specific things together to make a big program. If they can think about one thing at a time and break it down that way, it'll be easier for them to think about a whole program and put it together. We've worked this way on animation and how to put a story to it.

Dan also tried to build links between the programming work and the math curriculum:

> The Apple can use "setxy" commands to draw lines. You can vary the shape by varying the coordinates. I have been giving them experience with coordinates, which is also part of the third-fourth grade curriculum, so I'd be doing it with them anyway. I want them to have this experience so that they can have it as a tool and as something that is part of the curriculum. We can do this as part of the math curriculum and also to advance their knowledge of the computer.

At this point in the year, Dan was unclear about how much the children understood and, consequently, about how he should be helping them.

By the end of the first year, Dan recognized the necessity for a theory of Logo instructional support and had accumulated enough experience to begin to develop one. Some of the problems of the first year's work were revealed in his account:

> I was teaching programming skills piecemeal, and expected them to find a use for that skill. I hoped they'd come up with the picture. I realized near the end that I should show them the results of having the skill and then see what

they do with it. After the demonstration I would say, "You have to do such and such."

Based on his experiences with two classes of children, Dan began to make his theory of instruction for Logo explicit. Both he and Jeff decided that there was a need to teach specific skills in a coherent sequence (e.g., what is a program, what is a variable, recursion, conditionals, tests); to context the skills in sample programs; to provide support for further developing their ideas; and to come back and talk about results. Encouragement to practice the skills was seen as important because

> It was rare for children to go beyond [their initial efforts]. They somehow stay pleased with things as they are, the passive approach. They want immediate results, so they pick small goals and are pleased with themselves.

Dan also decided that he wanted to include information about the history and function of the technology in the general culture as a part of the programming work, thereby offering a perspective for the children that would help them to see how this work fit into the world.

By the end of the year, Jeff reported that it was difficult to have group discussions about the computers because the uninterested children reacted negatively to the idea. Some didn't like the precision required for doing things on computers; others were interested in spending their time elsewhere. Throughout the year, Jeff had attempted to provide support to the children as needed in order to advance their work. He estimated that about 85% of the teaching was done individually or with two or three children. During much of this time, Jeff remained committed to the idea that the children would learn Logo most successfully through developing their own projects. His efforts to engage the uninterested children included project suggestions, teaching skills by demonstrating interesting programs, and giving children programs to modify.

Unlike the younger children, computer sharing was not popular among the older group: "It just didn't connect with what they wanted to do." Because he found that disk housekeeping was a problem—the children couldn't find their work on the disks—Jeff resolved to teach good file-saving techniques and the importance of documenting programs during the second year. He also felt that teachers needed a good deal of support in order to carry out the Logo agenda:

> The skills a teacher needs are monumental. The kids says, "I'd like to do this," and sometimes I have no idea how to do it. So I said, "Let's think of a simple thing, a part of it." I was afraid that was dishonest—I had that happen many times. We need to get expert help. It's not like helping the kids to write a story, where I'm never at a loss.

The First Year: Reflections on Cognitive Skills and What the Children Learned

During the first year, the teachers shifted their focus from Logo as a learning environment for general problem-solving skills to Logo as a context for learning about programming and computers. One reason for this shift was that the teachers were accumulating evidence that caused them to reinterpret the value of Logo:

1. There were large individual differences among children in interest and skill with Logo.
2. Many children had difficulty "putting the pieces together" into projects.
3. Many children reached "plateaus" of skill and didn't seem to be motivated to advance.
4. Many children had a relatively shallow grasp of the functioning of the language and were not flexible in applying what they learned in one context to a new problem.

Individual Differences. Both teachers noticed and were concerned about the wide variation in the children's commitment to working with Logo. At the end of the year, they estimated that about one-quarter of the children were very much involved in the work, one-half were moderately involved, and one-quarter were not at all interested. The teachers were concerned that many of the unenthusiastic individuals were girls (e.g., Hawkins, Chapter 13, this volume). Given their expectations about Logo's broad appeal for children, the teachers were surprised at the effort required to motivate children. They had great difficulty in getting the uninterested children involved in the work. In this effort, the organizing idea was to help children find a project or goal for themselves as a means of getting into the system; the learning of skills was subordinated to the articulation of goals:

> Another problem is that not every kid has a project that they're working on—that was my goal at the beginning. I haven't insisted because of practical pressures. Also, because some of the kids need a lot of play, a lot of directed play...I was heading for everyone having a project real soon, but I've changed that. This is *my* learning about the process. [Jeff, in November]
>
> *   *   *   *   *
>
> Trying to get kids who are not interested in projects on their own to get interested—that has been my struggle all along. I've been trying to get them to find activities that they're interested in. [Jeff, in February]
>
> *   *   *   *   *
>
> My biggest task is to get kids interested who aren't doing very much. It's similar to writing in that I focus on helping kids to develop skills. [Jeff, in June]

By the end of the first school year, both teachers were beginning to voice concerns about the possibility that, in contrast to the idea that Logo was, per se, an exciting and beneficial environment for all children, certain prior skills or interests might be prerequisites for enthusiastic engagement with Logo:

> A lot of abstract thinking is required. I wonder about limitations on people's ability to do programming. Maybe some people can do it and some can't [do it] as well because of the highly symbolic abstract nature of it. It may be a misconception that people need to learn how to program computers to survive in the world. It may be a very limited field, more inaccessible than I thought— maybe it's not like reading that anyone can do. . . . I have no impression that it changed the thinking of kids, but I don't feel that what I did with computers was particularly successful, so maybe it wasn't a fair test. And it could be that the kids that were good were already thinking that way. [Jeff, in June]
>
> * * * * *
>
> Kids who do logical thinking develop programming skills. I now think that the reverse is unlikely. [Dan, in June]

Making Programs from Pieces. From the beginning of year 1, Dan was particularly concerned with his observation that, although many children learned individual commands or techniques, they had difficulty putting them together into coherent programs:

> Even though they have all these pieces of things that they know they can do, it is very hard for most of them to put all these pieces together—it only happened in two or three cases. [Dan, in October]
>
> * * * * *
>
> I began to demonstrate actual programs to them rather than just techniques. The kids weren't putting the pieces of the techniques together to make wholes. Some kids, yes, but for the most part kids were having a hard time seeing all the pieces and taking the big step. And even when they do, they'll get satisfied and go no farther. [Dan, in February]

Jeff also reported that putting commands together to construct programs became increasingly difficult for many children as the year progressed and the programs became more complex. Translating an idea into the code required to execute it was a difficult task for both children and teachers. The children often changed their goals to accommodate the program, rather than trying to rewrite the code in order to achieve their original goals.

Plateaus of Skill. Both teachers reported what they found at first to be a strange phenomenon: Many children reached a "plateau" of skill, sometimes quite early in their learning, and were content to continue constructing programs at that level. The teachers then realized that this could be said of many areas of the curriculum, but that it was especially true of the programming work with its individual-project focus. This was particularly demanding of the children because it required them to be self-motivated in learning about and adapting new tools to their own purposes. The teachers directed their efforts at encouraging the children to do variations on their work, and offering them new concepts that they might incorporate into their work, thereby gaining new skills.

Depth of Knowledge. The teachers also found that most children did not have a very deep understanding of many of the commands or the structure of programming, and thus were not flexible in applying particular commands or concepts to new problems. As discussed above, the teachers began to realize that it was increasingly unclear to them just what "full" understanding of the language entailed: How deep did the children's understanding of the functioning of the system have to be? As they thought about this problem, both teachers expressed as their overall goal that children be able to use the concepts flexibly. The core of their implied definition of expertise was that a child should be able to accomplish what he or she wants to do in programming the computer. However, by the end of the year, most children were well below this functional level.

> Some kids know commands as nonflexible units; others can use the same command as a tool. I see differences between kids in using a command as a sophisticated tool and using it without clear understanding. [Jeff, in February]
>
> * * * * *
>
> There is a gap between what kids want to do and the skills they need to do it. Some programs have to be very complex to do simple things. [Jeff, in June]
>
> * * * * *
>
> I would like them to understand the instructions...if the kids had an idea, they would be able to do it. [Dan, in February]

The First Year: Reflections on Self-Initiated Learning

As noted above, the second idea that guided the incorporation of Logo into the classrooms was that it would support self-guided, expressive learning. Logo was an environment where children could learn complex, logical skills through a medium that allowed child-centered expression, as opposed to teacher-directed learning of component skills. Although they made significant modifications, the teachers remained committed to the organizing framework of child-selected Logo projects throughout the 2-year experiment. The following account summarizes the issues they encountered as they reinterpreted the value of Logo as a tool for self-initiated learning.

During the pilot period, the teachers had begun to realize that the children were having difficulty developing their own goals for Logo—a considerable problem for a learning experience firmly rooted in self-motivated expression. But they were committed to the strategy that the children be given access to Logo and then make their own decisions about what they wanted to do with it:

> I see the computer as another area of the curriculum, an area that it's very much up to them what they want to do. I would never want to give a kid something to do on the computer that the kid would say, ''No, I don't want to do that.'' I'd rather it remain optional until they have adequate command of the language....I would like the kids to be motivated to learn, so they can decide if the computer is something they want to express themselves with. [Dan]

Throughout the first year of the experiment, the teachers struggled with the problems involved in maintaining the self-initiated framework for learning, while becoming increasingly aware of the complexity of the learning skills required in this domain. Many children had to struggle with both the computer skills and finding their own goals for the work. This theme remained a constant and unresolved tension throughout the experiment:

> I didn't give them a basic introduction. Basically I wanted to get kids thinking about a project. I'd leave that up to them, but I realize from last year that they really need a lot of structure for their thinking about what to do on the computer. Their imaginations seem to stop at a certain point. It's sort of shocking for me to see that. [Dan, in October]

But the self-initiated orientation was valued by the teachers, who saw it as especially powerful for those children who became engrossed in the programming work:

> With their programs I have rarely said where I want them to go. Part of the reason is that kids have their own ideas of where they want them to go. It generally happens that kids say, ''I'm done.'' Kids don't say that with computers. If they do a program, they want to play with it and improve it. It's a new material and a new type of work. It's more self-directed and kids can work absolutely alone. They might ask more difficult questions though, and that's something that doesn't happen in other parts of the curriculum. [Dan, in February]

By June, Dan was expressing more need for structure and teacher input to children's programming work:

> The best results were in the last two months when I insisted on a project, and my having input into it. More people were interested and they asked more questions. It's not a tool you can just hand over to kids and have them express themselves, as I'd expected.

Thus, while maintaining a commitment to the self-initiated framework, Dan was beginning to interpret Logo less as a context for solely self-guided expression, and more as requiring some structured guidance of discovery from the teacher.

Jeff also reported that children were having difficulty in formulating goals for themselves, and that some simply abandoned the work. He found that he had to carefully think through what was appropriate for the children to attempt, and then develop ways to support the work they chose to do:

> I've been having them work at the computer exploring the possibilities of computers, and not giving them specific tasks, encouraging projects of various sorts. If I see them working on something, I might ask them if they'd like to try such and such, and I would teach them a technique. I haven't pushed the kids to move on. . . . I am realizing what is feasible and what is not. In the beginning, kids took on things that were too ambitious. Recently, I've been more careful about getting them to go little by little.

By the end of the year, Jeff felt that the fully self-initiated learning framework worked well for only a few children: "If they developed a good project, the work was enjoyable and intellectually challenging. But not many kids did that sort of thing." Significantly, Jeff added, "I didn't teach it in the right way." Jeff's interpretation of his role in the enterprise had undergone significant revision—from a tool that "taught" itself, to a topic that required careful teaching.

By the end of the first year, both teachers were uncomfortable with the child-centered, self-discovery pedagogy embodied in the Logo rhetoric. They felt that the radical version of this approach—child-initiated goals with support from the teacher only when necessary—had worked well for only a small number of children. Difficulties for other children were attributed to two factors: First, the children had difficulty developing goals in this new medium. Unlike other domains, they brought little world-knowledge of what could be done with Logo. "Social studies was much more contexted than Logo programming—in social studies children have ideas already about what it's possible to do." Second, the teachers were not satisfied that they had adequately solved the problem of what it was necessary for the children to know, and of how to support Logo learning in the classroom.

Summary of Year 1: What is Logo?

At the end of the first year, a critical question was being asked by both teachers and children in the two classrooms: Is Logo a legitimate part of the work of the classroom? For the teachers, this meant two things: What is Logo teaching, and what is its role in relation to curriculum?

Initially, the teachers had believed that the children might learn general problem-solving skills. This belief gave way to doubt about the generality of such skills, and a new question emerged: What is the importance of computer programming itself as a topic?

The second interpretation of the legitimacy of Logo concerned the way Logo was taught. How does it relate to other areas of the curriculum? Is it a "real" subject, and what instructional requirements and techniques are appropriate?

> Even in parts of the curriculum they're very excited about, I have to direct them. I have to give them a sense of what's next. With a lot of kids they can develop a sense of what's next with the computer, but for the kids who aren't good with the computer, the decision as to whether to learn it is very personal, and until I make the decision to make it part of the curriculum, then it will remain a private area. It's now a self-directed experience. [Dan, in February]

> * * * * *

> Next year it'll be a subject kids are responsible for. I'll teach particular skills, talk about results, concept-oriented. [Dan, in June]

> * * * * *

> It's different. There haven't been failures because I haven't imposed goals on their work. It's completely child-directed. They're doing it, but I wouldn't force them to do it. My goals are very flexible, very different for each child, much more tailored to what they like. My goals for the academic work have been much more uniform. There is a sense of direction in academic work, uniform direction that there isn't in computers. [Jeff, in November]

> * * * * *

> One thing I'm struggling with is, what is my role vis-a-vis the computers outside the individual format? The other thing is, how do the techniques which I use in other teaching apply? Are they relevant? [Jeff, in February]

The work of the children reflected the ambiguity of the status of Logo in the classroom. For them, the question of its legitimacy concerned the lack of clarity about what the activity was, and their responsibility for working at it. The radically self-initiated style of the work was uncomfortable for many children because it was so different from the more structured tasks of the classroom that they were used to. There was no formal presentation of material, no group lessons, no task requirements, and no evaluations. Because the children were not sure of the legitimacy of the Logo work in the school environment, they didn't know how much effort they should devote to learning it:

> There were kids who were losing interest. They were receiving a double message. I wanted computers to be part of their work, yet it was optional. Kids would reach a problem in their work, and they would be less inclined to push through it in the way they might with other work because I didn't make them. [Dan, in February]

* * * * *

Some kids felt, "Isn't it funny we can just fool around with this?" [Dan, in June]

Jeff also reported that some "kids didn't feel that it was a legitimate part of their work. Others saw it as an intrusion."

Thus, over the course of one school year, both teachers began to assimilate Logo into the complex pattern of learning that was already established in their classrooms. Logo-out-of-the-box was problematic because teachers found it too complex for children to master without systematic support. The radical self-discovery pedagogy of Logo gave it an ambiguous status vis-a-vis the more structured learning tasks of the classroom because it was unclear where the responsibility for getting the work done rested and, indeed, what the work itself should be.

By the beginning of the second year, Logo learning began to take on some characteristics of learning and teaching in other curriculum areas. However, the teachers recognized the overall nature of the interpretive problem they were struggling with:

> I have a clear idea of culture such as it is, past culture, of what it means to be an educated person in terms of all different subject areas. In terms of the computer, it's not part of our culture, it's something new so I don't have clear ideas of what kids should or should not know. In a sense, I can be much more conceptual about computers than I can about other kinds of work because society as a whole doesn't know yet what it wants to do with computers. [Jeff]

SECTION 2. THE SECOND YEAR:
THE DEVELOPMENT OF AN INSTRUCTIONAL STRATEGY

During the second year of the experiment, the teachers began to provide a particular type of structure to Logo learning based on their experiences with effective edcuation in other subject areas. Unlike the first year, when the teachers were committed to adopting Logo in the manner advocated by its developers, the second year saw Logo being adapted to the shape of the existing classroom learning context. Logo was also offering new perspectives to the teachers about the teaching of cognitive skills. While they viewed programming as a "subject" requiring precise, analytic skills, the classroom work continued to be seen as more like social studies and writing and less like math and grammar; the core of Logo learning remained organized around self-initiated programming projects. Because of their belief that this sort of analytic skill required a structured, sequenced curriculum, both teachers developed a parallel "track" where concepts were "formally" taught and children were held accountable for learning certain concepts and doing assigned tasks.

Over the course of year 1, Dan's thinking about learning Logo underwent a major shift in focus from a belief that the structure of Logo naturally supported children's discovery of programming concepts with little instructional intervention necessary, to an effort to develop a means for systematically supporting the learning of important programming concepts.

The Second Year: Revisions for Classroom Work

By the second year, Logo was seen as a tool for learning about computers, with the emphasis on programming. There was no longer any talk about the acquisition of general problem-solving skills. Although there was still some ambivalence about its ultimate value for all children, by the end of the experiment both teachers felt that learning programming in Logo was valuable for many children:

> Programming can be a good idea, to give kids control over the computer, how the computer is working, invest their own ideas in what is happening. There were few kids who I thought it was totally worthless for. [Dan]

Jeff also felt that Logo was valuable, even if no broader goals were achieved through its practice:

> My thinking now is that what thinking kids have to do to make up programs is a worthwhile, useful exercise. I don't know about its application or impact on other thinking, but even if there were none it wouldn't bother me. So I'm giving them skills, making sure they understand them.

Jeff decided to work out a sequence of skills to present to the children. His concern was that children missed concepts or misunderstood some things, and thus could not proceed. Therefore, he began the year by assigning the children lessons and tasks for practicing these skills. At the same time, the children were required to develop their own projects: "This year's structure is designed to teach skills. Kids who are facile with the computer can do what's assigned in five or ten minutes, and then do their own projects." The assignments were designed to ask children to use concepts in contexts similar to, although not identical with, the ones in which they were taught. Jeff felt that these assignments would be diagnostic tools to help him understand what was going on with individual students' knowledge development. Jeff continued to find it difficult to help kids develop their own project ideas, to give them "germs" from which larger projects could grow.

Requirements for documentation were laid out so that the children and Jeff could easily find their programs. Children were required to keep a card file of their work.

At the beginning of the second year, the teachers were no longer defining Logo primarily as a medium for self-expression, but as a curricular topic with particular concepts and skills. Both teachers devised plans for the second year's work:

> My plan is to teach programming skill in sequential order. Last year I taught things when kids needed it or were bored; this year I'm teaching in a particular order, it's more coherent. It's arranged so that the computer is work. [Dan]
>
> *   *   *   *   *
>
> This year there will be a weekly computer period. I will teach skills in a directed way, with equivalent importance to other subjects. There will be less time just free with computers in classrooms. I'll work out a sequence of developing skills. I'll teach record-keeping techniques. [Jeff]

Thus, in the second year, like Jeff, Dan decided on a squence in which he presented Logo concepts and held weekly lessons for the entire class. The lessons were accompanied by worksheets that the children could use for reference. The children were required to develop their own projects, but Dan also gave them programs that he asked them to look at and modify. In effect, there were parallel learning activities going on with Logo which sometimes intersected. Children learned skills through the formal lessons, and worked on their own projects during assigned work periods. Sometimes the new information was incorporated into the ongoing, self-initiated work, and sometimes it was not. Dan was hoping to develop a conceptual framework for the children and an organized repertoire of skills, which they could draw on as needed. Dan continued the practice of embedding techniques and concepts in working programs, as well as the group sharing where children demonstrated and explained their work to each other. He recognized the need to draw children's attention to the details of a program in order to develop functional capacity with a technique:

> I think that by giving them more of an opportunity to think about what's happening and see how it works, we can make those difficult steps. I've been focusing a lot on looking at the program and really reading what I'm putting in front of them—to think about what it's going to do before it runs. Thinking about how I demonstrated things in the past, I'm sure I typed things on the screen and told them what was going to happen and then did it—not making sure they're reading the words, not making sure they know the significance of each part, and not giving them the opportunity to practice before they've gotten it themselves.

Dan felt that it was important for the children to be able to share their work and knowledge publicly, that such opportunities added to the importance and coherence of the work for the children:

> So I found that I had started giving them reinforcement in the way that I do with other subjects all the time but sort of never really did with the computer. The thing that gets the most response from the kids if you're teaching is still to give everybody the opportunity to give an answer. So that if you have a

wide open question where anybody can contribute anything to it, kids will always respond—that's how we try to teach a lot of things. Allowing kids to read through a program over and over again—what's this line going to do. Five or six kids will raise their hands because they want to be able to say what it will do, and they feel good that they can say it and nobody objects.

They're very interested in sharing something. The importance is not so much the product but in saying, "I worked on this and I want to show this to you." Same thing happens with computers as happens with their stories. They get very involved in it. They pay very close attention to each other's work. They don't say "no" to each other's work because there's too much of a personal connection. They have a better understanding than adults do sometimes. They can empathize with the kid.

The learning experience in the classrooms during this year was designed to address some of the problems that the teachers had observed during the first year's work. In November, for example, Dan discussed his intention of helping the children to deepen their knowledge of Logo in order to enable them to use it flexibly:

They can't understand why what's happening is happening. So they are working out their own problems, their own programs, but they're not getting much out of it. I want to make what they know more coherent to them. Like last year, Kathy made a program with eight variables but it wasn't clear to her what she was doing. Kids don't ask why things do what they're doing. In that program she would just throw anything in. There was nothing systematic about figuring out why those numbers worked.

Dan reported that this lack of pursuit of understanding was not limited to learning with the computer:

Function is so important, so much more important to them than understanding. If they're reading a story and they come across a word they don't know, it doesn't matter to them if they can still understand the story. But if it's a focal point in the story, hands shoot up right away. Kids won't ask why things are the way they are in math. If they're working on the abacus and I say that 8 times 7 equals 56, no one asks why.

Thus, Dan decided that programming was analogous to other subject areas, where teacher support and direction were essential to the development of depth of knowledge.

Jeff also cited the development of deeper understanding as a goal of his work with Logo:

A major concern from last year was that kids didn't understand things and that inhibited their performance on the computers. This year I'm going to be more thorough in the instruction I provide, so I help kids who would otherwise drop out—the kids who missed concepts and couldn't proceed. I want to make sure the kids get the skills to build upon.

An additional problem that both teachers noted during the first year was the difficulty children had in putting the pieces/commands of Logo together into programs: "With the computer, it's an arbitrary logic. It's very difficult for them to put the pieces together on their own. It's hard not to function as a mediator." Thus, they began to present programming techniques in the context of working programs to demonstrate the function of a piece within a whole.

In order to delivery sequenced information to children about critical programming concepts, the teachers set up situations that encouraged children to think through in detail what was happening as programs were constructed and run, and they helped children to develop project ideas. The notion of long-term projects selected by individual children continued to be a dominant framework.

By the middle of the second year, Dan was talking about the organization of learning in terms of the kind of structure that was needed to help the children acquire difficult concepts. He was no longer reliant on the "natural organization" of the material, but recognized that he as a teacher had to organize the presentation to help kids see clearly and avoid misconceptions:

> Whereas last year I would probably have introduced it [variables] as a technique, the past few months I've been trying to think about how they would understand it best. Not just from how the computer works, but how they would understand it best....It's building up each step logically, what you need to do before you do the next thing.

The teaching of Logo was beginning to be interpreted as analogous to other subject areas where a teacher has to structure the material in accordance with his or her theories of children's learning: "It's forced me to sit down and think, well, I have this sequence of skills, and what comes first and when...it makes me think of how to flesh out each concept."

During this year, Jeff's formal lesson structure broke down because of the limited time he had available for teaching, and because of the resistance of the children to these lesson formats. Jeff also began to feel that there was little relationship between the lessons and what the kids were doing on their own:

> I realized that the lessons were too rigid, meaningless to some because they were too difficult. For others they didn't fit with what they wanted to do.

> When I gave lessons or taught techniques, many kids didn't care if they understood or not. Some wanted to do sophisticated things but I didn't have the skills, so I taught them pieces....The sequence of concepts didn't work. It was too fast for some and too slow for others. It went from drawing to relative direction, commands, absolute direction, variables, recursion, changing variables, conditionals, print. I realized the lessons weren't faring well when there were no interesting projects.

Jeff reported that for the second half of the year he gave no work-sheets or assignments. Techniques were demonstrated—"short things to learn"—and individual projects were again the major emphasis. Jeff felt that it was a mistake to try to get all the children "moving at the same speed": "Programming is like math. You could not teach a group of 26 children all the same math."

At the end of the second year, Jeff was again disappointed in the year's work. He felt that few interesting projects had resulted, and was concerned at the number of children who had "dropped out" of the programming work. Like Dan, he was not sure how to bring together the disparate elements of learning Logo given the constraints of the classroom. He felt that Logo should be based on functional learning through an individual project focus, yet the children needed a frame-work to master difficult concepts and skills in order to do their independent work. He found the task of helping children identify appropriate projects to be difficult and frustrating. Because the children learned in different ways and at different speeds, whole-group lessons were prob-lematic. In addition, Jeff continued to feel that the legitimacy of the work was still an issue among the children:

> There were changes from the previous year. I tried to make it clear that the computer was a subject. I set aside periods for it. But even this year, few children thought of it as a subject. The older kids knew about tests for schools, and they talked a lot about that. They're not tested in Logo like they are in other things. If I did it again, I would do something like evaluation of skills. I would do more group teaching.
>
> *   *   *   *   *
>
> There are some kids who still have trouble, and obviously I have to con-tinue to think about how to connect them. There's an enormous range, from kids who are very good to kids who can barely make a program. Some kids pick up an idea and do all kinds of things with it. They explore. Others—it's as if it truly is an alien medium to them. [Jeff, in May]

By the end of the second year, Dan felt "like the pieces are fitting to-gether." He began to observe that the children were using skills they had learned earlier in the year in both individual and group projects. For example, one group of children was creating a solar system program that used a lot of different techniques: "They finally found a reason to use some of the things we'd been talking about."

While he felt that there were several different levels of ability repre-sented in the classroom, Dan also believed that proficiency and interest were more widespread than the previous year. He characterized the year as one in which he had been doing a curriculum and group lessons, and therefore didn't have much time left over to individualize things. The promise of Logo had been just that: a learning environment where the pace and sequence would accommodate very different individual interests and needs. When it became clear to Dan that the language was too complex for the children to learn without considerable structured support, he focused in the second year on a way to offer that structure to the class as a whole. The issue of how to provide an overall framework and yet deal with each student's level of understanding was an unresolved one for Dan in light of time constraints in the classroom:

> I feel that I have to have more time to figure out ways of involving them all in solving a problem. There was always a clear difference among children but I wanted to ignore it for the sake of time. It's very hard to get away with not differentiating—I don't like to do it. I've never used grouping where they're grouped according to skills. The first time I've ever done it is with math, so maybe I should do computer when they're already grouped that way. When I get more abstract now, fewer kids can follow. I want to make time for the good kids—some kids are so good at things, I'd like more time to work with them individually just to see what's going on. For less good kids I need to figure out ways to help them—to see what's going on and figure out ways to get them to participate, not necessarily in the group, but in doing something productive for them—that's still the hardest. To work with anyone on the computer takes an enormous amount of time. That's why I'm talking about splitting them up into groups. I see there's a real need to focus independently on the kids who really know the skills, and then to meet in some way the needs of the kids who don't know the skills. I've been working on a sophisticated level, sort of pushing them. That means the kids who can't get pushed are lost.

The Second Year: Reflections

Throughout the second year, the teachers reflected on their role in relation to Logo as they tried to assimilate it into their classrooms in a structured way. Their original perceptions of what Logo as a fully self-initiated learning experience could offer to children, and their subsequent awareness of the need to make it a structured, legitimate, and accountable part of the classroom work, created a tension about their understanding of their own roles that continued to be an issue at the end of the second year. During this year, in contrast to the first year, Logo was defined by the teachers as a new curriculum area, thus giving it legitimacy in relation to other classroom work.

Dan felt that his commitment to sequence and structure in the learning of Logo helped him to better understand what was going on with the children. He reported that he was forced to think through the requirements of learning the language. Dan also felt that his commitment to providing a coherent learning structure allowed the children to feel more comfortable; Logo was defined in terms that legitimized it in children's eyes as part of their appropriate work in the classroom setting.

It's different from last year, primarily in my perspective. I feel like we're going somewhere. I don't know if the kids feel the way I do. I feel that they're going to end up with something. [Dan, in November]

* * * * *

This year it seems less of a problem to help kids figure out what to do on the computer—in fact they really seem to have ideas. I think it has a lot to do with my attitude toward teaching it, that it is a subject I expect them to be responsible for, a lot to do with the coherency with which things are taught. It's forced me to sit down and think—I have this sequence of skills, and what should come first, how to flesh out each concept. It's building each step logically: What do you need to have before doing the next step? [Dan, in January]

Dan reported that throughout the year most of the children were more engaged in understanding the details of program construction than they had been during the first year:

The kids demonstrate what they're working on and they explain it to other kids....Kids will ask, "Let me see the program." To me it's a sign that they're thinking about how it's happening, that they would ask. It didn't really happen last year that kids would ask what it looks like.

At the end of the year, Dan summarized his strategy and agenda for the children: He had decided to lay out the programming concepts and techniques in a sequence and present them to the children in meaningful contexts. He discovered that it was best to introduce each new concept as part of a program that interested children—a problem situation. This gave the children an idea of how it worked in context and what it was good for. He felt that it was important to combine two things: presenting concepts in a clear way, and doing problem-solving work with the children. Self-discovery-based learning was problematic because the ideas inherent in Logo needed to be clearly and carefully pointed out:

This year I had an agenda, and let them take part in it as they wanted to. Last year I was more involved in their individual work—seeing how I could help them rather than giving a general framework. It was more hectic last year, giving pieces of information that did not fit together.

Overall, Dan was pleased with the development of this teaching strategy and the engagement and accomplishment of the children during the second year. However, he still pondered the paradox inherent in his role in this structured yet self-discovery-based learning situation:

Sometimes the kids have the right idea of what ought to work on the computer, but the syntax is so exact—the right idea but the wrong set of words, and there are no books that are useful to them. It's a very funny situation because it really makes a myth out of what Papert is saying. Even though kids feel very much in control, very much involved, it's made my role as a teacher much more traditional in a funny sort of way. I've tried in the lessons to give some idea of the structure of the language, but still I'm the dispenser of the information. I still have to say, "This is how it works." It's different in other areas—I can ask them a question about how people coming over from Europe in 1600 would manage to live, and from the knowledge they have and from speculation, they could come up with some very good ideas and they can have a discussion. We can't really do that with the computer now. That's actually something I'm trying to do now—thinking of more open questions that have to do with computer logic but not necessarily with the exact answer. [Dan, in June]

Jeff was less satisfied than Dan with the Logo experiment during the second year. This was perhaps partially due to the fact that Jeff was on half-time paternity leave during the year and had to accomplish a great deal during his limited time with the children, partially to the fact that he found it difficult to engage many children, and partially to the age difference between the classrooms. Jeff found that the structured sequence he had planned did not work well: Many of the children were resistant to organized lessons about Logo. Throughout the year, a dominant theme in relation to his teaching role was the large individual differences he saw in interest and ability, and the conflict between letting children follow their own interests and holding them accountable for learning the programming skills:

> This year, I tried to make clear that the computer was a subject and set aside periods for it. But even this year, few kids thought about it as a subject like others. They weren't tested in Logo, and they know they have tests in other subjects. Many kids didn't like the lessons, but when there were few organized things, kids dropped out. [Jeff, in June]

Jeff found that he had difficulty providing both organized lessons and the project ideas that grew out of these lessons as germs for long-term programming commitments. He continued to grapple with the need for some structured learning, and the fact that individual children assimilated and made use of information at different rates. Like Dan, Jeff remained committed to the organizing framework of individual programming projects where children pursued their own goals as a means of learning. But he had difficulty with organizing the information-giving so that children could make use of it in their own way and at their own pace:

> Another part of my approach is thinking that if I just let kids fiddle and play with it, they'll run out of things because they don't know what to do. So I wanted to give them techniques, project ideas. And they were very conscientious about it—they always did what I gave them. There were kids who got techniques out of it, but there were kids who didn't understand, so my going on with what I thought was this curriculum was a problem. In math, I have a curriculum, and the fact that they don't perfectly understand or can't manipulate all the concepts doesn't mean that I don't go on because they do

get some of it. The difference with computers is that having experienced it isn't enough to apply it to your own work, just as an artist who had some exercises in perspective couldn't use it unless he or she played with it a lot. You need much more experience than just a lesson with it. [Jeff, in May]

* * * * *

So what I decided about three months ago is that I couldn't teach a whole group—that just didn't make any sense at all. I had decided in the beginning of the year that I could do that. I wanted to make it into a piece of the curriculum, into something that the kids felt was part of their work. Doing it in this very "projecty" way—kids following their own interest—I was having a lot of trouble making them feel that this was work they had to do. Most things aren't run that way; most classroom activities are much more assigned. So I felt I had to structure their work more and give it direction. What happened was that in giving them direction, I was trying to get them all moving at the same speed and that just wasn't working. It's not like social studies—I would never divide the class into more and less mature groups because the thinking about people, even if it takes place at different levels of maturity, has important commonalities. There's a core of understanding about what a person is that abstract symbolic information lacks. [Jeff, in June]

Thus, at the end of the second year, Jeff also confronted a paradox: His understanding of the necessary pedagogical structure for learning an abstract symbol system (leading to considerations of sequence, accountability, and ability grouping) was in conflict with a commitment to the importance of self-initiated, discovery-based learning:

It's very difficult to tell what is going on with kids' understanding of computers, and this is true for kids who are good and those who are not. I haven't yet built up a way of analyzing what happens when I give them a task and what it means to succeed. . . . [Consequently] I don't intervene much in their work.

CONCLUSION

The analysis of Logo in classroom practice was undertaken to understand how Logo was assimilated to classroom use over time, and how particular issues were confronted and resolved as teachers worked with it in the complex learning situation of schools. Such an analysis is critical to understanding the impact of Logo in a general way and might be helpful to teachers and other practitioners. The perspective here, however, is a research perspective: What overall themes and problems appeared, and what was their course of expression in the teacher dialogues? I have made use of the teachers' voices as they expressed the general themes I discerned; nonetheless, the research ear was selective. Others, coming to the material with different questions and goals, would have heard different things. With these caveats, certain conclusions emerge for me from these materials.

First, the teachers vacillated over the course of the two years between two poles in their interpretation of Logo: Logo as an environment for discovery learning, where students could freely explore with minimal guidance; and the belief that some formal structure was necessary for effective learning. The teachers' enthusiasm for the discovery-learning pedagogy of Logo was tempered by some of their experiences with students' classroom learning. They tried different forms of structure, from informal lessons to the beginnings of a formal curriculum sequence in the second year. However, the tension between free exploration of Logo and structured learning sequences was never fully resolved. There were different solutions at different times and for different circumstances. For example, one teacher thought more structure in the form of project ideas and technique-teaching might help to resolve the problem of sex differences in learning (see Hawkins, Chapter 13, this volume).

Second, there were large individual differences among the students in their interest in and accomplishments with Logo over the course of the two years. Some students were highly motivated by Logo, became "experts" in aspects of the language, and produced substantial projects. Other students remained uninterested in Logo over the school year and learned little more than the most basic commands of the language. The teachers were puzzled about how to involve these students in such a way that they would become personally motivated to learn through Logo.

Third, Logo is a complex, symbolic, rule-based system requiring significant time and cognitive effort to master (see Hawkins & Kurland, Chapter 14, this volume). In the classrooms, students had difficulty understanding the concepts or logic underlying some of the Logo commands necessary to accomplish even relatively simple projects (e.g., conditional statements). Students also had trouble understanding when and how to apply some of the programming concepts, as well as how to use the fundamental programming technique afforded by Logo of decomposing a large program into functional subparts, or procedures.

Fourth, the integration of Logo into the ongoing work of the classroom was problematic because its status and legitimacy were never clarified. Teachers tried to resolve two issues: Is Logo a legitimate part of the curriculum? And, if so, does it fit in as programming or math, or does it belong elsewhere? What can students be expected to learn from their efforts involving Logo: specific programming or math concepts, general problem-solving skills, or both? Teachers also observed confusion on the part of the students, who observed that Logo was being treated differently from other classroom subjects. The accountability that students had come to expect to "legitimize" their work, such as formal requirements and assessments of what was being learned, was missing in their work with Logo. Consequently, it appeared that they often chose to put less effort into it.

In sum, the assimilation of this educational innovation over two years proved to be a process of adaptation and refinement—of both the innovation itself and the way the teachers thought about their work. The experience of these two teachers offers part of a story, and helps to concretize the issues confronting teachers seeking to make use of the potential of Logo.

AUTHOR NOTES

This research was supported by a grant from the Spencer Foundation.

The teachers who so insightfully and willingly reflected on their work made this analysis possible. My thanks as well to the students in their classrooms, and to Jeffrey Arons, Barbara Dubitsky, Kathy Fiess, Shelley Goldman, Roy Pea, and Karen Sheingold.

CHAPTER 2

TEACHERS' ADOPTION OF MULTIMEDIA TECHNOLOGIES FOR SCIENCE AND MATHEMATICS INSTRUCTION

Laura M.W. Martin

APPLYING TECHNOLOGIES TO SCIENCE AND MATHEMATICS INSTRUCTION

At present, there is a greal deal of national concern about the quality of science and mathematics instruction, particularly in elementary and middle schools. Because science is rarely well integrated into the curriculum, many children lose interest in this subject early in their school careers. In science and mathematics, the material covered often appears to be both irrelevant to the students' daily life and not intriguing enough to study for its own sake. In many instances, the teachers themselves are underprepared and uncomfortable with teaching basic concepts.

In recent years, curricular goals in these domains have been undergoing change. Science and mathematics educators have been calling for a problem-solving approach (National Council of Teachers of Mathematics, 1980; National Science Teachers Association, 1982). In the case of science, this means greater emphasis on scientific method and on ways to motivate inquiry and investigation among children; in the case of mathematics, motivation and more flexible use of concepts are the hoped-for outcomes. Educators recognize that preservice and inservice training for teachers will have to reflect this new emphasis in the near future (National Council of Teachers of Mathematics, 1980; National Science Teachers Association, 1982).

While materials that deal with science and mathematics in enriched ways have been available for some time, they have not taken hold in all or even most schools. Materials alone do not seem to solve the problem of teacher adoption of new methods (Berman & McLaughlin, 1978). However, as we have pointed out elsewhere (Sheingold, Martin, & Endreweit, Chapter 4, this volume), the advent of new technologies is likely to provide leverage for school change in a way that hands-on science kits and problem-solving games do not, if only because of the enormous interest they have for educators, parents, and students.

Two concepts have been particularly useful in the analysis and understanding of the technology-adoption process in schools. The first calls attention to the technology itself, for its ability to provide multiple levels of entry to the teachers and students who use it (Levin & Kareev, 1980). A technology that provides different routes for accomplishing the same activity can accommodate a range of individual approaches to problem solving. The second concept calls our attention to the broad and complex contexts within which learners, teachers, and technology function. This "embedded-context" analysis requires us to look beyond an individual child's carrying out a particular task in order to understand how learning is supported and tasks are carried out in the classroom (Laboratory of Comparative Human Cognition, 1985). These two notions—multiple-entry-level technology and embedded-context analysis—can help us to describe and understand the factors affecting classroom change mediated by the introduction of technology.

Multiple Levels of Entry
The idea of offering several paths into an activity means that both experts and novices can use a software program for their respective purposes, which, in some cases, is accomplished by building levels of complexity into the program. For example, with certain software, once a set of parameters becomes comfortable for the user, s/he may select more complex options that provide corresponding gains in program control or flexibility. In other cases, multiple entry into an entire medium, such as the microcomputer, may be designed. The different kinds of user participation required, for example, by a computer-assisted instruction (CAI) program and by a turtle-graphics environment result from different amounts of user support or program structure. In a classroom, a range of structure may suit the needs of different users of the same computer (Riel, Levin, & Miller-Souviney, 1984) or the different needs of the same user.

The Voyage of the Mimi materials, created at Bank Street College, are an example of technology designed to accommodate the multiple needs of people. This system distributes access to potentially instructive experiences across different media. We will examine how such a system can contribute to the particular goal of making science and mathematics relevant to both teachers and their students.

The Embedded Contexts of Learning

The second notion that has import for the technology-adoption process is the understanding that learning tasks may be viewed as occurring within embedded contexts, each of which influences performance on the tasks (Laboratory of Comparative Human Cognition, 1985). On a simple level, one can document that a teacher's use of a microprocessor is often determined by the routes through which machines are introduced (e.g., by a teacher-enthusiast) into the classroom (Hess & Miura, 1984). Less directly, institutional factors have been seen to exert influence at the individual level on decision making about children's educational needs (Mehan, 1984a). Thus, in order to understand adoption of educational technology that appears to depend on teacher attitudes and experience, it may be necessary to analyze the process as part of district "organizational procedure" (Mehan, 1984a), rather than as teacher choice. In this regard, the current work points to district procedures that are influencing the use of technology by individual teachers in their classes.

In order to specify how district procedures influence classroom change, we look for the presence of support for teacher learning as it becomes structured in the context of a more comprehensive goal, usually formulated at the district level. The larger goal will necessarily have an impact on technology adoption by defining what constitutes feedback and support.

The current framework is consistent with what studies have found to be factors relevant to the adoption of innovation in schools (Berman & McLaughlin, 1978; Hord & Loucks, 1980). As we shall see, the themes of multiple-entry points and embedded context allow us to describe the initial stages of a developmental process that took place among individual teachers attempting to improve their classroom practices through the use of educational technology, and among districts attempting to improve instruction across schools.

This chapter reports preliminary findings from a training project that introduced teachers to *The Voyage of the Mimi,* a multimedia package for teaching science and mathematics. Some of the assumptions behind the development of the package and the goals of the teacher training are described as they address current concerns about science and mathematics instruction generally.

THE VOYAGE OF THE MIMI MATERIALS

We begin by providing background on *The Voyage of the Mimi* materials and the related Mathematics, Science and Technology Teacher Education Project (MASTTE), and then briefly describe the results of the training program. The major focus of the chapter is a discussion of the effects of (a) the various media that comprise the *Mimi* materials on classroom instruction, and (b) the organizational features of the school systems themselves on the adoption and diffusion of these materials. The concept of multiple-entry-level technology helps us to understand the first set of effects, while the notion of embedded context is useful for understanding the second.

In 1981, with funding from the U.S. Department of Education, the Bank Street College Project in Science and Mathematics began the development of a multimedia program using video, computer, and print materials that was aimed at helping children gain a better understanding of science, mathematics, and technology. This program, *The Voyage of the Mimi*, has been available on the commercial market since the spring of 1985.

The designers of *The Voyage of the Mimi* worked from several conceptual premises which addressed the issues of what would stimulate change in science and mathematics practices in schools. These premises related to the effects of the media on users, both teachers and children.

First, the developers were concerned with providing the children with concrete and affective experiences, and then moving to more abstract activity. As a result, the centerpiece of *The Voyage of the Mimi* is a 13-part television drama that portrays the adventures of a group of young scientists who are studying whales off the coast of New England. During the course of the show, viewers see the crew conducting scientific "experiments" and solving technical problems. Each episode is accompanied by a documentary showing scientists engaged in their work, thereby offering students and teachers a chance to apply their story involvement to a real problem domain.

Four different computer modules covering concepts related to the scientific voyage allow children to experience simulation of navigation instruments, a microworld ecosystem, a tool for measuring and graphing physical events, and a programming environment. Although researchers are only beginning to study the effects of these types of computer-mediated experience on learning outcomes, it is presumed that such activities on a microcomputer give children experience in linking concrete and abstract problem dimensions in ways otherwise unavailable in classrooms. For example, the "Whales and Their Environment" module includes hardware and software that allows a microcomputer to measure and record temperature, light, and sound. The possibility of relating measurement and representation of measurement directly with the laboratory tool accompanying the *Mimi* provides special connections that are not readily demonstrated with graph paper and thermometers.

The *Mimi* package includes a book version of the television show with classroom activity suggestions and additional factual information, as well as books to accompany the microcomputer modules. The latter present information related to the module content, computer-based and noncomputer-based activities. Thus, the print materials both iterate information available from the video and microcomputer, and in some cases present new facts, experiments, and puzzles. In many instances, the specific activities available through the print materials make a bridge to the recording and interpreting of information and to the use of notation systems, both central to science learning.

Second, because of their belief in the importance of demonstrating to children the social nature of doing science, the *Mimi* developers showed people working together, provided materials that allow children to work cooperatively and productively in their thinking, and presented open-ended topics of interest to both scientists and children. The developers assumed that the fact of shared questions and interests would become an important part of the discovery experience for the children; for example, very little is known about whales, and it was found that a large cross-section of children are fascinated by these mammals.

Third, the *Mimi* package takes into consideration the teacher's participation in the enactment of science. Designed to be supplementary to regular curricula, the *Mimi* materials contain no scope or sequence requirements or suggestions. At the same time, however, a teacher's manual gives suggestions for activities in class, discussion topics, vocabulary, and work on concepts related to the *Mimi* themes in ways that are designed to broaden teachers' notions about science and mathematics. Information about whales is also provided for the teacher in the manuals; no assessment materials are. More importantly, the materials were designed to establish an exciting context and reason for teachers to teach science and mathematics, something not ordinarily available. As one teacher described her typical science lesson:

> I had a book with questions and an experiment to answer each one. "What is the purpose of a reservoir?" Then you have them build a reservoir and figure out the purpose. That's the curriculum. Six or seven questions per unit.

The *Mimi* materials, in contrast, invite the teacher to be an active explorer in the learning situation by being responsible for much of the organizational and motivational work, which is dependent on technological tools.

THE MATHEMATICS, SCIENCE AND TECHNOLOGY TEACHER EDUCATION PROJECT

Although the materials were designed to be implemented by teachers without specific training, and since this was the first commercially available package of its kind, it was not apparent what pattern of activities would develop in the classrooms of the teachers who used them. The designers felt that it would be important to support their innovative program by specifically training teachers to make the most of the integrated media and subject matter.

The Bank Street College Mathematics, Science and Technology Teacher Education Project (MASTTE) was undertaken in order to address the needs of teachers using *The Voyage of the Mimi*. Its purpose was to develop a training model for upper-elementary and middle-school teachers that would focus on the use of both new and old educational technologies to promote science and mathematics instruction.

The training was designed to meet teachers' personal needs for an explanation of the concepts and materials in the *Mimi* package, for models of appropriate pedagogical methods, for ideas for handling changes in classroom activity, and for building broader systemwide adjustments to the new program. During its first two phases, the MASTTE project utilized a combined workshop, demonstration, and discussion format for a week of training, and provided participating districts with support after training in the form of site visits and phone contact with Bank Street field staff.

The MASTTE Research Program

In the spring of 1985, researchers from the Center for Children and Technology began to look at what was being accomplished by teachers and district personnel in their schools as a result of their training experience, and at the factors that might be influencing implementation of the materials and program. Further, in an effort to determine the extent of the information made available by each technology in instructional situations, the researchers asked about the nature and content of the activities that were being conducted, whether the activities were consistently utilized in all classes, and what elements made districts judge the program worth continuing.

Between March and June, the research staff of the MASTTE project visited 16 classes on an average of four visits to each. Structured observation forms were used in the classrooms, and field notes were taken. All teachers and staff developers were interviewed toward the end of the school year. The two Bank Street field trainers who were providing support for the districts were asked to maintain logs describing each of their site contacts in participating districts. The Bank Street staff were periodically interviewed by the researchers.

Many issues concerning science and mathematics instruction arose as a result of the first phase of our work (March-June, 1985). The focus here, however, is on the technology: how it was seen to influence what was done in classrooms, and what in turn influenced its use. General and specific patterns that emerged in this sample of classes will be described and some reasons for the patterns offered.

MASTTE Training Week Participants

In February of 1985, during the first phase of the MASTTE Project, 16 classroom teachers (grades 4, 5, and 6) and ten staff developers from four New York area districts were introduced to *The Voyage of the Mimi* in a week-long training session.

A pretraining questionnaire surveyed the participants' general teaching experience and technical background, as well as their views about instruction. The average number of years of teaching experience among participating teachers was 14; staff developers averaged 17.2 years. All participants had taken more college courses in science than in mathematics, with only five teachers and two staff developers having taken mathematics in college. The staff developers had more experience with computers than did the teachers, six having taught computer work to others.

According to their responses on the questionnaire, teachers and staff developers had different views of the need for schools to improve science and mathematics programs. Teachers tended to stress availability of resources; for example, the need for more lab equipment and teaching kits. Staff developers' perceptions were varied, with some consensus that teachers needed more hands-on experience in order to improve programs. Methodological and support structure needs were rarely mentioned.

In a subsequent interview, one teacher expressed a basic dilemma:

> I never had to teach elementary science and I was bored with it. The curriculum they give you—no books, not a reference material—you have to find everything. Then you have to put it at a 3.6 reading level. It's frustrating. By then, you don't even want to do it any more.... When I said science [to the children], it was boredom.

RESULTS

The Impact of the Program on Teachers

All 17 teachers and nine staff developers in the phase 1 sample, regardless of background, were highly pleased with the materials, in large part because the format allowed an entry point for everyone. As one teacher put it: "I find the materials very useful and they suit my style of teaching. But my style is not everybody's style."

The open-ended nature of the materials related directly to the teachers' abilities to reach the students. One teacher expressed it this way: "With the variety of materials, they're able to reach every kid, whereas before, if you used one type of material, you were not reaching everybody.'' The teachers whose schedules allowed them to choose when to teach science (all but two) reported that as a result of participating in the MASTTE project they were teaching more science in their classes. At each site, it was decided that classes would visit the aquarium, the natural history museum, beaches, and marinas. School librarians, computer teachers, science teachers, art teachers, and parents became involved in providing support for the project. Principals in each district reported that their veteran teachers were newly inspired by working on *Mimi* activities. Children who had never before shown an interest in science, or indeed, in a couple of cases, in school at all, were fascinated by the *Mimi*. A fifth grade teacher reported of one child: ''All of a sudden his mother said he's interested in science, he wants to be a doctor...he wants to go into research.''

In class after class, we observed and heard of virtually 100% time-on-task for the whole class during *Mimi* lessons. Teachers felt that since the video showed the functional context of the scientist's task, it motivated the children to ask questions and provided a framework for the teachers to arrange experiments and activities. One teacher reported her surprise at the children's eagerness to see the documentaries; they felt that the programs ''answered some of their questions.''

Other teachers emphasized the significance of these materials for showing children a fuller context for asking scientific questions and for using problem-solving tools:

> I was surprised they got some of the concepts that they did, like hypo-thermia...since they are fourth graders. We did convection and conduction, and when I tried to do that earlier with the science textbook, it was impossible.

It is clear that the teachers' efforts were highly reinforced by student attentiveness. Children even volunteered for extra work; they gave up gym, art, lunch, recess, and before- and after-school time to do science activities. ''I've had them actually say to me, 'Can we skip art and continue with *The Voyage of the Mimi*'!''

These are indeed powerful materials. Considering the demands placed upon the teacher by the multimedia format—utilizing new technologies in new ways, arranging experiences of scientific process, and tackling subject matter in new contexts—it is clear that they can be motivated to engage in a complex process of change. We conclude that because of the features of multiple-entry level inherent in the current approach to materials and training, the demands on the teachers we observed were likely to be regarded by them as manageable, even revitalizing. It is not surprising, therefore, that every district planned to expand its use of the materials during the subsequent school year.

The Effects of the Integrated Media on Instructional Situations

An assumption of the developers of *The Voyage of the Mimi* was that each of the media employed in the program would provide a unique channel for information to reach the children. Less articulated were assumptions about the effects of the media on lesson organization. Despite schools' typically inflexible science and mathematics lesson structures (whole-group learning and individual "seatwork"), segmented (as opposed to integrated) curriculum, and set time periods, the technological vehicles of the *Mimi* package affected the social arrangements of learning. In fact, some of the most interesting results of our observations pertained to these effects. Moreover, they have profound implications for the availability of information in classroom settings. Video, computers, and print materials offered teachers a choice of how to introduce science and mathematics content. This multiple-entry system supported the teachers in the early stages of developing teaching objectives to promote inquiry and to integrate science and mathematics. The media held the interest of children and teachers alike as teachers began to assimilate, or "own," the goal of stimulating children's curiosity and knowledge.

Television

In the middle-school years, the impact of televised information can be as powerful as 3-dimensional experiences are for younger children. Because the children can comprehend visual narrative and because they learn from modelled behavior, they seem to remember and to be very attentive to what they see on the video screen (Greenfield, 1984). Children can readily access science and mathematics concepts and problem-solution strategies when they are presented in a televised format. As one teacher commented: "Certainly watching something about whales, watching it on TV, is just wonderful. Going from concrete to abstract... it took over the lesson much better than I could do." Another teacher observed:

> I saw them sitting there in that room today, looking as if they were there... you're not smelling the salt air, you're not touching [a whale], you're not even on a ship...but I think they're *there*. The viewing was far more of an experience for them than it was for me.

Referring to the video episode in which the captain of the vessel *Mimi* develops hypothermia, a teacher remarked:

> Why do these kids get so involved in hypothermia? That's because that's CT's [a character's] grandfather that's lying there unconscious on the beach. They're totally involved in that. It could be their grandfather or friend or parent ...and that's where TV has it all over a book.... [Referring to the documentary accompanying another episode] You could read about Mt. Washington until

you're sick of reading it, but. . .when Ben [the actor who plays CT] is knocked over and cannot walk because the wind is so strong and the meteorologist has to grab him, that's more graphic than anything you ever read. . . .I think TV is great.

The teachers we observed held different theories about television's contribution to education. Some felt that video was not the "concrete" experience that the developers were claiming it to be: "It's recreational; reading is educational." Another, describing what was a widely reported phenomenon, said:

> When they [the students] go to the reading and the words [after seeing the video], they recall far more than I thought they would, and it makes the reading more interesting. . .they want to take the books home.

Television was used as a motivator and tool, as a lesson text, and as a reward, according to what teachers felt the video could accomplish. Some teachers noted that "Viewing interest is intense even at the second viewing"; and "My kids act as if it's a reward"; but one felt that

> to see *The Voyage of the Mimi* for a second or third year, I would have trouble with that. Even theoretically, yes, they could get things that they missed the first time. I think it would be too costly, time-wise.

Yet, despite the range of attitudes, the video was used regularly and this caused changes in learning arrangements. When members of the research team visited the MASTTE classes, they were most often shown a television-viewing and discussion session. The reasons for this may lie in what the teachers thought the visitors expected, or in the fact that they might have been more comfortable conducting this type of lesson. However, what was most striking in these sessions was the rapt attention of the children during the viewing and the subsequent discussions.

During those lessons that were configured around the video segments of the *Mimi*, shifts occurred to change the usual patterns of lesson organization. First, chairs were pulled out of alignment and grouped closely together. Second, children sat or draped themselves on the chairs or desks in relative disarray, rather as if they were in their own living rooms. In many classes, children would consistently get their *Mimi* books out without teacher direction in order to follow the video. This kind of informality was also reflected in the class members' interactions. The usual turn-taking and discourse patterns were often disrupted; the teacher and the children talked over the video, commented (not just answered or asked questions), and failed to bid for the floor in the style that generally characterizes a lesson. Informal interactions occurred even in cases where teachers did carry on formal questioning during the video sequences, sometimes stopping the machine in order to pose questions to the students. However, when video viewing took place in the auditorium, little informality was noted.

It may be that the relaxed or home-like features of television viewing have learning implications for children who are not at ease with the classical whole-group, teacher-led lesson format. Television viewing may encourage more open-ended exchanges, more personal involvement in the material, and a less teacher-centered focus, all of which may contribute significantly to children's learning. It has also been suggested that if the television channel carries the "facts," the teachers may be freed to ask the children other kinds of questions (J. Black, personal communication, 1985).

Microcomputer Modules

While the use of television in the classroom was a new experience for some of the teachers, the microcomputer was for all both a novel teaching tool and an unfamiliar medium. During the training period, the teachers' reactions to computers ranged from eager to amused to hesitant, and all but one learned to use the software.

The Voyage of the Mimi modules that were available to the teachers—"Introduction to Computing" and "Maps and Navigation"—were not equally utilized. Based on Logo, "Introduction to Computing" incorporates prompts which the developers felt would be of more help to the children in understanding the features of the programming language than would a free Logo environment (Hawkins & Kurland, Chapter 14, this volume). In schools that had a Logo curriculum already in place, the teachers did not see the advantage of the module (except, in one case, for use with young children not yet using Logo), despite their positive comments about how the software could facilitate work with programming concepts. However, one lab teacher regularly used the software, even in non-*Mimi* classes. The fact that teachers who were not familiar with Logo also tended not to use the module might be accounted for in two ways: First, this module was not as strongly emphasized in the training week as was the "Maps and Navigation" module. Second, with the exception of two whale search games, the module's programming exercises were not as clearly integrated with the *Mimi* content or with the reading matter on computer history. Teachers recognized that this software did not build directly upon concepts in the show.

The "Maps and Navigation" module, in contrast, was used in all classes. It clearly created junctures for teachers and children to interact around *Mimi* topics by demanding the use of certain concepts within the "whole task" (Mehan, 1984b) of the navigation game. The children in the classes we studied willingly gave up such activities as recess, lunch, art, and gym for chances to play the simulation games, and thus came in contact with the educational opportunities believed to exist there. One teacher said:

> I'm supposed to be teaching them some foreign country in social studies. I found out nobody in this class knew anything about geography. Well, we're not going to any foreign countries till we know how to get there. And this particular navigation thing is perfect for me.

"Maps and Navigation" is made up of three navigation games designed to teach latitude and longitude, speed/time/distance calculation, and triangulation with a radio direction finder. A fourth game in the module, "Rescue Mission," simulates a navigation problem whose solution depends on students' coordinating their use of a variety of "instruments," as well as a map and a parallel ruler, and on choosing their procedures in a strategic sequence. The games are designed to be played in teams.

Teachers have reported that children have gained fluency with the concepts embedded in the games, although direct instruction about rate calculation, measurement techniques, and reading screens appears to be necessary. Another outcome concerns the organization of learning partners that occurred when children used the software. While the introduction of the machines did not cause any of the MASTTE teachers to reorganize the physical or temporal arrangements that were in place for lessons (see Mehan, 1985), several teachers felt they could tolerate "noise" and so allowed pairs of children to play navigation games while others in the class worked at their seats. Also, teachers who demonstrated how to use the computer in front of the class sometimes had children assisting at the keyboard or reading the screens: "When I introduce a game, I'll do all the different techniques that they need and then I'll let them work on it."

Since all the teachers taught whole-group lessons and this did not change, and since the computers were used, small groups of children were allowed to use the computers primarily during free time (i.e., lunch, recess, and before and after school). Only occasionally did certain teachers allow pairs of children to work at the computer during whole-group lessons. Both for those who planned some computer use during their lessons and for those who didn't, novel peer configurations at the computer were noted: "I let my brighter ones work on it first, and then when they've mastered it, I mix up groups." Either by design or spontaneously:

- Boys and girls were seen to work together for the first time.
- More experienced children taught less experienced children.
- "Quicker" learners worked with "slower" learners.
- Children paced themselves, recording their own activities.

- Children distributed tasks cooperatively, for instance, taking the role of keyboarder, scribe, or strategist.

Interesting shifts in thinking occurred for some teachers who used the computer in front of their classes. During a training discussion on inquiry lessons, one teacher made clear his view that teachers must know all the answers before conducting a lesson. As a result of his making errors while demonstrating the use of the computer for his class, he later told his colleagues in the district about the value of "learning along with the kids." Two teachers who controlled the computer in whole-group lessons reported that they were using computers at home for the first time as a result of getting familiar with the machine in school. A staff developer reported that an experienced teacher asked for advice after an unsuccessful lesson: "I think the fact that teachers are open to changing their ways of teaching is really admirable for people who've been in the system for a long time." Thus, although the essential structure of the lessons did not change, the computer caused changes and reexamination of social arrangements within the familiar structures.

Print Materials

In contrast to the novel arrangements generated through the use of the video and microcomputer, the lessons organized around the *Mimi* print materials were consistently traditional. Specifically, we saw lessons in which children each took a turn in reading a paragraph; children followed along with the teacher; children looked for answers to the teacher's questions in the text; children were instructed to do the activity in the book; children were instructed to answer the questions in the book.

We may suppose that for teachers the children's books, the teacher's manual, and the computer software guidebooks all represented a familiar school format and thus tended to be used in ways similar to other printed materials. It is possible that the more familiar "school-like" format of the print materials allowed some teachers a comfortable entry point into the content of the *Mimi* package. Most of the teachers in our sample thought that the print materials were excellent: "If the children are able to prepare first with the books, they pick up a lot more [from the video]." Interestingly, several teachers noted that the video caused the books to become valuable to the children. A few teachers, however, did not find the print materials useful or special: "The thing they [the children] liked least was the textbook because that's like everyday work."

In addition to making new information available to classes by causing a rearrangement of instructional exchange, the media caused the teachers to reexamine their lesson objectives by eliminating some traditional sources of feedback. All teachers were left to their own devices for evaluating the activities resulting from the use of the media. One teacher hoped to develop a "process" test, but was disappointed that he was only able to devise a "fact" test. Some teachers managed to test vocabulary, at the same time recognizing that this was not the point of the *Mimi*. A couple of teachers, expressing some bewilderment about how to conduct assessment, gave assignments to the children and simply kept track of whether or not the work had been completed. One of these teachers had each child demonstrate to her that s/he was able successfully to play a computer game before the child was allowed to try another.

Television viewing and computer use, as well as the discussion and questioning that accompany them, do not easily lend themselves to formal assessment. "Testing is not in the spirit of the *Mimi*," said one teacher. Thus, while all the teachers found a way to integrate the media into their classes, the media demanded that they use new or more individually referenced means of assessing how the lessons suited their purposes. The different lessons engendered by the media may eventually help teachers work towards the goals of science and mathematics inquiry by encouraging a focus on process and problem solving.

The Effect of School Systems on the Adoption of New Technologies

The enthusiasm we witnessed among teachers is not enough to maintain the momentum for a project such as MASTTE. The adoption and diffusion of technological innovation in classrooms demands district-level as well as classroom-level planning (Berman & McLaughlin, 1978; Loucks & Zacchei, 1983). As each district attempted to adopt and incorporate new and integrated technology, constraints were revealed that operated upon both districts and individual teachers. Among the MASTTE sites, district-level planning was shaped, first, by the nature of the district's initial goals for participating in the project, then by the processes by which information was exchanged as the project was implemented and, finally, by the bases on which support and diffusion came to be structured in the district.

Goals for Participation in the Project

In order to help maintain the effectiveness of the new program in the districts, the MASTTE training program included opportunities for the participating school personnel to develop and clarify program plans and devise strategies for organizing district-level support.

We found that the freedom to experiment afforded by the *Mimi's* multiple-entry design seemed to be the key to individual teachers' acceptance and use of integrated technologies: "I can use my strengths"; "It's good for myself and my background." However, as with any innovation, in order for individual experiences to affect practices across a district, the experimentation had to occur in districts which (a) could incorporate the project's goals into their own, and (b) had mechanisms for detecting and supporting professional growth among staff. In other words, the elements that sustained individual teachers as they changed their instructional practices resulted in district change when those elements became part of a district's plan for improving science and mathematics instruction.

The districts participating in the MASTTE project varied greatly in structure and, therefore, in how they addressed the problem of change. They represented a cross-section of New York area districts, including urban and suburban schools, districts with more or less extensive tax bases, school populations with a variety of ethnic backgrounds in different proportions, and districts of varying size:

District M is a large, central-city school district serving a mixed ethnic population, primarily hispanic and black. The participant schools varied in the extent to which they used educational technology. The personnel sent for training came from three levels of the system: classroom teachers from two sites, a school computer coordinator, and a district science coordinator who served 23 schools. District M was contacted about participation in the training program through the central office, as were the other districts. Yet, two teachers selected to attend were under the impression that they would be participating in a social studies program. Although District M did not articulate any districtwide plans for the MASTTE work, it did express a desire to expand the computer technology program in one of the participating schools.

District B, a large district in one of the boroughs, also serves a mixed ethnic population and has limited technology in its schools. Teachers from three schools and two district-level staff developers (Mathematics/Computer and ESL/Special Education) responsible for 28 schools were sent for training at Bank Street. Before the project began, the staff developers organized a school board meeting, which was attended by selected principals and included several PTA presentations about the project. The staff developers worked with the explicit goal of improving science, mathematics, and technology capabilities throughout the district.

South Bay is a small, working-class district in a suburb serving a mixed ethnic community. Only building-level personnel—teachers, science coordinators, and one computer coordinator—were sent to Bank Street for training. The district office, notably the superintendent's assistant, gave the project classes ''carte blanche,'' that is, exemption from regular curriculum requirements and priority on equipment use. This district has a strong CAI program and an exemplary mathematics program. Its participation in the MASTTE project was part of a 3-year effort to upgrade district science programs.

Chesterfield is a small, upper-middle-class district in a wealthy suburb. A district mathematics facilitator and a science facilitator, both experienced with computers, attended the training week at Bank Street; teachers could not be spared from the classrooms. Technological resources are readily available in Chesterfield, and the district has an elaborate inservice program. All classes above the third grade have computers. The facilitators planned to organize their own inservice program on using the materials immediately after the Bank Street training week. This district was interested in exploring the integrative possibilities of the *Mimi* materials.

Results indicated that defining a goal for district participation in the project before training began was a necessary precondition for later diffusion of the *Mimi*. Surprisingly, the degree of a district's or school's technological advancement prior to the program had no relation to the extent of diffusion: Those who were determined to make the program work organized the needed equipment, while some sites with adequate technology did not expand the program.

In our sites, goals were critical because they legitimated and clarified implementation activities. Of the four participating districts, the three (District B, South Bay, and Chesterfield) that had clear ideas about why they wanted to introduce technology into their science and mathematics programs were able to develop districtwide implementation plans for the coming school year. These three districts organized their own inservice programs, which were slated to begin before school reopened in September. In District M, where the goal of the project had been and continued to be unfocused despite training and the enthusiasm of the teachers, technological innovation was not diffused on a districtwide basis, and barely so within the schools.

Personnel Responsible for Implementation

Carrying out district goals involves training personnel who are regarded as key in the implementation process. Depending on whom the districts chose to send for training, initial support for using the new materials varied. At most sites, strong connections to the central office proved to be important for the effective implementation and diffusion of the project.

One of the city districts (District B) sent central office staff developers for training, with the result that for the first time in that district a link was established between classroom teachers and the central office. For the teachers, "there was a response [from the district]. A living being who said 'yes' [to experimentation] instead of 'why didn't you?'" Previously, the teachers had not even been aware that the district had staff developers, let alone ones who could offer positive support.

This responsiveness was somewhat unexpected since, according to our informants, the two city districts we worked with operate heavily on favoritism and have few resources for staff development. The staff developers have many schools to work with and little authority; the teachers are often at odds with the district about obtaining the things they need for their classrooms. Thus, it was encouarging that staff developers were able to forge links with the teachers in that context.

In the other city district of our sample (District M), the staff developers sent for training did not work together. One was the computer coordinator of his school; the other worked in schools throughout the district, but not out of the central office where decisions are made. The support that these staff developers were able to provide for teachers was limited or nonexistent since they themselves had so little support from and not much access to those responsible for allocating resources in the district. Consequently, acquisition of and access to equipment was difficult to organize at the beginning of the project.

One suburban district in our sample (Chesterfield), which sent district-level facilitators to training, has the resources to offer many courses and workshops at the district office. The teachers are encouraged to design inservice programs for their colleagues, and money is available for attending professional conferences. Teachers were given time off for district training in using the materials, staff developers conducted demonstration lessons and, generally, resources were made available to *Mimi* classes. In contrast, the other suburban district (South Bay) sent only building-level personnel for training. Although this district has resources, there are few interschool or centralized professional activities; individual teachers are encouraged to pursue professional development on their own. Each building in South Bay was provided with equipment at first, but then was left to organize its own materials and support for the *Mimi* work. This became relatively hard to do for those MASTTE teachers who worked alone in schools.

Thus, in Chesterfield and District B, implementation was overseen by trained staff developers who worked out of the central office. Their positions facilitated the teachers' getting the materials needed to undertake the project. In South Bay and District M, implementation proceeded independently in each school building involved in the project. South Bay building personnel, however, had a clear framework from the district in which to carry out their work and were assisted in implementing the program.

Feedback on Implementation

Responsibility for implementing the program, for assessing feedback from this experiment in technology adoption, and for delineating the next steps of implementation was distributed differently in the districts. Support for continued experimentation with the technology and for its diffusion also differed, depending on how heavily teachers' and staff developers' classroom experiences weighed and on the strength of the communication lines to decision makers.

All districts considered the informal, positive reactions of teachers and staff developers, and the increased amount of science activities in classrooms as evidence of the success of the *Mimi*. When the time came for deciding what direction the program would take in the coming year, two of the districts (South Bay and Chesterfield) made decisions about the diffusion of the materials at the central office level, with teacher input considered in varying degrees. Chesterfield had in place a planning and review structure for teachers and staff developers with which to formally assess the program. Although the two Chesterfield staff developers, in conjunction with the Assistant Superintendent of Instruction, drew up a diffusion plan before consulting the teachers, teacher input, in the form of rating scales and discussion, was eventually used to verify and justify this plan.

In South Bay, decisions about expanding the use of the *Mimi* technology for the coming school year also were made centrally, but without systematic teacher or staff developer input. The opinions of project participants were heard at a group meeting by the Assistant Superintendent for Instruction but, based on their knowledge of the district, MASTTE participants doubted that their comments would carry weight in the district office. According to some of the South Bay people involved, making diffusion decisions without teacher input might work against the nature of the materials. The teachers felt that excluding them from decision making meant that budgetary or standard curriculum considerations were determining the use of the materials, thus overriding what the teachers had decided was relevant to their students. These feelings were expressed despite the fact that South Bay MASTTE participants were enlisted to train their colleagues for the coming year. The teachers felt that, by having the program and the use of particular materials mandated for the coming year, their professionalism had been challenged: "I feel some resignation about the whole thing."

Good communication lines to decision makers did not necessarily mean that central office control was exerted. In District B, for example, the staff developers used their knowledge of the system's workings to keep the program fluid for those teachers who were devising their own ways of using the materials. The District B staff developers, through private discussions and at meetings, helped district administrators and principals to understand that teachers needed support for exploring the best ways of utilizing the materials. In the meantime, the staff developers organized ways to provide meaningful feedback to administrators at a later date.

In District M, which neither had clear communication lines nor delineated central goals, interested teachers at each site pursued the project as best they could. In one school, the principal took active interest in the materials and sought to involve the science and computer teachers, as well as other classroom teachers, in the work. In the other school, the computer coordinator, who had attended training, introduced the materials to several new classes and planned some training for them. At both sites in District M, the teachers' positive experiences have kept the project alive in the absence of district support.

Teacher Support

Teachers are professionals who require short-term and long-term support, especially when asked to change their professional practices. In our sample, district histories of administrative interest in teachers' needs, of professional treatment of teachers, and of decision making affected the implementation of the new technology.

For example, one teacher in District M said:

> No one has mentioned to me or Ms. D, "How's it going?" or "Is there anything I can do to help?" There hasn't been one word—well, one: "Did you get the computer?" That was the extent of it. Not "if you're using it," not "how the children are reacting to it," "what materials did you get," nothing.

The teachers in this district struggled to maintain the momentum of their commitment.

We found that the informed involvement of administrators was essential for supporting teachers' feelings of professionalism: Teachers felt that they could earn genuine recognition, were more likely to argue successfully for innovations, and could trust that their needs would be met in the future. Without such involvement, none of these teacher benefits was assured.

Some of the participants felt that the administrators in their districts did not really understand what the project was about. Teachers in two districts expressed resentment of what one teacher called "the white glove brigade"—administrators who were interested in publicity on technological developments in the district, but who made no effort to acquaint themselves with the actual work being done.

In the districts where administrators and parents were informed and involved in the adoption process, more activities and more extended activities were taken up by teachers during the first stages of implementation. The range of projects envisioned for the future was also greater in those districts.

One way in which district administrators could be helpful to teachers without being fully acquainted with the details of the project was to provide them with material support. However, their own roles (e.g., obtaining resources, cutting red tape) needed to be specified, and they did have to be generally familiar with the project goals. We found, too, that administrative and parental involvement was not necessarily related to an efficient process for obtaining equipment. Information short-cuts were benign only when there was a central support structure for teachers, such as a communications network. These support structures served as a guarantee that teachers' classroom equipment needs would be dealt with by someone who had access to a decision maker and could thus be an advocate. For the current group of teachers, a strong support mechanism was already in place in two of the districts; in a third, two district-level staff developers working together were able to construct a support system.

Diffusion

Although we found clear district goals to be important for undertaking innovation, there was some evidence that creating a central district implementation plan may have limited the range of innovations possible with the materials, and restricted the advantages afforded by the multiple-entry approach. By June of 1985, three months after the materials were introduced, the two suburban districts considered the pilot stage of the program to be over. The district coordinators knew what they wanted from the materials; that is, they decided which *Mimi* materials and activities were appropriate for particular grade levels and curriculum strands. In South Bay, for instance, it is now required that the *Mimi* be taught in fifth grade; in Chesterfield, a decision dictating the use of the *Mimi* will be made at the end of the 1986-87 school year. In both districts, teachers in grades not using the video episodes are still experimenting with the software modules, but within limits defined by the central office. In South Bay and Chesterfield, too, certain computer modules are to be used only in specific grades; video use in Chesterfield is restricted to one grade.

Personnel in both districts felt that the program was robust and efficient, and had confidence in their district's ability to deal with any problems that might arise, including procuring new equipment and training teachers in the use of technology.

The two city districts have maintained a ''pilot'' state of affairs concerning program implementation, one by default (District M) and the other deliberately (District B), in part because the staff developers supervising the program felt that three months was not enough time to fully evaluate its utility across grades and teachers. District B staff feel confident that the technology will eventually effect broad changes, but their approach is to involve the school and parent community through demonstration and education.

CONCLUSION

The science and mathematics materials comprising *The Voyage of the Mimi* attempt to address the pervasive problem of why these topics are often deemed irrelevant in a child's life. They do so by contexting science and mathematics concepts in a story and in integrated mixed-media activities for the classroom. Their effectiveness in achieving their aim needs to be understood in light of their impact on how teachers organize information systems for their students within the whole-school context. As we saw in the few months of the program, the presence of the new technologies does not automatically prescribe the nature of the task for the teacher who is involved in motivating problem-solving activity on the part of the student.

Teachers were able to tolerate a wide range of conditions for working with *The Voyage of the Mimi* materials, despite the fact that many of their situations were far from ideal. The flexibility of the materials themselves, both in terms of their content and format, seemed to contribute to the flexibility with which they were used by the teachers in such a broad range of circumstances. While this made it necessary for staff developers to deal with each teacher's situation as an individual case, it may prove to be a more efficient outcome overall, since teachers felt they came to "own" the program; they could adapt lessons as they wished without feeling they were violating a prescribed sequence, skipping content, or underutilizing the materials.

As teachers become comfortable with the content of the materials, we anticipate that they will become more open-ended in their lesson arrangements (Guskey, 1986). As judged by the reports we received from the teachers, the multimedia materials, with suggestions for classroom use provided through training, inspired them to begin enrichment of their science instruction. Teachers in every district reported that the responses of their students to the materials were more powerful and consistently more positive than any they had seen. Not surprisingly, the increased attempts by teachers, following training, to use the materials for integrated science and mathematics activities revealed a set of teaching practices that are not always functional for subject integration. In many classrooms science is taught as a corpus of facts, and mathematics is a discrete subject dealt with from 10:00 to 10:45: "Math class is a separate class." Our observations suggest that the possibility of revising these practices is likely to depend less on verbalizations of alternative philosophies than on the mobilization of district resources that help teachers accommodate the developing interests of the children, the excitement of the classes, and their own increasing confidence.

In the classrooms we visited, the teachers' work seemed to be as much influenced by the technology as the technological applications were shaped by the teachers. Multiple routes into the materials for both inexperienced and experienced teachers meant that the materials could be utilized in some fashion by almost anyone. It is likely that the materials brought teachers into contact with factors that will encourage their further development as teachers of science and mathematics, namely: children's high interest; topics of interest to themselves; the legitimation of unanswered questions, which makes the teacher a learner too; and resources necessary for building a full program.

The school systems we studied significantly influenced and defined the project goals for the teacher. They delimited, to greater and lesser degrees, the boundaries of what was possible in individual classes by shaping the larger goals and human resources within which teachers explored the relatively uncharted territory of integrated technology. Whether or not schools were equipped with technological resources was of secondary relevance to what was possible (cf. Shavelson, Winkler, Stasz, Feibel, Robyn, & Shaha, 1984). Rather, the school systems impinged on the adoption, diffusion, and richness of the program by dint of their organization of goals, communication, teacher support, and decision making. Individual experimentation by teachers in classrooms had different impacts depending on the context of the wider system in which it occurred.

The content and concepts of science and mathematics are not easily accessible for either children or teachers, but we found the teachers very willing to change how children gain access to such information. According to observations made during three months of classroom visits following the MASTTE training program, adopting integrated technologies as tools for change as well as for learning can be a promising enterprise. We are continuing to investigate factors that seem to influence the adoption process, and to determine the ways in which training can address them systematically.

AUTHOR NOTES

This chapter is based on work carried out by the research staff of the Bank Street College Mathematics, Science and Technology Teacher Education Project, directed by Regan McCarthy, with resources provided by the National Science Foundation. The contributions of Mary McGinnis and Maxine Shirley to the research process were invaluable. The insights shared with us by the project training staff, Marilyn Quinsaat and Bill Roberts, and by the classroom teachers are also gratefully acknowledged.

CHAPTER 3

FUNCTIONAL ENVIRONMENTS FOR MICROCOMPUTERS IN EDUCATION

Denis Newman

INTRODUCTION

For the last several years, researchers at the Center for Children and Technology have been conducting a program of research on the use of computers in education. One of the central themes of this research is that the computer is a tool that can be used for a variety of functions or purposes. Thus, we talk about the computer operating within a "functional learning environment" (FLE). Here, functional means that the learning activities have a function or purpose from the point of view of the child. In this chapter, I discuss three projects undertaken at Bank Street College in which we implemented and studied such environments. These studies raise fundamental questions about the design and implementation of FLEs, particularly the relationship between the children's purposes and those of their teachers. Coordination of divergent purposes within a FLE turns out to be a critical factor in the success of classroom microcomputer activities.

While research on microcomputers is relatively new at Bank Street, concern for FLEs is quite old. Since its beginning in 1916, the college has been at the forefront of the progressive education movement founded by John Dewey. A central theme in Dewey's (1902, 1938) writing on education is the notion that classroom activities must be related to the child's experiences, interests, and goals. This was a radical proposal for an era in which the teacher stood at the front of the class and lectured or conducted drills. Although the general notion has found wide acceptance in United States schools in recent decades, many teachers find it impossible to implement because of limited resources, materials, and training. It is the hope of many people in the field of educational computing, including staff at Bank Street, that the microcomputer can be a resource for engaging children's interest and fostering a more creative learning process.

In the sections that follow, I first describe the notion of a FLE in more detail, and then present observations about three projects that have tried to create FLEs. These projects concern the use of the Logo language in Bank Street classrooms, a project on science and mathematics education, and the creation of a network of microcomputers. In each case, the observations illustrate the importance of coordinating the goals of children and teachers.

FUNCTIONAL LEARNING ENVIRONMENTS

We start with two assumptions: (a) that children are intrinsically motivated to work on tasks that are meaningful to them; and (b) that the most effective educational environment is one that provides meaningful tasks; that is, tasks that embody some function or purpose that children understand. While some children enjoy learning about a particular topic "for its own sake," in most cases facts and skills are best learned in connection with larger tasks that give them significance or meaning. In this way, not only are children motivated to master the facts and skills, but they have a framework in which to understand the cultural significance of the facts and their relation to other facts. For example, a science project in which children attempt to answer specific questions about whales and their habitats by constructing a database provides an environment for learning scientific categorization schemes as well as specific facts about whales. It can also demonstrate to the children the variety of resources—such as textbooks, encyclopedias, and films—that are available in our culture for obtaining facts, and confront them with the need to cull information from several sources.

Our assumptions, however, leave two fundamental questions unanswered. First, we must understand where the goals that the children are interested in come from: Are they inventions of the children or are they imposed by the teacher? Second, we must understand the relation between the goals that children undertake in the classroom and the tasks they will be confronted with in the real world outside of school. Unless students can apply the knowledge and skills they have acquired in school to tasks outside the classroom, any FLE will have been for naught.

Our approach to the first issue takes a middle position between the idea that the teacher must impose problems and the idea that children must invent their own classroom activities. On the one hand is the traditional view of education, and on the other is a radical version of the child-centered approach to education based on interpretations of the writings of Dewey as well as Piaget (1973b).

It is very clear that Dewey felt that the purely child-centered approach was as erroneous as the traditional view that the teacher must impose the classroom tasks. The teacher has very important responsibilities, which include suggesting tasks and presenting to the children alternative interpretations of problems. In many respects, Dewey's approach is more consistent with the socio-historical approach to child development presented in the recently published writings of Vygotsky (1978) and Leont'ev (1981), in which the importance of the teacher-child interaction is emphasized, than with the universalist approach of Piaget, which deemphasizes the cultural context (Laboratory of Comparative Human Cognition, 1983). According to these theorists, the child's initial attempts to solve an arithmetical problem, write a story, or operate a computer program are carried out in interaction with teachers or more experienced children. What the child internalizes is not what the expert says, but a version of the interactions that constitute the joint activity. Thus, without coercion, these interactions guide children toward the cultural interpretation and significance of the tasks in which they are engaged (Newman, Riel, & Martin, 1983).

Meaningful tasks may come from a variety of sources. One source is the spontaneous ideas of the children themselves: Most children have some topic which they simply "like." However, for most school topics this source may not be the most important. Teachers can make classroom tasks meaningful by showing children their significance in terms of a variety of uses for the skills involved, or in terms of the adult world they will be entering. The FLE created in this way can be a simulation of a real problem (e.g., role-playing commercial transactions as a context for doing arithmetic calculations), or it can be a real problem (e.g., actually selling food at a school fair to raise money to buy a classroom computer). The FLE can also be of a more abstract nature (e.g., a geometric problem can provide a meaningful context for calculating the size of an angle, providing that geometry itself has meaning within the children's experiences), A teacher can create interesting FLEs by crossing traditional discipline boundaries (e.g., by showing how geometric concepts such as triangulation can be used in geography to solve navigation problems).

Our approach to the second issue—the relationship between classroom and real-world goals—is closely related to the first. We suspect that the usability of school learning in later life is inseparable from the variety of FLEs in which it is embedded. Being able to see the same fact from multiple perspectives (i.e., recognizing the different uses it can have) engenders a flexible approach to acquiring knowledge that would otherwise be absent. This flexibility makes it possible to adapt the knowledge to new functional environments that cannot be specifically anticipated in the classroom.

Microcomputers can play a very useful role in FLEs because of their capacity for simulation and because they themselves are important tools for the solution of a variety of interesting real-world problems. They also provide fluid and manipulable symbol systems in which many interesting abstract problems can be represented and solved. But they cannot be expected to function on their own. A teacher must build the bridges between the tool, the school task, the thinking skills, and their functional significance for the culture beyond the classroom.

LOGO IN A CLASSROOM

Logo is a programming language popularized by Seymour Papert (1980) and colleagues. According to Papert, Logo is an environment in which children can learn fundamental mathematical concepts and powerful problem-solving methods without the intervention of teachers. Papert takes his inspiration from Piaget, who has argued forcefully that

> each time one prematurely teaches a child something he could have discovered for himself, that child is kept from inventing it and consequently from understanding it completely. (1970, p. 175)

One of Piaget's (1965) earliest examples was the game of marbles played by boys from preschool to adolesence. In Switzerland, where Piaget studied the game, adults were not involved. The children learned from each other. Not only did the children master the complex rules of the game, but they came to understand that the rules were not absolute but a matter of convention and agreement among equals. The same kind of process is at the heart of Papert's claims for Logo: Without the imposition of adult authority and adult ideas, children can come to an understanding of the nature of concepts such as recursion that are as fundamental to programming as cooperative agreement is to games with rules. Of course, the peer play group for marbles included undisputed experts; the same may not be true for programming, which is seldom mastered by young children. This weakness in the analogy might lead us to question peer interaction as a basis for learning programming.

The initial interest in Logo at Bank Street, however, was not in testing its adequacy as a peer group FLE but with quite a different question. Researchers from the Center for Children and Technology set out to see if experience with programming would enhance planning skills in children. It was a reasonable hypothesis since writing a program is like creating a plan for the computer to execute. The question was whether there was any transfer from the activity of programming to other experimental tasks that also required making a plan of action but did not involve computers.

The researchers arranged to do their study in two classrooms at Bank Street's School for Children (SFC). The SFC teachers, both highly committed to the child-centered approach to education, were eager to try out

Logo and the pedagogy developed by Papert. Neither teacher was an expert programmer, although each had taken a course with Papert prior to the study. They were, however, experts in creating FLEs for children and approached the new task with enthusiasm.

For two years, the researchers observed and interviewed the children and teachers in the third and sixth grade classes. Pre- and post-tests were administered using a chore-scheduling task based on the work of Hayes-Roth and Hayes-Roth (1979). The findings concerning the transfer of Logo experience to the experimental planning tasks were very clear: The researchers found no effects at all (Pea & Kurland, 1984a). By the time the researchers compiled their data, however, the negative findings came as little surprise. Observations of the children as they interacted with Logo and with each other showed that very little planning was involved in their programming practices. Thus, there was little reason to expect programming to make children more planful.

As Pea (1983) observed:

> Much more common was on-line programming, in which children defined their goals, and found means to achieve them as they observed the products of their programs unfolding on the screen. Rather than constructing a plan, then implementing it as a program to achieve a well-defined goal, and afterwards running the implemented plan on the computer, children would evolve a goal while writing lines of Logo programming language, run their program, see if they liked the outcome, explore a new goal, and so on. . . . In most cases, children preferred to rewrite a program from scratch rather than to suffer through the attention to detail required in figuring out where a program was going awry. As one child put it when asked why she was typing in commands directly rather than writing a program: "It's easier to do it the hard way."

From the children's point of view, Logo was for the most part an interesting classroom activity, although there were certainly differences among the children in their level of interest and in the amount of programming they learned. But, despite their enthusiasm, they did not explore the more conceptually challenging aspects of Logo in the course of their discovery learning. They were essentially "playing." In Piaget's (1962) terminology, assimilation was dominating accommodation; that is, the goal was assimilated to the procedures rather than the procedures being accommodated to a set goal. Whatever worked became the goal retrospectively.

From the teacher's point of view, the children were engaged in the Logo activity but were not learning to program. Experiments involving the better Logo programmers showed that few had correct understanding of such central concepts as flow of control, conditionals, or recursion (Kurland & Pea, 1985). As time went on, the teachers began to question the discovery-oriented approach to teaching programming. It became clear to them that Logo could not just "happen," but that they, the teachers, had to have an idea of what they wanted the children to get out of the activity: Goals had to be set, activities had to be formulated, and the teachers had to come up with effective ways of getting their ideas across to the children. The teachers themselves wrote a book based on their efforts to make Logo part of their classrooms. Their experiences while attempting to follow the radical child-centered approach advocated by Papert suggests that in the case of complex symbol systems, the educational activity must be guided by more mature members of the culture.

When an activity is made functional from the teacher's point of view, the children's activity may change. Those who follow Papert's child-centered approach fear that the activity will lose its intrinsic motivation once teachers decide they want to teach programming. This should not be the case if the teacher's role is to guide rather than to impose the activity. However, important changes can result when the activity becomes part of the children's schoolwork. For example, children were often observed working cooperatively while doing Logo. The children's interviews indicated that the relatively high level of cooperative work was a result of the activity's not being seen as part of the official schoolwork (Hawkins, 1983). There is some concern, even in Bank Street classrooms where a high value is placed on cooperation, that children will be less cooperative when the activity is no longer perceived as play and they have to be accountable to a teacher. FLEs must be functional for both teachers and children for education to happen. The coordination and optimization of these functions, however, remains a difficult issue that demands the attention of educators.

SIMULATING A FUNCTION:
THE VOYAGE OF THE MIMI

Another illustration of the importance of the teacher in the structuring of a FLE is found in Bank Street's Project in Mathematics and Science Education. Materials developed by the project include a television series, software simulations, and workbooks, all of which emphasize the process and tools of scientific work. My focus here is on one aspect of the project in which a FLE is based on a multimedia simulation of a navigation problem. While the content is more specific than is the case with Logo, the use of the content is still conditioned by the teacher's interpretation of its function.

A television series, The Voyage of the Mimi, tells the story of an expedition to study whales off the New England coast. A group of scientists and their teenage research assistants charter a schooner captained by an old sailor. Although the boat is old-fashioned, it is equipped with elec-

tronic navigation equipment, as well as computers and other sophisticated scientific gear. Thirteen episodes take the expedition through a
series of adventures in which the crew learns a lot about the sea, whales,
navigation, survival in the wilderness, and each other. In one episode, a
bad electrical connection causes several instruments to malfunction. The
captain suspects that they have been moving faster than his knotmeter
indicates, so he has one of the assistants use the battery-operated radio
direction finder to establish their position. The assistant calls down the
compass bearings for two beacons while the captain plots the position of
the boat on the chart. He finds that they are actually much closer to dan-
gerous shoals than he had thought. This episode illustrates a functional
environment for navigational equipment, as well as for geometry-related
skills concerned with intersecting lines and measurement of angles.

A simulation created as part of this project engages the same skills in
a similar FLE. The game "Rescue Mission" simulates a navigational
problem in which the players must determine their own position using a
simulated radio direction finder, locate the position of a ship in distress
using chart coordinates, and then plot a course toward the ship. A simulated radar screen, binoculars, and compass are also available to indicate
the current location of the ship. Children play in teams, each attempting
to be the first to get to the distressed ship.

The episode described above was designed to show how navigational
instruments and geometrical concepts function in a real problem. It
engaged children's interest both because they could identify with the
teenage characters and because of the emotional and dramatic tension of
the narrative. The "Rescue Mission" game builds on the understanding
of navigational instruments, and adds the motivation of peer interaction
and the fantasy goal of rescue. Together with the print materials—workbooks and study guides to be used in the classroom—the show and software provide the basis for FLEs for a number of school-relevant subjects.
However, as we saw with Logo, the teacher plays an important role in
determining the nature of the software experience.

Char (1983; Char, Hawkins, Wootten, Sheingold, & Roberts, 1983)
carried out formative research to guide the design of the classroom
materials. Working in fourth, fifth, and sixth grade classrooms, she
observed the way the teachers used the materials and the children's responses to them. From the children's point of view, the materials were a
success. They enjoyed the TV show and were excited by the software
simulation. Interviews with the children showed that after seeing *The
Voyage of the Mimi* and playing "Rescue Mission," most understood the
functions of the navigational tools and the concepts of plotting positions
at the level needed to win the game.

From the teachers' point of view, the results were mixed. The teachers
in the study represented a wide range of expertise in their own science

and mathematics training and in their use of classroom microcomputers. These teacher differences in training and computer expertise appeared to lead to differences in their interest in and perceptions of the "Rescue Mission" simulation. Some considered it limited to the function of teaching about navigation, while others found a variety of uses for it across the whole elementary curriculum. For the latter, the simulation and the navigation unit functioned as a jumping-off place for teaching about geometry, mathematical measurement, estimation, the history of the whaling industry, geography, and literature.

Interestingly, it was the teachers less familiar with computers and the teachers responsible for a wider variety of subjects (i.e., those who taught more than math or science) who found "Rescue Mission" most useful. In contrast, the science and math specialists, who were also more familiar with computers, were less receptive to the game's long-term use. Char (1983) points out that these teachers used computers primarily for programming instruction and were not accustomed to software that presented specific content. Perhaps as a result, the navigational content seemed to them to comprise the primary educational function of the need to make explicit the full educational potential of the simulation to those teachers familiar with computers, as well as to those who are computer-naive.

The formative research on *The Voyage of the Mimi* materials clearly indicates the extent to which teachers shape children's exposure to materials through the FLEs they set up. It is not sufficient for software developers to create activities that embed important educational facts and concepts. A computer program per se constitutes a very limited FLE. The program must be interpreted by a user or a teacher who understands its significance for a variety of culturally important contexts. Like any tool, a program is most useful in the hands of someone who knows how it can be used.

THE FUNCTIONS OF NETWORKING FOR CHILDREN AND TEACHERS

The third project, one that will help to illustrate the coordination of teachers' and children's goals in FLEs, has just begun at Bank Street. However, we can draw on the experience of researchers Margaret Riel and James A. Levin of the University of California at San Diego (USCD) for examples of how networking can function as a FLE. Networking is a general term for communications systems that link up computers. Most microcomputers, when enhanced with a piece of hardware known as a modem, can send and receive messages, text, and even programs to and from other computers over phone lines. Networking is becoming a popular pastime among young computer users who call up computerized bulletin board systems to read messages from other people, leave messages about topics of interest, and exchange software.

We at Bank Street are interested in finding out if networking can be used as a FLE for writing and communication skills. Can we take advantage of children's strong motivation to communicate with their peers to create environments in which children can practice writing and learn to write better? An experimental FLE at UCSD gives reason to be optimistic. The "Computer Chronicles" (Riel, 1983) operated between schools in San Diego and Alaska, several of which were located in isolated areas. Children wrote news stories using a word processor, which were then sent to the other participating classrooms. In each site, the children, with their teachers' help, composed a monthly newspaper drawing on both local stories and those coming from distant places. In many cases, children edited the stories that came in "over the wire" just as newspaper reporters would do. In fact, the frequency of editing someone else's work for style and meaning using the word processor was much higher than is often the case when children write their own stories using the same technology (Quinsaat, Levin, Boruta, & Newman, 1983). Thus, the production of a newspaper became a FLE that not only encouraged children to write, but also provided a context for the editing and revision of their own work as well as the writing of others.

The "Computer Chronicles" shows the potential for networking as the basis for a FLE. It also illustrates a feature of FLEs that have been suggested as important by our other examples: the coordination of the goals of children and teachers. From the children's point of view, the activity was interesting because they were able to communicate with peers who lived in interesting and exotic places (Alaska and southern California, depending on your point of view). From the teachers' point of view, the activity provided a context in which children could practice writing and were motivated to edit and revise their work. These goals were not identical, but neither were they in conflict. It was because the teachers wanted an activity that would encourage writing and revision that they set up the newswire data, thus giving the children a chance to communicate with interesting peers. However, without the specific structuring, it is unlikely that the children would have engaged in editing each other's writing.

CONCLUSION

Three examples of FLEs have illustrated the importance of the teacher in creating and interpreting children's learning environments. While computer software can play an important role in FLEs as a tool, they should not be expected to carry the whole burden of education. Teachers are needed in order to interpret the tools in terms of classroom goals and the larger culture outside of school. Our examples have all been drawn from elementary schools where the need is especially clear. We suspect that as children develop, the role of the teacher as interpreter or as someone to present another side of the story is gradually internalized, with the result that the mature college student can be expected to use books and manuals to discover multiple points of view on many subjects. Yet, even mature students require the insights of experts when the subject matter is particularly complex.

Our focus on the teacher is not meant to detract from a concern for the children's point of view. Obviously, a FLE cannot work unless it makes contact with the children's interests and experiences. A well-designed FLE is one that coordinates children's and teachers' points of view so that both the children and the teachers can achieve meaningful goals.

AUTHOR NOTES

Paper presented at the conference on Microcomputers in Education, Tokyo Institute of Technology, Tokyo, Japan, January 8, 1984.

CHAPTER 4

PREPARING URBAN TEACHERS FOR THE TECHNOLOGICAL FUTURE

Karen Sheingold, Laura M.W. Martin, and
Mari E. Endreweit

EDUCATION IN THE AGE OF TECHNOLOGY

In 1980, a team of researchers from Bank Street College spent several months studying the implementation of microcomputers in three very different school systems. The purpose of the study was to identify issues that cut across the specifics of implementation in each district (Sheingold, Kane, & Endreweit, 1983). The issues identified then included: differential access to microcomputers; emergence of new teacher and student roles (teacher buffs and student experts) in response to microcomputers; the lack of integration of microcomputers into elementary classrooms and curricula; the inadequate quantity and quality of software; the inadequate preparation of teachers for using microcomputers; and the lack of incisive research on the effects and outcomes of the instructional use of microcomputers.

In 1986 all of these issues remain relevant. In most cases, they are more critical now than they were five years ago, since the number of microcomputers in schools has increased independently of solutions to the problems of quality software, effective teacher training, or research. While each of these issues deserves its separate analysis, the focus of the current report is on teachers—in particular, teachers in urban schools.

Urban school systems must meet the educational requirements of large, heterogeneous, relatively poor populations at a time when employment and resource patterns are undergoing major shifts. Although job opportunities in the cities are currently decreasing, analysts expect a labor shortage in the next decade (Bernstein, Therrien, Engardio, Wise, & Pollock, 1985). Despite a tapering in population growth (United States Department of Commerce, 1982–83), the big city districts still have the largest pupil enrollments in the nation (National Center for Education

Statistics, 1980). These districts recognize that if their students are to be part of the future work force, they must share in the educational advantages afforded by the new technologies.

Addressing the unique features of urban schools and urban school populations is critical in planning for the widespread use of electronic innovations. Unfortunately, however, the needs of cities have not been adequately targeted by hardware and software designers and manufacturers, by policy makers, or by researchers. In describing how school systems are helping teachers to prepare for the future, our report seeks to contribute to explorations about how technology may help the students.

To inform the report, we gathered information by reviewing research, conducting phone interviews with teachers and computer personnel in many large school districts, and having in-depth discussions with experienced teachers and teacher trainers in the New York metropolitan area. Since we could not visit school districts to observe and evaluate teacher training, our findings to date are provocative and suggestive, not definitive.

We begin with the assumption that how teachers are educated with respect to the new educational technologies will prove to be critical in shaping education in the next ten years. Teachers are faced with a work situation that is changing rapidly. They must become acquainted with the possible directions the technology can take and be prepared to design and experiment with options that make sense for them and their students. We argue that programs of staff development are needed that do nothing less than make teachers important builders of the school of the future. All of this is particularly important in urban schools, where a long history of inequality of educational opportunity for poor and minority students threatens to repeat itself in the domain of technology.

In what follows, we examine how training and technology issues are handled in current programs. We discuss how they might be handled to prepare teachers for the future, especially in the urban setting. Our discussion necessarily leads us to explore the workplace and visions of technology uses and users both at work and at school. Finally, we draw conclusions and make recommendations.

PREPARING STUDENTS FOR THE FUTURE

The introduction of microcomputers into this nation's public schools has proceeded at a pace exceeding predictions. Between 1981 and January 1984, the number of school districts with microcomputers almost doubled, and the percentage of districts with microcomputers rose from 38.2 to 75 (Quality Education Data, 1984). Even more dramatically, the number of schools with microcomputers more than tripled in that period, from around 14,000 to more than 55,000. In the fall of 1983, Quality Education Data counted almost 300,000 microcomputers in the nation's schools. It is generally accepted that there are now at least one million.

Were hardware acquisition our only measure, we could safely conclude that some important innovation was under way. What makes this conclusion uncertain is that the rate of change in education is usually slow, while that in computer technology is very fast. School administrators know that the computers they purchase today will soon be superseded by newer models. Teachers know that the software they are learning to use will soon be replaced by something else. While some teachers are very enthusiastic about the new technology and its potential for student learning, others assume that computers will go the way of many previous educational innovations—into the closet.

The closet scenario is unlikely, however, given the large investment already made in microcomputer technology nationwide, the rapidly decreasing cost of the technology, and the powerful forces outside of school —parents and the work place—that are placing microcomputers in a prominent educational position.

As for parents, it is hard to think of any previous educational innovation that has so captured their determination and energies. In many communities, parents have taken the lead in bringing microcomputers into the schools, through pressure on school and district administrators and through their own fundraising efforts. Many parents believe that computers hold an important key to their children's future, that if their children do not have opportunities to use computers in school, many doors to the job market will be closed to them. Some of the same thinking lies behind the commitment of many schools to programs of "computer literacy" (Center for the Social Organization of Schools, 1983–84; National Academy of Sciences, 1984). Since computers are becoming an ever-present technology in today's society and the work place, so the argument goes, students should know what they do as well as how to use and program them.

TECHNOLOGY AND THE WORKPLACE

But just what *is* the connection between knowing about computers and getting jobs? And what are the likely effects of technology on the work place? The Bureau of Labor Statistics projections (see Lewis, Fraser, & Unger, 1984; Riche, Heckler, & Burgan, 1983) prompt some analysts, such as Levin and Rumberger (1983), to conclude that technology will deskill workers, resulting in large numbers of low-level jobs (food service workers, janitors) and relatively small numbers of "high tech" jobs. Others (e.g., Noyelle, 1984a) argue that although jobs may be downgraded in status (salary, benefits, and chances for promotion), technology will result in a simultaneous upskilling; that is, many jobs not in high technology industries per se will require greater conceptual skills.

Several things are clear, regardless of which viewpoint one takes in the work-force debate. High technology jobs are not likely to be a significant portion of the work force ten years from now. These jobs represented 6% of the work force in 1982, the same percentage as in 1972 (Riche et al., 1983). While many workers will be using computers in the 1990s, few will be high technology scientists and engineers; rather, they will use computers as powerful tools to accomplish work-relevant tasks. Technology in the future is likely to restructure jobs within particular settings in ways that are sometimes radical and not easily predicted from current economic models (Botkin, Dimancescu, & Stata, 1984).

Work in the nation's cities is changing significantly and the job market is narrowing. Heavy industry in the mid-Atlantic region, which in the past employed urban school graduates, is becoming roboticized. Even when a decline in the heavy industry jobs that previously went to city youth is balanced by expansion of light industry jobs in the surrounding suburbs, the city's high school graduates may not be moving to those jobs. In the last ten years, for example, New York City has lost thousands of jobs that previously went to youth (Noyelle, 1984c). At the same time, white-collar employers such as insurance companies and banks have computerized many entry-level clerical tasks and, more importantly, eliminated a level of "back-office" jobs that used to link entry-level jobs to middle-management and executive jobs (Noyelle, 1984a,b; Noyelle & Stanback, 1984). Many service jobs—in hospitals, schools, and municipal systems—are being streamlined by technology (Levin & Rumberger, 1983).

With technology restructuring some jobs, eliminating others, and creating new types of work altogether, no one can look forward to doing the same type of job for life or to a traditional "ladder" toward upgraded job categories (Noyelle, 1984b). In this age of technology, neither employers nor educational reformers (Goodlad, 1984; Sizer, 1984) are calling for students to learn technical skills.

For today's work place, employers want high school graduates to have

> the ability to read, write, reason, and compute; an understanding of American social and economic life; a knowledge of the basic principles of the physical and biological sciences; experience with cooperation and conflict resolution in groups; and possession of attitudes and personal habits that make for a dependable, reasonable, adaptable, and informed worker and citizen. (National Academy of Sciences et al., 1984)

Employers rely on the schools to teach these general intellectual and social skills and are willing to take on the responsibility of detailed technical training themselves (National Academy of Sciences et al., 1984; Noyelle, 1984b).

These changing prospects emphasize the necessity for students to learn "movable" skills that enable them to adapt easily to new situations. Generalizable skills of literacy, problem solving, decision making, and communicating take on greater importance in preparing students to work. In earlier times, many business transactions were divided into separate clerical tasks and a complete paper-work process was not carried out at one location. With computers, complete transactions can be carried out by one person. But that individual must understand the goals of the transaction, its component parts, and the relations among these components (Noyelle, 1984a).

Partly because of the ways in which technology is transforming the work place, general intellectual skills and comprehensive literacy are now necessary goals for mass education (Resnick, 1985). To the extent that computers can be enlisted in the service of these critically important educational goals, their impact on education will be significant. For those students who wish to have computer science or engineering as an option for their future, being able to study the computer per se (e.g., programming, computer science) may be appropriate. But using the computer as a tool to achieve goals of learning, thinking, and literacy is likely to be of greater relevance to the needs of most students.

ISSUES FOR URBAN SCHOOLS

Preparing students for the future presents particular problems for the schools in large urban settings. While the general goals of education in the inner city are no different from those elsewhere, factors such as limited resources, the large sizes of districts, and the special needs of relatively poorer student populations have contributed often to very different educational experiences for inner-city children and their suburban counterparts. Lower test scores, higher dropout rates, and poorer employment prospects are a few of the indicators of the widespread inequities faced by city youth.

Familiarity with the computer, now considered part of a "good education" (Johnson, 1982), has been seen both as a means to remedy educational inequities and as a potential source of greater inequities. Concerns among parents and educators about equity of access to computers means that urban systems are spending a lot of money to make sure schools, particularly high schools, are technologically equipped. While large school districts have led the way in acquiring microcomputers for instructional purposes, in the 1983–84 school year urban schools were somewhat less likely than wealthy suburban schools to use microcomputers (69.1% to 72.6%) (Quality Education Data, 1984). In addition, districts with approximately 50% minority students were less likely to have microcomputers than were districts with minority enrollments of less than 25% (68.4% compared to 81.0%) (Quality Education Data, 1984).

Equal opportunity to have contact with computers is only part of the issue. The funding by which urban systems often acquire hardware may limit machine uses (Sheingold, Kane, Endreweit, & Billings, 1981). Such restrictions may work against the best educational interests of students in at least two ways. First, where uses are limited to remedial tasks or to drill, emphasis in mastery of basic skills becomes the central academic goal for students. In contrast, students in suburban schools are more often using computers in the service of more comprehensive literacy and reasoning goals (Center for the Social Organization of Schools, 1983–84). Thus, the use of computers can perpetuate a system in which more privileged students are expected and helped to achieve more generalizable literacy skills than are their less privileged counterparts. Second, the machines may be limited to business courses (i.e., word processing, spreadsheets) and programming courses. This makes it likely that girls and boys will have different access to the technology (see Hawkins, Chapter 13, this volume).

A prevalent source of student alienation from school occurs in the mismatch between patterns of learning in the school and home. Some educators foresee that the computer, being a new and relatively undefined entity for everyone, may offer an opportunity for students, teachers, and parents jointly to decide and describe common educational approaches. In order to avoid computers' becoming yet another arena of mismatch, several large school systems have developed strong parent involvement components, allowing parents to borrow machines and thus work on computer-related school tasks with their children (Chion-Kenney, 1984).

TEACHING IN AN AGE OF TECHNOLOGY

While there has been a great deal of discussion about the potential of new technologies for the education of students, less has been said about the ways in which technology may affect teachers and the profession of teaching. What is true for students is also true for teachers: They need preparation for being learners in a dramatically changing field, and they need additional training necessitated by transformations at their work place. At this point, exactly what forms the retraining takes must rest on a range of untested assumptions, just as curricular innovations do. We can, however, attempt to anticipate the changes to come from what we know about computers, their entry into schools, and the rapidity with which they are changing (Olson, 1984).

Futuristic thinking is always risky; whatever we predict will almost certainly be wrong to some degree. But for education and technology, it is more risky *not* to think about the future. Many believe that the power of this particular innovation is likely to transform education radically (e.g., Dede, 1983; Podemski, 1984). While some possibilities are exciting, others are profoundly problematic. Here, it will be useful to distinguish between projections that are based on what is already in place and more visionary speculations about the teacher and school of the future (asterisked sections).

Developers are already at work on information-management systems for students, complex performance analyzers, authoring systems with which teachers can customize programs, and telecommunicative linking of classrooms. Widespread use of such tools would affect the content, structure, and organization of schools, and thus the role played by the teacher.

Curriculum and Teaching

The content of school curricula (e.g., in mathematics) is already changing and is likely to change further as a result of an assessment of what students ought to know and need not know in a computer age (National Council of Teachers of Mathematics, 1980). More generally, the greater emphasis on thinking and learning skills, which educators are calling for (Adler, 1983; Resnick, 1985), may be heightened by the move to include computers in schools. If access to vast amounts of information is made possible through the technology (i.e., large databases accessible via telecommunications), then learning of facts may become relatively less important than learning how to search, query, make sense of, and evaluate information. While these skills are currently being taught, they are neither given high priority nor are they commonly well defined as curricular goals. Researchers are only beginning to study the organization of inquiry, research, problem solving, and decision making in classrooms (Hawkins, Char, & Freeman, 1984).

> * As curriculum changes, the role of teachers may shift from that of providers of content-specific information to facilitators of students' own information-organization skills (Sheingold et al., 1981). Instructional techniques might shift away from direct delivery of information toward greater emphasis on shaping students' mastery of information and their thinking skills—finding relevant information, solving problems, asking questions, thinking critically, and communicating ideas. The teacher of the future would need to know how to teach procedural and "metacognitive" skills.

Classroom Management

In the near future, a teacher may be managing something very different from a classroom full of students who are doing individual paper-and-pencil seat work, listening to a lecture, or engaging in large-group discussions (Center for the Social Organization of Schools, 1983–84). Computer simulations and many computer tool uses, for example, make possible and support students' joint problem solving (Mehan & Souviney, 1984). A teacher guiding students working together on computers in pairs or in groups requires observational and management skills different from the ones she normally applies, as well as new understandings about when and how to intervene in the student-based activity.

Effective use of computers as information-delivery systems in school settings may enable students to move through some academic content at an individual pace. Students may work alone much more than they do now, as some college students do in "self-paced" classes, or grouped with a few others in particular academic domains.

With the introduction of computer-based networks, "classrooms" could include students and teachers who are working together across long distances.

* To the extent that instruction becomes individualized, the usefulness of age-graded classrooms may be called into question (Berliner, 1984). It may be, too, that the location of learning can be wherever the technology is, namely, the home, library, or community center. Thus, the purposes and functions of school buildings may change (Levin & Kareev, 1980).

Measurement of Student Performance
In some schools, the computer manages simple instruction; that is, the computer keeps track of students' performances on drills. In two large urban areas we contacted, the basic mathematics and language arts curricula exist as exercises in a computer, accompanied by a set of diagnostic tests. Teachers test the children every two to three weeks to pinpoint weaknesses. The hoped-for outcome for this kind of assistance is that the teacher will be freed for more challenging work.

Computer-based activity of the more open-ended variety can provide teachers with new insights into what their students can do. Anecdotal accounts describe how teachers have learned new things about their students' capabilities as a result of observing them interacting with peers at the computer (Burns, Cook, & Dubitsky, 1982; Papert, Watt, diSessa, & Weir, 1979).

With a greater emphasis on skills of abstraction and comprehension, what student achievement consists of and how it is measured will need to change (Frederiksen, 1984). For example, the advent of the pocket calculator has meant that mathematical operations and estimation can be emphasized over calculation. Word processors have resulted in a new emphasis on the writing process, as opposed to spelling and penmanship. Standardized tests are already being altered to reflect new pedagogical goals (California State Department of Public Instruction, 1985; Eric Clearinghouse on Urban Education, 1984).

Determining whether a student is a good problem solver who can envision multiple solutions, plan solution strategies, and estimate outcomes is very different from counting how many problems a student answers correctly. A composition may no longer be judged simply by the number of spelling and grammatical errors it contains.

> * Through future "intelligent" computer systems, it may be possible to promote and diagnose student performance in new ways (Sheingold et al., 1981). Based on the student's performance, these systems might prompt the students to reconsider an answer, demonstrate a different process for solving a particular problem, or ask the student to indicate why she thought a particular response was correct.

Other types of intelligent systems might help teachers understand how students learn and solve problems by analyzing students' errors (Burton, 1981). Such diagnostic functions, if developed with the needs of teachers in mind, could help teachers zero in precisely and effectively on students' conceptual difficulties. In order to use such systems, however, the teachers would need to learn new ways of dealing with detailed information about aspects of students' cognitive performance.

The Role of Teachers in Shaping the Future

Three characterizations of the teacher in relation to the technology process may be distinguished. Each one has clear implications for training. As *bystander*, the teacher's role is considered irrelevant to or unchanged by the introduction of "teacher-proof" technology into classrooms. This naive view implies providing teachers with minimal computer-literacy and classroom-management training. *Consumer* roles attribute a gatekeeper function to the teacher, who is trained to decide which products to use from the array in the educational market. Finally, the characterization of the teacher as a *builder* derives from early classroom computer innovations in which individual teachers not only select but redefine learning activities using technology. In turn, significant ideas for revising the technology are generated from such onsite experimentation. This view implies a long-term professional development process of training rather than brief contacts with the new educational materials. If the teacher's role changes in ways suggested here, the teacher will have to *build* new ways of making learning happen in the classroom.

The work of teaching is likely to change with respect to curriculum content, classroom management, and student assessment as a result of the new educational technologies. Approaches to training that view the teacher solely as a bystander to or as a consumer of hardware, software, and curricula that others design may be completely inadequate to prepare teachers for the future. Perhaps more importantly, such approaches are unlikely to provide teachers a significant professional role in shaping that future. Technological transformations will be adopted by teachers to the extent that the technology is meaningful and integral to their teaching situations. This means that teachers must be encouraged as partners in the creative enterprise.

THE STUDY, ITS FINDINGS AND IMPLICATIONS

To ascertain the current state of school computer use and teacher retraining, a sample consisting of 28 nationally distributed districts was selected (see below). They represented cities ranging from 300,000 to over 7 million people, plus four large districts in either suburban or mixed urban/suburban/rural areas. Their school populations ranged from 45,000 to over one million. Minority students constituted 9% to 75% of the total school population in the districts (mean = 43.3%).

Districts Surveyed

Albuquerque, NM	Los Angeles, CA
Baltimore, MD	Manhattan, NY
Boston, MA	Memphis, TN
Chicago, IL	Milwaukee, WI
Cleveland, OH	New Orleans, LA
Dade County, FL	New York City, NY
Denver, CO	Oakland, CA
Detroit, MI	Philadelphia, PA
Fairfax County, VA	Pittsburgh, PA
Granite County, UT	San Diego, CA (TECC #15)
Houston, TX	San Francisco (TECC #5)
Indianapolis, IN	St. Louis, MO
Jefferson County, CO	Tuscon, AZ
	Washington, DC

Information about the computer programs of the selected sites was gathered in several ways. At 23 of the sites, a district person responsible for computer education was interviewed by phone. Five communities provided written materials. Finally, 18 people were interviewed who were employed by communities or involved in training or documentation of school computer programs. These interviews sought to elicit a description of implementation, the concerns of teachers, perceived obstacles, and ideas for interventions and activities that would support school systems in the development of educational computing.

Five general findings of our research have particularly significant implications for staff development. These include the fact of high demands for training, the development of "top-down" approaches to planning, a trend toward using computers as tools, the presence of complex equity issues, and the scarcity of resources for computers and for training in urban districts.

DEMANDS FOR TRAINING

The demands for training teachers in computer use are very high, from both the districts and from the teachers themselves. At least 50% of the districts surveyed wanted their secondary school teachers to integrate computer use into the existing curricula of their disciplines, and 75% mentioned the goals of computer literacy and awareness for all their teachers. Few teachers, however, are emerging from departments and schools of education with appropriate preservice training (J.F. Brown, 1983; Souviney, Martin, & Black, 1984). Fewer still have a level of computer skill that matches the needs of schools. Since there is a shortage of well-credentialed new teachers, the need for preparing teachers who are currently employed is great.

Several states have instituted requirements in computer competency for teacher certification and others are in the process of doing so, but in general participation in training is voluntary. In most cases, voluntarism is a necessity: Contracts do not permit mandatory training; districts are not equipped to handle large-scale training and are reluctant to pay for alternative classroom coverage for mandated released-time training. In inner-city schools, where educational continuity is already a problem because of a mobile student population and high absentee rates, teacher absence is seen as particularly undesirable. Compulsory training is therefore usually restricted to those who teach computer science and those responsible for implementing computer curriculum goals at certain grade levels. Districts do encourage participation in training programs by offering recertification credit, graduate credit, and monetary rewards.

Even under a voluntary system, districts are finding no lack of participants for the programs they offer. While some teachers are skeptical about the value of technology, many wish to learn computer skills, and some districts report that they can't keep up with the demand. Several districts claim to have already trained thousands of teachers. Some districts are having such difficulty keeping up with the demand for computer training that they are requiring formal application, principal recommendations and, in some cases, fees.

Voluntarism has specific advantages in the implementation of computer goals. It allows teachers to become engaged with computers at their own pace, to select their own entry point, and to choose among a variety of courses on the basis of personal interest. In this way, they are more likely to formulate meaningful goals and to achieve them (Oakes & Schneider, 1984).

The negative side of this approach is that there may be a poor match between the training available and the classroom situation teachers must face. Teachers sometimes receive training that they cannot put to use in their classrooms, and the result is frustration. Even when teachers can use what they have learned, their training is often too inadequate to make them competent users of computers. In addition, there appears to be little articulation of needs special to urban educators on the part of those responsible for teacher training.

Given the innovative potential of computers, the patterns of change in their use, and the uncertainty about how best to train students and teachers, it seems important to foster district commitment to "staff development"—long-term professional growth in the field—rather than to "inservice training"—immediate, quick immersion (Lieberman, 1984). To use the technology effectively, teachers need the chance to learn and experiment over a long period of time with support from other teachers, administrators, and experts. Such a long-term approach, with continuing support for training, is most likely to ensure that the training will be assimilated and that the technology will be put to its best use (Nathan, 1984).

"TOP-DOWN" APPROACH

Many school systems are adopting a top-down approach to planning, in which the teacher is the consumer of a plan developed and implemented by specialists and administrators at the central office level. Large city school systems, which must deal with up to a million students and thousands of teachers, tend to see central planning as the only sensible choice. They are also highly responsive to local pressure and to demands for accountability, and it is easier to be accountable when programs are designed and controlled at the central office level.

Twelve of the districts surveyed have already committed themselves to firmly developed and, in several instances, highly specified computer education plans. Of these, eight are to be implemented over 3- to 5-year periods. In some cases, specific computer applications are being written into curriculum guides.

The top-down approach is a disturbing trend. The large-scale, uniform, and prescriptive quality of such an approach may rigidify the use of technology in schools long before the educational potential of the technology has been developed and researched. Training programs that are driven by the need to institute change all at once, on a large scale, may well be less adaptive in the long run than training arising from classroom needs and individual teachers' vision of what they want to do with computers (Berman & McLaughlin, 1978).

When such planned programs of districtwide computer use and teacher training are developed in district offices, teachers are essentially left out of the process, although teacher representatives may sit on district advisory boards. Yet the experienced and thoughtful teacher, given a brief acquaintance with the possibilities of computers, can contribute greatly to decisions about how, or whether, to use them. As we have seen, some of the most imaginative and successful uses of the computer in schools today have come from teachers who were willing to redesign learning activities to take advantage of the technology, or who discovered new dimensions in the technology that could be shaped and revised for use in education.

Teachers should be central participants in and builders of the future of technology in education, not solely the recipients of decisions made by others, either in the area of training or in tool design. Specifically, they should be supported and encouraged to adapt computers to their own and their students' purposes, to explore the ways in which technologies can alter what happens in the classroom, and to share what they do and what "works" with other teachers. Their influence should be felt on what gets created and marketed for schools during the process of development, not after. Teacher-development programs must support teachers to shape and engage in "experiments" with technology, experiments that can inform and influence the future of technology in education. For districts with large numbers of poor and minority students, such an approach will make possible local design and implementation of programs that may be of particular benefit to such students, and to their teachers.

TRENDS TO TOOL USES OF COMPUTERS

The focus of educational uses of computers has shifted from computers as objects of study (programming and computer literacy) to computers as tools for learning. While programming is still a popular activity at the secondary level, its importance is increasingly questioned in the lower grades, and only 20% of the districts surveyed defined their educational computing programs as a computer literacy curriculum for K-12 students. The current school goal is the integration of computers throughout the curriculum.

The most frequently cited activity is word processing, which is no longer confined to courses intended to prepare students for careers in business. The computer is slated to become a writing tool of the English Department and of remedial education, and in places where there is adequate equipment, of the social studies, the sciences, and other disciplines.

Another frequently reported computer activity is database management. The use of popular commercial systems is still taught in computer science and business courses, but electronic filing systems are also turning up in social studies and science, home economics, and health education. Some school systems are creating local databases that students can access through a local area network (LAN). Others allow students to go ''on line'' through telecommunication systems to access large, nationally available databases.

The use of electronic spreadsheets is another computer skill that is beginning to be more widely taught. Business-course students in high schools are the primary target for this training, but spreadsheet packages are also turning up in high school math and science classes, and anywhere else that students need to manipulate interdependent, quantitative variables and teachers understand the applicability of the spreadsheet as a problem-solving tool.

Concurrent with repeated shifts in computer use, teacher training is reported to have entered a new phase, a phase in which priority is placed on applications of the computer. In the long run, such emphasis may promote smaller scale, more personalized training programs, since applications lend themselves to multiple uses.

We remain skeptical of the quality of the current state of training and implementation of tool uses in schools. Using software that was not designed for the classroom environment creates instructional difficulties (Hawkins & Kurland, 1984). In a series of classroom-based studies on the use of database management software in Northeast school districts, it was noted that ''few schools are currently using them, even fewer are using them with students in classsrooms, and only a handful of teachers are making substantial or creative use of the software'' as thinking tools (Hawkins et al., 1984). Rather, in the schools visited, the software was often used to illustrate business uses of software. It was not integrated into the ''business'' of classroom learning.

Despite these difficulties, the refocusing of the goals of school districts on tool uses and on the integration of computers with curriculum are encouraging developments. Accomplishing these goals, however, makes much more serious the role of long-term staff development. Using computers effectively as tools in the classroom requires rethinking how some kinds of work get done in the classroom—both the content and the social context of that work (Sheingold et al., 1983).

EQUITY IN ACCESS TO COMPUTER EDUCATION

The largest school districts have been leaders in the rapid increase in the use of microcomputers for instructional purposes. This year, students in large high schools of the nation's largest school systems are virtually certain to have access to an educational computing program. Junior high school students in large schools in these systems are the next most likely to have organized access to computers. Elementary school students are still the least likely to use computers in their school programs (Quality Education Data, 1984). School systems that have multiyear plans for computer purchase and program development tend to start at the high school level and work down year by year, reasoning that the younger pupils will eventually have their opportunity for computer exposure.

A widespread concern for achieving computer-access equity for inner-city students has meant that, in spite of limited response in general, schools are spending a lot of money in this area. But while urban high school students are now probably just as likely to be in contact with computers as are suburban students, students at elementary levels are not (Quality Education Data, 1984). Favoring secondary over elementary students may accentuate inequities. The kinds of skills that educational analysts hope computers will promote are acquired early in the educational career—that is, before high school (Goodlad, 1984). By the ninth grade, a selection process is in place, eliminating choices of careers and courses for some students, especially for minority ethnic groups and for girls in general.

Moreover, inequities may exist in *how* computers are used. More advantaged students are more likely to use computers in ways that promote new learning, while less advantaged students are more likely to use them for drill (Eric Clearinghouse on Urban Education, 1984; Mehan & Souviney, 1984). To the extent that computer use is increasingly being infused into the curriculum, it may address the problem of equity of access. For example, where word processing is taught only as part of business education, it becomes the domain of female students. Where database management is part of a computer science elective, boys are overwhelmingly the recipients of the training (California Basic Education Data Systems (1982–83). But when these skills are introduced as part of English, social studies, or some other part of the curriculum compulsory for all students, the situation changes. Many students—boys and girls, minority and majority, at all achievement levels—are at the keyboard learning computing skills along with their subject area studies.

Urban schools face special problems in integrating computers with the curriculum. Lack of equipment, security concerns, class size, and teacher training availability are some. For some communities, too, there is a critical lack of bilingual software, as well as a lack of support for developing these educational tools (Diaz, 1984; Moll, 1985).

For a teacher trying to meet the many educational and social needs of urban students, computer training that is perceived as useful is vital lest the technology be rejected as one more burden. With fewer resources for staff development in the inner cities than in more affluent districts, there is good reason for concern that skepticism on the part of teachers about the utility of computers will inadvertently be reinforced and that the hardware now in place will not be utilized to its fullest capacity.

SCARCITY OF RESOURCES

Predictably, many communities cite insufficient funds as a major obstacle to implementing computer programs in the schools. The school districts sampled are some of the largest in the country, and they are beset by general budget problems: loss of population, a weakened tax base, loss of federal funds, and budget-capping by the state. They must try to respond to the social and financial inequities that exist among different areas of the community, as well as between inner-city populations and those of the suburbs.

The cost of providing computers is tremendous. State and federal funds have been inadequate to meet even minimal needs. In many districts, Chapter I funds have been used to equip compensatory education programs, but access to such programs is limited to those students eligible by reason of school failure and low socioeconomic status. Chapter II funds (federal funds administered as block grants through the states) are more flexible and have been used by several districts. The level of state funding specifically targeted for computer programs varies greatly.

Community resources also vary widely. In a district with a concentration of business and industry, local businessmen may cooperate in "adopt-a-school" programs, providing such support as equipment donations, technical consulting, and summer employment for students. Some districts have large research universities supporting experimental programs; some have active parent groups that take the lead in organizing, equipping, and consulting for the school's computer program. In many districts, however, limited funding has resulted in difficult decisions about allocating equipment, especially when the district includes both low-income areas and more affluent schools where some equipment is already in place.

Federal and state funding for training is less available than money for the purchase of hardware. In fact, it is rarely available. Moreover, in many places expertise for training is in short supply. While, in some districts, universities and schools of education have been able to provide training resources, for the most part Higher Education lags far behind the school systems themselves in understanding and responding to the need for training.

Finally, resources for well-researched quality software have not been forthcoming, either from government or from commercial sources (National Academy of Sciences, 1984). There are great limitations in the programs geared for school use, as well as in the research-based knowledge about how to create programs most useful for students' learning and teachers' effectiveness. Here, again, we see the need for teachers' perspectives and expertise to inform research and development efforts (Lesgold & Reif, 1983).

CONCLUSIONS AND RECOMMENDATIONS

Our analysis of the retraining needs of teachers in urban schools for using computer technology has resulted in a complex story, with both encouraging and sobering themes. On the positive side, large urban systems are committed, as are their suburban counterparts, to making computer education available to their students and training accessible to their teachers. Moreover, there is a widespread and intense demand for training on the part of teachers. Since such training is almost always undertaken voluntarily, the demand indicates high interest and enthusiasm.

In addition, there is a marked shift in priorities for how students and teachers use computers toward tool uses of the computer and integration of the computer with the curriculum, in contrast to earlier emphases on the computer as an object of study and as a device for drill and practice. These are encouraging trends, since tool uses appear more likely to support the kind of learning, problem-solving, and information-management skills required of citizens and workers in the information age.

On the negative side, resources are severely limited. Many systems are unable to meet the local demand for equipment and training and do not foresee any improvement in the funding picture. It is also not clear in what ways issues related to schooling for urban poor and minority groups are being taken into account in the training of teachers and in plans for school use of computers. Issues of concern to minorities and the poor—such as cultural differences, differences in family demographics and in home support for school activities, lack of resources, and limited job prospects—are often ignored by decision makers and leadership in the field of educational technology. Definition is needed as to what *are* the best ways to use the technology to meet the needs of these students and their teachers for valuable educational experiences. Finally, and perhaps most distressing, is the trend toward top-down, short-term teacher training and program implementation in many large districts. While this trend is understandable, it may well undermine what the districts seek to achieve—improvement in the quality of education.

Although there are many recommendations we could make, we restrict them to those that bear directly on improving teacher training and on addressing specific needs of urban schools.

1. *Identify, support the development of, study, and disseminate effective models of staff development.* Such effective programs of staff development for computer education should include goals to support urban school efforts to improve student preparedness for the future, provide teachers with flexibility for coping with future developments in educational technology, and involve teachers as shapers of how technology is used in the schools. They would best be designed to:

- ensure that at least some of what teachers learn will be directly put to use in classrooms;
- include extensive support and consultation systems for teachers, both during and after training, through special meetings, in-class consultation, opportunities to visit other sites and attend conferences, and use of electronic networking;
- encourage professionalism in teachers by drawing on their skills to shape educational uses of technology and by providing voluntary, tailored training options, access to state-of-the-art technology, feedback mechanisms by which they can reflect on their practices, and dissemination of information on technology and educational changes.

2. *Identify and support the development of effective higher education programs to create new expertise and new leadership in the field of practice, research, and development of educational technology for the urban setting.* Higher education should be providing in-depth education to urban practitioner-leaders and trainers, to those who have or wish to have policy-making positions, and to those who wish to make research and/or development in the field of educational technology their careers. The development and implementation of such programs deserve encouragement and support.

3. *Design, implement, and study small-scale experimental projects with particular relevance for urban schools.* Large-scale, comprehensive programs are often prohibitively expensive, difficult to implement and learn from, and less responsive to teachers' needs. What is needed now are small-scale, clearly focused, experimental projects in technology adoption by schools for which there are adequate resources to do a good job of implementation. Building on local involvement and enthusiasm, they should include support for helping participants reflect on and learn from what they do as they do it, and for assessing the extent to which project goals were met. Such experiments should also provide for imagi-

native and powerful avenues of dissemination for the models. Examples of ideas that might form the core of such experiments include: (a) using technology to promote comprehensive literacy in urban schools; (b) using computer networking to support teacher communication within and among districts; (c) involving parents in school activities with their children via computers; and (d) introducing urban schools and teachers to state-of-the-art software and hardware under development, whose design they could both learn from and influence.

There are no quick, short-term, or inexpensive solutions to the problems of helping teachers in urban schools to use technology and assuring that the technology is put to the best use for the students in these schools. And technology alone, even put to its best use, cannot be expected to remedy the many deep problems that beset urban schools. But at this moment in our history, if there is a lever for renewal of education in this country, it is the microcomputer. Teachers who can use the technology in the interests of their urban students can be a major force in helping their students to function effectively as citizens and workers in the technology age.

AUTHOR NOTES

We are grateful to the Ford Foundation for its support of this work and of the preparation and dissemination of this paper. The content is solely the responsibility of the authors. We wish to express our appreciation to the many district administrators who generously took the time to talk with us, to the Bank Street College Computer Outreach staff, and especially Stephen Shuller, who shared experiences and insights with us, and to the teachers and researchers who contributed their observations to this effort. Nina Gunzenhauser provided invaluable editorial help.

CHAPTER 5

BEYOND BASIC SKILLS: LITERACY AND TECHNOLOGY FOR MINORITY SCHOOLS

Warren Simmons

A changing economy and world have introduced a new standard of literacy that poses a critical challenge to schools serving educationally disadvantaged blacks and Hispanics. Throughout history, the definition of literacy in Western societies has been shaped by social, economic, and technological forces, such as the invention of the Greek alphabet (Have-lock, 1976), the development of the printing press (Eisenstein, 1979), and the 17th century Protestant education movement (Resnick & Resnick, 1977)—and today, by electronic word processing, publishing, and telecommunications (Levin, 1982; Pea & Kurland, in press).

The criteria used to define literacy in the United States are being transformed by structural shifts in the economy, such as the growth of service industries (e.g., legal, health, and finance-related businesses), technological advances in computers and electronic automation, and by global social problems such as population control, hunger, and human rights. These changes have important implications for both the objectives and methods of teaching, implications that threaten to reverse the educational gains made by minority students in recent years.

ECONOMIC CHANGES

The rapid growth of service and high-technology industries (e.g., computer hardware and software industries) coupled with the decline of heavy manufacturing industries (e.g., steel and textile industries) have created new types of jobs and new demands for literacy in the work place. Since 1980, the labor force has lost five million blue collar jobs while witnessing the rapid expansion of service occupations—nurses, secretaries, legal assistants, financial advisors (Bastian, A., Fruchter, N., Gittell, M., Greer, C., & Haskins, M., 1985).

A significant feature of the emerging service occupations is their dependence on oral and written communication skills and the ability to use technology as a tool to manage and distribute information (Sheingold, Martin, & Endreweit, Chapter 4, this volume). Walberg (1984) estimates that job-related reading activities ''may constitute a quarter or a third of adult work and currently amount to about $500 billion per year in compensated adult time'' (p. 2). The increasing role of literacy and technology in the work place has fostered a host of predictions about the skills individuals will need to become productive workers and citizens, both now and into the next century.

REDEFINITION OF LITERACY

Over the past five years, a plethora of reports, commissions, and surveys has attempted to delineate the literacy requirements of what is commonly referred to as the information age or society (Sheingold et al., Chapter 4, this volume). Despite the number of reports on this subject and their diverse motivations and sources, there has been a considerable amount of agreement regarding present and future skill priorities. These generally include the ability to (a) comprehend a wide range of familiar and unfamiliar texts, (b) communicate effectively both orally and in written form, (c) think critically and reason logically, and (d) solve problems and make decisions (e.g., National Academy of Sciences, 1984; National Commission on Excellence in Education, 1983).

The importance attributed to extensive reading, oral, and written communication skills for the majority of citizens represents a significant rise in the standard of literacy applied to the general population. After World War I, for example, the literacy criteria for the general population (as opposed to an educated elite) for the most part involved the ability to answer questions, follow directions, and derive meaning from relatively simple texts (Resnick & Resnick, 1977). The literacy standards currently being applied across the population have in the past been limited to those interested in postsecondary education as opposed to entry-level employment after completion of high school.

Society's increasing need for a highly skilled and literate population has placed a great deal of pressure on an educational system whose ability to meet existing, as opposed to new, standards has been widely criticized. Employers faced with a shrinking entry-level employment pool and $40 billion in annual training expenditures are expressing an increased interest in and dissatisfaction with the quality of schooling

(Educational Commission of the States, 1985; Walberg, 1984). Educational statistics, such as a decade-long decline in college admissions test scores (The College Board, 1985b), an increase in the high school dropout rates for white students (Educational Commission of the States, 1985), and a downward trend in the reading proficiency of 17-year-olds (National Assessment of Educational Progress, 1985) have been taken as evidence that the nation's schools are graduating students who lack the skills needed to lead productive lives.

This negative depiction of the results of schooling has been reinforced by qualitative analyses of schooling, which show that students spend little time engaged in activities that might promote the problem-solving, oral, and written communication skills that are critical features of many new occupations (Goodlad, 1984; Sizer, 1984). Moreover, direct comparisons of the literacy requirements in a range of occupations and those faced by students in high school indicate that job-related reading tasks are more demanding and involve a greater variety of materials than do school-related reading tasks (Mikulecky, 1982).

In response to declining school performance and the observed discontinuities between literacy in school and at work, proponents of the school reform movement have proposed a 2-pronged approach to school improvement: (a) the implementation of policies and curricular changes that will strengthen students' basic skills; and (b) the introduction of curricular innovations that will enhance students' attainment of higher order literacy, thinking, and problem-solving strategies (e.g., National Commission on Excellence in Education, 1983). The first of these recommendations has had a significant impact on educational policy and practice in schools nationwide; the second, much less so.

SCHOOL REFORM AND MINORITY EDUCATION

Unfortunately, the crisis atmosphere in education has obscured the educational gains achieved by minorities during the so-called decline era. The late 1960s and early 1970s marked the beginning of compensatory education programs and the spread of school integration efforts in areas outside the South. The positive impact of these efforts on minority education is mirrored in a variety of statistics. For instance, there was a slight decline in high school dropout rate for blacks between 1971 and 1981 (The College Board, 1985a). College enrollment rates for blacks and Hispanics also increased during the 1970s. Furthermore, from 1977 to 1982, the average verbal and mathematical SAT scores of blacks and Hispanics increased, while for the most part national averages continued a decline begun in the late 1960s (The College Board, 1985a,b).

MINORITY EDUCATIONAL STATUS IN THE 1980s

The outcomes mentioned above speak to the progress made by minorities in response to educational programs designed to meet their needs. Despite this progress, a significant gap remains between educational attainment of white and minority students. For example, according to the latest national assessment (National Assessment of Educational Progress, 1985), an average black 17-year-old reads about as well as a 13-year-old white student. In light of the continuing minority achievement gap, recent cutbacks in aid to compensatory education, and a reduced commitment to equity in education, it appears that the era of "school excellence" is relegating the educationally disadvantaged to a "second-class" form of school participation. For example, the weakened commitment to compensatory education and equity may have contributed to the recent decline in minority college enrollment and the rise in the high school dropout rate among younger (14- and 15-year-old), as opposed to older (15- to 18-year-old), minority youth (National Center for Education Statistics, 1984). These trends suggest that in its initial stages the excellence movement may be doing more harm than good to minority education.

MINORITY EDUCATION AND THE
REFORM MOVEMENT

The apparent trade-off of equity for excellence is tied to the distinct differences in the way excellence recommendations have been implemented in minority and majority schools. The two central aims of the reform movement—renewed attention to basic skills, and the development of higher-order competencies—have been applied unevenly across minority and majority schools. Minority schools have devoted a large portion of their resources and energies to strengthening students' basic skills while, concomitantly, their counterparts with predominantly white enrollments have devoted significantly more attention to advancing higher-order abilities.

The prevalence of this pattern is evident in the stratification of computer use in white and minority schools. Surveys of computer use in schools reveal that in schools with large minority enrollments, computers are used primarily to provide basic-skills instruction delivered by drill-and-practice software (Center for the Social Organization of Schools, 1983-84; Shavelson, Winkler, Stasz, Feibel, Bobyn, & Shaha, 1984). In contrast, computer use in majority schools is characterized by an emphasis on the use of computers as tools to develop higher order literacy and cognitive skills and as objects of study (e.g., instruction focused on computer literacy and programming) (Center for the Social Organization of Schools, 1983-84).

The basic-skills approach (traditional or computer-based) to literacy instruction in minority schools has been criticized for undermining student achievement in three areas: (a) computer literacy, (b) learner initiative and motivation, and (c) advanced levels of literacy.

COMPUTER LITERACY

The extensive use of drill-and-practice basic-skills software in minority schools reduces opportunities for students and staff to obtain higher levels of computer literacy. This type of software limits the level of expertise required for use; that is, users participate in preestablished exercises and do not actively define or control the sequencing of computer operations. These restrictive features constrain users' abilities to control the technology and acquire deeper insights into the flexibility of its operation and its power (Mehan & Souviney, 1984; Pea & Kurland, in press).

LEARNER INITIATIVE AND MOTIVATION

Competency-based programs, which receive extensive use in minority schools, are examples of a paper-based form of instruction that also limits users' (i.e., students and staff) control of learning or instruction, and thereby their insights into the broader purposes of literacy. Both types of competency-based curricula (computer-based and paper-based) have been faulted for undermining student interest by focusing on the acquisition of isolated sets of skills (e.g., spelling, phonics, learning vowels and consonants) with little reference to their broader purposes, and providing few opportunities to apply skills to tasks other than those tied to the curriculum (e.g., reading newspapers or the classics) (Mehan & Souviney, 1984).

ADVANCED LEVELS OF LITERACY

Finally, the weight given to traditional or computer-mediated basic skills instruction in minority schools has been criticized for fostering a 2-tiered national curriculum that furnishes a basic education for minorities while offering a fuller range of learning opportunities to other students (Laboratory of Comparative Human Cognition, 1985; Sheingold et al., Chapter 4, this volume).

The preoccupation with basic skills in minority schools is especially surprising and troubling given the results of the latest national assessment and a recent report by the National Science Foundation (1985) on minorities and women in math and science. More than 80% of the black and Hispanic 13- and 17-year-olds tested in the last national assessment achieved scores at or above the Basic Proficiency Level, a level defined as the ability to "locate and identify facts from simple informational paragraphs, stories, and news articles" and to "make inferences based on short, uncomplicated passages" (National Assessment of Educational Progress, 1985, p. 15).

The results for minority achievement at higher levels were far less encouraging. Forty-five percent of the 17-year-old white students tested obtained reading proficiency scores at or above the Adept Level; that is, the ability to comprehend, analyze, and summarize complex written information on familiar and unfamiliar topics (National Assessment of Educational Progress, 1985, p. 15). Less than 20% of the black and Hispanic 17-year-olds tested achieved scores at or above this level. These test results demonstrate that while the literacy gap between whites and minorities has been narrowed at lower competency levels, the gap between minority and majority students' performance is widening at more advanced levels of ability.

This view receives further support and elaboration in a National Science Foundation (1985) report on science and math achievement, which indicates that while blacks and Hispanics report taking as many years of math and science as their white counterparts in junior high and high school, significantly fewer blacks and Hispanics enroll in advanced science and math courses such as trigonometry, calculus, chemistry, and physics. Furthermore, when compared to white students, blacks and Hispanics are more likely to be enrolled in general, as opposed to academic, courses during high school.

These findings, together with the recent National Assessment of Educational Progress data, indicate that there is a widening gap between the educational achievement and experiences of whites and minorities, particularly at more advanced levels of school curricula and performance. This alarming educational problem is not being and cannot be addressed by basic-skills curricular priorities in minority schools, priorities out of step with the skill demands of the information society and the educational needs of blacks and Hispanics. Moreover, the National Assessment of Educational Progress definition of Adept Reading Proficiency is remarkably similar to analysts' descriptions of the basic literacy requirements of the information age (National Commission on Excellence in Education, 1983). The emergence of the information society, then, has not only expanded the upper limits of literacy, it has altered the meaning of literacy at all levels. As a result, the concept of basic literacy in the information age is roughly akin to the definition of an advanced reading level in the industrial age.

The pace of curricular change in education usually lags behind other educational innovations. As a result, the basic-skills objectives adhered to by many minority schools do not correspond to recent changes in the meaning of basic literacy rendered by economic, technological, and social developments. Curricula that employ a linear basic skills approach to literacy instruction—that is, one that begins with basic and proceeds to cover progressively more complex skills—are still in wide use despite these developments and recent research that has advanced our understanding of the nature of literacy.

COGNITIVE RESEARCH ON LITERACY

The linear approach to reading instruction is tied to the strong influence of formal, as compared to functional, models of literacy on curriculum developers. For example, developmental (i.e., formal) theories of reading (Chall, 1983; Gates, 1947) outline reading generally in terms of movement through a series of stages ordered by the complexity of the skills which are their determining features, and by the presupposition that higher stages, which encompass more complex skills, depend on mastery of lower ones. Chall's (1983) 5-stage model of reading, for instance, begins with an initial reading phase characterized by a focus on learning the associations between letters and their corresponding sounds in spoken language, and proceeds through four higher stages: (a) reading to develop coding fluency; (b) reading to learn new information; (c) reading that involves dealing with multiple viewpoints; and (d) reading that leads to the construction of new knowledge and ideas.

As a developmental/hierarchical framework, Chall's model outlines a bottom-up progression of skill acquisition based on the order in which skills first appear. When applied to the reading process, stage models can lead to the false impression that processing also occurs in a linear bottom-up fashion. This notion has been dispelled by cognitive analyses of reading done in the last ten years.

Cognitive research on reading has shown that decoding (e.g., recognizing words) and comprehending written language involves the coordination and use of literal (decoding) and interpretive (comprehension) processes. Word recognition, for example, is largely accomplished through the use of literal processes (e.g., perceptual) that use textual cues (e.g., individual letters and letter strings) to translate written symbols into spoken language. These translations, however, also are guided by the reader's prior knowledge: Readers use their knowledge about text to develop hypotheses concerning the words that are likely to appear next (Adams, 1980; Lesgold, 1983; Perfetti, 1983). The relative importance of top-down (application of interpretive processes followed by literal ones) and bottom-up (literal followed by interpretive) processes in decoding, then, depends on the reader's familiarity with the text. When material is relatively unfamiliar, decoding may depend largely on deciphering textual cues (letter strings); where there is a significant overlap between text information and prior knowledge, the latter can act to facilitate processing at lower levels.

The reader's familiarity with the text can also influence the level of top-down and bottom-up processing when comprehension is the goal of the activity. A number of studies demonstrate that the meaning of text is derived from the inferences made by relating written discourse to prior knowledge (Bransford, Barclay, & Franks, 1982; Schank & Abelson, 1977; Spiro, 1980). Some degree of decoding must, of course, occur to allow the reader to relate information on the page to knowledge in memory, but without making connections between presented and previously acquired information, his or her understanding of the material is bound by the resources provided by the text.

EDUCATIONAL IMPLICATIONS

Cognitive research on reading has furthered our understanding of the role and importance of prior knowledge in both decoding and comprehension. A view of reading as a generative activity in which individuals actively construct the identity and meaning of text has also emerged from this research. One of the most general and straightforward educational implications of recent findings is that reading instruction should encourage students to use their knowledge as a resource for interpreting text. However, this seemingly simple recommendation requires the use of materials and instructional strategies that (a) encourage active rather than passive orientations to literacy, (b) represent students' experience and knowledge, and (c) promote analytic and inferential reasoning.

Many existing instructional materials and strategies, particularly those employed in basic-skills programs, fail to meet these requirements. Basic skills reading texts usually present exercises designed to develop isolated sets of decoding skills (e.g., phonics, spelling, grammar, vocabulary development). Generally speaking, this approach devotes little attention to the influence of text content and organization on the reader's motivation to learn, his or her ability to apply prior knowledge to the task at hand, and the extent to which the text elicits interpretive cognitive skills (Markman, 1985; Simmons, 1985).

In many ways, the well-noted inability of sizable numbers of students, especially minorities, to make the transition from literal to interpretive reading skills in third or fourth grade (Chall, 1983; Labov & Robbins, 1973; Laboratory of Comparative Human Cognition, 1985) attests to the failure of basic literacy materials and instructional strategies to move students beyond basic skills. This problem has prompted several research and demonstration efforts that use cognitively based curricula to promote interpretive literacy skills among educationally disadvantaged minority students.

INNOVATIVE LITERACY PROGRAMS

The Kamehameha Early Education Program (KEEP) and a series of literacy projects in rural North Carolina described by Heath (1983) are excellent examples of literacy programs which strive to integrate literal and interpretive skill instruction in the early grades. Both programs combine a concern for integrating lower and higher order literacy skills instruction with a sensitivity to the importance of creating learning environments that do not conflict with the culture of the community.

The KEEP program was initiated in the early 1970s as an effort to improve the reading achievement of Hawaiian children descended from the original Polynesian inhabitants of the islands (Tharp, 1982). In its early stages, the program adopted a phonics-oriented approach that met with little success. After testing and subsequently rejecting a series of hypotheses that would account for the phonics method's failure (e.g., possibility of dialect interference, lack of appropriate cognitive skills), the KEEP staff developed a comprehension-oriented program guided by cognitive/linguistic research on literacy and ethnographic analyses of relevant aspects of community life (e.g., parents' and children's attitudes toward schooling, community uses of literacy, organization of learning in community settings).

The revised program featured small-group reading lessons, which allowed teachers to relate to children in ways that were compatible with adult/child interaction in informal learning situations (i.e., those occurring in the community). Teachers were encouraged to demonstrate warmth and control, and to emphasize mutual participation in the lessons by creating opportunities for children and teachers to perform activities together (e.g., teacher and student take turns narrating a story) (Au & Jordan, 1981).

In addition, the lessons were structured in Experience-Text-Relations (ETR) sequences which helped children to apply and learn a process for interpreting stories that mirrors strategies used by more advanced readers. Lessons began with discussions about information and ideas related to the material to be read, with the goal of building and clarifying children's knowledge in reference to the story. The next step entailed the joint narration of the story by two or more people. Finally, lessons ended with teachers leading discussions about children's interpretation of a story utilizing its content and their own knowledge, and/or questions regarding the story's theme.

Comprehension-oriented KEEP reading lessons produced significant gains in Hawaiian children's performance as measured by standardized reading achievement tests (Tharp, 1982). In addition, the program also benefited students who were not ethnic Hawaiians, though to a lesser extent.

Heath's work with teachers in rural parts of North and South Carolina showed a similar concern with designing culturally compatible methods of instruction. Heath participated in a project to increase the writing skills of black and white, junior and senior high school students reading on a third to fifth grade level (Heath, 1981). The effort was guided by the belief that effective writing instruction must be based on the uses of writing in students' present and future lives. Qualitative analyses of writing in the community and prospective work settings of the students were done to identify local literacy practices and attitudes toward writing, and to see how these differed from classroom practices and teachers' beliefs.

These analyses indicated that the local community and work environments offered little motivation for learning to write. The recreational activities of the students, however, did involve cases of writing, and the project used these instances as a foundation for expanding students' writing skills by focusing classroom instruction on everyday uses of writing. For example:

> [The] students were asked to talk about the writing of others which created problems for them or their parents. Immediately they pointed out that information about social services, warranties and guarantees, and regulations related to housing were "too tough" to read. When their parents asked agents in local institutional offices to explain these writings, they talked in the same language in which the documents were written. Students were asked to try to rewrite these sources and to interview each other on the meanings of the documents in order to pinpoint specific questioning techniques needed in these "clarification episodes." Teachers stressed that certain "legal" documents used special language for the protection of the parties involved; other documents were not legal and could be rewritten. Initially, the students rewrote documents they brought from home or local community social service offices. These efforts took the students into several useful areas of language study. They challenged the merits of readability tests and basic word lists; they examined high interest-low level readers to determine their characteristics. They tried to determine what made reading "easy"—words or length of sentences, construction of discourse units or printing format and use of illustrations. (Heath, 1981, pp. 41–42)

In summary, this project engaged students in writing and learning about literacy (reading and writing) by starting with familiar content and discourse and moving gradually to analyses of school-related material and talk (Laboratory of Comparative Human Cognition, 1985). The introduction of everyday literacy materials and problems into the classroom raised students' understanding of and desire to learn about literacy, and increased teachers' appreciation of their students' concerns and abilities.

The KEEP program and the writing project described by Heath (1981) were the result of the combined and intensive efforts of researchers and practitioners to improve the achievement of educationally disadvantaged students. Both enterprises used research to identify patterns of social interaction, areas of prior knowledge, and forms of communication that were culturally meaningful and relevant to the goals of instruction. This information was then used to design classroom activities that helped students make connections between literacy and important aspects of their lives, and reading and writing skills and their impact on comprehension and effective communication.

The Kamehameha project and the writing project described by Heath demonstrate the importance of research to the design of effective literacy curricula for educationally disadvantaged youth from minority cultures. Most schools serving minority communities, however, lack the resources and guidance needed to embark on extensive research and demonstration projects similar to those described above, or to ferret out the instructional implications of recent research on literacy. In addition, the application of new literacy technologies in minority schools has thus far been limited to a few, mainly exploratory, efforts.

LITERACY TECHNOLOGIES FOR MINORITY SCHOOLS

During the past five years, word processing software for children has been augmented by database programs (e.g., The Bank Street Filer and the QUILL Library), graphics programs (e.g., The Bank Street StoryBook), speech synthesis programs (e.g., the Talking Screen Textwriter), and text-design prompters (e.g., Interlearn's Expository and Narrative Writing Tools) to motivate and guide children's acquisition of reading and writing subskills. The QUILL Planner, for instance, contains text prompts that help users generate ideas and identify topics for writing. The QUILL Library and The Bank Street Filer can be used to store new words and their definitions, and to compile categories of information that can be used as a writing resource. Voice synthesis programs such as the Talking Screen Textwriter enable children to explore the relationships between sounds and individual letters or letter strings. And, finally, software combining graphics with word processing capabilities (e.g., The Bank Street StoryBook) allow children to compose text and represent its content pictorially. In addition, through electronic storytelling, children can manipulate temporal and spatial relations between words and text (e.g., control the sequence in which sentences or paragraphs and the adjoining graphics are presented) to build suspense or emphasize an idea.

The amount of guidance or support provided by the software use and integration of various features varies with the educational philosophy favored by the developers. The Bank Street Writer, for instance, features a user-transparent design to facilitate use by novices as well as those who are more experienced. It is also an entirely open-ended tool that can be adapted by teachers or students for a number of uses. Other programs, such as QUILL and Interlearn's Interactive Writing Tools, furnish multiple levels of support based on the user's competence, or a teacher's judgment about an individual's ability (Rubin & Bruce, in press).

These types of writing tools are just beginning to be used in schools to improve the literacy skills of educationally disadvantaged minority youth. Thus far, research and demonstration projects using discovery-learning writing tools (e.g., The Bank Street Writer) and those that take a more directed approach to learning (e.g., QUILL) have produced promising results. For example, Riel (1983) used a set of text prompters and a word processing program (The Writer's Assistant) in an exploratory study aimed at improving the writing skills of educationally disadvantaged elementary school students (fourth and fifth graders) in San Diego. The text-prompting programs were used to develop students' prewriting skills (e.g., generating ideas and guiding questions, setting goals and priorities) and to stimulate the production of text. Students used The Writer's Assistant to compose, organize, and revise their writing.

Riel used a laboratory, as opposed to a classroom-based instructional model. The students left their classrooms to attend the Mental Gymnasium, a lab where they could exercise and develop their skills. The writing activities in the Mental Gymnasium were organized around the production of articles for a classroom newspaper, the "Computer Chronicles," and a newswire involving schools in California and Alaska. Comparisons of children's writing prior to the project and six months after its implementation were used to assess the project's impact on children's writing skills. The analysis used the average length of the children's stories as an indicator of their writing ability. At the end of six months, the average length of children's stories had increased to 63 words, as compared to 29 words on the pretest. Moreover, Riel reported striking changes in children's attitudes toward writing: the students were much more confident and knowledgeable about their writing during the posttest than they had been on the pretest.

Riel's work indicates that writing software that offers multiple levels of support for prewriting, composing, and revision can advance some aspects of children's writing when used in a laboratory setting by staff familiar with computers. However, the generalizability of these findings is restricted by the small number of participants in the project (8), the lack of a comparison group, and a fairly limited set of outcome measures (students' attitudes toward writing and the average length of writing sample in pre- and post-test sessions). In addition, Riel's work does not address the impact of computer-based writing activities on performance measures used by school systems and parents alike to gauge the effectiveness of instruction and the ability of students—standardized reading tests.

Research done by Pogrow (1985), however, does suggest potential benefits in this area. Pogrow used a variety of writing tool software, including The Bank Street Writer and Speller, Kidwriter, and Wordmaster, in a project to promote higher order thinking skills (HOTS) among educationally disadvantaged children in an elementary school in Arizona. Students in the HOTS project attended a computer lab staffed by teachers trained by the HOTS project team. During the lab, children engaged in computer-based writing, reading, math, and simulation activities intended to promote planning, problem-solving, and logical reasoning skills. Standardized tests of reading achievement were included in the measures used to assess the project's impact after two years. Although detailed analyses of the results are not yet available, the preliminary findings indicate that the test scores of HOTS students increased significantly over the 2-year period.

CONCLUSION

HOTS and the Mental Gymnasium represent seminal attempts to improve the literacy skills of minority and educationally disadvantaged children through the use of computers, writing tool software, and innovative learning arrangements and materials. Although much of the research has been limited, results suggest that interactive writing tool software, cooperative learning arrangements, and culturally salient learning activities can be used to increase students' participation in literacy and expand their awareness of the processes involved (e.g., setting goals, applying their own knowledge to interpret or produce text).

Thus far, the research has been less clear about the impact of computer-based writing activities on the development of cognitive skills related to literacy, and on performance on indicators valued by schools (e.g., standardized tests). Part of the ambiguity here is due to the limited duration and scope of the work undertaken. These studies have been small-scale efforts involving one or two classrooms. In addition, the attention of researchers has often been divided between studying the ways in which computer-based writing activities mediate the development of literacy and formatively evaluating the software under development (e.g., Barnhardt, 1985; Riel, 1983). These potentially competing goals cloud the objectivity of some of the work that has been done, and lessen the attention given to such issues as the extent to which processes learned and attitudes exhibited during computer-based writing activities are transferred to other situations where writing takes place.

POTENTIAL FOR CHANGE ON A LARGE SCALE

A popular approach to the use of computers in minority schools has been their placement in specially created "laboratories" outside regular classrooms. This means of intervention has limited our understanding of the feasibility and effectiveness of integrating the technology into regular classrooms for use by teachers and students. The computer laboratory approach lends support to the unfounded assumption that the educational conditions and practices in minority schools are intractable and thus require the development of learning "sanctuaries" that function outside the regular classroom.

This approach demeans the ability of regular classroom teachers and does little to build their computer expertise or alter their approach to education. We know from research that simply placing computers and computer tools in classrooms does not guarantee their effective use (Michaels, 1985; Shavelson et al., 1984). Teachers in general, but particularly those in minority schools, need support to accommodate the technology to existing conditions and demands. These demands include such factors as classroom size (students per classroom, as well as physical space for computers), student and teacher competencies, academic objectives and materials, computer and software resources, and areas of conflict and consistency between school and community experience.

A program designed to improve minority education on a sizable scale should start by upgrading the skills and knowledge of teachers. This would involve building their ability to understand and apply new technologies and models of literacy for educational purposes. It would also involve reducing barriers between school and community experience by drawing upon the latter as a resource for student learning and literacy. Such efforts should also be concerned with providing information to developers about the adequacy of existing software and what elements to include in the design of new software that would best meet the needs of students and teachers in minority schools.

Finally, parents, community leaders, and social scientists attuned to the realities and needs of minority schools and youth have to pay special attention to the educational imperatives of the information age, along with the recommendations set forth by proponents of school reform. Excellence should be a goal for all of our nation's children, though somewhat different routes to it may need to be created. Thus far, our schools are following a map drawn without adequate routes for educationally disadvantaged minority children.

PART II

TECHNOLOGY AND THINKING PROCESSES

CHAPTER 6

MAPPING THE COGNITIVE DEMANDS OF LEARNING TO PROGRAM

D. Midian Kurland, Catherine A. Clement,
Ronald Mawby, and Roy D. Pea

INTRODUCTION

Vociferous arguments have been offered for incorporating computer programming into the standard precollege curriculum (Luehrmann, 1981; Papert, 1980; Snyder, 1984). Many parents and educators believe that computer programming is an important skill for all children in our technological society. In addition to pragmatic considerations, there is the expectation among many educators and psychologists that learning to program can help children develop general high-level thinking skills useful in other disciplines, such as mathematics and science. However, there is little evidence that current approaches to teaching programming bring students to the level of programming competence needed to develop general problem-solving skills, or to develop a model of computer functioning that would enable them to write useful programs. Evidence of what children actually do in the early stages of learning to program (Pea & Kurland, 1984b; Rampy, 1984) suggests that in current practices programming may not evoke the kinds of systematic, analytic, and reflective thought that is characteristic of expert adult programers (cf. Kurland, Mawby, & Cahir, 1984).

As the teaching of programming is initiated at increasingly early grade levels, questions concerning the cognitive demands for learning to program are beginning to surface. Of particular interest to both teachers and developmental psychologists is whether there are specific cognitive demands for learning to program that might inform our teaching and tell us what aspects of programming will be difficult for students at different stages in the learning process.

In the first part of this chapter, we explore factors that may determine the cognitive demands of programming. In the second part, we report

103

on a study of these cognitive demands conducted with high school students learning Logo. The premise for the study was the belief that, in order for programming to help promote the development of certain high-level thinking skills, students must attain a relatively sophisticated understanding of programming. Therefore, we developed two types of measures: measures to assess programming proficiency; and measures to assess certain key cognitive abilities, which we hypothesized to be instrumental in allowing students to become proficient programmers. The relationship between these two sets of measures was then assessed.

Issues in Determining the Cognitive Demands of Programming

One of the main issues in conducting research on the cognitive demands of programming is that the term "programming" is used loosely to refer to many different activities involving the computer—activities ranging from what a young child seated in front of a computer may do easily using the immediate command mode in a language such as Logo, to what college students struggle over even after several years of programming instruction. Contrary to the popular conception that young children take to programming "naturally" while adults do not, what the child and the adult novice are actually doing and what is expected of them is radically different. Clearly, the cognitive demands for the activities of the young child and the college student will also differ. Thus, what is meant by programming must be clarified before a discussion of demands can be undertaken.

Defining programming and assessing its cognitive demands are problematic because programming is a complex configuration of activities that vary according to what is being programmed, the style of programming, and how rich and supportive the surrounding programming environment is (Kurland et al., 1984; Pea & Kurland, 1984b).

One consequence of the fact that programming refers to a configuration of activities is that different combinations of activities may be involved in any specific programming project. These activities include, at a general level, problem definition, design development and organization, code writing, and debugging (see Pea & Kurland, 1984b). Different combinations of activities will entail different cognitive demands. For example, a large memory span may facilitate the mental simulations required in designing and comprehending programs. Or analogical reasoning skill may be important for recognizing the similarity of different programming tasks and for transferring programming methods or procedures from one context to another. An adequate assessment of the cognitive demands of programming will depend on analyses of the programming activity and examination of the demands of different component processes.

Specifying Levels of Programming Expertise

In assessing the cognitive demands of programming, specifying the intended level of expertise is essential since different levels of expertise entail different cognitive demands. In many Logo programming classrooms, we have observed children engaging in what we term "brute-force paragraph" programming, or what Rampy (1984) has termed "product-oriented" programming. This style is analogous to so-called spaghetti programming in BASIC: Students decide on desired screen effects and then write linear programs, lining up commands that will cause the screen to show what they want in the order in which they want it to happen. Students do not engage in problem decomposition or use the powerful features of the language to structure a solution to the programming problem. For example, if a similar shape is required several times in a program, students will write new code each time the effect is required, rather than writing one general procedure and calling on it repeatedly. Programs thus consist of long strips of Logo primitives that are nearly impossible to read, modify, or debug, even for the students who have written them. Although students may eventually achieve their goal, or at least end up with a graphics display with which they are satisfied, the only "demands" we can imagine for such a linear approach to programming are stamina and determination.

Thus, as a first step in determining the cognitive demands for learning or doing programming, we need to distinguish between *linear* and *modular* programming (i.e., between learning to program elegantly and efficiently, and using a style that emphasizes the generation of effects without any consideration of how they were generated).

The beginner's linear style of constructing programs, whether in Logo or BASIC, contrasts with modular programming—a planful process of structured problem solving. Here, component elements of a task are isolated, procedures for their execution developed, and the parts assembled into a program and debugged. This type of programming requires a relatively high-level understanding of the language. Modular programming in Logo, where programs consist of organized, reusable subprocedures, requires that students understand the flow of control of the language, as well as such powerful control structures as recursion and the passing of values of variables between procedures. The cognitive demands for this kind of programming are different from the demands for linear programming, as are the potential cognitive benefits that may result from the two programming styles.

Distinguishing Between Product and Process

In assessing the demands for different levels of expertise, however, it is important not to equate level of expertise with the effects the students' programs produce. We must distinguish product from process (Werner, 1937). We have seen very elaborate graphics displays created entirely with brute-force programming. One characteristic of highly interactive programming languages such as Logo and BASIC is that students can often get the effects they want simply by trial and error; that is, without any overall plan, without fully understanding how effects are created, without the use of sophisticated programming techniques, and without recognizing that a more planful program could be used as a building block in future programs.

Furthermore, in school classrooms we have often seen students borrow code from each other, and then integrate the code into their programs without bothering to understand why the borrowed code does what it does. Students therefore can often satisfy a programming assignment by piecing together major chunks imported from other sources. Although such "code stealing" is an important and efficient technique widely employed by expert programmers, an overreliance on other people's code that is beyond the understanding of the borrower is unlikely to lead to a deeper understanding of programming. Therefore, if we simply correlate students' products with their performance on particular demands or programming proficiency measures, we are likely to find the correlations greatly attenuated.

Compensating Strategies
Identification of the cognitive demands of programming problem is further complicated by the fact that any programming can be solved in many ways. Different programmers can utilize a different mix of component processes to write a successful program. This allows for high levels on some abilities to compensate for low levels on others. For example, a programmer may be deficient in the planning skills needed for good initial program design, but may have high levels of skills needed to easily debug programs once drafted. Thus, it will not be possible to identify the unique set of skills that are necessary for programming. Instead, different programmers may possess alternative sets of skills, each of which is sufficient for programming competence.

The Programming Environment
The features of the programming environment may also increase or decrease the need for particular cognitive abilities that are important for programming. We cannot separate the pure demands for using a programming language from the demands and supports provided by the instrumental, instructional, and social environments. For example, an interactive language with good trace routines can decrease the need for preplanning by reducing the difficulty of debugging. Similarly, implemen-

tations of particular languages that display both the student's program and the screen effects of the code side by side in separate "windows," such as Interlisp-D, can reduce the difficulty in understanding and following flow of control.

The instructional environment can reduce certain cognitive demands if it offers relevant structure, or can increase demands if it is so unstructured that learning depends heavily on what the students themselves bring to the class. For example, understanding the operation of branching statements of the IF-THEN-ELSE type requires an appreciation of both conditional logic and the operation of truth tables. If students have not yet developed such an appreciation, doing programs that require even simple conditional structure can be very confusing. However, with appropriate instruction, an understanding of how to use conditional commands in some limited contexts (such as conditional stop rules to terminate the execution of a loop) can easily be picked up by students. Thus, in the absence of instruction, conditional reasoning skill can be a major factor in determining who will learn to program. However, with instructional intervention, students can pick up enough functional knowledge about conditional commands to take them quite far.

Instruction is important in other ways as well. It has been our experience that students are very poor at choosing programming projects that are within their current ability and at the same time will stretch their understanding and force them to think about new types of problems. They are poor at constructing for themselves what Vygotsky has described as the "zone of proximal development" (Rogoff & Wertsch, 1984). Consequently, too little guidance on the part of the teacher can lead to inefficient or highly frustrating programming projects. On the other hand, too much teacher-imposed structure can make projects seem arbitrary and uninteresting, with the result that they are less likely to evoke students' full attention and involvement. Finding the right balance between guidance and discovery will have a major impact on the kinds of cognitive abilities students will have available to them when engaging in programming tasks.

Finally, the social context can mediate the demands placed on an individual for learning to program, since programming—particularly in elementary school classrooms—is often a collaborative process (Hawkins, 1983). The varying skills of student collaborators might enable them to create programs that any one of them alone could not have produced. While teamwork is typical of expert programmers, it raises thorny assessment problems in an educational system that stresses individual accountability.

In summary, several factors complicate the identification of general cognitive abilities that will broadly affect a child's ability to learn to program. In asking about demands, we must consider level of expertise, the impact of supportive and/or compensatory programming environments, and the role of instructional and social factors that interact with children's initial abilities for mastering programming.

ANALYSIS OF THE COGNITIVE DEMANDS
OF MODULAR PROGRAMMING

Two central motivations for teaching programming to precollege students are to provide a tool for understanding mathematical concepts and to develop general problem-solving skills. But achieving these goals requires that students learn to program extremely well (Mawby, 1984). To use a language like Logo to develop an understanding of such mathematical concepts as variable and function requires that students learn to program with variables and procedures, generate reusable code, and understand the control structure of the language. Students must also become reasonably good modular programmers before Logo can be effective in teaching problem solving or planning. A rational analysis of the cognitive requirements of designing and comprehending modular programs suggests that students will first need to be skilled in *means-ends procedural reasoning* and in *decentering*.

We would expect procedural reasoning ability to be one of the important skills underlying the ability to program, since programmers must make explicit the antecedents necessary for different ends and must follow all the possible consequences of different antecedent conditions. Designing and following the flow of control of a program necessitates understanding different kinds of relations between antecedent and consequent events, and organizing and interrelating the local means-end relations (modules) leading to completion of the program. Procedural reasoning thus includes understanding conditional relationships, temporal sequencing, hypothetical deduction, and planning.

Decentering also may be an important skill in programming, since programmers must distinguish what they know and intend from what the computer has been instructed to execute. This is important in both program construction and debugging: In the former, the program designer must be aware of the level of explicitness required adequately to instruct the computer; in the latter, he or she must differentiate between what the program should do from what it in fact did. We have found that such decentering is a major hurdle in program understanding at the secondary school level (Kurland & Pea, 1985).

On the basis of this rational analysis, we designed a study to investigate the relationship of measures of procedural reasoning and decentering to the acquisition of programming skill.

METHOD

To investigate the relationship between these cognitive abilities and programming competence, we studied novice programmers learning Logo. Logo was chosen in part because of the high interest it has generated within the educational community, and in part because the Logo language has specific features that support certain important thinking skills. For example, the strategy of problem decomposition is supported by Logo's modular features: Logo procedures may be created for each subpart of a task. The procedures may be written, debugged, and saved as independent, reusable modules and then used in combination for the solution of the larger problem. Efficient and planful problem decomposition in Logo results in flexibly reusable modular procedures with variable inputs. While the same can be true of languages such as BASIC, the formal properties of Logo appear to be more likely to encourage students to use structured programming.

PARTICIPANTS AND INSTRUCTIONAL SETTING

Participants in the study were 79 eighth to eleventh grade female high school students enrolled in an intensive 6-week summer program designed to improve mathematics skills and introduce programming. The goal of the program was to improve students' mathematical understanding while building their sense of control and lessening their anxiety about mathematics (see Confrey, 1984, and Confrey, Rommney, & Mundy, 1984, for details about the affective aspects of learning to program). Those admitted to the program were generally doing very well in school and had high career aspirations, but were relatively poor in mathematics and in some cases experienced a great deal of mathematics-related anxiety.

Each day the students attended two 90-minute mathematics classes, as well as lectures and demonstrations on how mathematics is involved in many aspects of art and science. Each student also spent 90 minutes a day in a Logo programming course. The teachers hoped that the programming experience would enable students to explore mathematical principles and thus lead them to new insights into mathematics. The guiding philosophy of the program, which influenced both the mathematics and Logo instruction, was constructivist. This Piagetian-inspired philosophy of instruction holds that a person's knowledge and representation of the world is the result of his or her own cognitive activity. Learning will not occur if students simply memorize constructions presented by their teachers in the form of facts and algorithms. Thus, students were expected to construct understandings for themselves through their direct interactions with and explorations of the mathematics or programming curricula.

The Logo instruction was given in small classes, with the students working primarily in pairs—that is, two students to a computer. There was a 6:1 student-teacher ratio and ample access to printers and resource materials. In order to provide structure for the students' explorations of Logo, the program staff created a detailed curriculum designed to provide systematic learning experiences involving the Logo turtle-graphics commands and control structures. While the curriculum itself was detailed and carefully sequenced, the style of classroom instruction was influenced by the discovery-learning model advocated by Papert (1980). Thus, students were allowed to work at their own pace and were not directly accountable for mastery of specific concepts or commands. The instructors saw their primary role as helping students develop a positive attitude toward mathematics and programming. In this respect, the program seemed by our observations to have been very successful.

The emphasis of the course was on learning to program. The teachers repeatedly called attention to the underlying mathematical principles at work in the assignments, and at the same time tried to bring students to an adequate level of programming proficiency. Thus, the curriculum was designed around a series of "challenges" (i.e., worksheets) which the students were to work though systematically. These challenges included creating graphics using Logo primitives, unscrambling programs, predicting program outcomes, and coordinating class projects to produce large-scale programs. It was assumed that the students would find the challenges and the opportunity to work at the computer enjoyable, and would as a result be largely self-motivated.

MEASURES

We were interested in how students' level of programming proficiency would relate to the specific cognitive abilities that our earlier analysis had indicated to be potentially important. We therefore developed the following measures of cognitive performance and programming proficiency:

Cognitive Demands Tasks

Two cognitive demands tasks were developed and administered to students at the beginning of the program. The first, procedural flow of control, was designed to assess students' ability to use procedural reasoning in order to follow the flow of control determined by conditional relations. In this task, students had to negotiate a maze in the form of an inverted branching tree (see Figure 6.1). At the most distant ends of the branches were a set of labeled goals. To get to any specific goal from the top of the maze, students had to pass through "gates" at each of the branching nodes. The conditions for passage through the gates involved

Figure 1. Procedural flow of control task to assess students' ability to use procedural reasoning.

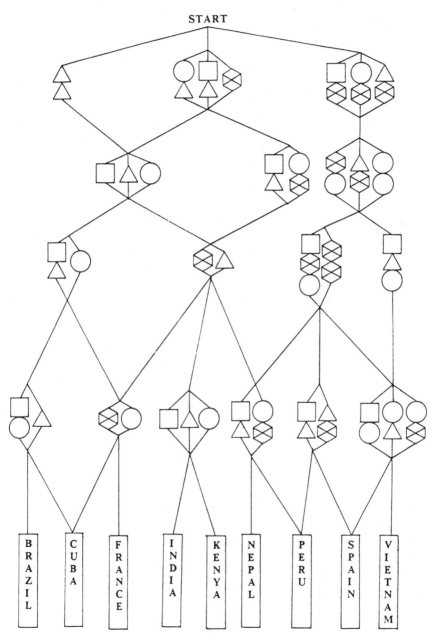

satisfying either simple or complex logical structures (disjunctive or conjunctive). Passage through gates was permitted by a set of geometric tokens with which the student was presented at the beginning of each problem. Each gate was marked with the type(s) of tokens required to gain passage. For example, a circle token allowed students to pass through a circular gate but not through a square gate. If they had both a square and a triangle token, they could pass through a joint square-triangle gate but not through a joint square-circle gate.

The task consisted of two parts. In the first part, students were presented with five problems in which they had to find paths through the maze that did not violate the conditions for passage through the gates. They were given a set of tokens and asked to discover all the possible goals that could be reached with that set.

In the second part of the task, we designed two problems, based on a more complex maze, to add further constraints and possibilities for finding the optimal legal path to the goals. Unlike part 1, at a certain point in the maze students could choose to trade one kind of token for another. In addition, as they passed through each gate, they forfeited the token that enabled them to get through it. This feature introduced additional planning and hypothetical reasoning requirements, since the students had to foresee the sequential implications for choosing one path over other possible paths. This task allowed for several possible solutions that met the minimum requirements of the task (i.e., reaching a specified goal). However, some solutions were more elegant than others in that they used fewer tokens. Thus, it was of interest to see whether students would choose to go beyond an adequate solution to find an elegant one.

The task was designed using non-English symbolisms so that verbal ability and comprehension of the IF-THEN connectives would not be confounding factors. In natural language, IF-THEN is often ambiguous, its interpretation depending on context. We therefore did not include standard tests of the IF-THEN connective in propositional logic because computing truth values, as these tests require, is not strictly relevant to following complex conditional structures in programming.

The procedural flow of control task, therefore, involved a system of reasonable, albeit arbitrary and artificial, rules not easily influenced by the subjects' prior world knowledge. The nested conditional structure of the tree and the logical structures of the nodes were designed to be analogous to the logical structures found in computer languages.

The second cognitive demands task was designed to assess decentering as well as procedural and temporal reasoning. In this debugging task, students were to detect bugs in a set of driving instructions that had supposedly been written for another person to follow. Students were given the set of written directions, a map, and local driving rules.

They were asked to read over the directions and then, by referring to the map, catch and correct bugs in the direction so that the driver could successfully reach the destination. In order to follow the instructions and determine their accuracy, students had to consider means-ends relationships and employ temporal reasoning. They had to decenter by making a distinction between their own and the driver's knowledge. The kinds of bugs students were asked to find and correct included:

Inaccurate information bug. Instructions were simply incorrect (e.g., telling the driver to make a righthand turn at a corner instead of a left).

Ambiguous information bug. Instructions were insufficiently explicit to enable the driver to make a correct choice between alternative routes (e.g., telling the driver to exit off a road without specifying which of two possible exits to use).

Temporal order bug. One line of instruction was given at the wrong time (e.g., telling the driver to pay a token to cross a toll bridge before indicating where to purchase tokens).

Bugs due to unusual input conditions and *embedded bugs,* in which obvious corrections failed because they introduced and/or left a bug (e.g., telling the driver to make a detour in response to a rush hour traffic rule, but failing to note that the obvious detour violated a second traffic rule).

Programming Proficiency Tasks

In order to determine skills in modular programming, we developed measures for three aspects of programming proficiency: flow of control, program decomposition, and reusability of code. In designing the test, we were concerned less with students' knowledge of individual commands than with assessing their comprehension of the overall strucure of the language and the pragmatics of programming. The test consisted of three parts: one production task and two comprehension tasks.

Production task. The production task was a paper-and-pencil test designed to assess students' skills in planning, problem decomposition, and features of programming style such as the conciseness and generality of procedures. Students were shown a set of seven geometric figures, represented in Figure 6.2.

The students were instructed to select five of the seven figures and write Logo programs to produce them. The task called for students first to indicate the five figures they would write programs for, and then to number them in the order in which the programs were to be written. It

Figure 2. Program production task to assess students' skills in planning, problem decomposition, and features of programming styles.

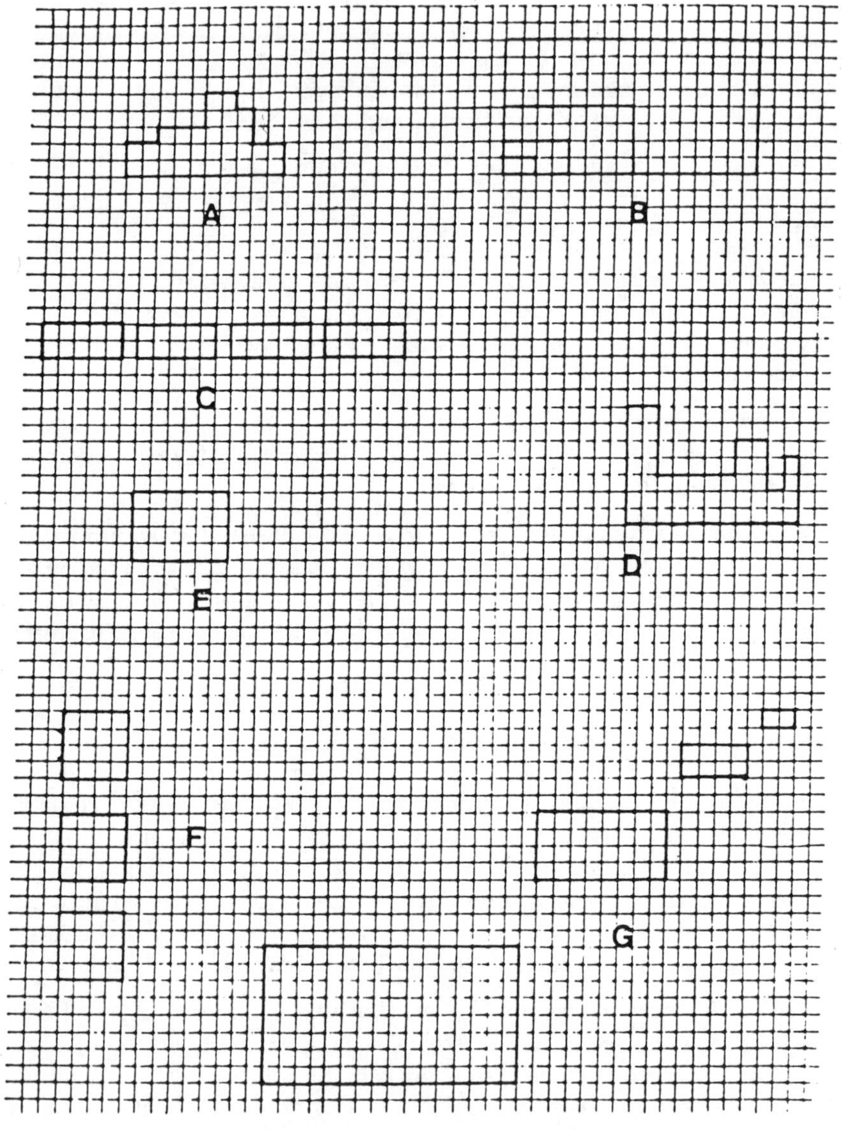

was hoped that this instruction would encourage the students to plan before writing their programs. Students were free, however, to alter the choice and/or order of their figures once they began to code. For each of their five programs, they were to write the code and give the run command needed to make the program produce the figure.

The task sheet included an area labeled "workspace," analogous to the Logo work space, in which students would write the procedures to be called by their programs. The layout of the task sheet, two sample problems, and explicit instructions made it clear that once written in the work space, the procedures were available to all programs.

The task was designed to encourage planning for modular procedures that could be reused across programs. In fact, figures B, C, E, F, and G could be programmed by writing three general-purpose procedures. An optimal solution would be to write a procedure with two variable inputs to produce rectangles, a "move over" procedure with one input, a "move up" procedure with one input, and then to use those three procedures in programs to produce figures B, C, E, F, and G. Also, Figures B and G could be most efficiently produced using recursive programs, although recursion was not necessary.

Figures A and D were included as distractor items. Unlike the other five figures, they were designed *not* to be easily decomposed and could not easily be produced with code generated for any of the other figures.

The task could be solved by planful use of flexible modules of code. It could also be solved in many other ways, such as writing low-level, inelegant linear code consisting of long sequences of FORWARD, LEFT, and RIGHT commands, thereby never reusing modules of code. We were particularly interested in this style dimension since a linear solution gives no evidence that the student is using the Logo constructs that support and embody high-level thinking.

Comprehension tasks. Each of the two comprehension tasks presented four procedures: one superprocedure and three subprocedures. The students were asked first to write functional descriptions of each of the procedures, thus showing their ability to grasp the meaning of commands within the context of a procedure. Then they were asked to draw on graph paper the screen effects of the superprocedure when executed with a specific input. To draw the screen effects, students had to hand simulate the program's execution, thus providing a strong test of their ability to follow the precise sequence of instructions dictated by the program's flow of control.

In the first comprehension task, the superprocedure was named TWOFLAGS and the subprocedures were CENTER, FLAG, and BOX. Figure 6.3 presents the Logo code for the procedures and a correct drawing of the screen effect of TWOFLAGS 10.

The second comprehension task included procedures with two inputs, and a recursive procedure with a conditional stop rule. The task was designed to make the master procedure progressively harder to follow. The superprocedure was named ROBOT, and the three subprocedures BOT, MID, and TOP. Figure 6.4 presents the Logo code and correct drawing of the screen effects of ROBOT 30 25.

Figure 3. First Logo comprehension task with correct drawing of the resulting screen effects.

Logo Prodedures   Drawing of Screen Effects

                                   TWOFLAGS 10

```
TO CENTER
  PENUP
  HOME
  PENDOWN
END

TO FLAG :X
  FORWARD 15
  BOX :X
  CENTER
END

TO BOX :SIDE
  REPEAT 4 [FORWARD :SIDE RT 90]
END

TO TWOFLAGS :X
  CENTER
  FLAG 15
  PENUP
  RT 90 FORWARD 20 LT 90
  PENDOWN
  FLAG :X
END
```

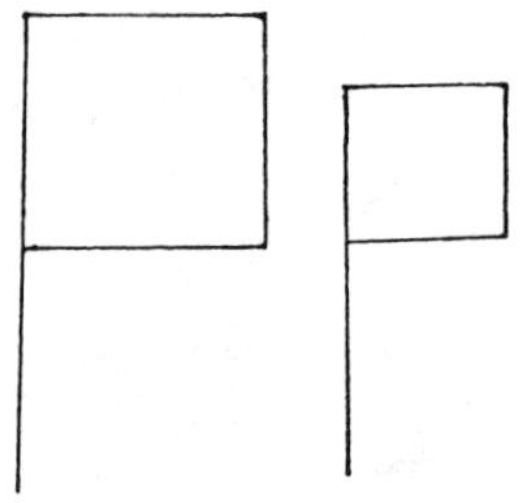

Both programming comprehension tasks were designed as paper-and-pencil tests that did not require the use of the computer. Students were given a sheet that listed the programs, a sheet on which to write their descriptions of what procedure would do, and graph paper on which to draw their predictions of what the program would do when executed.

PROCEDURE

The cognitive demands measures were administered to the students on the first day of the program, along with a number of mathematics, problem-solving, and attitude measures (see Confrey, 1984, for a discussion of the attitude measures). The students were tested together in a large

Figure 4. Second Logo comprehension task with correct drawing of the resulting screen effects.

Logo Procedures

Drawing of Screen

Effects of ROBOT 30 25

```
TO BOT :X :Y
  FORWARD :X
  RT 90
  FORWARD :Y
END

TO MID :X :Y
  BOT :X :Y
  RT 90·
  BOT :X :Y
END

TO TOP :X
  IF :X 5 RT 90 BACK 10 STOP
  REPEAT 4 [FORWARD :X RT 90]
  FORWARD 5 LT 90
  TOP :X - 10
END

TO ROBOT :X :Y
  HT
  MID :X :Y
  BACK 15 LT 90
  BOT :X - 10 :Y - 15
  RT 90 PU FORWARD 50 PD
  TOP :Y - 10
END
```

auditorium. Instructions for each test were read by the experimenters, who monitored the testing and answered all questions. Students were given 17 minutes for the procedural reasoning task and 12 minutes for the debugging task.

In the final week of the program, the students were administered the Logo proficiency test. Testing was done in groups of approximately 30 students each. Again the experimenters gave all the instructions and were present throughout the testing to answer students' questions. Students were given 30 minutes for the production task and 15 minutes each for the comprehension tasks.

RESULTS

Programming Proficiency Tasks

To use Logo as a tool for high-level thinking, one must employ relatively sophisticated Logo constructs, such as procedures with variable inputs and superprocedures that call subprocedures. To write and understand Logo programs using these language constructs, one must understand something about the pragmatics of writing programs and have a good grasp of Logo's control structure; that is, how Logo determines the order in which commands are executed. The empirical question addressed here is whether students can develop such an adequate understanding after five weeks (approximately 45 hours) of intensive Logo instruction.

Comprehension tasks. Assessments of Logo proficiency at the end of the course indicated that mastery of Logo was limited. On the TWOFLAGS task, 48% of the students correctly drew the first flag, which required simulating the execution of TWOFLAGS through its call to FLAG in line 2. But only 21% correctly drew the second flag, with 19% of the students correct on both flags (showing that in almost all cases performance was cumulative).

One-third of the students were partially right on the second flag. Analysis of errors on this flag indicated that more students had trouble following the flow of control than keeping track of the values of the variables. An error in *place* on the second flag suggests that the student's simulation did not execute all the positioning lines of code, especially the call to CENTER in the last line of FLAG. This reveals an error in flow of control. An error in *size* on the second flag suggests that the student did not correctly pass the variable from TWOFLAGS to FLAG to BOX.

On the ROBOT task, 65% of the students correctly drew the body of the robot, which involved simulating the execution of ROBOT through its call to MID. Thirty-seven percent correctly drew the leg, which involved following the execution through ROBOT's call to BOT in line 4. TOP is a recursive procedure with inputs to ROBOT of 30 25; it executes three times. The first time TOP draws the head, the second time it draws the nose, and the last time it draws the mouth and then stops. Sixteen percent of the students correctly drew the head, 13% succeeded with the nose, and only 2% were able to follow the program execution all the way through to the mouth. The cumulative percentages were within 3% of these absolute percentages.

Again, analysis of the errors of students who were partially correct showed that more of them correctly passed the values of variables than followed the flow of control. In partially correct drawings, the parts of the robot were more often correctly sized than correctly placed.

The students' written descriptions of the procedures in both the TWOFLAGS and ROBOT tasks showed that many had a general, albeit vague, understanding of the procedures. Often students seemed to understand the code in that they gave adequate glosses of individual lines. But when tested by the drawing task, many revealed that they did not understand Logo's control structure well enough to trace the program's execution. This became especially clear when the order of the lines in a listing of the program differed from the order in which the lines were executed.

Some students failed to grasp the fact that, since variable values are local to the procedure call, values can be passed among procedures under different names. Even more failed to understand the most basic fact of flow of control: After a called procedure is executed, control returns to the next line of the calling procedure.

Production task. In the production task, students made very little use of variables and reusable subprocedures. While most are able to generate these figures, many did so following the linear programming style. Only 21% of the students avoided both distractor items. An additional 35% avoided either A or D singly. Thus, 44% of the students wrote programs for both A and D. Given a low level of programming proficiency, choosing the distractors was reasonable because, by design, linear programs for the distractors were easier than linear programs for figures B and G (and comparable to C and F).

Among the possible approaches to the task are analytic and synthetic decomposition. By analytic decomposition, we mean analyzing a single figure into component parts, writing procedures for the parts, and having the program call the procedures. By synthetic decomposition, we mean decomposition of the entire problem set into components, writing procedures for the parts, and then having each of the five programs call the appropriate modules of code. Note that while the five nondistractor figures contain only rectangles, the rectangles are of different sizes. Thus, high-level synthetic decomposition, unlike analytic decomposition, requires a general procedure with variable inputs for producing the rectangles.

Students were much more likely to use analytic than synthetic decomposition. In fact, 88% wrote, used, and reused a procedure at least once, thus giving evidence of some analytic decomposition. However, only 20% of the students gave evidence of synthetic decomposition by using a procedure for more than one program.

Figure 6.5 and Table 6.1 provide more detail on the features used by Logo students to produce the individual figures. In the analysis represented by Figure 6.5, we wished to know, for each figure, whether

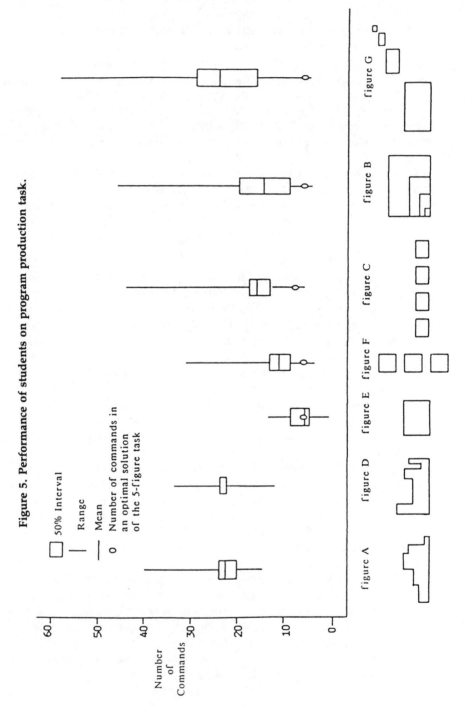

Figure 5. Performance of students on program production task.

120

Table 1
Performance of Students on Program Production Tasks

Performance (percentages)	Figures						
	A	B	C	D	E	F	G
% who did it	73	60	96	51	91	91	31
workable program	86	47	85	90	91	80	48
variables used	5	43	10	2	14	12	40
repeat used	8	49	65	2	49	84	78
recursion used	0	4	0	0	0	0	8

students could write code to produce it and whether they could correctly use REPEAT, variables, and recursion. The REPEAT command is the simplest modular feature in Logo. Variables go further in transforming procedures into reusable *functions*, making the procedure more general, and hence more useful. Recursion is an extremely powerful Logo construct in which a procedure can call on copies of itself from within other copies. These features of Logo make modular code possible, and thus support problem decomposition strategies.

The number of commands used to produce the program is a good summary indicator of style. For these tasks, elegant programs use few commands. We counted each use of a Logo primitive as one command. Each procedure call was counted as one command, and on the first call to a procedure the commands within the procedure were counted. On subsequent calls to that procedure only the call itself was counted.

The graph at the top of Figure 6.5 displays several statistics concerning the number of commands used: the range, the mean, and the region containing the middle 50% of the scores. For comparison, we also include the number of commands used in an optimal solution of the task as a whole. This particular optimal solution synthetically decomposes the five rectangular figures with three subprocedures, and produces the programs in the order E, F, C, B, G.

The figures fall into three groups: the distractors A and D; C, E, and F; and B and G. As noted, nearly half of the students chose figures A and D, and 90% of the students who chose these figures were able to write a Logo program to produce them. As expected from the design of the figures, less than 10% of these programs used variables or REPEAT. Most of the code was low-level, brute-force style, which could not be reused in other programs. Thus, while the students wrote programs to produce the figure, their programming style gave no indication that they were engaged in the high-level thinking that Logo can support.

The group of figures C, E, and F was chosen by over 90% of the students, and nearly 90% of these wrote workable programs. More than half of the students correctly used REPEAT, Logo's simpler, within-procedure modular construct. Less than 15% of these programs correctly used variables. This more elegant, across-program construct was largely ignored. As a result, most students needed more than the optimal number of commands to write programs for Figures F and C.

Figures B and G were chosen by the least number of students (60% and 31%, respectively), and proved to be the most difficult since only half of the students wrote workable programs. These programs used REPEAT and variables relatively often (REPEAT: 49% in B, 68% in G; variables: 43% in B, 40% in G). Thus, it seems that the skilled students who chose these figures did quite well. Of the other students who chose these figures, about half did not attempt to use variables, and half used variables incorrectly. Again, because few students did synthetic decomposition, most programs had more than an optimal number of commands.

No one tried to write a recursive program for any of the figures except B and G, and fewer than 10% of the students who chose figure B or G wrote correct recursive programs. This powerful Logo construct was conspicuous by its absence.

What factors may have kept these students from using the powerful and elegant features of Logo? It is unlikely that students did not notice the geometrical similarity among, for instance, figures C, E, and F. But in order to do a synthetic decomposition of the task, it is necessary to write procedures with variables. Moreover, coordinating subprocedures in a superprocedure requires a good understanding of Logo flow of control. Performance on the comprehension tasks showed that students had a fair understanding of individual lines of Logo code, but had difficulty in following program flow of control.

Cognitive Demands Tasks
There was a fairly broad range of performance on the cognitive demands tasks (Mawby, Clement, Pea, & Hawkins, 1984). Many students showed moderate or high levels of reasoning skills as assessed by these tasks, and a few found the tasks fairly difficult.

Procedural flow of control task. The two parts of this task were examined individually. The first part included a series of problems for students to solve, each of which posed a different set of constraints and/or goals for going through the maze. Difficult problems required a more exhaustive testing of conditions than did the others (i.e., the given tokens satisfied many nodes early on). Some problems were best solved using alternate strategies, such as searching from the bottom up rather than from the top down. Performance was relatively low on the more difficult problems (30%–40% correct as opposed to 55%–70% correct on the less complex problems). This indicated that when many possibilities had to be considered, and there were no easy shortcuts to reduce the number of possibilities, students had difficulty testing all conditions.

In the second part, there were three levels of efficiency among correct routes corresponding to the number of tokens required to successfully reach the goal. Only 14% of the students on the first problem and 21% on the second problem found the most efficient route, while 41% of the students on the first problem and 79% on the second problem were unable to reach the goal at all. Few students tested the hypotheses needed to discover the most efficient route.

Debugging task. Table 6.2 shows the percentage of students detecting and correcting each of the four types of bugs in the task. As shown, inaccurate information and temporal bugs were easiest to detect and correct (72%–91% success). Students found it more difficult to successfully correct the ambiguous instructions. Only 48% were able to write instructions that were explicit enough for a driver to choose correctly among alternate routes. For the lines with embedded bugs, only 21% fully corrected the instructions; 40% caught and corrected one bug but not the other.

Results indicated that students had little difficulty detecting first-order bugs and correcting them when the corrections were simple, for example, changing a number or direction to turn. However, when students had to be explicit and exhaustively check for ambiguity and for additional bugs, they were less successful.

Relationship of the Demands Measures to Programming Proficiency

Analysis of the relationship between these cognitive demand tasks and the assessment of programming proficiency yielded an interesting set of

Table 2
Debugging Task

Bug Type	No Change	Catch No Fix	Catch Some Fix	Catch & Fix
	Task			
	% of students (n = 70)			
Wrong Instruction	3	6	na[a]	91
Ambiguous Instruction	11	41	na[a]	48
Temporal Order Bug	16	11	na[a]	73
Embedded Bugs	29	10	40	21

[a] not applicable

results. As can be seen in Table 6.3, the cognitive demands measures correlated moderately with composite scores on both tests of programming proficiency.

Examination of correlations with subscores on the programming production task showed that students' ability to write an adequate, runnable program was less highly correlated with cognitive demands measures than were appropriate use of variables, the use of subprocedures within programs, or the use of a minimum number of commands to write programs (one indication of program elegance).

Other subcomponents of the production task that we assumed would correlate highly with the cognitive demands measures—in particular, whether students reused procedures across several programs or used recursion—were not highly correlated. However, so few students engaged in either of these forms of programming that a floor effect may have masked this correlation. Interestingly, although few students used the more advanced programming techniques, many seemed to manifest sufficiently high levels of reasoning skill on the cognitive demands measures. Perhaps other knowledge specific to the programming domain is required in addition to the underlying cognitive capacity to reason in the ways we assessed.

In general, the correlations of the cognitive demands measures were higher with programming comprehension than with programming production. The design of the production task may have contributed to these findings. Students could write linear programs and still succeed on the task, and most did so. This was true even for those who at times in their class projects had utilized more advanced programming techniques. In contrast, the comprehension task required students to display

Table 3
Correlations of Demands Measures with Measures of Programming Proficiency

Demands Measures		Measures of Programming Proficiency						
		A	B	C	D	E	F	G
				($n=70$)				
Procedural Reasoning Part 1	A	—	—	—	—	—	—	—
Procedural Reasoning Part 2	B	.34[b]	—	—	—	—	—	—
Debugging Task	C	.38[c]	.27[b]	—	—	—	—	—
Math Level	D	.51[c]	.38[c]	.42[c]	—	—	—	—
Production Proficiency	E	.45[c]	.19[a]	.39[c]	—	—	—	—
Comprehension Proficiency	F	.54[c]	.50[c]	.45[c]	.59[c]	.26[b]	—	—
Teacher Rating	G	.30[b]	.20[a]	.22[a]	.37[c]	.26[b]	.54[c]	—

[a] $p < .05$
[b] $p < .01$
[c] $p < .001$

their understanding of sophisticated programming constructs. Thus, while the comprehension task was better able to test the limits of programming novices' understanding of the language, a production task such as the one we employed may prove to be the better indicator of programming proficiency for students once they attain a more advanced level of ability.

We examined the relation between mathematics achievement level (assigned on the basis of grade point average, courses taken in school, and scores on mathematics tests administered on the first day of the program) and Logo proficiency. Mathematics level was as good a predictor of programming proficiency as the specific cognitive demands measures taken individually. However, when mathematics level was partialled out of the correlations, they all remained significant at the .01 level or better, with the exception of the correlation between part 2 of the procedural reasoning task and program production proficiency. Thus, our cognitive demands measures appear to tap abilities that are independent of those directly tied to mathematics achievement.

When both mathematics achievement and performance on our demands measures were entered into a multiple regression analysis, with Logo proficiency as the dependent variable, the multiple correlations were .71 and .52 for programming comprehension and production, respectively. Thus, one-quarter to one-half of the variability in tested programming proficiency was accounted for by mathematical understanding and specific cognitive abilities bearing a rational relationship to programming.

DISCUSSION

The present study was aimed at identifying the cognitive demands for reaching a relatively sophisticated level of programming proficiency. We examined students learning Logo in an instructional environment that stressed self-discovery within a sequence of structured activities, but with no testing or grading. Given this setting and the amount of instruction, we found that for the most part students managed to master only the basic turtle-graphics commands and the simpler aspects of the program control structure. While they gained some understanding of such programming concepts as procedures and variables, most did not develop enough understanding of Logo to go beyond the skill level of "effects generation." Thus, for example, although they used variables within procedures, they seldom passed variables between procedures, used recursion, or reused procedures across programs. There was little mastery of those aspects of programming requiring a more sophisticated understanding of flow of control and the structure of the language. Without this understanding, students cannot use the powerful Logo constructs which engage and presumably encourage the development of high-level thinking skills.

Nonetheless, we did find moderate relationships between the ability to reason in ways that we had hypothesized would be critical for advanced programming and performance on our measures of programming proficiency. The magnitude of the correlations indicated that the students who developed most in programming were also those who tended to perform better on tests of logical reasoning. However, our observations of the students during the course of their instruction and their performance on the Logo proficiency measures suggest that for many students the actual writing of programs does *not* require that they use formal or systematic approaches in their work. Programming can invoke high-level thinking skills, but such skills are not necessary for students to generate desired screen effects in the early stages of writing programs.

CONCLUSIONS

The field of computer education is in a period of transition. New languages and more powerful implementations of old ones are rapidly being developed, and more suitable programming environments are being engineered for both the new and established languages.

We can best assess the cognitive demands of programming when we are clear about our goals for teaching programming and how much we expect students to learn. However, to understand the cognitive demands for achieving a particular level of expertise, we must consider the characteristics of a specific language (such as its recursive control structure), the quality of its implementation, the sophistication of the surrounding programming environment (the tools, utilities, and editors available), and the characteristics of the instructional environment in which it is being presented and learned.

Our results indicate that certain reasoning abilities are linked to higher levels of achievement in learning to program, but that most students opt for a programming style that negates the need for engaging in high-level thinking or planful, systematic programming. Thus, the cognitive demands issue remains clouded by inherent characteristics of interactive programming languages, which promote the use of a trial-and-error approach to program production, and the particular characteristics of the instructional environment in which learning occurs.

In conclusion, we have argued that uncovering the cognitive demands of programing is far from simple. On the one hand, programming ability of one form or another is undoubtedly obtainable regardless of levels of particular cognitive skills. On the other hand, if by learning to program we mean developing a level of proficiency that enables programming to serve as a tool for reflecting on the thinking and problem-solving processes, then the demands are most certainly complex and will interact with particular programming activities and instructional approaches.

Programming can potentially serve as a fertile domain in which to foster the growth and development of a wide range of high-level thinking skills. However, if this potential is to be realized, studies are needed on two fronts:

First, more work is needed to discover what kinds of instructional environments and direction are best suited for achieving the many goals educators have for teaching programming to children of different ages. We are only beginning to understand how to teach programming. Indeed, many parents and educators who read *Mindstorms* (Papert, 1980) too literally are surprised that programming has to be taught at all. But the unguided, free exploration approach, while effective for some purposes, does not lead all students to a deeper undertanding of the structure and operation of a programming language, and thus does not lead them to use or develop such high-level thinking skills as problem decomposition, planning, or systematic elimination of errors.

Second, our ability to design effective instruction will depend in part on further experimental work to tease apart the roles various cognitive abilities play in influencing students' ability to master particular programming commands, constructs, and styles. A better understanding of the cognitive demands of using a programming language should help us to focus our instruction and identify those aspects of programming that will be difficult for students. While this study demonstrated a relation between conditional and procedural reasoning ability and programming, we conjecture that, at a more fundamental level, these tasks correlated with programming proficiency because they required the ability to reason in terms of formal, systematic, rule-governed systems, and to operate within the limitations imposed by such systems. We feel that this may be the major factor in determining whether students will obtain expert levels of proficiency. What remains to be determined is whether extended programming at proficiency levels below that of the expert require and/or help to develop high-level cognitive skills and abilities.

AUTHOR NOTES

The work reported here was supported by the National Institute of Education (Contract No. 400-83-0016). The opinions expressed do not necessarily reflect the position or policy of the National Institute of Education and no official endorsement should be inferred.

CHAPTER 7

INTEGRATING HUMAN AND COMPUTER INTELLIGENCE

Roy D. Pea

The thesis to be explored in this chapter is that advances in computer applications and artificial intelligence have important implications for the study of development and learning in psychology. I begin by reviewing current approaches to the use of computers as devices for solving problems, reasoning, and thinking. I then raise questions concerning the integration of computer-based intelligence with human intelligence to serve human development and the processes of education.

EXPERT SYSTEMS AND INTELLIGENT TUTORING SYSTEMS

Until recently, written texts have been the principal means for storing the knowledge needed to solve complex problems. Computers have provided a radically new medium for storing and making use of expert knowledge. Expert systems are programs that embody the knowledge of experts in making judgments in a field. Such systems emulate the reasoning and problem-solving abilities of human experts, and they are widely used as advisory aids in human decision making. They vary greatly in their representations of knowledge, its accessibility, its ease of modification, and in the degree to which it attempts to teach its user. Today, dozens of such systems serve as powerful conceptual tools for the extension and redefinition of human intellectual efforts in science, medicine, industry, programming, and education. Excellent accounts of existing expert systems and their growing importance are provided in Feigenbaum and McCorduck (1983). Prominent examples include MYCIN (Shortliffe, 1976), a medical expert system; MOLGEN (Friedland, 1979), an expert system used to design experiments in molecular genetics; and DENDRAL (Lindsay, Buchanan, Feigenbaum, & Lederberg, 1980), an expert chemistry system used in determining the molecular structure of unknown organic compounds. Expert systems are also used as aids in ill-defined creative tasks, such as the design of integrated circuits (Stefik & de Kleer, 1983).

The heart of the process of transferring expertise to the machine lies in reducing experts' know-how to chunks of knowledge specified, for example, in terms of productions or if-then rules; that is, if specific conditions are present in a situation, then a certain action is taken (Davis & Lenat, 1981; Hayes-Roth, Waterman, & Lenat, 1984). Methods for mining experts' knowledge are related to both the clinical interviewing techniques familiar to developmentalists and the think-aloud protocols common to cognitive psychology. The aim is to work with the experts to help them articulate what they know. Then, the domain-specific facts, algorithms, heuristics, general problem-solving strategies, and systematic understanding of a domain (e.g., causal laws, probabilities) that the experts have available can be codified in computer programs that mimic the solution of novel real-world problems at an expert level of performance. The system comes to emulate human expertise through recursive iterations that eliminate the differences between experts' judgments and those of the expert system.

The problem of transfer of expertise (Barr, Bennett, & Clancey, 1979) raises a host of developmental concerns:

> For an expert system to be truly useful, it should be able to learn what human experts know, so that it can perform as well as they do, understand the points of departure among the views of human experts who disagree, keep its knowledge up to date as human experts do (by reading, asking questions, and learning from experience), and present its reasoning to its human users in much the way that human experts would (justifying, clarifying, explaining, and even tutoring). (Barr & Feigenbaum, 1982, p. 80)

This passage implies that system users and knowledge sources (the "experts") are in relevant respects homogeneous in knowledge. However, the knowledge in an expert system and its power are not immediately accessible to a novice, much less to a child. Most expert systems act as advisers for consultation on specific problems. They can rarely solve problems autonomously. Thus, many techniques need to be learned in order to make effective use of expert systems.

Creating systems that children can use constitutes an important problem for education and developmental psychology. The developmentalist asks the reverse of the knowledge engineer's question: How can the expertise transferred from human adults to computers be transferred back by computer to the child? The adult version (how can novices effectively use and understand the problem-solving activities of an expert system?) is now being addressed in the design of intelligent expert systems. Intelligent expert systems give correct answers or useful advice in problem situations. They also use concepts and reasoning processes that resemble those that the system user might employ. A major problem in engineering such systems has been in creating facilities that can give an explanatory account, in terms that one expects from a human, of the reasoning that underlies the advice offered.

What is the potential for expert systems for human learning and development? Can expert systems eventually offer students better access to knowledge and opportunities for development than either most teachers or spontaneous experience alone can provide? We come closer to answering these questions by considering intelligent tutoring systems—systems that go beyond possessing expert knowledge and attempt to model both the student's knowledge and the learning process for acquiring expertise. These intelligent tutoring systems are designed to support students in gaining access to the expert system. For example, SOPHIE (Brown, Burton, & de Kleer, 1982) functions both as an expert system and as a teaching system in prompting the student to form and test hypotheses about an electronic power supply circuit. SOPHIE has two different modes: One poses troubleshooting problems for a single person; the other simulates a gaming situation in which one team sets a fault for another team to diagnose. In the solo mode, the system sets a fault for the student to diagnose in a power supply circuit. The student can measure voltages and currents in different parts of the circuit by asking questions of the system; the aim is to figure out which component is faulty. The system evaluates the student's hypotheses about the fault by analyzing what it has told the student up to that point about the values in different components of the system and by comparing these values with the values that would obtain under the student's hypotheses. This kind of comparison involves very sophisticated circuit simulation and fault propagation techniques. The same capabilities are used to tutor students in the team gaming option. Other systems that attempt to understand the user are DEBUGGY (Burton, 1982) and ACM (Langley, Ohlsson, & Sage, 1984), which diagnose students' procedural errors in base-ten subtraction; the WHY system (Stevens, Collins, & Goldin, 1979), which teaches the geographical aspects of rainfall distribution by initiating a Socratic dialogue; and Boyle and Anderson's (1984) system for teaching proof procedures in high school geometry, which explicitly tutors problem-solving strategies for the construction of geometric proofs. These systems vary in the degree to which their cognitive diagnostics are theoretically and empirically substantiated.

From a developmental perspective, the educational use of expert systems must be concerned with how the novice can be supported in learning from and making use of this form of knowledge storage. Certain types of expert systems must be guided by the need to address students' lack of knowledge about either the expert domain or the methods for operating the systems that use such information storage. An important task remains in creating systems capable of providing interactive environments that succeed in integrating students' intuitive theories of domain knowledge constructed through everyday experience, such as in physics (diSessa, 1983), with formal domain knowledge. Research is needed on how children's use of such systems affects the relation between cognitive development and learning. For example, how does the child novice differ from the adult novice for particular content domains, such as geometry? In the context of this question, such computer-based systems appear to have theoretical import for developmental psychology, in ways now to be addressed.

CHANGES IN VIEWS ON COGNITIVE DEVELOPMENT

After describing some characterizations of cognitive development as the construction of an invariantly ordered sequence of universal stages, I will review some recent challenges to these universal descriptions. These considerations will lead to an examination of potential uses of computer expert systems and intelligent tutoring systems for the reconceptualizing of cognitive development and to more drastic reformulations of the agenda for developmental studies.

Constructivism and Stages in Developmental Psychology

In recent decades, developmental psychologists have been preoccupied with the ongoing debate concerning research into stages of cognitive development. Driven by the seminal studies of Piaget (1983), developmental psychologists throughout the world have sought to substantiate and finely delineate the broad universal stages of cognitive development that Piaget proposed.

Piaget defined four broad stages of intellectual or cognitive development: the sensorimotor, the preoperational, the concrete operational, and the formal operational. Although recent formulations (Case, 1985; Fischer, 1980) differ in emphasis, they maintain a roughly comparable picture. Stages are major qualitative breaks in cognitive functioning that, according to Piaget (1973a), have four characteristics: First, they are ordered in sequence. Second, they are integrative, in that earlier stages are an integral part of later stages. Third, they are characterized by a "whole structure," which in the case of intelligence means by an underlying system of logical operations. Fourth, in any series of stages, there is a distinction between the process of formation and the final forms of equilibrium; that is, they are progressively constructed without total preformation.

In describing the formation of the stages, Piaget placed central emphasis on constructivism, the perspective that emphasizes the interaction of the endogenous character of the organism and environment in the organism's construction of progressively more advanced stages of knowledge. Piaget (1973a) emphatically contrasted the "spontaneous" or subject-initiated discovery, learning, and inventing that contribute to the construction of these broad systems of operations with "other" learning, such as the learning that occurs in schools:

> I have in mind only the *truly* psychological development of the child as opposed to his school development or to his family development; that is, I will above all stress the spontaneous aspect of this development, though I will limit myself to the purely intellectual and cognitive development. Actually we can distinguish two aspects in the child's intellectual development. On the one hand, we have what may be called the psychosocial aspect, that is, everything the child receives from without and learns in general by family, school, educative transmission. On the other there is the development which can be called spontaneous. For the sake of abbreviation I will call it psychological, the development of the intelligence itself—what the child learns by himself, what none can teach him and he must discover alone; and it is essentialy this development which takes time...it is precisely this spontaneous development which forms the obvious and necessary condition for the school development. (pp. 2–3)

As I will later suggest, symbolic activities with the computer may necessitate a reformulation of the concept of spontaneous learning, since the world of physical objects for child play and action is remarkably expandable through programmable symbols.

Challenges to the Piagetian Enterprise

There have been several areas of research that converge as problematic for Piaget's conceptions of development. I will review three fundamental areas: findings on the role of sociocultural factors in learning and development, on giftedness and prodigies, and on the role of knowledge in computer expert systems.

Piaget has been extensively criticized for underplaying the contribution of sociocultural factors to development (Rogoff & Lave, 1984). Contemporary work has been influenced by the theories of the Soviet psychologist L.S. Vygotsky (Laboratory of Comparative Human Cognition, 1983; Rogoff & Wertsch, 1984), who saw sociocultural factors as having important consequences on higher level cognitive development. Formal operations are nonuniversal, particularly in cultures without schooling, a finding that was troubling even for Piaget (1972). What Piaget described as spontaneous learning is apparently insufficient to enable humans to think in terms of operations on operations, the definition of formal thought. Educational processes of sociocultural transmission, especially those involving abstract symbolic systems such as logic, mathematics, and written language, play an essential role in the formation of such thought patterns (Laboratory of Comparative Human Cognition, 1983; Olson & Bruner, 1974).

Research inspired by Vygotsky has great significance for computer-based extensions and redefinitions of human intelligence. Vygotsky's (1978) dynamic conception of the "zone of proximal development" concerns phases in ontogenesis in which a child has partly mastered a skill but can act more effectively with the assistance of a more skilled peer or adult. The zone of proximal development is the region of skill effectiveness that lies between the child's independent functioning and the child's functioning with social support. Intelligence is viewed as a collective activity jointly accomplished between the child and more able others before the child can function intelligently on his or her own. In contrast to Piaget, Vygotsky (quoted by Rogoff & Wertsch, 1984) argued that

> instruction is only good when it proceeds ahead of development. It then awakens and rouses to life those functions which are in a stage of maturing, which lie in the zone of proximal development. It is in this way that instruction plays an extremely important role in development. (p. 3)

The central implication is that the problem-solving system formed by child and more competent others—broadened here to include computer systems—is an especially appropriate unit of analysis for studies of the development of problem-solving skills.

Findings on Giftedness and Prodigies

Further evidence against the universalist architecture of Piagetian theory is found in cognitive studies with children identified as gifted or prodigious in their performance in such domains as mathematics, music, chess, or composition. Research on giftedness and prodigy performances among children (Feldman, 1980, 1982; Gardner, 1983) demonstrates that such individuals are not in an advanced Piagetian stage of development across tasks but that they perform on Piaget-based measures much like their same-age cohorts, even as they outperform most adults in their forte. Prior attainment of the general logical structures defining the Piagetian formal operational period is not, as these exceptional individuals illustrate, necessary for high-level domain-specific intellectual performances.

According to Gardner (1983), a pluralistic approach to cognition, which focuses on the domain specificity of intellectual performances rather than on transdomain universal stages, posits that,

> irrespective of domains, there should (in proper Piagetian fashion) be a stagelike sequence through which any individual must pass. However, individuals differ greatly from one another in the speed with which they pass

through these domains; and, contra Piaget, success at negotiating one domain entails no necessary correlation with speed or success in negotiating other domains....Moreover, progress in a domain does not depend entirely on the solitary individual's actions within his world. Rather, much of the information about the domain is better thought of as contained within the culture itself, for it is the culture that defines the stages and fixes the limits of individual achievement. One must conceive of the individual *and* his culture as embodying a certain stage sequence, with much of the information essential for development inhering in the culture itself rather than simply inside the individual's skull. (p. 27)

This perspective on the development of intelligence has provocative implications for marrying the problem-solving capabilities of child and computer. Since there are distinct developmental trajectories for different content domains, rather than a general logical engine on which the development of cognitive skills in specific domains depends, then integrations are in principle possible between childhood thinking and expert or intelligent tutoring computer systems that provide developmental technologies. These integrations would serve as mental catalysts for engineering the development of high-level cognitive skills. The child would not need to await the development of general logical structures in order to become a powerful thinker.

The Role of Knowledge in Expert Systems
Similar arguments are provided by research on artificial intelligence (AI) systems. Cognitive scientists have found that extensive knowledge is necessary for expert-level performance in solving problems in every content area studied. Waldrop (1984) reached the conclusion that "the essence of intelligence seems to be less a matter of reasoning ability than of knowing a lot about the world." (p. 1279). This presents a clear problem for the Piagetian approach, in which the underlying logical schemes involved in the reasoning behind a task are considered to be the core of intellectual functioning. The principal mechanisms distinguishing what Piaget described as the stages of intelligence are, for example, defined in terms of the logical operations of reasoning characteristic of that stage. What is the role for knowledge? Here Piaget introduced the convenient abstraction of *decalage* in order to deal with the theoretically inconvenient differences in the average age at which, for example, the concept of conservation is acquired for the different materials of weight, volume, and number (different content domains). Specific knowledge is accorded a minor role.

What are we to do, then, with knowledge in an age in which intelligent behavior is being modeled by computers and in which reasoning mechanisms, although necessary, are far less important than the web of propositions and rules that define knowledge and cognitive skill? If the weak end of the machinery of cognitive development lies in building up the appropriately organized store of knowledge structures (Carey, 1984), how then can knowledge be better acquired? How can computers as intelligent tutoring systems and learning machines in their own right help the student to develop such knowledge?

Although in broad outline the interactionist perspective that Piaget offers may be correct, the three groups of studies just reviewed imply a different vision of what constitutes the interaction environment basic to learning and development and of what experiences warrant the description of spontaneous learning though solitary discovery. The culture, as expressed through more knowledgeable others, provides apprenticeship models for the development of cognitive skills and offers advice and hints to help structure the child's discovery space as he or she proceeds through the zones of proximal development. Left to her or his own spontaneous discoveries, the child as intuitive scientist arrives too often at theories of how the physical or mathematical world works that are at odds with appropriate formal theories (A.L. Brown, 1984; Gentner & Stevens, 1983). We find eroding the artificial distinction between what one discovers alone (what Piaget chauvinistically describes as true development) and what one discovers with the aid of others, however indirect that aid may be. Children need not—indeed, in most instances, they will not—reinvent through spontaneous discovery the conceptually adequate theories about the world that science has taken centuries to identify and formulate.

DEVELOPMENTAL THEORY AND HUMAN-COMPUTER SYSTEMS

In this section, I consider some major questions that the possibility of human-computer intelligent systems raises for developmental theory and some of the rich prospects they offer for psychological research and for the promotion of education and development.

Two possibly but not necessarily interconnected roles for the creation of such systems may be distinguished. The first is as research tool for developmental and cognitive psychology; the second is as educational tool. In terms of the first role, by configuring the system in different ways, different explanatory models of learning and development can directly be tested. These models might be concerned with one or another of several issues: assessing whether systems that give the student prompts to promote self-questioning, planning, and monitoring lead to more effective metacognition and learning to learn (J.S. Brown, 1984b; Palincsar

& Brown, 1984); ascertaining the kinds of prodevelopmental roles of conflict or of confrontation of "bugs" in student understanding in developmental reorganizations of knowledge systems (Siegler, 1983); testing our understanding of the heuristics that expert teachers use to model a student's understanding and providing new learning experiences and environments at the appropriate level (Collins & Stevens, 1982; Sleeman & Brown, 1982); and providing testing grounds for knowledge assessment and cognitive diagnostics and explicit tests of intervention hypotheses in training studies (Boyle & Anderson, 1984). In terms of the second role, for educational purposes, systems can be constructed to be used autonomously by students as tools for learning new fields of knowledge and for acquiring problem-solving and problem-defining skills for specific domains.

In the paragraphs that follow, major challenges to developmental psychology posed by the coupling of human and computer intelligence are roughly ordered from the conservative to the radical in their implications. At the conservative end, they merely carry forward modifications to the Piagetian enterprise; at the radical extreme, they portend the coevolution of human and computer intelligence.

Computers and the Zone of Proximal Development
It is possible that future versions of AI systems could serve as tools for helping children move through the zones of proximal development by extending the "social" environment for cognitive growth by interactively providing hints and support in problem-solving tasks like the ones adults provide. Computers playing this role will be the information age sequel to concepts of a zone of proximal development (ZPD), in which the adult human plays the tutorial role of coconstructing with the child his or her latent developmental capabilities. In this case, the zone of proximal development is traversed with the complementary capabilities of the human-computer system. However, unlike those who have conducted most ZPD studies, I do not assume that self-sufficiency is the telos of such learning activities. Many forms of cognitive activity may require the continuing intervention of an intelligent computer system, for effectiveness or because of their complexity. Similarly, not all cognitive tasks for which ZPDs can be arranged should be ones that the child is expected to internalize for subsequent solo performances. Solo performances are not realistic in terms of the ways in which intelligent activities are organized and accomplished in the real world. They are often collaborative, depend on resources beyond an individual's long-term memory, and require the use of information-handling tools. If we took away from practicing thinkers and practitioners what we take away from children to assess their cognitive functioning, scientists could not do science, mathematicians could

not do math, historians could not do history, and policy makers could not make policy. The level of task understanding necessary for the child alone is an empirical question that remains to be answered, domain by domain. For example, in arithmetical understanding, educators now emphasize estimation skills over calculation skills as the use of calculators has become widespread.

In terms of computer-based ZPD tools, there are two major ways of transforming the zone of learning environments in which interactions toward development emerge. First, microworlds, which are fairly conservative in their implications, can be created for the promotion of domain expertise; second, there are cognitive trace systems, which are more radical in their potential powers.

Microworld Pedagogic Systems

Pedagogic systems focus on cognitive self-sufficiency, much like existing educational programs, in contrast to pragmatic systems, which allow for precocious intellectual performances of which the child may be incapable without the system's support. We thus need to distinguish between systems in which the child uses tools provided by the computer system to solve problems that he or she cannot solve alone and systems in which the system establishes that the child understands the problem-solving processes thereby achieved. We can call the first kind of system pragmatic and the second pedagogic. Pragmatic systems may have the peripheral consequence of pedagogical effects; that is, they may contribute to understanding but not necessarily. The aim of pedagogic systems is to facilitate, through interaction, the development of the human intelligent system. While there is a grey area in between, and some systems may serve both functions, clear cases of each can be defined.

Pedagogic systems that use microworlds provide rich opportunities for development and learning. A microworld is a structured environment that allows the learner to explore and manipulate a rule-governed universe, subject to specific assumptions and constraints, that serves as an analogical representation of some aspects of the natural world. Microworlds have other properties that cannot be described here (Papert, 1980). Pedagogic systems can use microworlds to further redefine the objects of the spontaneous learning that Piaget considered integral to development when he argued that each time one prematurely teaches a child something he could have discovered for himself, the child is kept from inventing it and consequently from understanding it completely (Piaget, 1983). But discovery by oneself is not well defined, and interactive software can further blur the distinction. Computer objects could be programmed so that the child would be subtly guided to discover them. They could provide discovery situations that conflict with the inferred worldview of the child because they are "smart" with knowledge of the flawed theories that children construct en route to expertise. For such pedagogic systems to work in promoting learning and development, we need research on the prodevelopmental roles of conflict or disequilibrium and a theory of how and when hints toward discovery are successful (Sleeman & Brown, 1982).

Microworld pedagogic systems could provide environments enabling students to learn skills and knowledge in specific domains by observing modeling of the process of solving example problems, by doing, by discovery, and by instruction. An aim can be to replicate the coincidences (Feldman, 1980, 1982) of factors that appear to lead to prodigious cognitive performances. This involves providing suitable models, a learning environment with cognitively appropriate help facilities that embody cultural knowledge and that is sufficiently engaging to command the child's intensive efforts.

Pedagogic Cognitive Trace Systems

Pedagogic systems could also be created that transform what will happen in the learning environment in ways that cannot be anticipated without building prototypes and doing observations. Cognitive trace systems can provide a major lever for cognitive development by providing tools for reflection. The fundamental idea of a cognitive trace system is that the intermediate products of mind are externalized through the process of interacting with knowledge-based computer systems. These traces expand the cognitive work space to include a trail, as it were, of where one has been in an episode of problem solving. Thus, remembering where one has been does not interfere with ongoing processes of creation or problem solving. Such traces would provide richer sources for assessing the student's knowledge than any teacher only observing student behaviors without the system could ever process and use for effective instruction.

Cognitive trace systems may have dramatic consequences for how human beings develop cognitive skills. These systems are instances of the thinking tools provided by other symbolic media—writing, mathematics, logic, and programming—that render human thought processes external for inspection, analysis, and reflection and that have forever transformed our world of thought and action (Ong, 1982).

Three major functions can be imagined for such traces. First, for the child, an examination of these cognitive traces, possibly prompted by the computer at appropriate junctures of thought, could lead to an emergent awareness of errors in understanding. In some cases, this could also lead to an understanding of errors of execution, which misdirect the search for solution. Second, for the psychologist or teacher, such traces could be used to diagnose a child's understanding and potentially bug-ridden ideas of the domain under study and to identify the learning experiences that are necessary for instructional remediation. Third, for the computer, such traces could be used to build a model of the child's understanding and then provide next-step responsive environments.

A prototype of such a cognitive trace system has been built by John Seeley Brown and colleagues at the Xerox Palo Alto Research Center (J.S. Brown, 1984b). In this system, called AlgebraLand, the computer carries out low-level procedures for transforming equations while students focus on their strategies for choosing the procedures that the computer will perform on equations. The cognitive trace function is expressed in an updated topological graph of the student's problem-solving steps. With this trace path, the student can "read" the alternative solution paths that she or he tried in order to learn from experience why some were successful and others less so.

As Boden (1979) notes in discussing Piaget's work on the development of purposive self-knowledge, children can or try to do many tasks without knowing how they do so, often without being able to correct their failures. She discusses Piaget's (1976, p. 340) account of how consciousness moves from periphery to center, since deliberate action first involves awareness only of the goal and of whether success or failure occurs, "while the fact that the scheme that assigns a goal to the action immediately triggers off the means of affecting it may remain unconscious." Later, largely because of the child's search for the reasons underlying his or her errors, consciousness "moves in the direction of the central regions of the action in order to reach its internal mechanism: recognition of the means employed, reasons for their selection or their modification en route, and the like." Cognitive trace systems could act as prime movers toward the child's grasp of consciousness in different domains by contributing to the development of this metacognitive knowledge, so important for expertise (Brown, Bransford, Ferrara, & Campione, 1983). But, we first will need research to determine whether such cognitive trace facilities do indeed make developmental contributions.

Integrating Child and Computer Information-Processing Systems

It is now commonplace to note limitations in human symbol manipulation abilities. As Siegler (1983) observes, many

> processing limitations can prevent people from attaining their goals: limitations on the number of symbols that they can manipulate simultaneously, on the speed with which they can manipulate symbols, on the depth to which they can search memory, and on their resistance to interference, to name but four. (pp. 129–130)

It has become a central goal of cognitive and developmental psychology to document how we utilize strategies to overcome these processing limitations of short-term memory (through such mnemonic strategies as rehearsal, elaboration, and organization) and long-term memory (through books and other materials).

Integrating the powerful information-processing systems of the computer and the frail information-processing system of the human mind may be possible. If such integration is successful, it may have great consequence for cognitive development. Empirical studies during the past decade have extensively demonstrated young children's precocious understanding of such complex concepts as causality, number, conservation, proportions, and logical deduction in simplified task environments that avoid taxing the limits of their information-processing systems (for reviews, see Carey, 1984; Case, 1985; Donaldson, 1978). Yet it is still conventional wisdom that student access to many disciplines, such as statistics, must await a certain age. In principle, we may be able to close much of the gap between the information-processing capabilities of child and adult and ultimately of humans and computers by integrating our information-processing systems.

One central hope is that such integrated systems may provide a path out of the breakdowns of rational thinking that have been extensively catalogued recently and that appear to result in large part from the bottlenecks of human information processing. The work of Kahnemann, Slovic, and Tversky (1982) on judgment under uncertainty, of Wason and Johnson-Laird (1972) on the attentional bias to positive evidence in deductive reasoning, of Luria (1976) and Scribner (1977) on the empirical bias in logical reasoning, of Shweder (1980) and others on statistical thinking, and of Nisbett and Ross (1980) on errors in social judgment has revealed the widespread use of heuristics for thinking that leads to erroneous conclusions. We have already noted the nonuniversality of formal operational thinking, particularly in cultures without schooling. There should be more effective ways for people to develop these problem-solving powers. Too many people have trouble learning the formal rule- and model-oriented disciplines that pervade the modern information age—ranging from physics and mathematics to the genetic code in biology and computer programming—and the kinds of problem-solving skills required for job and life successes. We are so prone to errors of judgment, errors of reasoning, and lack of monitoring and evaluation in our decision making that most of us most of the time could usefully be propped up and reminded to become more effective.

Could AI systems be used to buttress these well-known human frailties? Could they serve educational processes of cultural transmission and redefinition in a computer age? With the integration of human and computer intelligent systems, we may be able to attenuate human processing limitations. One possible way of dealing with the problem posed by the cognitive interface between software and the child's mind is to work at providing the set of computational tools necessary so that intermediary cognitive work, which usually goes on in the child's mind and strains age-related memory and processing limitations, can become virtually perceptual work, unrestricted by such limits. The store and processes of the mind needed for problem solving can be those of the child-computer system, rather than of the child only. The cognitive work space could be expanded to include the computer screen and other computational devices.

With such systems, we may thus extend the forms of thought made possible by the symbols that Vygotsky (1978) describes as ''external memory aids'' to the mind—mathematics, written language, logic, and programming languages. For any content domain, from Siegler's (1983) balance beams to correlations, we should be able to build devices that enable children to circumvent the processing limitations that hamper their ability to engage in higher forms of reasoning and thinking, such as concrete and formal operational thinking. The principal caveat is that we have to show how such adjuncts to processing capacity can be designed and developed for specific knowledge domains. Only then will we find the practical obstacles to their effective use in childhood education.

Pragmatic Cognitive Tools for Higher Level Achievements

To go further, one can imagine the invention of powerful cognitive tools that would support problem solving in domains previously considered to be difficult or even impossible for young children. In other words, programs could be devised that would serve as ''cognitive props'' for complex problem solving. For example, by using these programs children who were not formal operational thinkers would solve abstract problems that require formal operations.

Dennett (1978) argues that when a system, such as a software system, gets sufficiently complicated, we change the focus of descriptions from physical to intentional properties. As observers, we adopt the intentional stance and describe the system as thinking, believing, and with other intentional terms. The same is true when we discuss human-computer systems. We adopt the expert stance by attributing to such systems expertise and intelligence that we normally reserve for the human adult. We say that the system is formal operational, or clever, or very good at solving algebra problems rather than focus on the individual as the unit of developmental analysis. In fact, we can extend the well-known Turing test, a thought experiment proposed by Alan Turing (1950), to the idea of human-computer intelligent systems. In this test, a blind evaluation question-and-answer format is used to determine whether an object possesses thought. However, the Turing test is nondevelopmental; that is, it does not distinguish qualitatively different levels of intelligence. Given a developmental revision, such a test might be used to evaluate behaviors of an integrated human-computer intelligence system. Consider a child who approaches a formal operational task. The child alone may not be formal operational in his or her thinking. However, working with the computer system, the child may indeed to able to successfully solve formal operational cognitive tasks (such as control of variables or proportional reasoning). The integrated child-computer system is evaluated by the Turing test as formal operational.

This argument rests on the genetic epistemology of symbol systems. What are the implications of a tool of human intelligence for cultural development? Just as other symbol systems, such as mathematics, logic, and written language, have transformed our intellectual powers, so in principle can intelligent computer systems transform them. The concept of intelligent human-computer systems is simply an extension of this generally recognized developmental empowering by symbol systems. What makes the computer unique is its potential for modeling human intelligence. As thinking tools, computers have considerably greater potential than tools of the past, because effective use of such intellectual tools as mathematics and written language is constrained by our limited memory and information-processing abilities (Minsky, 1983; Simon, 1977b). We now have extensive gaps between competence and performance in cognitive functioning, but these gaps may narrow when human and computer intelligence are married.

This argument contrasts with Piaget's contention that better teaching and earlier experiences of the right kind cannot lead to precocious intellectual performance. He responds to the so-called American question (of accelerated instruction) by criticizing Bruner's (1960) claim that any idea, problem, or body of knowledge can be presented in a form simple enough that any particular learner can understand it. Piaget (1971) argues that "intellectual growth contains its own rhythm. Speeding up cannot be indefinitely continued" (p. 21). Piaget's argument is essentially that education can at best accelerate stage development within certain limits. Successive reorganizations of knowledge exemplified by the stages are time-consuming and take much experience.

But we may resurrect these questions, since the potential of AI systems may change the terms of the acceleration debate. One may agree with Piaget's notions about the structural limitations to educational acceleration. However, Piaget's reservations were based on the performances of a solitary child. Yet children's problem-solving skills may be stretched beyond their potential when they receive aid from others, such as peers or adults. Performance in what Vygotsky called the zone of proximal development has important implications for intelligent tutoring systems that can in principle be extended to human-computer intelligent systems. It has even more radical implications for Piaget's objections to the American question.

The radical implications center on the capabilities of young children when supported by intelligent computer systems. Some developmentalists have been dissatisfied with the ZPD studies because they also view the solitary performance of the child as the fundamental unit for developmental analysis (seeing additional aids, coaching, and prompting by an adult as "cheating" in this respect), yet the issue becomes more controversial when the child is part of a human-computer intelligent system. Imagine a typical 9-year-old working with an expert system to solve formal operational problems on correlations that involve multiple variables. The child-computer system solves the problem through the integration of the computer and the child's currently functioning solitary intelligence. As already noted, the system would be considered formal operational by the criteria of the Turing test. What does this mean in terms of the child's intelligence?

At first, one is inclined to say that children are only as intelligent as they are capable of demonstrating alone, without the technological aid supplied by the computer. But this will not do. The reason is that this technological aid is similar to other aids that we readily allow and would never rip away from the child in our crudest assessments of a child's solo intelligence: such symbol systems as written language and mathematics. These systems are truly technologies, as are the symbolic artifacts of computer programs. If the child can use the computer symbol system as an aid in solving complex problems, it should be just as admissible as the thinking tools provided by written language (e.g., by note taking during arithmetic calculations, or by list making in a formal operational experiment). Like mathematical and language notation, the symbolic notations used in the computational environment provide a powerful means for the child's thinking.

The consequences of these integrations are profound for developmentalists (including Piaget) bound to the assessment of intelligence in solitary settings. We should consider what these new possibilities say about stage conceptions of human intellectual development. What types of problems will emerge in the student modeling necessary for integrating computer and human intelligence, and for developing usable programs from the child's perspective? As intelligent systems become widely available, what are the implications for the emergence of highly creative mental acts in the arts and sciences throughout society? What complex ethical problems will be raised by such fusions?

Systems for the Coevolution of Human-Computer Intelligence

Tikhomirov (1981) has asked the profound question of how the mediation of mental processes by computer differs from mediation by signs. For example, does the computer introduce qualitatively different changes into the structure of intellectual processes? And how can a new stage be distinguished in the development of human mental processes?

The most speculative but also the most spectacular possibility is that human and computer intelligence will coevolve. Perhaps only by joining the strengths of human intelligence with the strengths of the computer can the potential of either be realized. It will soon be necessary for any theory of learning and development to explain not only human or computer learning (Michalski, Carbonell, & Mitchell, 1983) and development but also their symbiotic union. This speculative discussion casts aside reservations about the need for human self-sufficiency in intellectual functioning, because integration between human and computer intelligence will be the norm in future decades. Just as the human body is no longer the major tool for physical labor, and just as a carpenter need not use only hand tools, so will mental functioning no longer be the sole province of the human mind.

To carry this speculation further, we can submit that computers will not always be so obviously external to humans in their functioning as mental tools as they now are. They may ultimately be use-transparent and serve as literal organs of intelligence, even to the extent of being integrated with the physical confines of the body, if we so desire. Hardware differences between the machinery of the mind and of the computer will be glossed over, and integration on the physical level will characterize human-computer intelligent systems. The insight comes from cognitive science: Intelligence does not need human hardware (the nervous system) to run; it is independent of hardware. The consequence is that an intelligence system (that is, a system that has the programs needed for achieving intelligent performances) need not be based in the nervous system. Until recently, we have conceived of human intelligence (realized through the nervous system) and artificial intelligence (realized through microcircuitry) as distinct. But these two intelligences can in principle be integrated, since the hardware differences need not serve as a barrier for a new hybrid intelligence. Already, microprocessors have been integrated with artificial limbs to provide a form of internal integration of human-computer systems. Of course, there are caveats: Complex ethical issues of personal identity, rights, and dominion will emerge. But we cannot begin such discourse without charting the possibilities.

It is important to observe that computers, as components of such systems, can serve to bootstrap human intellectual development under human control and choice. Just as adults have been able to solve complex problems with computers that they were unable to before, so children should be able to go beyond their current developmental capabilities with computer assistance. Human-computer intelligence systems will serve to extend and ultimately to reorganize what we think of as human imagination, intelligence, problem-solving skills, and memory.

CONCLUSIONS

As Tikhomirov (1981) reminds us, the computer only creates possibilities for human development, to be realized when certain technical, psychological, and social conditions are met. While I have argued that we have the technical capabilities needed for integrating human and computer intelligence, there are few exemplars to demonstrate that the psychological conditions of effective integration have been met. And, social conditions have not been adequately considered: What are the goals for computer use in our society?

One consequence of the information age is that what children will need to know to learn and develop will be drastically different from what our educational system now provides. Today, we spend decades learning the three Rs and memorizing facts that are often already outdated. A culture pervaded by AI-based developmental tools for all the basics, and also thinking tools in creative processes (such as design and invention) will lead to new definitions of intelligence. These definitions may highlight the skills that have long been the aim of a liberal arts education. Cognitive skills of information management; strategies for problem solving that cut across domains of knowledge; such metacognitive skills as planning, monitoring, and learning how to learn; and communication and critical inquiry skills will come to be valued more highly. Teaching the basic facts of the disciplines will not only not provide for an educated citizenry that can use the thinking tools of this age, but it will not even be feasible because of the information explosion.

In this chapter, there has been little opportunity to address the tough research questions that must be raised if we are to achieve success in the various levels of human and computer intelligence. Developmental research is needed to elaborate the theory of cognitive tasks, the theory of stages of competence by domain, and the theory of interventions and stage transitions (Resnick, 1984) integral to the creation of computer-based developmental tools. Too little is known about how stages of knowledge are transcended to become new and more adequate constructs. Also, we know little about the expert teaching that we hope such systems would model, although substantial progress has been made in unpacking procedures of inquiry teaching or Socratic dialogue (Arons, 1984; Collins & Stevens, 1982).

This enterprise will depend on interdisciplinary collaborative work among the computer and cognitive scientists who build AI systems and the developmental psychologists, content area specialists, and educators who know so much about how the work and play of learning and development take place. Such groups can together study learning and developmental processes while simultaneously providing tools to transform the very activities of learning and development. There are no precedents. The printing press had profound cognitive and social consequences, especially in education (Eisenstein, 1979), but its effect will not compare with the consequences of interactive information tools that function with the basic currency of human thought processes, the symbol.

CHAPTER 8

ON THE COGNITIVE EFFECTS OF LEARNING COMPUTER PROGRAMMING

Roy D. Pea and D. Midian Kurland

There are revolutionary changes afoot in education, in its contents as well as its methods. Widespread computer access by schools is at the heart of these changes. Throughout the world, but particularly in the U.S.A., educators are using computers for learning activities across the curriculum, even designing their own software. But virtually all educators are as anxious and uncertain about these changes and the directions to take as they are optimistic about their ultimate effects. "Now that this admittedly powerful symbolic device is in our schools," they ask, "what should we do with it?"

We believe that educators and social scientists are at an important watershed in American education. Important new opportunities abound for research and development work that can influence directly the quality of education. Hard questions are emerging about the *design* of educational activities that integrate the computer with other media. The volatile atmosphere of choices for schools (and parents), as new hardware and software appear daily, calls for principles and knowledge that educators can use, derived from systematic empirical studies in laboratories and classrooms, of how children learn with these new information technologies. We also need theoretical debates on the aims and priorities for education in an information age. We believe that a developmental approach to the understanding of information technologies will be required, one that incorporates the new insights of cognitive science, and that will guide both research on, and design of, computer-based learning environments. Such a discipline of developmental cognitive science would merge theory and practice to dovetail the symbolic powers of human thinking with those of the computer in the service of human development.

In this essay our goals are considerably more modest, but nonetheless a timely subtask of the larger enterprise. Our aim is to examine two widespread beliefs about the mental activities engaged by programming a computer and their expected cognitive and educational benefits. The two beliefs are polar opposites and neither is acceptable. Together, they express the two predominant tendencies in thinking about learning to program today.

The first belief is linked to an atomistic, behaviorist tradition that views learning narrowly. This is the traditional and deeply engrained idea that learning is simply an accumulation of relatively autonomous "facts." On this view, what one learns when learning to program is the vocabulary of commands (primitives) and syntactic rules for constructing acceptable arrangements of commands. This belief underlies most programming instruction. Its other facet is that what one learns when learning programming is just a programming language.

The contrasting belief, in part a reaction to the first belief, is that through learning to program, children are learning much more than programming, far more than programming "facts." It is said that children will acquire powerfully general higher cognitive skills such as planning abilities, problem-solving heuristics, and reflectiveness on the revisionary character of the problem-solving process itself. This belief, although new in its application to this domain, is an old idea in a new costume which has been worn often before. In its common extreme form, it is based on an assumption about learning—that spontaneous experience with a powerful symbolic system will have beneficial cognitive consequences, especially for higher order cognitive skills. Similar arguments have been offered in centuries past for mathematics, logic, writing systems, and Latin (e.g., Bruner, 1966a; Cole & Griffin, 1980; Goody, 1977; D.R. Olson, 1976; Ong, 1982; Vygotsky, 1978).

The intuitively plausible claims for the cognitive benefits of programming have broadened in scope and in public attention. Although evidence does not support these claims as yet, their presumed validity is nonetheless affecting important decisions in public education, and leading to high expectations for outcomes of programming in the school and home. In the current climate of uncritical optimism about the potential cognitive benefits of learning to program, we run the risk of having naive "technoromantic" ideas become entrenched in the school curriculum by affirmation, rather than by empirical verification through a cyclical process of research and development. Already at the pre-high school level, programming is taught primarily because of its assumed impacts on higher cognitive skills, not because proficiency in programming is itself an educational goal. This assumption takes on added significance since several million pre-college age children in the U.S.A. are already receiving instruction in computer programming each year, and France has recently made programming compulsory in their precollege curriculum, on a par with mathematics and native language studies.

With the rapid rise in the teaching of programming, it has become critical for decision makers in education to understand how programming is learned, what may be the cognitive outcomes of learning to program, what levels of programming skills may be required to obtain different types of outcomes, and what the relationships are between the cognitive constraints on learning to program and its cognitive consequences. Research directly addressing these questions is only beginning.

Throughout this chapter, we highlight major issues and fundamental complexities for researchers in designing studies responsive to these critical questions. We discuss these issues in terms of a hybrid developmental framework, incorporating cognitive science and developmental psychology, and review relevant research in cognitive science and its cognate disciplines. This synthesis recognizes the inadequacies of either an extreme knowledge-building account of learning to program, or the naive technoromanticism that postulates spontaneous higher order cognitive skills as outcomes from programming experiences. Although claims about the spontaneous cognitive impacts of programming have an intuitive appeal, we show them to be mitigated by considerations of factors involved in learning and development. We also demonstrate how, embodied in practice, the fact-learning approach to programming often leads to incomplete programming skills. Cognitive studies of what expert programmers know, the level of the student's programming skills, the goals and purposes of those learning to program, the general difficulty of transferring "powerful ideas" across domains of knowledge, all contribute to our rejection of these two views. Programming in the classroom *may* fundamentally alter the ways in which learning and cognitive development proceed. But we must examine whether such bold claims find, or are likely to find, empirical support.

We have felt throughout our analysis of these issues that a developmental perspective that incorporates the seminal work in the last decade of the interdisciplinary field of cognitive science will illuminate our understanding of the potentialities of information technologies for advancing human cognition. Fundamental contributions to thinking about and concretely establishing the educational roles of information technologies could be gained from the synthesis of these two important theoretical traditions.

Developmental theorists such as Piaget and Inhelder (1969), Werner (1957), and Vygotsky (1978) have provided accounts of developmental processes with profound implications for the roles of technologies in education. On all these views, cognitive development consists not of an accumulation of facts, but of a series of progressive reorganizations of knowledge driven by the child's active engagements with physical and social environments. In these views, learning (i.e., the accumulation of new knowledge) is important for driving the developmental processes, but at the same time is mediated by the current developmental capabilities of the learner.

In the field of cognitive science during the last decade, researchers in the constituent disciplines of cognitive psychology, computer science, linguistics, anthropology, and philosophy have begun intensive collaborative research projects (e.g., Gentner & Stevens, 1983; Greeno, Glaser, & Newell, 1983; Norman, 1981). The combination of careful analysis of cognitive processes and the techniques of computer simulation has led to important new insights into the nature of mental representations, problem-solving processes, self-knowledge, and cognitive change. Cognitive science has revealed the enormous importance of extensive, highly structured domain-specific knowledge and the difficulty of developing general-purpose problem-solving strategies that cut across different knowledge domains. Also, within particular domains, cognitive science research has been able to specify in great detail the naive "mental models" held by novices, such as Aristotelian beliefs about objects in motion, which are often very resistant to change through spontaneous world experiences (Gentner & Stevens, 1983).

Cognitive science shares with the older tradition of developmental psychology a concern with how new learning must be integrated with prior knowledge, but it transcends earlier work in analyzing problem-solving and learning processes for specific knowledge domains, and finds little role for general structural principles invoking "stages."

For a student interacting with a programming environment, for example, a developmental perspective would indicate the importance of studying how these students' current knowledge of the computer system is organized, how they regulate and monitor their interactions with it, and how their knowledge and executive routines affect the ease or pace of acquisition of abilities to use new programming constructs. Also, it would investigate the students' exploration of the system, and the ways that they are able to assimilate it to their current level of understanding and to appropriate it in terms of their own purposes, including play and competition. Learning to use the programming language may require successive developmental reorganizations not only of the students' naive understanding of the language being learned, but also of the computer system as a whole. Complex cognitive changes are unlikely to occur through either spontaneous exploration or explicit instruction alone, since students must be engaged in the task in order to interpret the new concepts. This perspective suggests that rather than arguing, as many currently are, over global questions such as which computer language is "best" for children, we would do better in asking: How can we organize learning experiences so that in the course of learning to program students are confronted with new ideas and have opportunities to build them into their own understanding of the computer system and computational concepts?

In complementary terms, cognitive science raises such important questions as: How can common systematic misconceptions in particular domains of knowledge be diagnosed and remediated through either informal or formal learning activities? For example, what does a student specifically need to know in order to comprehend and use expert strategies in designing a computer program? What component mental processes are engaged in programming activities?

The synthesis of developmental cognitive science focuses on diagnosing the mental models and mental processes that children as well as adult novices bring to understanding computer programming, since these models and processes serve as the basis for understanding transformations of their systems of knowledge as they learn. Beyond the typically agenetic cognitive science, a developmental cognitive science would ask: How are the various component mental processes involved in expert programming constructed and reconfigured throughout ontogenesis, and accessed and organized during problem-solving episodes? Through what processes of reorganization does an existing system of thought become more highly developed? Through what learning activities in what kinds of environments does the novice programmer develop into an expert? Developmental cognitive science asks how the mind and its ways of knowing are shaped, not only by biological constraints or physical objects, but by the available cultural interpretive systems of social and educational interaction. As we shall see, the currently available research is impoverished in response to these questions, but current progress in understanding the development of mathematical and scientific thinking (reviewed, for example, in Siegler, 1983) leads us to be optimistic about the prospects for comparable work on the psychology of programming.

The critique of the literature on learning to program that we present below has been strongly influenced by this developmental cognitive science perspective. We do not adopt the usual computer programming perspective assuming that all programming students are adults or have the same goals as mature learners. Instead, the perspective is geared to the learning experiences and developmental transformations of the child or novice adult in interactive environments. The kinds of preliminary questions that we ask from this perspective in addressing the question: "What are the cognitive effects of learning to program?" lead us to draw on studies from diverse fields that we see as relevant to a developmental cognitive science of programming, and we have categorized them according to the topics of "What are the developmental roles of contexts in learning to program?" "What is skilled programming?" "What are the levels of programming skill development?" and "What are the cognitive constraints on learning to program?" First, however, we will begin by examining the bold claims about the effects of learning to program.

CLAIMS FOR COGNITIVE EFFECTS
OF LEARNING TO PROGRAM

Current claims for the effects of learning programming upon thinking are best exemplified in the writings of Papert and Feurzeig (e.g., Feurzeig, Horwitz, & Nickerson, 1981; Feurzeig, Papert, Bloom, Grant, & Solomon, 1969; Goldstein & Papert, 1977; Papert, 1972a, 1972b, 1980; Papert, Watt, diSessa, & Weir, 1979) concerning the Logo programming language, although such claims are not unique to Logo (cf. Minsky, 1970).

Early Claims

Two key catalysts underlie beliefs that programming will discipline thinking. The first is from artificial intelligence, where constructing programs that model the complexities of human cognition is viewed as a way of understanding that behavior. In explicitly teaching the computer to do something, it is contended that you learn more about your own thinking. By analogy (Papert, 1972a), programming students would learn about problem-solving processes by the necessarily explicit nature of programming, as they articulate assumptions and precisely specify steps to their problem-solving approach. The second influence is the widespread assimilation of constructivist epistemologies of learning, most familiar through Piaget's work. Papert (1972a, 1980) has been an outspoken advocate of the Piagetian account of knowledge acquisition through self-guided problem-solving experiences, and has extensively influenced conceptions of the benefits of learning programming through "a process that takes place without deliberate or organized teaching" (Papert, 1980, p. 8).

Ross and Howe (1981) have summarized Feurzeig et al.'s (1969) four claims for the expected cognitive benefits of learning programming. Initially, most outcomes were postulated for the development of *mathematical* thought:

1. that programming provides some justification for, and illustration of, formal mathematical rigour;
2. that programming encourages children to study mathematics through exploratory activity;
3. that programming gives key insight into certain mathematical concepts; and
4. that programming provides a context for problem solving, and a language with which the pupil may describe his own problem solving. (Ross & Howe, 1981, p. 143)

Papert (1972b) argued for claims (2) and (4) in noting that writing programs of Logo turtle geometry is a

> new piece of mathematics with the property that it allows *clear discussion* and *simple models of heuristics* [such as debugging] that are foggy and confusing for beginners when presented in the context of more traditional elementary mathematics [our emphasis].

He provides anecdotes of children "spontaneously discovering" phenomena such as the effects that varying numerical inputs to a procedure for drawing a spiral have on the spiral's shape. He concludes that learning to make these "small discoveries" puts the child "closer to mathematics" than faultlessly learning new math concepts.

Recent Claims

We find expanded claims for the cognitive benefits of programming in a new generation of theoretical writings. In *Mindstorms*, Papert (1980) discusses the pedagogy surrounding Logo, and argues that cognitive benefits will emerge from taking "powerful ideas" inherent in programming (such as recursion and variables) in "mind-size bites" (e.g., procedures). One of the more dramatic claims is that if children had the extensively different experiences in thinking about mathematics that Logo allows: "I see no reason to doubt that this difference could account for a gap of five years or more between the ages at which conservation of number and combinatorial abilities are acquired" (p. 175). Papert is referring to extensively replicated findings of a large age gap between the early conservation of number (near age 7) and later combinatorial abilities (e.g., constructing all possible pairings of a set of different colored beads, near age 12).

Feurzeig et al. (1981) provide the most extensive set of cognitive outcomes expected from learning to program. They argue that

> the teaching of the set of concepts related to programming can be used to provide a natural foundation for the teaching of mathematics, and indeed for the notions and art of logical and rigorous thinking in general.

Learning to program is expected to bring about seven fundamental changes in thought:

1. rigorous thinking, precise expression, recognized need to make assumptions explicit (since computers run specific algorithms);
2. understanding of general concepts such as formal procedure, variable, function, and transformation (since these are used in programming);
3. greater facility with the art of "heuristics," explicit approaches to problems useful for solving problems in *any* domain, such as planning, finding a related problem, solving the problem by decomposing it into parts, etc. (since "programming provides highly motivated models for the principal heuristic concepts");
4. the general idea that "debugging" of errors is a "constructive and plannable activity" applicable to any kind of problem solving (since it is so integral to the interactive nature of the task of getting programs to run as intended);
5. the general idea that one can invent small procedures such as building blocks for gradually constructing solutions to large problems (since programs composed of procedures are encouraged in programming);
6. generally enhanced "self-consciousness and literacy about the process of solving problems" (due to the practice of *discussing* the process of problem solving in programming by means of the *language* of programming concepts[1]);
7. enhanced recognition for domains beyond programming that there is rarely a single "best" way to do something, but different ways that have comparative costs and benefits with respect to specific goals (learning the distinction between "process" and "product," as in Werner, 1937).

Asking whether programming promotes the development of higher cognitive skills raises two central issues in developmental cognitive science. First, is it reasonable to expect transfer across knowledge domains? Even adult thinkers are notorious for their difficulty in spontaneously recognizing connections between "problem isomorphs," problems of identical logical structure but different surface form (Gick & Holyoak, 1980; Hayes & Simon, 1977; Simon & Hayes, 1976), and in applying strategies for problem solution that they have developed in one context to

---

[1] Hopes that learning the concepts and language that underlie programming will change the way a learner thinks of nonprogramming problems recalls the strong formulation of the Sapir-Whorf hypothesis: that available linguistic labels constrain available thoughts. The strong form of this hypothesis has been extensively refuted (e.g., Cromer, 1974); only a weak version is consistent with evidence on language-thought relationships. Available labels in one's language may facilitate, but are neither necessary nor sufficient for particular forms of thinking, or conceptual distinctions. Categories of thought may provide the foundation for linguistic categories, not only the reverse. The same point applies to the language of programming.

new problem forms. With problems of "near" transfer so acute, the possibility of spontaneous transfer must be viewed cautiously. In later discussions, we provide a tentative developmental model for thinking about relations between different types of transfer beyond programming, and different levels of programming skill.

The second and related question is whether intellectual activity is guided by general domain-independent problem-solving skills or by a conjunction of idiosyncratic domain-dependent problem-solving skills (Goldstein & Papert, 1977; Newell, 1980; Simon, 1980). An extensive literature on metamemory development indicates that the tasks used to measure the functioning of "abstract thinking" are inextricably linked to the specific problems used to assess metacognition (e.g., A.L. Brown, in press). As Ross and Howe (1981) note, "in most problem-solving tasks, it is impossible to apply the supposed context-free skills without initially having essentially domain-specific knowledge." Within domains, however, better performances by learners are commonly accompanied by reflection on the control of their own mental activities (Brown, Bransford, Ferrara, & Campione, 1983).

THE DEVELOPMENTAL ROLE OF CONTEXTS IN LEARNING TO PROGRAM

For a developmentalist, there is a major problem pervading each of these characterizations of the effects on higher thinking skills expected from learning to program. Programming serves as a "black box," an unanalyzed activity, whose effects are presumed to irradiate those exposed to it. But questions about the development of programming skills require a breakdown of the skills into component abilities, and studies of how specific aspects of programming skill are acquired. They require especially serious consideration of the developmental roles played by the contexts interpenetrating the black box: the programming environment, the instructional environment, and the relevant understanding and performances of the learner.

The question of the role of contexts in learning programming is complex because programming is not a unitary skill. Like reading, it is comprised of a large number of abilities that interrelate with the organization of the learner's knowledge base, memory and processing capacities, repertoire of comprehension strategies, and general problem-solving abilities such as comprehension monitoring, inferencing, and hypothesis generation. This lesson has been etched in high relief through intensive efforts to develop artificial intelligence systems that "understand" natural language text (e.g., Schank, 1982; Schank & Abelson, 1977). Skilled reading also requires wide experience with different genres (e.g., narrative, essays, poetry, debate) and with different goals of reading (e.g., reading for gist, content, style). As reading is often equated with skill in decoding, learning to program in schools is often equated with learning the vocabulary and syntax of a programming language. But skilled programming, like reading, is complex and context-dependent, so we must begin to unpack the contexts in which programming is carried out and learned.

Environments in which children learn to read are usually overlooked because adequate environments (e.g., plenty of books, good lighting, picture dictionaries, good readers to help with hard words, vocabulary cards, phonics charts) are taken for granted. By contrast, good programming environments are not generally available to schools. Determining how children develop programming skills will not be possible without due consideration of the programming environment in which learning and development take place, and of how learning activities are organized.

Programming Environment
The distinction between a programming language and a programming environment is crucial. A programming language is a set of commands and rules for command combinations that are used to instruct the computer to perform specified operations. The programming environment, on the other hand, is the larger collection of software (operating systems and programming tools) and hardware (memory, disk storage, hard copy capability) available to the programmer. It can include an editor program to facilitate program writing, code revising, and copying useful lines of code from one program to another; debugging aids; elaborate trace routines for following the program's flow of control; automatic documenters; cross-reference utilities for keeping track of variables; and subroutine libraries.

Good programming environments (e.g., those most extensively developed for working on large computers in Lisp and PL/I) make the coding aspect of programming far more efficient, allowing the programmer to concentrate on higher level issues of program design, efficiency, and elegance. In contrast, the programming environments provided for today's school microcomputers are so impoverished (typically consisting of only a crude editor and limited trace functions) that entering the code for a program and just getting it to execute correctly is the central problem.

Finally, despite vigorous arguments about the educational superiority of different programming languages, there are no data on whether different languages lead to significant differences in what children need to know prior to programming, or what cognitive benefits they derive from it. Although such differences between languages may exist, they do not affect our point, since these differences can be manipulated radically by restructuring the programming environment. Attention is best directed to general issues about programming, rather than to those that are programming language specific.

Instructional Environment

While features of the *programming environment* are important for learning to program, how successfully a child will master programming also depends on the *instructional environment* and the way in which resources such as computer access time and file storage are allocated. Each of these points concerns the context of cognitive abilities, which we know from cognitive science and developmental psychology to be critical to the level of performance achieved in cognitive tasks (for reviews, see Brown et al., 1983; Laboratory of Comparative Human Cognition, 1982).

Deciding how to introduce programming and assist students in learning to program is hampered today by the paucity of pedagogical theory. That current "fact-learning" approaches to programming instruction are inadequate has become apparent from studies of the kinds of conceptual errors made by novice programmers instructed in that way. For example, novice adult programmers reveal deep misunderstandings of programming concepts, and of how different lines of programming code relate to one another in program organization (Bonar & Soloway, 1982; Jeffries, 1982; Sheil, 1980, 1981; Soloway, Bonar, & Ehrlich, 1983; Soloway, Ehrlich, Bonar, & Greenspan, 1982). As expected from what they are taught, they know the vocabulary and syntax of their programming language. Their misunderstandings are much deeper (Jeffries, 1982), such as assuming that all variables are global (when some may be specific to one procedure), and expecting that observing one pass through a loop allows them to predict what will happen on all subsequent passes (although the outputs of programming statements which *test* for certain conditions may change what will happen during any specific loop). Research by Mayer (1976), L.A. Miller (1974), and Sime, Arblaster, and Green (1977) has revealed that adult novice programmers have a difficult time generally with the flow of control concepts expressed by conditionals (for a review of these findings, see duBoulay, O'Shea, & Monk, 1981). These conceptual difficulties, even among professional programmers, have been lamented by such programming polymaths and visionaries as Minsky (1970) and Floyd (1979) as due to problems with how programming is taught. Too much focus is placed on low-level form such as grammar, semantic rules, and some preestablished algorithms for solving classes of problems, while the *pragmatics*[2] of program design are left for students to discover for themselves. Interestingly, these complaints about writing programs are similar to those voiced about how writing in general is taught (e.g., Scardamalia & Bereiter, 1983).

What do we know about conceptual problems of children learning to program? Problems similar to those of adult novices are apparent. To take one example, in our research with 8- to 12-year-old Logo programmers (Kurland & Pea, 1985), we find through their think-aloud protocols and manual simulation of programs that children frequently adopt a systematic but misguided conception of how control is passed[3] between Logo procedures. Many children believe that placing the name of the executing procedure within that procedure causes execution to "loop" back through the procedure, when in fact what happens is that control is

---

[2] One may distinguish for (artificial) programming languages, just as in the case of natural languages, between three major divisions of *semiotics*, or the scientific study of properties of such signaling systems (Crystal, 1980). These three divisions, rooted in the philosophical studies of Peirce, Carnap, and Morris, are:

> *Semantics*, the study of the relations between linguistic expressions and the objects in the world which they refer to or describe; *syntactics*, the study of the relation of these expressions to each other; and *pragmatics*, the study of the dependence of the meaning of these expressions on their users (including the social situation in which they are used). (p. 316)

Studies of natural language pragmatics have focused on the

> study of the *language* from the point of view of the user, especially of the choices he makes, the *constraints* he encounters in using language in social interaction, and the effects his use of language has on the other participants in an act of communication. (p. 278)

Although there are important disanalogies to natural language, a pragmatics of programming languages concerns at least the study of programming language(s) from the viewpoint of the user, especially of the (design) choices that he or she makes in the organization of lines of programming code within programs (or software systems), the constraints that he or she encounters (such as the requirements of a debuggable program that is well documented for future comprehension and modification) in using programming language in social contexts, and the effects that his or her use of programming language have on the other participants (such as the computer, as ideal interpreter, or other humans) in an act of communication involving the use of the programming language.

[3] The concept of "flow of control" refers to the sequence of operations that a computer program specifies. The need for the term emerges because not all control is linear. In linear control, lines of programming instructions would be executed in strict linear order: first, second, third, and so on. But in virtually all programming languages, various "control structures" are used to allow nonlinear control. For example, one may GOTO other lines in the program than the next one in BASIC, in which case flow of control passes to the line of programming code referred to in the GOTO statement. Because a program's flow of control may be complex, programmers often utilize programming flowcharts, either to serve as a high-level plan for creating their program, or to document the flow of control in their program.

passed to a *copy* of the executing procedure. This procedure is then executed, and when that process is complete, passes control back to the procedure that last called it. Children adopted mental models of flow of control which worked for simple cases, such as programs consisting of only one procedure, or tail recursive procedures, but which proved inadequate when the programming goal required more complex programming constructions.

In other developmental studies of Logo programming skills (Pea, 1983), even among the 25% of the children (8- and 9-year-olds; 11- and 12-year-olds) who were extremely interested in learning programming, the programs that they wrote reached but a moderate level of sophistication after approximately 30 hours of on-line programming experience during the year. Children's grasp of fundamental programming concepts such as variables, tests, and recursion, and of specific Logo primitive commands such as REPEAT, was highly context-specific. For example, a child who had written a procedure using REPEAT which repeatedly printed her name on the screen did not recognize the applicability of REPEAT in a program to draw a square. Instead, the child redundantly wrote the same line-drawing procedure four different times. We expect that carefully planned sequences of instruction will be important to ensure that programming knowledge is not "rigid" (Werner, 1957), or "welded" (Shif, 1969) to its contexts of first learning or predominant use. Such rigidity is a common finding for early developmental levels in diverse domains (Brown et al., 1983).

More broadly, in the National Assessment of Educational Progress survey of 2500 13-year-olds and 2500 17-year-olds during the 1977–1978 school year (National Assessment of Educational Progress, 1980), even among the small percentage who claimed to be able to program, "performance on flowchart reading exercises and simple BASIC programs revealed very poor understanding of algorithmic processes involving conditional branching" (cited by R.E. Anderson, 1982, p. 14).

Educators often assume that adult programmers are not beleaguered by conceptual problems in their programming, but we have seen that they are. Once we recognize that programming by "intellectually mature" adults is not characterized by error-free, routine performances, we might better understand difficulties of children learning to program, who devote only small amounts of their school time to learning to program.

These findings lead us to two central questions about programming instruction, which we define broadly to include the direct teaching provided by educators as well as the individual advice, modelling, and use of metaphors with which they support instruction and learning. How much instruction, and what types of instruction, should be offered? How much direct instruction is best for children to learn programming is a controversial question (e.g., Howe, 1981; Papert, 1980). At one extreme, schools teach programming as any other subject with "fact sheets" and tests; at the other, they provide minimal instruction, encouraging children to explore possibilities, experiment, and create their own problems to solve. This second approach, popularized by Papert (1980), argues that little overt instruction is necessary if the programming language is sufficiently engaging and simple to use, while at the same time powerful enough for children to do projects that they find meaningful. Though this discovery-learning perspective is not universally shared, even by Logo devotees (Howe, 1981), it has had a pervasive influence over uses of Logo by schools.

What *type* of instruction should be offered, and *when* in the course of programming skill development specific concepts, methods, and advice should be introduced are also critical questions. Two central factors are implicated by cognitive science studies. One is the current mental model or system of knowledge that the student has available at the time of instruction. A second is the goal-relevance of the problem-solving activity required of the student. On the first point, there are no careful studies of the success of different instructional acts as a function of a student's level of understanding for programming akin to those carried out by Siegler (1983) for such concepts as time, speed, and velocity. At a more general level, Mayer (1979, 1981) has shown that a concrete conceptual model of a programming system aids college students in learning BASIC by acting as an advance organizer of the details of the language. With the conceptual model, learners were able to assimilate the details of the programming language to the model rather than needing to induce the model from the details.

On the second point, we would ask how compatible are the teacher's instructional goals with children's goals and purposes in learning programming? Recent developmental cognitive science and cross-cultural studies of cognition (e.g., A.L. Brown, 1982; Laboratory of Comparative Human Cognition, 1983) have shown that assessing task performance within a goal structure familiar to the person is necessary for determining the highest developmental level of an individual's performances. For learning to program, goals of the programming activity need to be contexted for the child in terms of other meaningful and goal-directed activities, connecting either to everyday world affairs, to other aspects of the curriculum, or to both. Papert (1980) has described this as "syntonic" learning. For example, in our studies Logo classroom children found two contexts especially motivating: creating videogames and simulating conversations. The most intensive and advanced programming efforts were in the service of children's goals such as these. Dewey's (1900) point about the importance for *any* learning that developments in the new skill serve as more adequate means for desired ends thus again receives new support. A similar emphasis underlies the successful use of electronic message and publishing systems in classrooms (e.g., Black, Levin, Mehan, & Quinn, 1983; Laboratory of Comparative Human Cognition, 1982). Embedding computer programming activities of increasing cognitive complexity in children's goal structures may promote learning to program and support the transfer of what is learned in programming to problem-solving activities in other domains.

Our point throughout this section has been that programming is not taught by computers or by programming languages but by teachers, with the aid of the supports of a programming environment. How effectively children of different ages and with different background knowledge learn programming will be contingent upon the capabilities of their teachers, the appropriateness of their learning activities to their current level of understanding in programming, and the features available in their programming environment. Studies to date have not incorporated these considerations that a developmental cognitive science perspective recognizes as central.

WHAT IS SKILLED PROGRAMMING?

How to define and assess the constellation of skills which comprise programming has long been a major problem for industry (Pea & Kurland, 1984b), and is becoming so for schools. We define the core sense of programming as the set of activities involved in developing a reusable product consisting of a series of written instructions that make a computer accomplish some task. But in order to move from definition to instruction, one must begin to unpack ''programming skill,'' in contrast to the black-box approach to programming prevalent in schools. Promising moves in this direction have already been provided by careful analyses of what expert programmers *do*, and what types and organizations of knowledge they appear to have in memory that they access during programming. This research strategy, characteristic of cognitive science, has revealed significant general features of expert problem-solving skills for diverse domains, such as algebra (Lewis, 1981), chess (Chase & Simon, 1973), geometry (Anderson, Greeno, Kline, & Neves, 1981), physics (Chi, Feltovich, & Glaser, 1981; Larkin, McDermott, Simon, & Simon, 1980), physical reasoning (deKleer & Brown, 1981), and writing (Bereiter & Scardamalia, 1982), and it is providing new insights into components of programming skill. In terms of what a programmer *does*, a set of activities is involved in programming for either novices or experts, which constitutes phases of the problem-solving process (e.g., Newell & Simon, 1972; Polya, 1957). These activities, which may be invoked at any time and recursively during the development of a program are: (a) understanding the programming problem; (b) designing or planning a programming solution; (c) writing the programming code that implements the plan; and (d) comprehension of the written program and program debugging. An extensive review of these cognitive subtasks of programming may be found in Pea and Kurland (1984b).

In terms of what an expert programmer knows, findings on the knowledge schemas, memory organizations, and debugging strategies which expert programmers possess are of particular interest. Recent studies of programmers characterize high-level programming skill as a giant assemblage of highly specific, low-level knowledge fragments (Atwood & Ramsey, 1978; R.E. Brooks, 1977). The design of functional "programmer's apprentices" such as Barstow's (1979) Knowledge Based Program Construction, and Rich and Shrobe's "Lisp programmer's apprentice" (Rich & Shrobe, 1978; Shrobe, Waters, & Sussman, 1979; Waters, 1982), and the MENO Programming Tutor (Soloway, Rubin, Woolf, Bonar, & Johnson, 1982) has involved compiling a "plan library" of the basic programming schemas, or recurrent functional chunks of programming code that programmers are alleged to use. Observations of programmers support these introspective analyses of chunks of programming knowledge. Eisenstadt, Laubsch, and Kahney (1981) found that most novice student programs were constructed from a small set of program schemas, and Jeffries (1982), in comparing the debugging strategies of novice programmers and graduate computer science students, found that experts saw whole blocks of code as instantiations of well-known problems such as calculating change. Soloway and colleagues (Bonar, 1982; Ehrlich & Soloway, 1983; Johnson, Draper, & Soloway, 1983; Soloway & Ehrlich, 1982; Soloway, Ehrlich, Bonar, & Greenspan, 1982; also see Kahney & Eisenstadt, 1982) postulate a model in which programmers use recurrent plans as chunks in program composition, and identified such plans in programs written by Pascal novices (e.g., the "counter variable plan"). But for developmental cognitive science we will need studies of how students mentally construct such plan schemas from programming instruction, experience, and prior knowledge.

A related aspect of programming skill is the set of rules that experts use to solve programming problems, but again we lack genetic studies. In an analysis of a programmer's think-aloud work on 23 different problems, R.E. Brooks (1977) demonstrated that approximately 104 rules were necessary to generate the protocol behavior. Similarly, Green and Barstow (1978) note that over a hundred rules for mechanically generating simple sorting and searching algorithms (e.g., Quicksort) are familiar to most programmers.

A third aspect of programming skill is the ability to build detailed "mental models" of what the computer will do when a program runs. An expert programmer can build dynamic mental representations, or "runnable mental models" (Collins & Gentner, 1982) and simulate computer operations in response to specific problem inputs. The complexities of such dynamic mental models are revealed when skilled programmers gather evidence for program bugs and simulate the program's actions by hand (Jeffries, 1982). Not all program understanding is mediated by hand simulation; experts engage in global searches for program organizational structure, guided by adequate program documentation, a strategy akin to what expert readers do (A.L. Brown, 1983; Brown & Smiley, 1978; Spiro, Bruce, & Brewer, 1980). How individuals develop such rich procedural understandings is currently unknown.

Expert programmers not only have available more knowledge schemas, strategies, and rules applicable to solving programming problems, but they perceive and remember larger chunks of information than novices. The classic Chase and Simon (1973) finding of short-term memory span advantages for chess experts over novices for meaningful chessboard configurations but not for random configurations has been replicated for programming (Curtis, Sheppard, Milliman, Borst, & Love, 1979; McKeithen, Reitman, Rueter, & Hirtle, 1981; Sheppard, Curtis, Milliman, & Love, 1979; Shneiderman, 1977). For example, McKeithen et al. (1981) found that experts clustered keyword commands according to meaning (e.g., those functioning in loop statements), whereas novices clustered according to a variety of surface ordinary language associations (such as orthographic similarity and word length), intermediates falling between the two. Similarly, Adelson (1981) found that recall clusters for experts were functionally or "deeply" based; those of novices were based on "surface" features of programming code. This is a major developmental transformation, but we do not understand how it occurs. DiPersio, Isbister, and Shneiderman (1980) extended this research by demonstrating that performance by college students on a program memorization/reconstruction task provides a useful predictor of programming test performances.

It is also a widely replicated finding that expert programmers debug programs in different ways than novices (Atwood & Ramsey, 1978; Gould, 1977; Gould & Drongowski, 1974; Youngs, 1974). Jeffries (1982) found that program debugging involves comprehension processes analogous to those for reading ordinary language prose. Experts read programs for flow of control (execution), rather than line by line (as text). But how do programmers shift from surface to deep readings of programs as they develop debugging skills?

In conclusion, we make one important observation. Expert programmers know much more than the facts of programming language semantics and syntax. However, the rich knowledge schemas, strategies, rules, and memory organizations that expert programmers reveal are directly taught only rarely. Many students appear to run aground in programming for lack of such understandings. This does not mean that they could not be taught, but for this to take place effectively will require considerable rethinking of the traditional computer science curriculum. These cognitive qualities appear instead to be a consequence of an active constructive process of capturing the lessons of program writing experience for later use.

LEVELS OF PROGRAMMING SKILL DEVELOPMENT

To date, observations of level of programming skill development (cf. Howe, 1980) have been extremely general and more rationally than empirically derived. Accounts of novice-expert differences in programming ability among adults coupled with observations of children learning to program provide a starting point for developing a taxonomy of levels of programming proficiency. This taxonomy can guide our research by providing a developmental framework within which to assess a student's programming expertise and make predictions for types of transfer beyond programming as a function of a student's level of expertise.

We believe that at least four distinct levels of programming ability can be identified that have distinct implications for what types of skills might transfer as the result of their achievement. These levels represent pure types and may not be characteristic of an individual, but they capture some complexities in what it means to develop programming skills. We view these levels only as guides toward more adequate characterizations of the development of programming abilities. Further differentiation will inevitably be required, in terms of the cognitive subtasks involved in the levels, and refined sublevels.

Level I: Program User
A student typically learns to execute already written programs such as games, demonstrations, or computer-assisted instruction lessons before beginning instruction in how to program. What is learned here is important (i.e., what specific keys do, how to boot a disk, how to use screen menus), but does not reveal how the program works or that a program controls what happens on the screen. For many computer users this level is sufficient for effective computer use (e.g., for word processing, game playing, electronic mail). But to be more in control of the computer and able to tailor its capabilities to one's own goals, some type of programming is required.

From this level we would expect relatively little transfer beyond computer use, but some transfer on computer literacy issues. For example, given sufficiently wide exposure to different types of programs, a student would be expected to know what computers are capable of doing, what they cannot do, and fundamental aspects of how they function in their everyday lives. As users, then, children might learn when computers are appropriate tools to apply to a problem.

Level II: Code Generator

At this level the student knows the syntax and semantics of the more common commands in a language. He or she can read someone else's program and explain what each line accomplishes. The student can locate "bugs" preventing commands from being executed (e.g., syntax errors), can load and save program files to and from an external storage device, and can write simple programs of the type he or she has seen previously. When programming, the student does very little preplanning and does not bother to document his or her programs. There is no effort to optimize the coding, use error traps, or make the program usable by others. A program created at this level might just print the student's name repeatedly on the screen or draw the same shape again and again in different colors. The student operates at the level of the individual command and does not use subroutines or procedures created as part of other programs. This level of understanding of the programming process is sufficient for creating short programs. But to create more useful and flexible programs, the student needs to progress to at least the next level.

At level II, more specific types of computer literacy related transfer would be expected. Students should develop better skills for dealing with more sophisticated software tools of the type which are rapidly permeating the business world. Computer-naive users of office information systems, even calculators, have many problems (e.g., Mann, 1975; Nickerson, 1981) and construct naive, error-ridden mental models of how they work (Mayer & Bayman, 1981; Newman & Sproull, 1979; Young, 1981). Knowledge characteristic of this level may be required to attenuate these problems. Sheil (1980, 1981) provides compelling arguments that most systems require low-level programming if the user wishes to take advantage of system options, a basic competency he has designated as "procedural literacy."

While potential computer literacy transfer from low-level programming exposure seems a reasonable expectation, what types of cognitive transfer should occur from this level of programming expertise is disputable. Our observations of children programming at this level suggest that some appreciation of the distinction between bugs and errors, degrees of correctness, and the value of decomposing program goals into manageable subparts may develop and transfer to other domains, but that a student's attention is typically so riveted to simply getting a program to work that any appreciation for more general cognitive strategies is lost.

Level III: Program Generator
At this level the student has mastered the basic commands and is beginning to think in terms of higher level units. He or she knows that sequences of commands accomplish program goals (e.g., locate and verify a keyboard input, sort a list of names or numbers, or read data into a program from a separate text file). The student can read a program and explain its purpose, what functions different parts of the program serve, and how the different parts are linked together. The student can locate bugs that cause the program to fail to function properly (e.g., a sort routine that fails to correctly place the last item in a list) or bugs that cause the program to crash as a result of unanticipated conditions or inputs (e.g., a division-by-zero error when the program is instructed to find the mean of a null list). The student can load, save, and merge files and can do simple calls to and from files from inside the main program. The student may be writing fairly lengthy programs for personal use, but the programs tend not to be user-friendly. While the student sees the need for documentation, he or she does not plan programs around the need for careful documentation or clear coding so that the program may be maintained by others. For this general level, one can expect to identify many sublevels of programming skill.

Within this level of expertise, students should develop some appreciation for the process of designing a successful program. Such understanding has potentially powerful implications for their work in other domains, particularly if such relationships are explicitly drawn by the teacher for students, or exemplified in other domains. However, it appears from our classroom observations and interviews with teachers that for students to spontaneously transfer computational concepts or language constructs used in one area of programming to other programming projects is a major accomplishment. Ideas about when to use variables, or the value of planning, as in designing program components so that they can be reused in the future, and following systematic conventions (such as beginning all graphics designs at their lower left corner) to make merging components into programs easier are all important accomplishments at this level that should not be taken for granted.

Level IV: Software Developer
Finally, at this level the student is ready to write programs that are not only complex and take full advantage of the capabilities of the computer, but are intended to be used by others. The student now has a full understanding of all the features of a language and how the language interacts with the host computer (e.g., how memory is allocated or how graphics buffers may be protected from being overwritten). When given programs to read, the student can scan the code and simulate mentally

what the program is doing, see how the goals are achieved and how the programs could be better written or adapted for other purposes. Programs are now written with sophisticated error traps and built-in tests to aid in the debugging process and to ensure that the program is crashproof. Beyond writing code accomplishing the program's objective, the student can optimize coding to increase speed and minimize the memory required to run a program. To decrease the time needed to write programs, he or she draws heavily on software libraries and programming utilities. Finally, he or she often crafts a design for the program before generating the code, documents the program fully, and writes the program in a structured, modular fashion so that others can easily read and modify it. Major issues in software engineering at high sublevels within this level of expertise are discussed by Thayer, Pyster, and Wood (1981).

It is at this level of programming sophistication that we would expect to see most extensive evidence for cognitive transfer. The student can distance himself or herself sufficiently from the low-level coding aspects of program generation to reflect on the phases and processes of problem solving involved. The issues of programming which the student is concerned with at this level—issues of elegance, optimization, efficiency, verification, provability, and style—begin to transcend low-level concerns with program execution, and may lead him or her to consider wider issues. The need at this level to be conscious of the range of intended users of programs forces the student to take the audience fully into account, a skill that has wide applicability in many other domains, such as writing.

Implicit in these distinctions between levels of programming skill and their linking to predictions about types of transfer is a theory of programming at odds with the naive technoromanticism prevalent in educational computing. While it is conceivable that even low levels of programming skill are sufficient to produce measurable cognitive transfer to nonprogramming domains, we contend that on the limited evidence available, this would be unlikely. Students who can barely decode or comprehend text are not expected to be proficient writers. Similarly, we doubt that students with a low-level understanding of programming and the skills that programming entails will write functional programs or gain insights into other domains on the basis of their limited programming skill.

COGNITIVE CONSTRAINTS ON LEARNING TO PROGRAM

Beyond asking what general cognitive characteristics may be prerequisite to or substantively influence a child's learning to program, some ask what "developmental level" children must be "at" in order to learn from programming experiences. The concept of developmental level at the abstract theoretical planes of preoperational, concrete operational, and formal operational intellectual functioning has proved to be useful for instructional psychology in understanding children's ability to benefit from certain types of learning experiences (e.g., Inhelder, Sinclair, & Bovet, 1974). But the very generality of these stage descriptions is not suitably applied to the development of specific domains of knowledge such as programming skills.

We have two reasons for not pursuing the development of programming skills in terms of Piagetian developmental levels. First, there is strong evidence that the development and display of the logical abilities defined by Piaget is importantly linked to content domain (Feldman, 1980; Gardner, 1983; Piaget, 1972), to the eliciting context (Laboratory of Comparative Human Cognition, 1983), and to the particular experiences of individuals (Price-Williams, Gordon, & Ramirez, 1969). Since it is not apparent why and how different materials affect the developmental level of children's performances within Piagetian experimental tasks, it is not feasible to predict relationships between learning to program and performances on the Piagetian tasks. Our second objection is that learning to program has neither been subjected to developmental analysis nor characterized in terms of its component skills that may develop, although such analyses are necessary for articulating measures that indicate the availability and developmental status of these skills for particular learners.

While no research has been directly aimed at defining the cognitive prerequisites for learning programming, at least six factors are frequently mentioned: mathematical ability, memory capacity, analogical reasoning skills, conditional reasoning skills, procedural thinking skills, and temporal reasoning skills. These cognitive abilities, each of which has a complex and well-researched developmental history, are presumed to impact on learning to program, and could be promising directions for research.

Mathematical Ability
Beyond "general intelligence," programming skill is said to be linked to general mathematical ability. Computers were first developed to help solve difficult mathematical problems. Although many computer uses today are nonmathematical (e.g., database management, word processing), the notion persists that to program one must be mathematically sophisticated. Media accounts of children using computers in schools have perpetuated the belief that programming is the province of math whizzes. Although we doubt that math and programming abilities are related once general intelligence is factored out, mathematical ability

cannot be ruled out as a prerequisite to the mastery of certain levels of programming skills.

Processing Capacity

Programming is often a memory-intensive enterprise requiring great concentration and the ability to juggle values of a number of parameters at a time. Individual differences in processing capacity are thus a likely candidate for influencing who becomes a good programmer. Forward and backward span tasks, and more recently developed transformational span measures (cf. Case & Kurland, 1980; Case, Kurland, & Goldberg, 1982) assess how much information one can coordinate at a given moment, and appear to index processes basic to learning. Performances on such tasks have reliably correlated with general intelligence, Piagetian developmental level, and ability to learn and use problem-solving strategies (e.g., Hunt, 1978).

Analogical Reasoning

A student may have background knowledge and capacities relevant to programming and yet neither connect them to the programming domain, nor transfer knowledge acquired in programming to other domains. This ''access'' of knowledge is absolutely fundamental to learning and problem solving throughout life (e.g., A.L. Brown, 1982). Transfers of knowledge and strategies, both ''into'' and ''out of'' learning to program, may depend on analogical thinking skills. Tasks designed to measure abilities for engaging in analogical thinking (e.g., Gick & Holyoak, 1980; Sternberg & Rifkin, 1979) may predict level of programming development and transfer outcomes. Mayer (1975, 1981) argues that students learn programming by comparing the flow of control intrinsic to computational devices to that of physico-mechnical models that they already possess. Also, duBoulay and O'Shea (1976) and duBoulay et al. (1981) have successfully used extensive analogical modelling to explain computer functioning to novice 12-year-old programming students.

Conditional Reasoning

Working with conditional statements is a major part of programming, since they guide the operation of loops, tests, input checking, and other programming functions. It is thus reasonable to predict that a student who has sufficient understanding of conditional logic, the various ''if . . . then'' control structures and the predicate logical connectives of negation, conjunction, and disjunction, will be a more successful programmer than a student who has trouble monitoring the flow of control through conditional statements.

Procedural Thinking

Several kinds of quasi-procedural[4] everyday thought may influence how easily a learner masters the "flow of control" procedural metaphor central to understanding programming, including giving and following complex instructions (as in building a model), writing or following recipes, and concocting or carrying out directions for travel. Presumably, learners more familiar with these linear procedures, analogous to the flow of control for computer operations expressed as instructions in a computer program, will more readily come to grips with the "procedural thinking" touted as a central facet of programming expertise (Papert, 1980; Sheil, 1980). However, the development of procedural thinking has been little studied to date.

Temporal Reasoning

The activity of temporal reasoning is related to procedural thinking, but with a distinct emphasis. Creating and comprehending programs requires an understanding of the temporal logic of sequential instructions: "it is the intellectual heart of learning how to program" (Galanter, 1983, p. 150). In teaching programming, Galanter says:

> The central theoretical concept that guided this effort was that classical forms of spacial-geometric-pictorial thinking must be augmented, and occasionally replaced, by temporal-imaginative-memorial logic. The child must learn to substitute an inner temporal eye for the outer spacial eye. (p. 163)

Going somewhere in the program *next*, running one subroutine or procedure *before* another, ensuring one counter does not exceed a certain value *until* another operation is performed—these fundamental operations all require temporal understanding. Yet understanding temporal terms is a major developmental achievement, a challenge for children younger than 7 to 8 years (e.g., Friedman, 1982; Piaget, 1969). Futurity also presents complex conceptual problems for the planning activities involved in programming, such as imagining outcomes of the possible worlds generated by program design options (Atwood, Jeffries, & Polson, 1980), or the "symbolic executions" while writing programming code (R.E. Brooks, 1977).

---

[4] What is "quasi-procedural" rather than "procedural" about giving and following task instructions, directions, and recipes is that unlike procedural instructions in a computer program, there is often *ambiguity* in the everyday examples, such that the instructions, directions, and recipes are not always unequivocal in meaning. They are also not constrained by strict *sequentiality*. One may often choose to bypass steps in a recipe or set of instructions, or reorder the steps. Neither option is available in the strict procedurality of programmed instructions. Yet similarities between the everyday cases and programming instructions are compelling enough to make their designation as quasi-procedural understandable.

In sum, the cognitive constraints on developing programming skills are currently unknown. Although a developmental cognitive science perspective predicts that a student's attainable level of programming skill may be constrained by cognitive abilities required in programming, no studies relate level of programming skill to the abilities we have described. Children may have conceptual and representational difficulties in constructing dynamic mental models of ongoing events when the computer is executing program lines that constrain their level of programming skill. Also, systematic but "naive" mental models or intuitive epistemologies of computer procedural functioning may initially mislead children's understanding of programming, as with adult novices. Since learning to program is difficult for many students, there is a serious need for research findings that will guide decisions about tailoring programming instruction according to a student's relevant knowledge prior to learning to program.

EVIDENCE FOR COGNITIVE EFFECTS OF PROGRAMMING

We now return to evidence for the claims for broad cognitive impacts of programming experience, with greater awareness of the complexities of learning to program and issues of transfer. In sum, there is little evidence for these claims.

Dramatic accounts have been offered of how some school-aged children's thinking about their own abilities to solve problems is transformed through learning to program (e.g., Papert et al., 1979; Watt, 1982; Weir, 1981; Weir & Watt, 1981). Important social interactional changes have been demonstrated in classrooms where children are learning Logo programming (Hawkins, Sheingold, Gearhart, & Berger, 1982), and for some children programming is an important and deeply personal intellectual activity. Similarly, many teacher reports focus on social and motivational rather than cognitive aspects of this experience (Sheingold, Kane, Endreweit, & Billings, 1981; Watt, 1982). It is not yet clear what the cognitive benefits of programming for such children may be in terms of the transfer claims reviewed earlier.

On the cognitive side, Ross and Howe (1981) have reviewed ten years of relevant research to evaluate Feurzeig et al.'s (1969) four general claims on the cognitive impacts of programming. The relevant research has been with Logo, and in nonrepresentative private schools. Below we summarize Ross and Howe's review, and integrate summaries of other studies relevant to these claims. In terms of our account of levels of programming skill and expected transfer outcomes from them, we must caution that studies so far, including our own, have an important limitation. They have all looked at what we have designated as high-level or cognitive-transfer outcomes, expected to emerge only at the higher levels in our account of programming skill, whereas the levels of programming attained by the students in these studies were low because they only did six weeks to a year or so of programming. In other words, there has been a mismatch of "treatment" and transfer assessments because of a failure to appreciate the different kinds of transfer to investigate and their likely linkage to different kinds of transfer to investigate and their likely linkage to different levels of programming skill. For example, there are no studies that have assessed the low-level transfer or application of programming concepts such as "variable" in different types of programming within a language (e.g., graphics versus list processing in Logo), or from one programming language to another, or of computer literacy outcomes.

First, there are no substantial studies to support the claim that programming promotes mathematical rigor. In a widely cited study by Howe, O'Shea, and Plane (1979), researchers who were highly trained programmers spent two years teaching Logo programming to eleven 11-year-old-boys of average or below average math ability. The first year they studied Logo, the second math with Logo, each boy working for one hour per week in a programming classroom. After two years, when Logo students were compared to nonprogrammers (who on pretest had significantly better scores on the Basic Mathematics Test, but equivalent scores on the Math Attainment Test), they had improved in Basic Math enough to eliminate the original performance gap with the control group, but fell significantly behind on the Math Attainment Test. Such global math score differences do not support the "rigor" claim. The oft-cited finding is that the Logo group learned to argue sensibly about mathematical issues and explain mathematical difficulties clearly, but the finding is based only on differences in ratings of Logo and control students in teacher questionnaires (Howe et al., 1979). The reliability of such ratings is questionable, since the math teachers should have been blind to which students learned Logo.

Second, there are no reports demonstrating that programming aids children's mathematical exploration. Reports by Dwyer (1975) for children learning BASIC, and Howe et al. (1979), Lawler (1980), and Papert et al. (1979) for those using Logo, do document children's goal-directed exploration of mathematical concepts such as "variable" on computers. Though encouraging, since math exploration and "mathland" play are likely to support math learning, studies have not shown any effects of math exploration during programming outside the programming environment.

Third, although Feurzeig et al. (1969) suggest that the twelve 7- to 9-year-old children to whom they taught Logo came to "acquire a meaningful understanding of concepts like variable, function and general procedure," they provide no evidence for the claim that programming helped the children gain insight into these mathematical concepts.

Finally, we ask whether programming has been shown to provide a context and language that promotes problem solving beyond programming. Papert et al. (1979) conducted a Logo project with sixth graders for six weeks, and reported anecdotes that children engage in extensive problem-solving and planning activities in learning programming. Whether such activities had cognitive effects beyond programming was not studied. However, Statz (1973) carried out a study to assess this claim. Logo programming was taught to sixteen 9- to 11-year-old children for a year. Statz chose four problem-solving tasks with intuitive, ill-specified connections to programming activities as transfer outcome measures. The experimental group did better on two of these tasks (word puzzle and a permutation task), but no better on the Tower of Hanoi task or a horserace problem that Statz had designed. She interprets these findings as mixed support for the claim that learning Logo programming promotes the development of more general problem-solving skills.

Soloway, Lochhead, and Clement (1982), in reaction to the finding (Clement, Lochhead, & Monk, 1979) that many college science students have difficulty translating simple algebra word problems into equations, found that more students solve such problems correctly when they are expressed as computer programs rather than as algebraic equations. They attribute this advantage to the procedural semantics of equations in programs that many students lack in the algebraic task. This effect is much more restricted than the increments in general problem-solving skill predicted by the cognitive transfer claims.

A very important idea is that not only computer programs, but one's own mental activities can lead to "buggy" performances and misunderstandings. Tools for diagnosing different types of bugs in such procedural skills as place-value arithmetic (Brown & Burton, 1978; Brown & VanLehn, 1980; VanLehn, 1981) have resulted from extensive programming efforts to build "bug diagnostic systems" (Burton, 1981). One may argue that the widespread recognition that systematic bugs may beset performances in other procedural skills, such as high school algebra (Carry, Lewis, & Bernard, 1979; Matz, 1981), reflects a kind of transfer beyond programming. No evidence indicates that programming students demonstrate such transfer.

Planning in advance of problem solving, and evaluating and checking progress in terms of goals, are important aspects of a reflective attitude to one's own mental activities (Pea, 1982). We have seen that the development of planning abilities is one major predicted cognitive benefit of learning to program. We therefore developed a transfer task for assessing children's planning (Pea & Hawkins, 1984). We reasoned that a microgenetic method (Flavell & Draguns, 1957) allowing children to develop multiple plans was comparable to the rounds of revisions carried out during programming, and would allow for a detailed study of planning processes. Children planned aloud while formulating, over several attempts, their shortest-distance plan for doing a set of familiar classroom chores, using a pointer to indicate their routes. We gave the task twice, early and late in the school year, to eight children in each of two Logo classrooms (8- and 9-year-olds; 11- and 12-year-olds), and to a control group of the same number of same-age children in the same school. There were six microcomputers in each classroom, allowing substantial involvement with programming.

As in related work on adults' planning processes by Goldin and Hayes-Roth (1980; also B. Hayes-Roth, 1980; Hayes-Roth & Hayes-Roth, 1979), our product analyses centered on "plan goodness" in terms of metrics of route efficiency, and our process analyses centered on the types and sequencing of planning decisions made (e.g., higher level executive and metaplanning decisions such as what strategic approach to take to the problem, versus lower level decisions of what route to take between two chore acts). Results indicated that the Logo programming experiences had *no* significant effects on planning performances, nor on any of the plan efficiency or planning process measures (Pea & Kurland, 1984a). Replications of this work are currently under way with children in other schools (Kurland, Pea, Clement & Mawby, in press).

CONCLUSIONS

As our society comes to grips with the information revolution, the ability to deal effectively with computers becomes an increasingly important skill. How well our children learn to use computers today will have great consequences for the society of tomorrow. The competence to appropriately apply higher cognitive skills such as planning and problem-solving heuristics in mental activities both with and without computers is a critical aim for education. As one contribution to these issues, at the beginning we argued for and then throughout documented the need for a new approach to the pervasive questions about the cognitive effects of computer programming. This approach, which we characterize as developmental cognitive science, is one that does not merely adopt the common perspective that computer programmers are all like adults, but is instead geared to the learning experiences and developmental transformations of the child or novice, and in its research would be attentive to the playing out of those processes of learning and development in the instructional and programming environments in which the novice gains expertise.

So, can children become effective programmers and does "learning to program" positively influence children's abilities to plan effectively, to think procedurally, or to view their flawed problem solutions as "fixable" rather than "wrong"? We have shown that answers to these questions depend on what "learning to program" is taken to mean. We reviewed cognitive science studies revealing that programming involves a complex set of skills, and argued that the development of different levels of programming skill will be highly sensitive to contexts for learning, including processes of instruction, programming environment, and the background knowledge the student brings to the task. We found few studies that could inform this new understanding, although many promising research questions were defined from this perspective.

We dismissed two prevailing myths about learning to program. The myth embodied in most programming instruction that learning to program is "learning facts" of programming language semantics and syntax is untenable, since it leads to major conceptual misunderstandings even among adult programmers, and since what is taught belies what cognitive studies show good programmers do and know. These studies have direct implications for new content and methods for programming instruction that are under development in several quarters. Studies of learning to program and of transfer outcomes are not yet available for cases where instruction has such nontraditional emphases, for example, on task analysis and problem-solving methods that take advantage of what we know expert programmers do. We also delivered arguments against the second myth, of spontaneous transfer of higher cognitive skills from learning to program. Resistance in learning to spontaneous transfer, and the predicted linkages of kinds of transfer beyond programming to the learner's level of programming skill were major points of these critical reviews.

So, when thinking about children learning to program, what levels of skill can be expected? Reports of children learning to program (Howe, 1981; Levin & Kareev, 1980; Papert et al., 1979; Pea, 1983), including the learning disabled, the cerebral palsied, and the autistic (Weir, 1981; Weir & Watt, 1981), suggest that most children can learn to write correct lines of code (level II in our account). This is no small achievement since writing grammatically correct lines of code is all that many college students of programming achieve in their first programming courses (Bonar & Soloway, 1982). This level of programming skill may depend on the same abilities necessary for learning a first language.

However, for programming skills that are functional for solving problems, "grammatical" programming alone is inadequate; the student must know how to organize code and "plan schemas" to accomplish specific goals. Development to these higher levels, where one becomes facile with the pragmatics of programming, may require strategic and planful approaches to problem solving that are traditionally considered "metacognitive," and more characteristic of adolescents (Brown et al., 1983) than primary school children. Further, the experience of the child in an elementary or junior high school program who spends up to 30 to 50 hours per year programming is minuscule when compared to the 5,000 hours which R.E. Brooks (1980) estimates a programmer with only three years of experience has spent on programming. Since it appears unreasonable to expect children to become advanced programmers in the few years available to them in most school programming courses, our educational goals should be more realistic and achievable. We do not currently know what levels of programming expertise to expect, but in our experience children who are programming experts are not common. There are thus large gaps between what is meant by learning to program in the computer science literature, and what "learning programming" means to educators interested in exposing this domain to children. These discrepancies should temper expectations for the spontaneous effects of children's limited programming experiences in school on their ways of thinking, at least for how programming is taught (or not taught) today. Whether research on learning to program with richer learning experiences and instruction will lead to powerful outcomes of programming remains to be seen. In place of a naive technoromanticism, we have predicted that the level of programming abilities a student has mastered will be a predictor of the kinds of concepts and skills that the student will transfer beyond programming. Although findings to date of transfer from learning to program have not been encouraging, these studies suffer in not linking level of programming skill to specific outcomes expected, and the critical studies of low-level transfer expected from levels I and II programming skills remain to be carried out. Even more importantly, with thinking skills as educational goals, we may be best off providing direct guidance that teaches or models transfers as a general aspect of highly developed thinking processes (Chipman, Segal, & Glaser, 1985; Smith & Bruce, 1981). For these purposes programming may provide one excellent domain for examples (Nickerson, 1982; Papert, 1980).

Throughout, we have emphasized how developmental research in this area is very much needed. We need empirical studies to refine our characterizations of levels of programming proficiency, extensive evaluations of the extent of transfer within and beyond programming in terms of different programming and instructional environments, and studies to help untangle the complex equation involving cognitive constraints, programming experience, and programming outcomes. We believe all of these questions could be addressed by careful longitudinal studies of the learning and development process by which individual students become proficient (or not-so-proficient) programmers, and of the cognitive consequences of different levels of programming skill. Such studies would provide far more relevant information for guiding the processes of education than standard correlational studies. A focus on process and the types of interactions that students with different levels of entering skills have with programming and instructional environments is critical for understanding how developments in programming skill are related to other knowledge. We are optimistic that others will join in work on these questions, for progress must be made toward meeting the educational needs of a new society increasingly empowered by information technologies.

AUTHOR NOTES

We would like to acknowledge with thanks the Spencer Foundation and the National Institute of Education (Contract 400-83-0016) for supporting the research reported here, and for providing the opportunity to write this essay. The opinions expressed do not necessarily reflect the position or policy of these institutions and no official endorsement should be inferred. Jan Hawkins, Karen Sheingold, Ben Shneiderman and a group of anonymous reviewers provided very useful critical discussions of the data and issues covered in this report.

CHAPTER 9

LOGO AND THE DEVELOPMENT OF THINKING SKILLS

Roy D. Pea, D. Midian Kurland, and Jan Hawkins

With the growing presence of computers in educational settings, questions about their importance and likely effects for children's learning have become a focal concern. Studies that draw conclusions about the impact of computers on children's development and thinking are beginning to emerge. It is important that we take a critical look at the contexts in which these studies are being carried out and at the assumptions that underlie them. Understanding the effects of any learning experience is a complex, multileveled enterprise. Ideally, studying how and what children learn in school contexts should allow for revisionary cycles in which variations in the important features of learning experiences and methods of measurement can be explored and improvements made. Too often this is not done.

For the past several years we have been carrying out a series of studies conducted to understand in detail one system for using computers with children that has received great attention in the educational community: teaching children to program through Logo. The Logo programming language is designed to be easily accessible to children (Abelson & diSessa, 1981), and experience with Logo is associated with general problem-solving abilities as well as with specific skills in programming (*Byte*, 1982; Coburn, Kelman, Roberts, Snyder, Watt, & Weiner, 1982; Papert, 1980). Our research was designed to answer questions about the cognitive and social impact of Logo in elementary school classrooms. One major strand of this work is summarized in this chapter: whether learning to program affects the development of other cognitive skills. An interwoven theme will be how our assumptions and understandings concerning the nature of programming and its necessary cognitive requirements changed as we became increasingly familiar with the programming "culture" emerging in the classrooms we were studying.

We began with a basic framework for conducting our work. Logo was a well-designed symbol system for programming. Many claims had been made about the power and uniqueness of this system as an environment in which children could explore through discovery learning and develop problem-solving skills that would spontaneously transfer beyond the practices of programming (Papert, 1980). Since this learning environment was being made available on a mass scale, it was important to examine these claims in the context of general use—elementary school classrooms. Our intent was to investigate the effects of Logo learning on cognitive skills (Pea & Kurland, 1984b), but we had the parallel problem of documenting the cocreation of Logo learning practices in classrooms by teachers and children in which cognitive skills were to be used. In the Logo discovery learning environment, how did children encounter new information? What were the problems that engaged them? How was Logo integrated into the work of the classroom?

In the next section we briefly review some of the key findings from one line of our research—the question of whether problem-solving skills were gained through Logo programming that transferred beyond programming practices. However, our main purpose will be to reflect on how these studies enabled us to look more closely at the distinction between the cognitive skills that *can* be practiced through some uses of formally elegant symbol systems such as Logo and the ways that these systems evoke particular practices in the classrooms.

RESEARCH SETTING

The studies took place over a 2-year period in one third/fourth grade and one fifth/sixth grade classroom in a private school in New York City. The children in the studies represented a variety of ethnic and socioeconomic backgrounds and a range of achievement levels. Many of the children were, however, above national norms in school achievement and came from upper-middle-class and professional families. Each classroom had six microcomputers during the 1981-1982 school year. In each class, children were learning Logo.

The teachers received intensive training in Logo. They had regular contact with members of the research staff as well as with the members of the team who developed Logo throughout the two years of the study. The computer programming activities during the first year were intended by the teachers to be largely child initiated so as to encourage the child-centered, Piagetian "learning without curriculum" advocated for Logo (Papert, 1980). While teachers in the first year of the study gave the children some simple instruction in Logo during the first several weeks and occasionally held group sessions to introduce new aspects of Logo during the year, their self-defined role was principally that of constructively responding to students' questions and problems as they arose. Students' primary activities were the creation and development of their own computer programming projects.

Teachers scheduled computer use for students in their classrooms so that everyone would have equal access—about two 45-minute work periods per week. There were additional optional times for computer use throughout the day—before school and during lunch periods—when computers were available on a first-come, first-served basis. Logs kept at each computer over the course of the year showed that, on the average, the children spent about 30 hours programming in Logo, although several spent as many as 60 hours.

The second year differed from the first in that both teachers decided to take a more directive role in guiding their students' explorations of Logo (see Hawkins, Chapter 1, this volume, for a more detailed description of the teachers' changing views of the role of programming in their classrooms). The teacher of the younger class gave weekly group lessons to introduce key computational concepts and techniques, and to demonstrate how they function in computer programs. The older students were also given more group lessons and were required to complete specific assignments centering on Logo concepts and programming methods, such as preplanning. In both classrooms, the focus of the work remained the development of individual programming projects.

In these classrooms, we carried out a number of studies concerning both cognitive and social questions. The studies we will focus on here concerned the effects learning to program had on students' *planning* skills. Before examining more closely why we chose planning as one of our key topics, we will briefly discuss the relationship of computer programming to the development of general thinking skills such as planning.

PROGRAMMING AND THINKING SKILLS

The current claims about effects of learning to program on thinking have been most extensively stated by Papert and Feurzeig (e.g., Feurzeig, Horwitz, & Nickerson, 1981; Feurzeig, Papert, Bloom, Grant, & Solomon, 1969; Goldstein & Papert, 1977; Papert, 1972a,b, 1980; Papert, Watt, diSessa, & Weir, 1979). Such claims are not unique to Logo, but have been alleged for programming in general (Minsky, 1970; Nickerson, 1982).

Two key catalysts appear to have contributed to the belief that programming may spontaneously discipline thinking. The first is from artificial intelligence, where constructing programs that model the complexities of human cognition is viewed as a way of understanding that behavior. The contention is that in explicitly teaching the computer to do something, you learn more about your own thinking. By analogy (Papert, 1972a), programming students would learn about problem-solving processes by the necessarily explicit nature of programming, as they articulate assumptions and precisely specify steps to their problem-solving approach. The second influence is the widespread assimilation of constructivist epistemologies of learning, most familiar through Piaget's work. Papert (1972a, 1980) has been an outspoken advocate of the Piagetian account of knowledge acquisition through self-guided problem-solving experiences, and has extensively influenced conceptions of the benefits of learning to program through "learning without curriculum" in "a process that takes place without deliberate or organized teaching" (1980, p. 8; also pp. 27, 31). (It should be noted that Piaget never advocated the elimination of organized teaching in schools.)

ON PLANNING

One of the claims made about the positive effects of programming on thinking has been in the area of planning (Feurzeig et al., 1981). From this framework it is believed that programming experience will result in greater facility with the art of "heuristics," explicit approaches to problems useful for solving problems in *any* domain, such as planning, finding a related problem, or solving the problem by decomposing it into parts.

Planning was selected as our principal reference topic because both rational analysis of programming and observations of adult programmers show that planning is manifested in programming in important ways. At the outset of our studies, there was little evidence of how this symbol system was learned by children in classroom settings. Since there was no information about practice in this "culture," we developed our transfer measures based on a rational analysis of the cognitive requirements of writing computer programs and from examination of the problem-solving activities of expert programmers in settings other than classrooms.

Examination of expert performance reveals that once a programming problem is formulated, the programmer often maps out a program plan or design that will then be written in programming code. Expert programmers spend a good deal of their time in planning program design (F.P. Brooks, 1982), and have many planning strategies available, such as problem decomposition, subgoal generation, retrieval of known solutions, modification of similar code from related programs, and evaluative analysis and debugging of program components (e.g., Pea & Kurland, 1984b). Does the effectiveness of planning become more apparent to a person learning to program? Does the development of planning skills for more general use as thinking tools become more likely when a person learns to program? And, fundamentally, does programming by its inherent nature entail planning as an unavoidable constituent process? These were the questions we set out initially to examine.

PLANNING AND PROGRAMMING

The core of computer programming is that set of activities involved in developing a reusable product consisting of a series of written instructions to make a computer accomplish some task. As in the case of theories of problem solving in general, cognitive studies of programming reveal a set of distinctive mental activities that occur as computer programs are developed. These activities are involved throughout the development of a program, whether the programmer is novice or expert, because they constitute recursive phases of the problem-solving process in any general theory of problem solving (see Heller & Greeno, 1979; Newell & Simon, 1972; Polya, 1957). They may be summarized as follows: (a) understanding/defining the programming problem; (b) planning or designing a programming solution; (c) writing programming code that implements the plan; and (d) comprehension of the written program and program debugging. We discuss each of these cognitive subtasks in detail elsewhere (see Pea & Kurland, 1984b).

One may raise the objection that it is possible to bypass planning in program development; that is, one may first make an initial reading of the problem and then compose code at the keyboard to achieve the task. Although such planning-in-action is certainly possible to produce some programs, it seemed likely that such a plan-in-action might create problems for the inexperienced programmer. While expert programmers can draw on their knowledge of a vast range of plans when creating programs (Atwood, Jeffries, & Polson, 1980; Soloway, Ehrlich, Bonar, & Greenspan, 1982), the novice programmer has neither the sophisticated understanding of programming code nor the experience of devising successful programming schemas necessary for engaging in planning-in-action.

What are we to make of these observations in terms of defining planning as a distinct cognitive subtask in programming? Is it optional? The answer to this question certainly has consequences for thinking about the cognitive outcomes of programming. However, in the absence of any actual observations of *how* novices, especially children (and particularly children engaged in a discovery-learning approach), create programs, it seemed reasonable to base our predictions about what the potential effects of programming for planning would be on a formal model of programming's entailments built on this adult model of expert programming.

ASSESSING PLANNING SKILLS

We were guided in the design of our studies by key features of planning processes (see Pea, 1982; Pea & Hawkins, 1984, for further details). Specifically, we felt the tasks should (a) represent situations that are congruent with what is known about plan construction, especially when planning is likely to occur, and (b) externalize the planning process to allow observers to see and record processes of plan construction.

With respect to the former, the planning context should (a) be one where a child might be expected to see planning as appropriate and valuable; (b) be complex enough so that the means for achieving a goal are not immediately transparent and the possibility of alternative plans is recognized; and (c) involve a domain where children have a sufficient knowledge base so that action sequences can be planned and consequences of actions anticipated.

With respect to the second point above, the task should reveal (a) whether alternatives are considered; (b) whether the planner tests alternatives by simulating their execution; (c) what kinds of revisions or debuggings of a plan are made; and (d) what different types and levels of planning decisions are made.

Planning is appropriately characterized as a revisionary process. As a consequence of considering alternatives, effective planners revise their plans. They work between top-down planning strategies, which create a plan from successively refining the goal into a sequence of subgoals for achievement in sequence, and bottom-up planning strategies, which note the emergent properties of the plan or the planning environment and add data-driven decisions to the plan throughout its creation (Hayes-Roth & Hayes-Roth, 1979; Pea, 1982).

We decided that a classroom chore-scheduling task, analogous to a planning scenario used by Hayes-Roth and Hayes-Roth (1979), met this series of requirements for a planning task. Nonetheless, it constituted a "far" transfer measure because it had very few *surface* similarities to programming—for instance, it did not involve a computer. We found from classroom observations that all children had to carry out certain classroom chores on a regular basis (washing the blackboards, watering the plants, and the like). The task was made novel by requiring children to organize a plan that would allow one person to accomplish all the chores. We designed a classroom map as an external representational model to support and expose planning processes.

A transparent Plexiglass map of a fictitious classroom was developed for the task (see Figure 9.1). Children were to devise a plan to carry out six major chores. The chores could be accomplished with a minimum of 39 distinct chore acts. Some of the acts are subgoals, because they are instrumentally necessary to accomplish others (i.e., the water can is needed

Figure 9.1 Diagram of classroom model, Study 1.

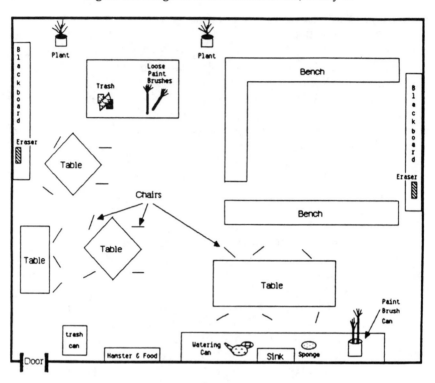

to water plants; the sponge is necessary for washing tables and black-boards). Finding the optimal sequencing of these chore acts is thus a challenging task.

STUDYING PLANNING SKILLS:
THE FAR TRANSFER TASK OF YEAR ONE

In the first year we videotaped children from the programming class-rooms individually (6 boys and 6 girls) and a matched set of same-age controls as they worked in this planning environment. Each child was told that the goal was to make up a plan to do a lot of classroom chores. The child was asked to devise the shortest spatial path for doing the chores, and that he or she could make up as many plans as were needed to arrive at the shortest plan. The child was instructed to think out loud while planning, and to use a pointer to show the path taken to do the chores. The child was given a pencil and paper to make notes (rarely used), and a list of the six chores to keep track of what she or he was doing. The same task and procedure was administered early in the school year, just as the students were beginning to learn Logo, and again four months later.

We were interested in examining three aspects of children's plans: (a) the plans considered as products; (b) the plan revisions children made in terms of the features that contributed to plan improvement; and (c) the planning process, especially in terms of the types and levels of abstraction of component decisions. On the basis of what programming was assumed to be, these areas were selected because we felt they were the ones most likely to differentiate between the programming and nonprogramming students. Complete descriptions of the analyses and results are available elsewhere (Pea & Kurland, 1984a). Here we will simply review the major findings.

Product Analysis

The sequence of chore acts for each plan was recorded, and the distance calculated that would be traversed if the plan were to be executed. Route efficiency for a plan was a function of the distance covered in executing the plan relative to the optimal distance for doing the chores. There were no significant differences in the mean number of plans attempted between children of different ages or between programming and nonprogramming groups.

Route efficiency score significantly increased with age, from first to last plan within session and across age groups. The Logo programming group, however, did not differ from controls for any plan constructed at the beginning of the school year or at the end of a school year of Logo programming. Finally, each *age* group, regardless of programming experience, improved in efficiency from first to last plan.

Our next question concerned *how* plan improvements were made. For the most part, we were able to characterize the children's substantive revisions of structure to improve their plans as resulting from "seeing" the chores differently over time (e.g., Bamberger & Schon, 1982; diSessa, 1983; Heller & Greeno, 1979).

More specifically, the initial formulation of our task as the carrying out of a set of *named* chores ("cleaning tables," "washing blackboards," "pushing in chairs") is a frame or set for problem understanding that must be broken for the task to be accomplished effectively. Performing each named task, in whatever order, is not an effective plan. Each chore must be decomposed into its component acts, and the parts must then be reconstructed and sequenced into an effective all-encompassing plan. The child's understanding of part-whole relations for the task is thus transformed during plan revision. To move toward the optimal solution of this planning problem, a child must reconfigure the chore "chunks" in terms of their spatial distribution on the classroom map. Major breakthroughs in plan structuring occur through discovering spatial clusters— from a list of named chores to a list of spatial *clusters* of chore acts.

Children's plans were analyzed in terms of these plan features. More efficient organization of chore acts into clusters was highly correlated to shorter plan distance for first and last plans in both sessions.

The mean plan cluster score significantly improved for each age group across plans and sessions, but Logo programmers did not differ from the control groups on any of these comparisons. The children reorganized their plans into more efficient clusters during the revision process whether or not they had programmed.

Process Analyses

We also wished to compared planning processes across children and plans. In creating their plans, did our Logo programmers engage in more advanced decision-making processes than the nonprogrammers, even though their plans were not more efficient? We examined the process of plan construction by categorizing each segment of the children's think-aloud protocols in terms of the type of planning decision being made and its level of abstraction (as in Goldin & Hayes-Roth, 1980; Hayes-Roth & Hayes-Roth, 1979).

For the process analysis, we asked whether the organization of the planning process in terms of the types, levels, and sequences of planning decisions was different for the programmers than for the nonprogrammers with respect to the following: (a) frequencies of different types of planning decisions; (b) decision-choice flexibility; and (c) relationships between the amount of "executive" and "metaplanning" activity during the planning process and decision-choice flexibility.

In brief, the Logo programming group did not differ from the control groups on any of the comparisons for types of planning decisions. Nonetheless, we found interesting differences in when and by whom such higher level decisions were made. Children made significantly more high-level decisions in their first plans than in their last in session 1, and older children produced more high-level decisions than did younger children. There were no age effects for the second session.

As a further index of planning processes, we determined the flexibility of a child's decision making during the planning process in two ways: (a) by looking at the number of transitions a child made between types of decision making while creating the plan, and (b) by looking at the number of transitions made between levels of decision making, irrespective of the decision type. For both sessions, the mean number of type transitions per plan is highly correlated with the mean number of level transitions per plan. The programmers did not differ from the nonprogrammers on these indices of decision-choice flexibility.

Relationship of Product to Process Measures

We also looked at how decision-making processes were related to the effectiveness of the plan as a product, and found that none of the process and product measures were significantly related. We also tested for a relationship between the frequency of high-level planning decisions and mean cluster scores. The nonsignificant relationships indicate that children revise their plans to accomplish the acts more efficiently without necessarily using (verbally explicit) metaplanning resources. Only for the last plan of the younger children in the first session are these variables significantly correlated.

DISCUSSION

On the face of it, these results suggest that a school year of Logo programming did not have a measurable influence on the planning abilities of these students. While an average of 30 hours of programming is small compared with what professional programmers or college computer science majors devote to such work, it is a significant amount of time by elementary school standards.

The failure of the programming student to show any advantage over nonprogrammers on the classroom planning task could have been attributed to any one of a number of possible sources. A prime concern was that our basic assumptions about programming, based on a formal analysis of its properties and expert programmer data, were inadequate for capturing what transpired in the classroom. Based on parallel ethnographic studies in Logo classrooms (Hawkins, 1983, Chapter 1, this volume), we were beginning to understand that the actual classroom practice of Logo had developed in ways that made programming activity quite different from what had been anticipated. For example, particular pieces of students' knowledge about specific programming concepts appeared to be tightly wedded to the specific contexts in which they were learned, unlike the knowledge of expert programmers. Programming constructs for the students had local functional meaning that they did not tend to generalize, even to other closely related programming problems. Although the planning task had features that made it formally similar to the characterization of planning in programming that was available in the literature on programming, the surface structure of the task was quite different from the way programming was actually done in the classrooms. Students may have failed to recognize the task as an opportunity to apply insights from programming.

Therefore, in the second year of the study we set out to create a new version of the planning task that resembled programming on its surface as well as in its deep structural features. Thus, for example, the new task, while not requiring any previous programming experience (therefore making it suitable for the control groups of students), consisted of a computer-based microworld environment similar to the programming environments with which the students were familiar, and provided on-line feedback on the success of planning efforts analogous to the feedback programmers get from executing their programs in the process of creating them.

In addition, most children appeared to do little preplanning in their programming work. Planning as a component of programming was introduced to the students, but not insisted upon, and possible program-planning aids (such as worksheets) were not explicitly provided. Students tended to write and revise their code in terms of the immediate effects that commands and sequences of commands produced.

The nature of the Logo programming environment changed during the second school year. At the end of the first year, teachers expressed disappointment with the quality of students' programming work, and decided to provide more structure to the learning environments for the second year. In addition to conducting "lessons" and group discussions on specific topics, teachers worked with children to develop more suitable individual projects, and at the beginning of the year provided some program-planning aids for the children. These aids, however, were seldom used. Students preferred to write programs interactively at the keyboard.

STUDYING PLANNING SKILLS IN A
NEAR TRANSFER PROGRAMMING MICROWORLD

In the beginning of the second year, the original planning task was administered to new groups of students in the two programming classrooms and to two same-age control groups. We found again that students' last plans were better than their first plans, and that there were no differences between the programming and nonprogramming groups at the beginning of the school year.

Near the end of the year, the new planning task was given. This revised task incorporated new design features that made the task bear a far closer resemblance to programming as it was practiced in these classrooms than did the Plexiglass map task. The new task consisted of four components: (a) a colored diagram of a classroom; (b) a set of goal cards, each depicting one of the six chores (such as wiping off the tables and watering the plant); (c) a microcomputer program that enabled students to design and check their plans with the support of the experimenter; and (d) a graphics interface that enabled students to see their plans enacted in a realistic representation of the classroom (see Figure 9.2).

The computer program created a graphics robot programming and testing environment within which children could develop their plans. The children could "program" a robot using a simple, English-like programming language, and then see their plan carried out.

The commands in the robot programming language consisted of a set of six actions (WALK TO, PICK UP, PUT DOWN, WIPE OFF, WATER, STRAIGHTEN UP), and the names for all the objects in the classroom. Each action-object pairing constituted a move in the plan. As the student talked through a plan while looking at the classroom diagram and goal cards, the experimenter keyed each move into the computer, which listed it for the student to see. If the student gave a command that could not be carried out at that point in the plan (e.g., telling the robot to wipe off the table before telling it to go to pick up the sponge), the computer

Figure 9.2. Diagram of classroom model, Study 2.

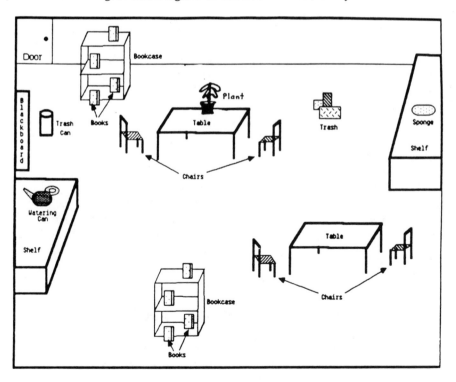

program immediately rejected the move and provided a precise context-specific error message on the screen (e.g., I'M NOT CARRYING THE SPONGE). If a student indicated that his or her plan was done when there was actually one or more chores still remaining, the program provided a message to this effect, and a list of the outstanding chores appeared on the screen. A message always displayed on the screen informed students that they could at any time ask to see the list of remaining chores or review their plan by having it listed on the screen. Together, these features ensured that all the students would develop runnable, albeit not necessarily optimal, plans.

The second part of the new classroom chore-scheduling task was a graphics interface designed to provide feedback to the student on the adequacy of his or her plan. There were four types of feedback: (a) a readout of the total time the student's just-completed plan would take if carried out in action; (b) a representation of a classroom displayed on a high-resolution screen, on which a step-by-step enactment of the student's plan could be carried out under the student's control; (c) a step-by-step readout of each move the student had entered and the time it took the robot to carry out each move; and (d) a hard-copy printout of the student's plan that could be referred to during subsequent planning attempts.

In individual sessions, children were told to imagine that they had a robot who could understand and carry out commands to perform classroom duties. Their task was to devise a plan for the robot to clean up a classroom in the least possible amount of time, covering the shortest possible spatial path. Students were told that they would create three plans, in which they would be able to improve on their previous plans (see Pea & Kurland, 1984a, for further details of the procedure). A clock inside the computer was used to record the intervals between the student's moves ("thinking time"). This enabled us to determine how reflective each student was while creating each plan, and where in the planning process the students spent time thinking.

Students were given as much time as they needed to think about what to do and to call out each individual move. The experimenter typed each move into the computer, where it was either accepted and added to the plan list or immediately rejected and the student told what was wrong. The computer did all the monitoring and error checking, and gave the only feedback the child received. When all the chores were completed and the robot was directed out of the classroom door, the program calculated and then displayed how long the just-entered plan would take.

In order to determine the effects of feedback from actual plan execution on revisions in later plans, two different task conditions were used.

Half of the students went on to do a second and then a third plan immediately upon completion of their first one. The other half of the students saw a representation of the classroom on the graphics screen after they had completed each plan. Simultaneously, the first move of the plan was printed on the text screen. The student was given a hand-held button that, each time it was pressed, took the program through the plan one move at a time. A line corresponding to each move was drawn to indicate the path the robot would follow in carrying out the plan, accompanied by the name of the move on the text screen (such as WATER THE PLANT). A time counter was displayed indicating the total time needed by the robot to carry out the plan up to the current move. The student's plan was printed out so that, when devising subsequent plans, he or she could see exactly what had been done on the earlier attempts.

We hypothesized that students with programming experience might differ from their nonprogramming peers in four major respects:

1. Programmers should be better planners overall. Therefore, lengths of plans for the programming students should be less than those for nonprogrammers.
2. Programmers should make more and better use of the feedback available, since programming teaches the utility of debugging partially correct procedures. This means that programmers should ask more often to see a listing of their plans (*review plan*) and refer more often to the list of remaining chores (*checklist*) than nonprogrammers. In addition, in the programming group, differences on these dimensions between students in the feedback and no-feedback conditions should be greater than in the nonprogramming group.
3. Programmers, relative to nonprogrammers, should spend more time early in their first plan thinking over alternative plans (i.e., significantly more *pauses* and longer mean *thinking time* in the first third of the first plan). On subsequent plans, their thinking time should become more evenly distributed across the plan as they concentrate on debugging different parts of it.
4. Programmers should seek to improve or debug their first plan through successive refinements in subsequent plans, rather than trying a different approach each time. This means that, relative to the nonprogrammers, the degree of similarity between successive plans for programmers should increase across plans.

Older students produced better (i.e., shorter) plans overall than did younger students. In addition, first plans were significantly different from both second and third plans, but the second and third plans did not differ significantly from each other. Even the best group did not produce optimal plans with respect to execution time. There were no differences between the programming and nonprogramming groups in the time their plans would take to carry out. In addition, there was no difference in their use of the available feedback aids such as checking over their sequence of moves or requesting to see a listing of the remaining chores. Students rarely used these features of the task environment, even though there was a message on the screen at all times indicating its availability. In addition, the group of students who executed their plans between each attempt tended not to spend much time watching the plan enactments, nor did they refer to the printed copy of earlier plans when creating a new plan. Plans were created without much attention to the details of previous attempts.

When the pause data (indicating thinking time) were examined, there were again no differences between the programming and the nonprogramming groups. Students paused to think more during the first plan than during their second or third, but the amount of time spent thinking in their second and third plans did not differ. When thinking time was broken down into thirds (beginning, middle, and end of the plan), it was found that more thinking time occurred in the beginning third of a plan than into the middle or end third. Thus, while the pattern of thinking time for the programmers conformed to what we had hypothesized, it did not differ as predicted from the pattern for nonprogrammers.

Finally, we examined the amount of overlap from plan to plan (plan similarity). The successive plans for all groups tended to overlap from plan to plan by 35% to 55%. Yet again there was no difference between the programming and nonprogramming students or between the students with and without benefit of feedback. Thus there was no evidence that the programmers were more likely to follow a model of plan debugging by successive refinement than nonprogrammers. Additional analyses indicate that students who modified previous plans, leaving larger portions intact, did not develop appreciably better plans than students who varied their approaches from plan to plan.

Discussion

On the basis of these results, we concluded that students who had spent a year programming did not differ on various developmental comparisons of the effectiveness of their plans and their processes of planning from same-age controls who had not learned to program. The results from this study are particularly striking because the computerized "near" transfer planning task was designed to have a strong resemblance to programming, including feedback in different representational media (picture of plan in execution, list of moves in plan, and so on), which, because of their planning experience, programmers might have used to greater advantage. The programming groups clearly did not use the cognitive abilities alleged to be developed through experience with Logo in these tasks designed to tap them.

What were we to conclude from these findings? That there does not appear to be automatic improvement of planning skills from learning Logo programming appeared clear, but why? Two major categories of potential explanations come to mind.

The first category concerns the design of the transfer tasks. There could be objections to the tasks we used and our resultant data. Perhaps these tasks did not tap planning skills. However, the tasks had greater surface validity, and the route efficiency measures in particular were developmentally sensitive. The developmental gap between actual performance and optimal performance could have been influenced by the greater development of planning abilities through programming. Yet whether or not a student programmed did not account for the variability we found in planning task performances.

Another objection to our planning tasks was that they were not close enough to programming tasks for the transfer of planning skills from the programming domain. But according to claims made about the general value of programming for thinking, transfer of the concepts and practices of planning to other problem-solving situations should occur *spontaneously*, not because of resemblances of the target task to the programming domain.

The second category of explanations concerns the nature of Logo programming. Here we may distinguish among four different kinds of arguments. First, there are problems with the Logo programming environment (*not* the instructional environment) as a vehicle for learning these generalizable cognitive skills. Second, the quality of learning about and developing such planning skills with the Logo discovery-learning pedagogy is insufficient for the development of generalizable planning skills. Third, perhaps the amount of time students spent in the Logo pedagogical environment was not sufficient for us to see the effects on planning of Logo programming experience.

On the basis of the two studies, we could not tease apart these first three alternatives. However, as we were simultaneously learning more and more about what the students were actually doing in the classrooms —what the *practices* of programming actually were—a fourth, and fundamentally different, interpretation of these studies became apparent.

To understand this interpretation it is useful to reflect on a set of issues similar to those we were pursuing in programming—those that relate to the cognitive consequences of *literacy*. The acquisition of literacy, like programming today, has long been claimed to promote the development of intellectual skills (Ong, 1982). Prominent historians and psychologists have argued that written language has many important properties that distinguish it from oral language, and that the use of written language leads to the development of highly general thinking abilities, such as logical reasoning and abstract thinking.

But studies bearing on this claim have traditionally been done in societies such as Senegal or Mexico, where literacy and schooling were confounded. Perhaps schooling is responsible for these changes in thinking, rather than the use of written language per se. In an extensive 5-year research program, Scribner and Cole (1981) examined the cognitive effects of literacy *independently* of schooling. The society they studied was the Vai, an African people who do not transmit literacy in the Vai language through formal schooling. Their reading and writing are practiced and learned through the activities of daily life. The Vai invented their written language a mere 150 years ago, and have continued to pass literacy on to their children without schools.

Like most psychologists, Scribner and Cole brought with them standardized psychological testing instruments and stimuli for experiments on concept formation and verbal reasoning. But as Scribner and Cole looked over their results from several years of work, they could see no general cognitive effects of being literate in the Vai script. For example, the literate Vai were no better than the nonliterate Vai in categorization skills or syllogistic reasoning.

Before continuing with their initial research strategy with a refined set of tasks, Scribner and Cole realized that there was a radically different way to think about their project, in terms of specific effects. They had begun by looking for general effects of literacy. But after several years of survey and ethnographic observations, they had also come to understand the tasks that Vai literates encounter in their everyday *practices* of literacy. The Vai use their written language primarily for letter writing, and for recording lists and making technical farming plans. New tasks were designed for assessing literacy effects that were based on those particular skills required by the literacy practices they observed.

Results from these studies demonstrated dramatic cognitive effects of literacy, but they were more local in nature. For example, letter writing, a common Vai literacy practice, requires more explicit rendering of meaning than that called for in face-to-face talk. A communication task where the rules of a novel board game had to be explained to someone unfamiliar with it revealed that performances of Vai literates were vastly superior to those of nonliterates on either version of this task.

Our results concerning the learning of programming can be examined from a similar framework (Pea, 1984). But for programming languages, unlike written language, we do not have the benefit of known historical and cultural changes that appear to result in part from centuries of use of the written language. In the absence of evidence about actual programming practices in these classrooms, we were guided by the rationale that "programming intelligence" and the kinds of programming activities carried out by adults would affect children too.

In addition to examining carefully the formal properties of programming and the planning tasks, we can also take a functional or activity-based approach to understanding our results. We can consider programming not as a *given*, the features of which we know by virtue of how adults do it at its best, but as a *set of practices* that emerge in a complex goal-directed cultural framework. Programming is as various and complex an activity matrix as literacy. Just as one may use one's literacy in Vai society to make laundry lists rather than to analyze and reflect upon the logical structures of written arguments, so one may achieve much more modest activities in programming than dialectics concerning the processes of general problem solving, planning, precise thinking, debugging, and the discovery of powerful ideas. One may, in particular, write linear brute-force code for drawing simple pictures.

From a functional perspective we may see that powerful ideas are no more attributes inherent ''in'' Logo than powerful ideas are inherent ''in'' written language. Each may be put to a broad range of uses. What one does with Logo, or written language, or any symbol system is an open matter. The Vai have not spontaneously gotten into the logical features of written language, philosophy, and textual analysis that written language *allows*. Likewise, most of our students—in these as well as others of our studies from grade school up through high school—have not spontaneously gotten into the programming practices (such as structured planful approaches to procedure composition use of conditional or recursive structures, or careful documentation and debugging) that Logo *allows*.

For the Vai, one could imagine introducing new logical and analytic uses of their written language. Similarly, one could imagine introducing to children the Logo programming practices many educators have taken for granted will emerge. In either case, we would argue that without some functional significance to the activities for those who are learning the new practices, there is unlikely to be successful, transferable learning.

It is our hunch that wherever we see children using Logo in the ways its designers hoped, and learning new thinking and problem-solving skills, it is because someone has provided guidance, support, and ideas for how the language *could* be used. The teachers in our studies began to work out such a supportive approach. They found this to be a complex enterprise because they found they had to think through the problems of what should be known about the system, and the sequence appropriate to comprehension. They also found that helping children to find functional goals for their Logo work was problematic throughout the two years.

There are many consequences of this more general account of what is involved in thinking about Logo as a potential vehicle for promoting thinking and problem-solving skills. A functional approach to programming recognizes that we need to create a *culture* in which students, peers, and teachers talk about thinking skills and display them aloud for others to share and learn from, and that builds bridges to thinking about other domains of school and life. Such thinking skills, as played out in programming projects, would come to play functional roles, not because of some abstract inherent characteristics of programming, but because of characteristics of the context in which programming gets embedded. Dialogue and inquiry about thinking and learning processes would become more frequent, and the development of general problem-solving skills so important in an information age would be a more common achievement of students.

Where are we left, then? It is encouraging that there are so many positive energies in education today. The enthusiasm for Logo as a vehicle of cognitive change is an exhilarating part of the new processes of education one can see emerging. But we must first recognize that we are visitors in a strange world—at the fringe of creating a culture of education that takes for granted the usefulness of the problem-solving tools provided by computers, and the kind of thinking and learning skills that the domain of programming makes so amenable to using, refining, and talking about together.

Learning thinking skills and how to plan well is not intrinsically guaranteed by the Logo programming environment; it must be supported by teachers who, tacitly or explicitly, know how to foster the development of such skills through a judicious use of examples, student projects, and direct instruction. But the Logo instructional environment that Papert (1980) currently offers to educators is devoid of curriculum, and lacks an account of how the technology can be used as a tool to stimulate students' thinking about such powerful ideas as planning and problem decomposition. Teachers are told not to teach, but are not told what to substitute for teaching. Thinking-skills curricula are beginning to appear, but teachers cannot be expected to induce lessons about the power of planning methods from self-generated product-oriented programming projects.

AUTHOR NOTES

We would like to thank the Spencer Foundation and the National Institute of Education (Contract 400-83-0016) for supporting our research and the writing of this chapter. The opinions expressed do not necessarily reflect the position or policy of these institutions, and no official endorsement should be inferred. Our colleagues at the Center for Children and Technology have contributed to these studies in the past several years, and we appreciate their help and support. Of course, our unnamed teachers and the Logo students deserve the lion's share of gratitude for their efforts throughout the research enterprise.

CHAPTER 10

THE MICROCOMPUTER AS A SYMBOLIC MEDIUM

Karen Sheingold

Picture a classroom of young children. There is a young boy in a smock, paintbrush in hand, excitedly putting brush to paper, creating his own work. The smell of the paint and the feel of the brush on paper are an integral part of his experience. Two young girls are building a farm in the block corner, discovering that their stable is not sufficiently large for 12 plastic horses to be housed there. In the book corner, a group of young children are creating a story together, which their teacher commits to writing.

What role could or should a microcomputer possibly play in such a lively environment where children are actively working with materials and inventing their own worlds? The computer, a piece of electronic "adult" technology, certainly doesn't smell like paint or feel like blocks. It is not an object in the world the way the class guinea pig is. Does it have a legitimate place in a classroom for young children, or, once it arrives, will it supplant these more important activities?

These are the kinds of questions on the minds of many educators of young children. They want to know whether children younger than 8 years of age should use microcomputers. I have been a witness to and a participant in many lively debates on this topic in the last few years. The intensity and passion with which views are expressed has led me to reflect on what underlies both the questions and their intensity. It is important to "unpack" these general questions to discover what the real issues are and how they can be addressed. The purpose of this chapter is to provide such an analysis.

In the absence of a substantial base of theory and research relating to young children's use of microcomputers, this analysis is difficult to accomplish. That no one knows much about what it means for young children to use microcomputers, however, provides an arena ripe for reflection, experimentation, debate, and cooperation among educators and researchers. Examining educators' questions about microcomputers leads inevitably and fruitfully into research questions, which then lead back into questions about educational practice. In the following pages I will suggest some reasons for the deep concerns I hear about using microcomputers with young children, and relate these to ideas about development, about what the microcomputer is or could be, and to how the power of this educational innovation is interpreted. Wherever possible, I will point to important research issues.

SYMBOLS AND REALITY

It is not possible to talk about young children or microcomputers without first talking about symbols. By a *symbol,* I mean anything that represents some kind of information. A word is a symbol because it refers to or denotes a thing, idea, or feeling. Symbols—pictures, numbers, words, gestures—convey meanings. *Symbol systems,* such as language, mathematics, and dance, are organized, complex, and related patterns of symbols that, taken together, comprise broad cultural systems of meaning. *Symbolic products*—stories, poems, songs, symphonies, scientific experiments—are the results of our active engagement with these systems. Symbolic products are created in particular media or materials.

There is a sense in which symbols are not "real." A picture of a tree, or the word *tree,* are not the same as the tree. Looking at a real tree is a different experience from looking at a picture of one or reading a story about one. Symbols are *about* the world and how we give meaning to it.

What does this have to do with young children and microcomputers? First among the concerns that I hear about young children's use of microcomputers is that this new technology is not real in the way other classroom materials are—such as paint, clay, crayons, or rhythm instruments. The microcomputer is fundamentally a symbolic machine. We use it to represent and manipulate symbol systems—language, mathematics, music—and to create symbolic products—poems, mathematical proofs, compositions. In this sense it is *about* the world and not *of* it.

But is a symbolic machine incompatible in some fundamental way with young children—with what they know, what they do, and how they learn and develop in the early years? What we know about early development, about how and in what realms children learn and develop during these years can help answer this question.

Early Symbolic Development

While for many years it was difficult to characterize development between infancy and the school years except in negative terms (the child is preoperational, illogical, and so forth), research in the last decade has modified this view in two significant ways. First, it has become clear that the young child is capable of many cognitive activities at first thought accessible only to older children. Researchers (Gelman & Baillargeon, 1983; Siegler, 1981) have shown that the ways in which tasks are structured for young children dramatically affect what they can demonstrate about what they know. In carefully designed situations, for example, young children reveal that they are not entirely egocentric or perception-bound (Gleman, 1978; Lempers, Flavell, & Flavell, 1977), and they can achieve some success on many tests of concrete operations (Donaldson, 1978; Siegel & Brainerd, 1978). What young children know, however, tends to be implicit rather than explicit. That is, these children demonstrate skills and knowledge that they are not aware of and cannot tell us about except by their actions in tasks of the psychologist's design.

The second way in which our views of early childhood have been modified is that there has emerged a more positive characterization of early childhood as a time of accomplishments in the development of symbolization (Gardner, 1983; Gardner & Wolf, 1979). During this period there is a genuine flowering of symbolic capacities and activities, such that by age 5 the child has "first draft knowledge" (Gardner, 1983, p. 305) of symbolization in language, pictures, 3-dimensional objects (blocks, clay), dance, music, and pretend play, as well as some number and logical knowledge. Between the ages of 5 and 7, children acquire the rudiments of notational systems—systems which themselves refer to symbol systems. So the child begins to learn a written language, which itself refers to a spoken language.

Symbolic Machine
The lack of "realness" that is attributed to the microcomputer derives, I believe, from the fact that the microcomputer is a symbolic machine. When children use a microcomputer they are interacting with symbols—words, numbers, pictures, graphic representations. But much of the activity young children naturally engage in is also symbolic—communicating with gestures, speaking, pretend play, counting, tapping a rhythm, singing, making a picture or a clay object. In the classroom described at the beginning of this chapter, the children were all making symbolic products—a painting, a block scene, a story. The symbolic nature of the microcomputer per se does not make it incompatible with or inappropriate for use by young children. One could, in fact, make just the opposite argument. To do so out of hand, however, would be to ignore the critical issue of *how* the child engages with a particular symbol system via the microcomputer.

There is a direct, active involvement of children with crayons and blocks that is assumed to be absent with the microcomputer. But is this absence intrinsic to working with a microcomputer? The image many people have of microcomputer use in schools reflects the drill-and-practice software that has dominated the educational software marketplace. Used this way, the microcomputer gives children questions to answer or problems to solve, and then tells them whether or not their answers are correct. In some cases, the drill and practice is "dressed up" to look more like a game, but the basic format is the same. For young children, a very large proportion of existing software is devoted to letter and number recognition.

This type of activity is relatively passive. Children respond to questions. Answers are correct or incorrect. There are few degrees of freedom in what they do, and no opportunities for invention, for shaping the medium to make their own products or achieve their own goals. This type of activity, however, is an extremely small and limited subset of the ways in which children can interact with the machine.

Within any given symbol system represented on the microcomputer, there are many different kinds of activities a child can do, some of which are more and some less constrained by the software itself. Take graphics, for example. A program can ask a child to do one of several things. One program might ask the child simply to detect correspondence among specific shapes. Another might provide an array of shapes and objects that the child can arrange in a design of his or her choosing. A third might provide the equivalent of paint and brushes and permit the child to create pictures or designs from scratch. Not only are these all different kinds of tasks requiring different skills, but the options open to the child increase as we move from the first program to the third. In both the second and third examples, the child can make something, rather than simply respond. At least in principle, the microcomputer is a medium that the child can use for making, doing, and creating.

Moreover, there are many different ways of giving information to the microcomputer, the keyboard being the most familiar as well as the most indirect. Mice, paddles, and joysticks, for example, are analog devices that make possible a direct mapping between the child's hand and finger movements and what happens on the screen. Many games make use of paddles and joysticks for controlling moves on the screen. Children can even manipulate directly what happens on the screen by touching it with a light pen. Special keypads have been developed for young children, and others could be, which have larger, fewer, and/or different symbols from what is on the keyboard. So, not only can the microcomputer be a medium for making and doing, but it can be more or less similar to other media with which the child is familiar.

The microcomputer is not one thing or one kind of experience, for young children or anyone else. Its flexibility presents a great challenge to our imaginations. The challenge is to determine whether and how the microcomputer can be made interesting, appropriate, and useful for young children.

POSSIBILITIES FOR MICROCOMPUTER USE WITH YOUNG CHILDREN

What would we have this technology be for the young child? What would we use it for? Such questions are difficult to answer in the absence of careful research and development work, but there are four possibilities that come to mind. Not an exhaustive list, these are examples of how we might think about using microcomputers with young children. I propose these as hypotheses to be tested, not as answers. First, we could use the microcomputer to acquaint the child with properties that are unique to it, such as dynamic movement and programmability, and thus provide experiences not possible with other classroom media. Second, we could use the microcomputer to support learning so that children can explore aspects of experience that would normally require skills they do not yet have. Third, we could use the microcomputer as a way for children to better understand what they do in other media. Fourth, we could use the microcomputer to help children gain a broader view of what the computer is as an important piece of technology in the world.

Exploring Unique Properties of the Microcomputer

There is no doubt that young children will approach the microcomputer as they do other new objects—with curiosity and excitement—and subject it to whatever means of exploration they have at their disposal so that it reveals its properties and ''secrets'' to them. But since the microcomputer is not just one thing, teachers must decide which software to use, which properties children might profitably explore.

One question that many educators ask themselves is whether or not microcomputer-based activity offers anything that is substantially different from what can be obtained in the classroom by other means. In its programmable and dynamic properties the microcomputer is different from most other media children with which interact. Introducing young children in simple ways to these properties may provide interesting learning opportunities. For example, children could explore the dynamic properties of movement by having a set of objects that they could cause to move on the screen in ways that they would specify. Children could convey their instructions via simple, specially designed input devices (e.g., keypads, mice, light pens). With a dynamic toolkit of shapes and movements, children could construct their own moving pictures and scenes. In this new medium, children could make something interesting to look at, play with, share with others, and redesign at will.

Programmability is another property unique to computers, and one to which I believe young children can be exposed in simple form. What might a young child learn about programmability? First, that a person can make a choice or give an instruction to the microcomputer to make something happen, and, second, that instructions can be combined to make a sequence of events occur. Programmability could be taught with respect to a number of different symbol systems, but graphics and music come to mind as ones that are likely to be particularly interesting for young children. These "simple ideas" about instructions and sequence could be introduced to young children without using programming languages per se.

These ideas that I refer to as *simple* are not necessarily so, and it will be important to discover whether or not young children are able to comprehend and use them with fluency. I have no doubt that young children will find it easy and interesting to give instructions to the microcomputer that result in events occurring on the screen. Many older children do. But there may be a problem in our interpretation of what is understood by the child. In working with older children, we find that they are capable of producing impressive arrays on the screen without having a flexible or deep understanding of the program that resulted in that array (Mawby, 1984; Pea, 1983). Programming languages are, it turns out, very complex symbol systems, the mastery of which takes much time and intensive effort (Kurland, Mawby, & Cahir, 1984: Pea & Kurland, 1984b). So, while I think it worthwhile to introduce young children to ideas about programmability, it is equally as important for educators and researchers to look carefully at what is actually learned and understood. We cannot assume that if a child can create some sequenced instructions on the microcomputer he or she "knows how to program."

Microcomputer as Cognitive Support
The second way in which it might be beneficial to use the microcomputer is as a support for or facilitator of activities that young children would not normally be able to do. It is widely assumed that there are sequences of skills that must be learned before being able to produce a symbolic product. So, in most cases one learns a musical instrument and musical notations before attempting to compose. Yet it is not clear that such skills are prerequisite to composing. While composing is generally reserved for a small segment of skilled musicians, we know that children as young as 2 years of age make up their own songs (McKernon, 1979). In a similar vein, one must be able to put letters and words on paper before being able to write a story. Again, it is not clear that composing with language depends on being able to form those letters and words. Young children are good at telling stories (Sutton-Smith, 1972), yet writing them down poses difficulties of many kinds. Can young children create these com-

plex symbolic products without having mastered the notational systems and all of the cognitive skills an adult or older child would bring to the enterprise?

A microcomputer might afford such opportunities. To begin with, much-simplified versions of existing word processors and music editors are required. Making such software simple enough and simple in the right ways is a significant design challenge. By allowing children to bypass some of the physical and cognitive obstacles in a particular arena, we may make it possible for them to enjoy creative experiences that would be difficult, if not impossible, to obtain without such support.

There is, however, another sense in which microcomputer-based work may serve to support and extend children's cognitive activities. It turns out that, for older children, microcomputer-based work in classrooms tends to be collaborative (Hawkins, Sheingold, Gearhart, & Berger, 1982; Levin & Boruta, 1983). Children work together and use each other as resources while they do such varied activities as programming, writing stories and articles, engaging in games and simulations, or simply figuring out how to get the microcomputer to work. This kind of joint activity provides a kind of "scaffolding" of the social environment for children to accomplish what they might not be able to on their own. Here we have the intriguing possibility that the microcomputer may serve as a kind of cognitive support, not by itself, but because of its impact on the social life of the classroom. When teachers allow it, microcomputer-based activities "invite" collaboration, which can assist accomplishments for children both as individuals and in groups.

Reflecting on Other Activities

> The computer, rather than being a superbrain, teaching us with its consistent and logical "thinking," is instead a fantasy world which, like a hall of mirrors, reflects back to us images of our commonsense ways of making *things* and making *sense*. (Bamberger, 1983, p. 1)

In these words Jeanne Bamberger proposed that we think about the microcomputer in yet another way—as a medium that can help us discover and reflect on what we already know intuitively. By playing with what we make in the microcomputer world, she suggested, we come to see familiar actions and objects in new ways.

She described, for example, how, in translating a drummed rhythm into a simple program for the microcomputer, we discover new properties of the rhythmic structure. Her general argument was that we have implicit knowledge about many things—how to clap a rhythm, build a block tower, draw a picture. Having to program that same activity on the microcomputer requires making explicit the knowledge that we have "in our muscles." In so doing, we know differently and better what we knew before.

Does this argument apply to young children? I think it does, if made more broadly. Since there is more than one way of knowing, giving children access to multiple ways of knowing may lead to better understanding in a particular domain (Dewey & Bentley, 1960). If some kinds of microcomputer experience offer ways of knowing that differ from what the child does with other media in the classroom, then it is precisely through the *connecting* of these related, but different, kinds of experiences that new learning may be possible.

To try but one example, let's give the child an opportunity to paint with a microcomputer. With a typical paint program, the child chooses a brush thickness and can even choose the type of pattern the brush will make as it moves around on the screen. Colors can be selected, mixed, and tried out. Shapes can be created and made smaller or larger. Many possibilities can be explored alone or in combination, erased, changed, or moved. Painting with the microcomputer could make children aware of choices and possibilities that they would otherwise accept as givens when they use paint and paper. With such rapid experimentation the child may make discoveries in microcomputer painting that enable him or her to attempt new things with paint and paper.

The flaw in this argument rests on *how* the child makes connections from one medium to another. Research conducted with older children at the Center for Children and Technology leads me to doubt that such connections will come naturally or easily. For example, children learning to program were often unable to apply a command or concept they had used successfully in one program to another program (Pea, 1983); that is, making connections *within* programming was difficult. Moreover, there was no general transfer of planning and problem-solving skills to a noncomputer task by children who had learned programming for a year, compared with those who had not (Pea & Kurland, 1984a). It follows, then, that if we are to use the microcomputer to help children see and reflect on connections from one medium to another, teachers will need to structure children's experiences and provide support to make this possible.

Microcomputer as Object

I want to conclude by going back to the original assumption about the microcomputer as something that is not truly real because it is a symbolic medium. There is, of course, a sense in which it is very real, and will become increasingly so for the young child. It is an object in the world, with its own physical and tactile properties. It is also a very powerful tool with which people can do many important and interesting symbolic tasks, from writing a book to designing a house to constructing a budget to communicating with people on another continent.

As children use microcomputers at home and in classrooms, they will develop their own ideas about what this machine is and what it is for (Mawby, Clement, Pea, & Hawkins, 1984). It will require serious and clever research to find out just how it is that young minds comprehend this peculiar and flexible object. There is no doubt, however, that children's notions will be influenced by the kinds of experiences they have had with the machine and the kinds of interpretations of it offered by teachers and peers. What they think it is and what they think it is for will, at least in part, reflect what they do with it and what they see others doing. Therefore, educational choices about how children use microcomputers in classrooms have implications for children's initial understanding of a significant piece of cultural technology.

My personal view is that I would like children to approach this machine matter-of-factly. I would want them to understand at some level that this is a tool that does more than one thing, that people use it for their own purposes, and that children, too, have a variety of purposes for which its use is appropriate. Such a view would be fostered in a classroom where the technology was treated matter-of-factly, where children were helped to use the machine in a number of ways, and where they could make use of it when they were interested or had something to do with which they thought the microcomputer could be of help.

In such a classroom the functionality and purposes of the microcomputer—the ways in which it helped teachers and students to do things, its connections to other classroom activities—would get worked out over time as uses were discovered, tried, and found to be productive. The microcomputer, then, would not be a thing apart. It would simply be another material for the classroom. As with other media, some children would find it more interesting than would other children. And there would be individual differences in the ways children chose to use the machine. In their imaginative play, children wouldn't "play computer," just as they don't "play telephone." Rather, they would incorporate the microcomputer into their play about other things.

SHAPING AN INNOVATION

I believe that the greatest source of concern about having microcomputers in classrooms for young children is that the microcomputer activities will *supplant* the many activities children do with "real" materials. Having a microcomputer in a classroom means, it is feared, these other activities will disappear in the face of their computerized versions. There is no doubt that working with materials is important for young children, and it would be unimaginable, not to say absurd, to have a microcomputer replace the water table, block corner, or pet rabbit.

What seems to underlie this concern is a sense that the microcomputer innovation has a life of its own proceeding at an intense, unstoppable pace. Such a fear is understandable when schools are acquiring microcomputers at an ever-accelerating rate, when parents are playing an active role in urging schools to buy microcomputers, and when advertisements for microcomputer hardware and software attempt to make us believe that serious cognitive deprivation and/or failure to get ahead in life will result if children do not have access to microcomputers at an early age.

On the other hand, this view implies that the technology will take over, that what teachers do or believe will not matter. Whatever research knowledge we have on this issue suggests quite the opposite—that what school systems and teachers do with computers—what they use them for, how they interpret them, how they present them to children—has an enormous effect on what happens in a particular system or classroom (Char, Hawkins, Wootten, Sheingold, & Roberts, 1983; Sheingold, Hawkins, & Char, 1984; Sheingold, Kane, & Endreweit, 1983). The technology does not have a life of its own, nor does it stand on its own. It is always used by people in a social context. Because it is such a flexible tool, people make choices in using it and thus shape its use in important ways. What teachers do *does* matter and will continue to matter. Teachers will help to share this innovation by their decisions about how to use this new technology, by their willingness to experiment with it and to share what they learn, and by their involvement in research and software development efforts. Finally, they will have an impact on this innovation by their willingness to say "no" to uses of technology that they believe are not in the best interests of young children.

As I see it, questions about whether and how microcomputers can be used by young children cannot be answered in the abstract. Nor can these questions be answered simply by putting currently available software into classrooms and "seeing what happens." There is a complex, cooperative enterprise called for among teachers, researchers, and developers. We need software that is well designed for the young child, teachers who are willing to experiment with interesting uses for it in their classrooms, and researchers who can ask insightful questions about the learning that the technology affords. With endeavors in place that are interactive among teachers, researchers, and developers, we will gradually be able to answer some of our questions about the use of microcomputers by young children. We will also discover new questions, which will require new research, development, and classroom implementation to answer. At each stage of this recursive process, we may learn more about questions that have always intrigued us—how it is that children learn and develop, how new technologies transform and support such learning, and how sensitive practitioners create effective learning environments for young children.

AUTHOR NOTES

I would like to thank my colleagues Jan Hawkins, Denis Newman, Roy Pea, and Edna Shapiro for their thoughtful comments on an earlier version of this chapter.

PART III

SHAPING THE TECHNOLOGY

CHAPTER 11

CHARTING THE COURSE: INVOLVING TEACHERS IN THE FORMATIVE RESEARCH AND DESIGN OF *THE VOYAGE OF THE MIMI*

Cynthia Char and Jan Hawkins

Over the last few years, there has been increased awareness of the critical role that teachers play in shaping the nature of students' computer experiences in schools (Char, 1983; Char & Tally, 1985; Hawkins, Char, & Freeman, 1984; Hawkins & Sheingold, 1985; Mehan, 1985; Michaels, 1984; Riel, 1984). The ways in which computers are incorporated into classrooms often bear a distinct stamp that reflects individual teachers' personal views and interpretations of the educational functions of the technology. This phenomenon has appeared across a variety of computer applications, such as in students' learning of a programming language or in their use of word processors, simulations, interactive videodiscs, and databases. For instance, one teacher might use database software as an example of a computer application in business, whereas, for another teacher, it might serve as a vehicle for encouraging students to think critically about concepts of information organization (Freeman, Hawkins, & Char, 1984).

The influence of teachers upon computer use, however, is only half the story. There is a system of mutual influences. Educational technologies can offer teachers opportunities for considering new kinds of learning goals and patterns of interaction for their students (Sheingold, Hawkins, & Char, 1984). For instance, since word processors can free students from writing out multiple copies of work by hand, teachers can focus greater attention on the process of revising and editing written prose, and on creating collaborative projects in classrooms, such as class newspapers.

Attention to this 2-way interaction has guided Bank Street's Project in Science and Mathematics. The project has produced an integrated multimedia set of materials for upper-elementary school children. At the core of the project is *The Voyage of the Mimi,* a television series that chronicles the adventures of two young scientists and their teenage crew on a whale research expedition.[1] Accompanying the television series are four learning modules, each featuring a different type of microcomputer software and assorted print materials: *Maps and Navigation* features a line of navigation simulation games, in which children apply various map reading and mathematical skills to solve navigational problems; *Whales and their Environment* features the "Bank Street Laboratory," a software package for gathering and graphing temperature, sound, and light data; *Introduction to Computing* features a series of software games to introduce concepts of computer programming in turtle graphics; *Ecosystems* features "Island Survivors," a software model for exploring the food chain, species populations, and the impact of human intervention on ecosystems.

Beginning with the formulation of the proposal for initial funding (Bank Street College, 1981), the project staff sought to use the potential of interactive technologies to introduce new ways of learning in schools —in this case, new forms of learning about science and mathematics that contrast with the common focus on rote learning of facts. The commitment to presenting students with an alternative approach to science and mathematics instruction guided the identification of the types of software to develop. The four applications chosen—a simulation, a data gathering and graphing utility, a programmable environment, and a computer model—would allow students to use computers in ways that scientists and mathematicians actually employ them for solving problems.

Furthermore, all of the applications were designed to encourage group interaction with the technology "because it provides a better approximation of the way computers are used in the real world, and it encourages cooperative social behavior rather than isolated use" (Bank Street College, 1981). This emphasis on group interaction and learning with the computer differs with the widespread application of drill-and-practice software, which assumes an individualized learning environment.

Integral to the research and design process has been the recognition of the significant influence of teachers upon the types of learning experiences students have with software. The interplay between these two forces—interactive technologies supporting new classroom practices on the one hand, and teachers actively interpreting and transforming software applications, on the other—clearly points to the importance of in-

---

[1] The project is currently producing the second season of *The Voyage of the Mimi,* which focuses on the Maya culture in the Yucatan and archaeology. This second series, accompanied by a new learning module of software, will premiere in 1988.

volving teachers in the software develoment process, particularly when the software is designed to be educationally innovative. Over the course of the project's 3-year development period for its first season, teachers contributed to the design of software materials in multiple ways: as curriculum advisors, as advisory panel members and reviewers, as field testers, and as codevelopers and members of design teams. In this chapter, we provide an overview of these different roles, the ways in which research staff coordinated teachers' involvement with and input into the ongoing production process, and the kinds of insights the project staff gained from teachers.

TEACHERS AS IN-HOUSE CURRICULUM ADVISORS

The in-house staff assembled at the start of the project consisted of a diverse, multidisciplinary team of production professionals (e.g., executive producer, director, script writers, software designers), formative researchers, and educators. Two educators were intensely involved in the initial development of the materials during the first year. One was a specialist in science; the other was a specialist in mathematics and computers. Each had considerable experience in the teaching of these subject areas to children, and to graduate students enrolled in teacher training programs. To help guide the early stages of prototype development, these educators worked with other staff members to formulate the parameters for the curriculum content to be covered by the project. The mathematics/computer specialist also designed and programmed the prototype version of the turtle graphics games.

TEACHERS AS REVIEWERS AND ADVISORY BOARD MEMBERS

Shortly after the inception of the project, the research staff established a teacher advisory board to serve as an outside group of reviewers. This panel met regularly over the course of the first year, and provided initial reactions to the curriculum ideas under development. The panel consisted of 14 teachers and educators, all of whom had worked with the targeted age group of 8- to 12-year-olds. Collectively, they represented a diverse range of school settings (e.g., public vs. private schools; self-contained vs. open classrooms), as well as a range of expertise in science, mathematics, and computers.

The teacher panel meetings provided staff with important feedback and recommendations from teachers early in the development process

(Roberts & Char, 1982). Based on their considerable experience with instructional films and television programs, the teachers pointed out what they felt distinguished superior science films from less notable ones, such as clear connections between scientific research and the impact upon people and society, and the avoidance of adult authority figures who constantly provide answers to questions and problems. The teachers also identified factors that would maximize the success of classroom viewing, such as the availability of videocassettes in addition to open-air broadcast, and 15-minute episodes to allow for pre- and post-viewing discussions in a 45-minute class period. These recommendations were incorporated into the series' final format and distribution plans.

In relation to the newer, less familiar medium of microcomputer software, the teachers voiced their concerns with some of the educational assumptions being made by the software designers regarding students' prior knowledge of certain science and mathematical concepts (e.g., mapping 2-point coordinate systems, angles). They stressed the important difference between feeling challenged and feeling inept. The teachers pointed out the need for multiple entry points for students of varying ability levels, which they felt could be provided in support print materials or hands-on experiences.

As a result of these comments by the teacher panel, along with later formative testing of the software with children, the final print materials presented a wide range of activities for children. Similarly, multiple entry points were incorporated into the final software design, with all three prototype software packages being expanded into a more comprehensive series of software games and activities (see later section for a description of the multiple-entry-point approach of the project software).

Teacher panel members also suggested that the prototype navigation software be modified so that more features were under user (teacher or student) control. Based on teacher recommendations and results from testing sessions with children, the final software product featured user control over the pacing and temporal length of software screen displays (rather than having them quickly vanish), over the number of commands per turn, and included the option of changing commands once they had been entered.

In addition to working with the teacher panel, the research team worked closely with over 1300 children during the first year to seek out their reactions to the various video and software materials under development. Given the preliminary nature of the materials (e.g., rough drafts of pilot scripts, buggy versions of software), researchers assumed a central role in these testing sessions to help "scaffold" the media experience. In this formative research, we were trying to identify problematic features and student misunderstandings of the software.

TEACHERS AS FIELD TESTERS

Upon completion of the development of prototype materials, we involved teachers and students in a major classroom field test (Char, Hawkins, Wootten, Sheingold, & Roberts, 1983) during the fall of the second year. The field test differed from the earlier *Mimi* formative studies in a number of respects. In addition to allowing us to see how the materials might be used in natural classroom settings rather than by individual or small groups of children outside the classroom, we focused more closely on teachers and their role. We were particularly interested in seeing how teachers chose to use the materials and how they evaluated their experiences. Thus, a new role for teachers emerged at this stage of the research and development process. In addition to the role of reviewers, like our advisory panel, teachers became more active participants in the formative research process. Rather than merely being subjects or informants who responded to questions asked by researchers, the teachers became agents of the software experience and provided numerous insights, suggestions, and innovative uses for the software. However, for teachers to have such a significant role, it was necessary for us to learn about and adapt to the everyday realities of school life.

METHODS

Thirteen teachers from the New York metropolitan area participated in the field test and, over the course of several months, tried out with their students the two pilot television episodes, prototype software, and print materials.[2] Drawn from seven different schools, all the classrooms were in the project's targeted age group of fourth through sixth grade, yet were diverse with respect to ethnicity, social class, urban/suburban location, and class size. As with our teacher advisory panel, the field-test teachers represented a wide range of teaching backgrounds and expertise. Roughly half of the teachers taught all classroom subjects to their students, while the rest specialized in the teaching of science, mathematics, and/or computer programming. The teachers also differed in the amount and type of computer experience they had had prior to the field test, ranging from no computer experience to knowledge of programming in BASIC or Logo and experience in teaching programming to children. The field test was unstructured in order to give teachers flexibility in

---

[2] Due to the extensive nature of the materials, each teacher was only responsible for one of the three software/print learning modules (i.e., navigation simulation, "Bank Street Laboratory," turtle graphics games) in addition to the television pilots. At the time of the field test, the fourth module on ecosystems had not yet been developed into prototype form.

using the materials and in their selection and organization of classroom lessons. We introduced teachers to the materials and asked that they be integrated into ongoing classroom work in whatever ways the teachers chose. Each teacher tested only one type of software with its accompanying print materials.

We employed a variety of measures to document and assess what happened in each classroom. In addition to conducting classroom observations and student interviews, and administering forms on which students indicated their reactions to the video and software, we obtained information directly from the teachers. At the beginning of the field test, the teachers filled out a background information form, describing such areas as their current science and mathematics curricula, the subjects they were responsible for teaching, and their past and present use of computers. Once they began using our materials, they completed forms in which they described and assessed the software after each day of use, as part of a written journal. At the end of the field test, in-depth interviews were conducted with individual teachers, during which they discussed at length their reactions to the materials.

PLANNING STAGE AND
INITIAL TEACHER ORIENTATION

Beginning with the planning stage for setting up the field test, we gained some important insights into the realities of schools. First, extensive research was required simply to locate appropriate field sites, where upper elementary school students and regular classroom teachers (as opposed to computer specialists) could have reasonable access to a computer for science-related activities. Schools often had limited computer resources or, frequently, a potpourri of hardware. Computers were often housed in a computer lab under the supervision of a computer specialist, rather than under the direction of a science teacher or a classroom teacher.

Our initial orientation meeting with the teachers was revealing; they required more training than we had anticipated. The meeting was originally intended as a briefing session for teachers to meet one another, and to learn about the objectives of our field test. Since we wanted to see if the print materials would suffice as preparatory support for our software, we did not want to provide hands-on, one-on-one training for the teachers during the meeting. Accordingly, we sent out the materials several weeks in advance of the meeting and told the teachers that, while we would be happy to answer questions about the materials, the major focus of the meeting would not be a teacher workshop on the project.

However, when the teachers arrived at the meeting, we learned that they were unprepared because it had been difficult for them to find both a free period and a free computer during the school day to review the materials. (In the case of some teachers, school buildings were locked shortly after 3:00 p.m., and the teachers were discouraged from staying late to review materials.) Thus, in order to be responsive to teachers' needs, the orientation meeting turned into a training session to provide teachers with the much needed hands-on experience with software. Furthermore, the inexperience and anxiety of some teachers concerning computers and software was also evident. The session ended up providing an important, highly personal context for learning, where teachers worked in pairs and researchers/trainers offered help and encouragement.

Therefore, both the site selection and the orientation meetings gave us an appreciation of the day-to-day concerns and practical constraints existing in schools. Even during the field-test planning stage, we learned a great deal about the limited computer, media, and teacher resources in most schools, the limited amount of time usually devoted to science and mathematics instruction, the considerable range in elementary school teachers' training and expertise regarding mathematics, science, and computers, and the importance of good teacher-training workshops and support.

TEACHER AND CLASSROOM FACTORS INFLUENCING SOFTWARE USE

As the fall field test progressed, and with an additional, less extensive classroom field test conducted in the spring, we began to appreciate fully the critical role of teachers in shaping children's software experiences. The teachers, having engaged in the day-to-day planning, implementation, and assessment of software lessons, gave us a vivid sense of what it was like to use these materials in the complex settings of classrooms— how they orchestrated the classroom activity, determined software use, and attempted to monitor and facilitate children's learning. The teachers' reflection on and articulation of their reactions to the software provided rich information regarding how the materials fit with their present and/or desired curriculum goals and teaching styles.

The field test allowed us to identify some of the important factors that influenced how the software was used. First, we found that the teachers' knowledge of science directly affected their recognition of the scientific concept and potential inherent in the software. For example, some of the teachers participating in the field test had limited formal science training, and tended to view science as a series of topics rather than as a coherent curriculum emphasizing experimentation and the scientific method. When presented with the "Bank Street Laboratory" (the data-gathering and graphing software utility), these teachers had difficulty seeing the software as a flexible data-gathering and graphing tool. They tended to demonstrate the software to the whole class rather than allowing students to use it themselves, and had some difficulty helping children with conceptual problems concerning heat and temperature. Their experiences with the software pointed to the importance of providing more extensive background information about the scientific concepts used in the software, and of providing sufficiently rich and varied suggestions for activities demonstrating the use of the tool.

One of the more intriguing findings of the field test was that teachers' familiarity with computers did not necessarily enhance software "success." One of the teachers who used the navigation simulation was a mathematics teacher with prior experience in teaching children computer programming, but had difficulty understanding the educational objectives of the navigation software. He chose not to become actively involved in monitoring or facilitating students' progress with the simulation, viewing it as an experiential learning activity with a self-sufficient and self-contained context. He also felt that the software was designed to teach navigation rather than our design objectives, which were map-reading skills, and mathematical concepts such as angles, degrees, measurement, and triangulation. Stated another way, he felt that navigation was the curriculum content rather than the vehicle through which to teach various mathematical skills. (Interestingly, the mathematical applications of the software were much more evident to our two generalist teachers, who had less expertise with computers and mathematics.)

The field-test teachers helped us to recognize that our simulation and data-gathering/graphing software appeared to fall into a curious spot between structured computer-assisted instruction and computer programming, and did not automatically rest in a conceptual niche of computer experiences commonly found in schools. This pointed to the importance of providing clear written material and, at a later stage, teacher-training workshops[3] (see Martin, Chapter 2, this volume) that would highlight for teachers the mathematical and scientific objectives of the software designed, and the overall educational approach of the project.

Second, we began to obtain a fuller sense of the multiple factors that influence teachers in how software is used. Through the field test, we learned firsthand that teachers often function in far from ideal teaching conditions: limited access to a computer, two brief science periods a week, 30 students vying to use the software during the same class period. Since our software was designed for use by more than one child

---

[3] Bank Street College received a grant from the National Science Foundation specifically to examine teacher-training issues surrounding the *Mimi* materials. The work of the Mathematics, Science and Technology Teacher Education (MASTTE) Project is reported by Martin (Chapter 2, this volume).

at a time (e.g., one of the navigation simulations can accommodate up to 12 children working in four teams of three), we found that our materials addressed both pedagogical concerns (i.e., the importance of children working collaboratively) and pragmatic concerns (i.e., maximizing children's access to limited computer resources). However, unless a school had enough computer and software resources to assure that all the students in a class could use software simultaneously, classroom management issues inevitably arose as the teachers tried to orchestrate computer and noncomputer activities. The scope of this "juggling act" was further heightened by the natural diversity among students in a classroom.

Findings from the field test, along with results from more intensive formative testing with children, were instrumental in helping to shape the final materials. Based on our research results, we undertook a major additional design effort regarding the modification and augmentation of the software prototypes and expansion of the print materials. Given the wide variability in students' backgrounds and experiences in science, mathematics, and computers, coupled with the realization that teachers will not always be able to monitor closely and assist children as they work with software, we created software that was multilevel or multiprogram in structure, and designed to offer many entry points for students. For example, to accompany "Rescue Mission," a fairly complex navigation simulation, we created three preparatory software games, each focusing on particular navigational or mathematical concepts, with a short, optional tutorial/demonstration section. A number of visual tools were also made available to aid in the particular navigational problem (e.g., being able to move a graphics distance scale to help figure out how far your boat is from an island; for a fuller description of the multilevel nature of the software, see Char, 1985).

Print materials were developed to provide parallel or supplementary activities for noncomputer-based learning. In recognition of the importance of teachers' individual discretion and assessment of their students' needs, these print materials were designed to be used as either an extension of or preparation for students' software experiences.

TEACHERS AS DEVELOPERS AND MEMBERS OF DESIGN TEAMS

In addition to being involved as advisory board members and field-test participants, teachers played another role in the project, namely, as developers and members of design teams during the third year. Two experienced classroom teachers served as primary writers for print materials. One was a classroom teacher who had taught computer programming to his middle-school students as well as to adult educators. The second teacher had previously developed a special unit on maps, navigation, and mathematics for his sixth graders. A third teacher, a fifth grade science teacher who had been one of our field-test participants, worked closely with a writer to select which experiments on heat, sound, and light should be included in the print materials that accompany the "Bank Street Laboratory." Given the expertise, interests, and teaching background of these individuals, they brought important insights to the *Introduction to Computing, Maps and Navigation*, and *Whales and their Environment* learning modules. Thus, rather than waiting until later phases of the formative evaluation process to have such expert teachers review existing software storyboards or manuscripts created by other software designers or writers, we incorporated the invaluable input these teachers provided into the design process itself, in the form of ideas and written drafts.

CONCLUSION

As the project evolved, we became increasingly aware of the complexities and substantial investments of time, energy, programming expertise, and creativity required to produce innovative, high-quality software that could be distributed on a large scale. At the same time, we learned a great deal about the important contributions that teachers can offer to the development process, and the multiple roles that teachers can play to influence the software that will ultimately be available to their classrooms.

In addition, we learned several lessons that should be applicable to other educational software development efforts:

1. Teachers comprise an important part of the intended school audience and play a critical role in shaping the nature of the software experience in classrooms. Given the interactive nature of software and the significant teacher interpretation and contexting needed when introducing innovative educational software, the teachers themselves are essential as consultants and contributors to the development process. They offer well-honed judgments regarding what children might like and understand, how students differ with respect to ability and learning styles, and how the subject matter and approach relates to existing curricula and classroom practices. They also offer sound judgments regarding what might constitute the best methods of presentation, and what might be do-able by and manageable to most classroom teachers.

2. It is important to encourage a continuing interplay and interaction among production staff, researchers, teachers, and students throughout the development process. It is highly advantageous to have a research team as permanent in-house staff to provide and coordinate continuous feedback from teachers and students to the production team, rather than limiting

research activities to the more typical, initial needs assessment of a project or the final summative evaluation of a product. In particular, we believe it is important to begin a dialogue between producers, researchers, and the target users early in the development process when teachers' and students' critical input can have maximum influence upon the direction and form of the software. If one waits until the later phases of software development, teachers' reactions will either have minimal impact on the final software package, given the considerable energy, money, and ego already invested in the product, or result in costly revamping of the software design. Thus, if one wishes to use field-test and other formative research results as serious input to software design decisions rather than largely as "beta test" citations in product advertisements, we strongly recommend that teachers and students be involved early in the research and development process. It is extremely valuable for producers and developers consistently to hear the voices of teachers and children in order to help guide the numerous, and often turbulent, phases of product development.

3. Teachers can play multiple roles in the research and design process: as *reviewers and advisors* throughout the different stages of product development; as *active participants and agents* in intensive classroom field tests; and as *actual developers and contributors* to the design of materials. Selecting teachers for particular roles is dependent upon the strengths and expertise of the specific teacher and on the particular needs of each stage of product development. The research staff will assume a key role in coordinating the teachers' involvement in the review and field-testing process, and in analyzing and synthesizing teachers' input and its implications for software revisions.

4. It is important to involve a wide range of teachers drawn from public and private schools, and from urban and suburban school districts: teachers who are familiar with computers as well as those who are computer novices, those who specialize in teaching science and mathematics, as well as those who are generalists and responsible for all subject areas. All of these factors can influence how software is interpreted, used, and valued.

It is important to acknowledge that the comprehensive nature of our research and development process could be viewed by some as luxurious in terms of time, finances, and staff resources. Nonetheless, we strongly urge that projects with limited budgets and/or tight production timelines consider less extensive ways of obtaining and incorporating teacher input. Teacher advisory boards and field tests of two or three classrooms (with perhaps less formal methods of assessment than ours) can still provide invaluable insights that help inform production decisions.

A concern voiced by producers and designers is that the video and software materials often are not yet in a form that is ready to be tested. We have found that both teachers and students can provide important reactions to even rough approximations of materials, such as storyboards and software mockups (i.e., software screens where full or partial programming has not yet been completed), if these materials are appropriately introduced and contexted by a researcher. Except for the initial period when a new project staff is going through the important process of identifying and coalescing the project's objectives, we strongly recommend that "the sooner the better" adage for formative testing be adhered to as much as possible in order to maximize the positive contribution of teacher and student input to final software design.

With educational software and the presence of computers in schools still in their infancy, it is difficult for software developers to understand how best to utilize the computer's graphic and interactive capacities to provide interesting educational avenues for children's learning. We believe that teachers not only can provide many specific suggestions about how a particular piece of computer software can be enhanced, but can help designers begin to gain a greater sensitivity to the needs and interests of teachers and students. Such an understanding is essential when designers wish to create materials that not only are educationally innovative and exciting, but also meaningful, usable, and legitimate for schools. Through such a collaboratiave venture among designers, researchers, and teachers, it is possible to create computer software that can provide innovative and valuable educational experiences for children and offer significant educational alternatives to children's learning in schools.

AUTHOR NOTES

Funding for the project was provided by the U.S. Department of Education (Contract No. 300-81-0375).

We wish to thank our colleagues who generously contributed to the formative research activities of the *Mimi* project: Tom Roberts, Bill Tally, Peggy Heide, Karen Sheingold, Jan Wootten, Midian Kurland, Mary Fitzpatrick, Marian Howard, Ellen Bialo, and Dick Hendrick. Special thanks are due to Sam Gibbon, director of the project, for his valuable comments, guidance, and support throughout the research. Finally, we extend our warmest appreciation to the many school administrators, teachers, and students who provided important insights into our research and design efforts.

CHAPTER 12

INTERACTIVE VIDEODISCS FOR CHILDREN'S LEARNING

Cynthia Char, Denis Newman, and William Tally

As McLuhan (1964) observed, when a new medium appears on the scene, our tendency is simply to transfer the content and approach of the old medium to the new one. Early radio programs, for example, were often broadcasts of vaudeville acts complete with sight gags. Early television mimicked radio in its primarily audio presentation of information. Videodisc technology provides a compelling recent example of this principle. A majority of videodiscs currently available contain movies, simply providing a higher picture-quality alternative to videotape. With a few very interesting exceptions, discs intended for educational use are simply storage and rapid-access devices for films, filmstrips, and slides (Char & Newman, 1985). The unique potential of the medium has yet to be realized in any substantial way. The Interactive Video Project, a research and development effort at Bank Street College, was organized to explore the value for schools of the unique properties of videodisc as an interactive medium. This chapter focuses on the findings of the research component of the project.

Unlike television and VCRs, videodisc players have not achieved popularity in homes or schools. Currently, one of their main uses is in military and corporate training, where they are often linked to microcomputers to create computer-assisted instruction (CAI) systems. The standard format is a 12-inch disc with capacity for 30 minutes of motion video or 54,000 still frames on each side (motion video plays at 30 frames a second). Videodisc players can access any frame randomly with a maximum search time of only a few seconds. Motion sequences can be played forward or backward at a wide range of speeds. Single frames can be displayed for any length of time without wear because the disc is read by a laser beam rather than by a magnetic head. This amazing flexibility, combined with the very high quality of the image compared to the familiar home VCRs, points to a potential for classroom use that is worth exploring.

Research on new media can have the same tendency as the medium under examination to mimic the old ways of doing things (Kelly & Gardner, 1981). Rather than focusing on the medium's distinctive powers and limitations, research on new media often echoes the questions and approaches of previous research. To avoid this tendency, we began with an analysis of the features and design options that make the medium unique. We sought out discs that clearly demonstrated these features so that we could use them in testing sessions with children and in classroom field tests.

The Interactive Video Project undertook a series of three studies, each with a distinct approach to the problem of identifying the unique potential of videodisc technology for children's learning. The first two laid the groundwork for the third study, a field test in four classrooms, which is the primary focus of this chapter.

The first study (Char & Newman, 1985) was a critical analysis of a variety of videodiscs currently available either as marketed products or as research or demonstration prototypes. We found that few of the educational videodiscs designed for children took creative advantage of the technology's unique technical features, such as its multiple audio tracks, freeze frame and slow motion options, and branching capabilities. In many cases, educational films, filmstrips, photo archives, and encyclopedias have been put on videodiscs with little concern for the unique power of the new medium, except as a medium for storage. Two types of videodiscs—simulations and visual databases—did provide significant and novel learning options to the user. With both types of applications, users are able to follow their own lines of inquiry in a semi-structured disc environment. This open-ended, yet supported, approach of making one's way through videodisc materials sharply contrasts with many traditional instructional materials and videodisc archives. For these materials, one is typically either confined to a strict teaching sequence or faced with a corpus of thousands of photographs lacking a clear or coherent indexing or organizational framework.

Two child-oriented discs designed for home entertainment—the *First National Kidisc* and *Fun and Games*—also were found to be exemplary in their use of the various video and audio options afforded by the medium. These discs were used as the test stimuli for our second study (Tally & Char, 1985). Having identified various ways in which disc designers have utilized special features of the technology to encourage new types of learner explorations of audio and visual materials, we sought to investigate whether children would recognize and could use this highly interactive potential of the videodisc environment. In this exploratory study, 9- and 10-year-olds worked in pairs with the two discs for at least two 40-minute sessions.

The study revealed that videodiscs can offer children a very different learning experience than that of linear television. Through experimentation with the disc, children learned to make use of many of the medium's novel visual and auditory options, such as slow motion, reverse motion, stepping through still frames, and selecting between two audio tracks. More importantly, the results indicated that children were able to apply such technical options to achieve particular learning goals, such as slowing down a segment to understand more fully a complex or rapid physical movement (e.g., someone pole vaulting or doing a card trick). In its flexibility, the videodisc medium also provided support for children's diverse interests and playing styles. Different children succeeded in working with the same set of visuals in distinctly different ways, and many invented their own games, apart from the intentions of the disc designers. For example, one of the segments was a high-speed, simulated drive through a New England town, offering intriguing scenic detail, a game component in which players had to quickly freeze the video whenever they saw a stop sign, and a trivia quiz based on the visual details of the scenery. Two boys who liked videogames each drove through the town twice in an attempt to improve their score by stopping at all the stop signs. In contrast, a pair of girls who liked playing with interesting human motions did not take the videogame aspect seriously, but saw a wealth of visuals to manipulate, such as making a dog walk backwards.

Furthermore, different children exercised a variety of individual strategies for the trivia quiz: intensely looking at the simulated drive and then trying to answer all of the questions; studying all of the questions first and then going through the segment; or tackling the questions one by one by flipping back and forth from the trivia section to the visual segment. These examples suggest that, in addition to delivering information and entertainment, videodiscs might serve as a vehicle for children's creative ingenuity and self-directed inquiry.

A STUDY OF THE USE OF VIDEODISC TECHNOLOGY IN SCHOOLS

Having determined some of the more innovative educational applications of videodiscs (i.e., databases and simulations) and that children enjoy and can spontaneously manipulate the visual and auditory options of the medium, we then conducted a third study (Char & Tally, 1985), to investigate the educational potential of the medium for children's learning in classroom settings. This intensive classroom-based study examined the potential promise and challenges involved in integrating videodisc technology into school curricula and practices. The research involved four teachers—two art teachers and two science teachers—and their students in three New York City schools. The teachers worked closely with our research team to modify and extend a set of existing art and sciences archival discs, and used the resulting materials in their classrooms over a 3- to 8-week period. It is this third study that constitutes the main focus for this chapter.

The study was distinct from previous videodisc research in three major respects: First, we investigated a variety of organizational formats of how interactive video might be incorporated into classrooms. As with our approach to disc design (Wilson, Newman, & Char, 1985), we were particularly interested in exploring several alternatives for placing students in greater control of their own learning paths, as well as in studying the roles that teachers play in facilitating children's learning. In contrast, the majority of previous videodisc studies (e.g., Brown & Newman, 1980; Bunderson, Olsen, & Baillio, 1981; Hoffmeister, Engelmann, & Carnine, 1985; Kehrberg & Pollak, 1982; McLaughlin, 1984) have focused primarily on teacher lecture modes and/or individualized CAI student work stations. In these models, the control resides either with the teacher or in the software program, and programs are typically based on a one student-one machine model of learning, with little acknowledgment of the teacher's role or that of other students.

Second, we examined how teachers and students regard videodisc technology in relation to the information resources they typically rely on, such as books and television. For example, how might a science videodisc offer something distinct and valuable not afforded by most science textbooks, films, or even hands-on science experiments? Thus, the study extended the analysis beyond the common focus on schools' audiovisual expenditures (e.g., Videodisc Design/Production Group, 1979), and examined how videodisc technology might match, and ideally surpass, the perceived strengths of other, more traditional media.

Third, we examined the early phases of integrating videodisc technology into the ongoing curricula and routines of classrooms. As other research we have conducted has shown (Char, Hawkins, & Freeman, 1985; Char, Hawkins, Wootten, Sheingold, & Roberts, 1983; Sheingold, Hawkins, & Char, 1984), the relationship between educational technology and the learning context is one of the complex, bidirectional influences: teachers significantly interpret and shape how new technologies are used in classrooms, while new technologies offer interesting possibilities for rethinking and reorganizing the goals and types of learning interactions that occur in classrooms.

Thus, we investigated in depth what is entailed in incorporating videodisc technology into classrooms. For example, how does videodisc technology and the learning it affords relate to traditional curriculum areas and modes of learning? How do requirements on teachers' time, lesson planning, materials development, and expertise compare with the requirements of more traditional media? Our intensive case-study approach to this question was in sharp contrast to focus-group studies of educators' reactions to videodisc demonstrations (e.g., Massachusetts Educational Television, 1981; Videodisc Design/Production Group, 1979) and anecdotal accounts of special learning centers removed from classroom settings (Ferralli & Ferralli, 1985).

Method

Sample and procedure. Four classrooms—two in art and two in science—from three New York City schools participated in the study. Both art classes consisted of 10- and 11-year-olds (roughly corresponding to fifth grade). The two science classes consisted of slightly older children, with 12- and 13-year-olds in one class (sixth/seventh grade) and 13- to 15-year-old eighth graders in the second. Three of the four teachers were highly experienced teachers, with 10 to 15 years of teaching background. The fourth teacher had taught for only four years but, unlike the others, had had previous home and classroom computer experience and encouraged students to use word processing and other utilities for their science reports.

We informed the teachers that we were interested in investigating a number of different models for using videodiscs in schools—as a visual resource for students' independent research projects, as a simulation or for educational game environments, as an aid for teacher lectures—and that we hoped they would consider implementing more than one model.

Following their agreement to participate in the study, we arranged an initial teacher interview with each of the four field-test teachers. The teachers were interviewed for about one hour in order to provide background information concerning their teaching experience, curriculum focus and goals, and types of media resources they used in their classrooms. They were then encouraged to spend some time becoming familiar with the contents of the discs that they would be using.

We chose five different, high-quality, visually rich discs in art and in science to be used in our field-test classrooms. For each of the five discs we created new software and/or print materials to transform these extensive picture resources into simulations, databases, games, and other classroom learning activities.

The art discs. Both art classes primarily used the *Van Gogh* disc, which contains a diverse assortment of chapters, including narrated motion video sequences describing the work and life of Van Gogh, large collections of still-frame photographs of paintings, and a "reference series" of still-frame images and accompanying text information, such as a sequence on Van Gogh's art techniques. The *National Gallery of Art Disc*, another archival disc, was used as supplementary material.

Based on teachers' input and some of our design ideas, we created a new piece of software to control the *Van Gogh* disc. The software augmented the disc-only experience in three ways: First, a "front end" and structure was created to change the chapter-based, book-like disc into a simulated museum visit. Options included such experiences as day trips, painting galleries, and an art library. Second, we created several new art portfolio groupings relating to the teachers' curriculum foci, such as *Humans in Motion* and *Studies* (i.e., different renditions of a particular work such as an ink drawing and oil painting of the same subject). A "Create your own portfolio" option allowed teachers and students to produce their own personalized file of paintings on the disc. Third, we created two original disc-based art games for students. In *Museum Mugshots*, children identified members of an art smuggling ring by matching a text description of a criminal with the correct portrait out of a "lineup" of paintings. In *Theo's Letters*, children assumed the role of Theo, Vincent's art dealer brother, and matched excerpts from Vincent's letters with the paintings that the passages described in order to determine which paintings should be sold and which stored.

The science discs. The eighth grade science class used two discs from the Space Archives series, *Apollo* and *Space Shuttle*. Each of the Space discs contains thousands of still-frame photographs as well as motion video sequences from various NASA space flights.

We created both print materials and software to accompany the Space discs. In *Lunar Gravity*, an activity resembling a laboratory experiment, students were asked to hypothesize whether objects on the moon would fall faster, slower, or at the same speed as objects on earth. Having done so, they tested their hypothesis by timing a video segment of an astronaut dropping a hammer and a feather onto the surface of the moon. They then compared the result with their measures of the time it took for a pencil to fall the same distance to the floor of the classroom. In *Orbit Adventure*, a fictional game environment, students had to guide a wayward spacecraft back to its mother ship or risk being burned up in the earth's atmosphere or stranded in deep space. In the course of the adventure, students encountered problems dealing with such topics as inertia, centripetal force, action/reaction, and thrust.

The science classroom of 12- and 13-year-old students used *Bio Sci*, a biology archive disc. *Bio Sci* contains numerous video clips from different educational biology films and thousands of still-frame images, including photographs of myriad plants, animals, and protozoa, and pictures of their natural habitats.

Initially, we had planned to use only the Space discs in both science classrooms, but found that the science curriculum in the younger class focused mainly on the biological sciences. Thus, rather than force an unnatural fit between the physics-oriented Space discs and the classroom's biological focus, we added *Bio Sci* to our sample of tested disc materials.

The development of new materials was least extensive for the *Bio Sci* disc as compared with the above-mentioned videodiscs. Used as a resource for a student research project, it was incorporated into a "mock hearing" class project to determine the fate of Central Park. In order to access images off the disc, a new paper index of relevant images (e.g., animal and plant species found in the park) was created to supplement the extensive print index of contents already accompanying the disc. (For a more detailed description of the tested disc materials, see Char and Tally, 1985).

Research Approach and Measures

Because the videodisc medium is generally unfamiliar to teachers, we did not assume that interesting materials could just be left in the classrooms to see what would happen. An explicit part of our research method was to provide several forms of support to the teachers and students to ensure that at least some of the unique potential was explored. Support took the form of creating lessons and activities, writing software to control the discs, and helping the teacher by supervising small groups of children. Without our taking this active role in the field test, the teachers might have used the materials in a very superficial way or not at all. By giving support during the field test, we were able to see the unique features of the medium and to gauge the amount and kinds of staff development, curriculum materials, and software that would be needed to make the new medium a viable part of the classroom.

Data collection for the field test was conducted in a variety of ways. Measures included initial teacher interviews, classroom observations and, at the completion of the field test, final interviews with each of the teachers and student interviews with approximately half of the students in each classroom.

Results and Discussion

We will outline the results of the field test in terms of the five models of videodisc use we observed across the classrooms. We will then turn to a discussion of three key issues surrounding the directions and success of videodisc use in schools: (a) ease of fit between the five videodisc models and traditional modes of classroom learning; (b) videodiscs as an alternative to traditional media; and (c) the role of the teacher in incorporating videodisc technology into schools.

Across the classrooms, five different models of using videodiscs were employed. As we had hoped, all four classrooms tried out more than one model. Each model possessed particular strengths, and differed from the others in the ways it was used to support student learning and in the ease with which it was integrated into regular classroom routines.

Teacher Presentation, or Teacher-Led Classroom Discussion

In this model, the videodisc provides provocative visual accompaniment for a teacher's lecture and/or a visual stimulus to elicit class discussion or lead into an upcoming nondisc-based activity. Thus, the disc is used in a way that is analogous to how a teacher might use a set of slides, images from an overhead projector, or a film.

All four teachers used the videodisc in this way, generally as the first type of videodisc experience for their students. For example, the art teachers used the *Van Gogh* disc as a lead-in to an art assignment on complementary colors, and as a topic for discussion concerning the artist's life and art techniques. Similarly, the two science teachers used the science discs to encourage students to offer scientific explanations for the phenomena they were observing.

Activity Stimulus

In this model, the videodisc provides the "raw data" for hands-on, non-technology-based activities. Rather than providing a lead-in to a nondisc activity, the images of the disc provide the object of study for the activity. Thus, the videodisc is used the way a teacher might use real objects or real physical phenomena.

Two of the teachers used the videodiscs in this way. One of the art teachers used a still-frame photograph as the basis for a still-life drawing activity, while one of the science classes used a *Space* disc motion sequence of an astronaut dropping a hammer and a feather on the moon as the basis for a timing experiment concerning lunar gravity.

Programmed Disc-Based Environments

In this model, the disc provides the photographs or motion footage for computer-driven simulations, games, or other problem-solving contexts. Thus, the disc program itself becomes the activity, much like a computer-based activity.

Such programs were created for and used by three of the four classrooms. Both art classes heavily used two art mystery games, which generated thinking and discussion around content and compositional aspects of paintings. The *Space* science students used an orbit adventure game, which provided the motivating context for grappling with such scientific principles as inertia and centripetal acceleration.

Visual Database

In this model, the disc provides an information resource for students for their own personal inquiry, much like a classroom and library resource such as a book, encyclopedia, film, or filmstrip.

Children in both art classrooms independently explored much of the contents of the *Van Gogh* disc. While this resource could have been used for students reports, it was used instead as a general body of information for children to examine freely, with no particular goal or assignment in mind. The science discs also could have served this database role if more computer software had been written to provide a coherent index and framework, or if there had been text frames to identify the different pictures. However, in their current form, they present more of a massive picture file than a stand-alone information resource for children.

Student Presentations

In this model, the disc provides a visual accompaniment to student reports to the class. Thus, as with the teacher presentation model, the disc is much like a set of slides or overhead projections to enhance an oral report.

The *Bio Sci* disc was used as a resource of visual images for students putting together hypothetical proposals for alternative uses for Central Park, and was presented as part of a mock community meeting in the school auditorium before an audience of parents, teachers, and children. The teacher using the Space discs also felt that it was important to have student presentations provide closure to the science unit. In this case, however, students presented the "programmed environment" that they had worked with in small groups rather than independently selected images to accompany an original oral report. Nonetheless, such a presentation generated a lot of student interest and lively discussion in the class.

In sum, the above five models differed with respect to the ways in which videodiscs were utilized as visual information resources in classroom learning. Furthermore, certain models (e.g., teacher- and student-led presentations) lent themselves to large-group instruction, while other models (e.g., programmed disc-based environments and visual databases) were more conducive to small-group work. In the next section, we will discuss the implications of these different models of videodisc use for their ease of implementation in the classroom. This discussion will center around three important issues: (a) ease of fit between the different models of videodisc use and traditional models of learning in the classroom; (b) videodiscs as an alternative to traditional media; and (c) the role of teachers in incorporating videodisc technology into schools.

ISSUES RELATED TO CLASSROOM IMPLEMENTATION

Ease of Fit Between the Different Models of Videodisc Use and Traditional Models of Learning in the Classroom

We found that large-group instruction and small-group learning with the videodiscs each had an important place in classrooms. Large-group instruction allowed the teacher to present classroom-wide, cohesive learning experiences to frame upcoming activities and focus classroom discussion, and to provide closure to units and student projects. In contrast, small-group work with videodiscs provided more student-controlled inquiry-driven and game-strategy-driven learning, and more active yet informal discussion among students concerning videodisc content. During our interviews with teachers, they discussed the relative advantages and disadvantages of the two formats of learning interaction.

As might be predicted, the videodisc models that allowed teachers to keep the classroom unit together were the most easily integrated into the existing classroom learning patterns, while those models requiring small groups of children working independently of their classmates were more challenging for teachers to orchestrate.

Regarding large-group instruction, all four teachers used the discs as audiovisual aids for lectures and class discussions. The two science teachers set aside class time for student presentations to the class, while an art teacher also had her whole class do a still-life charcoal drawing from a videodisc image.

Large-group instruction with the videodiscs during class time appeared to be, in part, a pragmatic outcome of the limited amount of time children actually spent in art and science classes. Art and science were taught as "special" subjects in the three field-test schools (as is done in many schools), where children left their regular classrooms to go to the art/science room for only one to three periods a week. As a result, the amount of time an individual child had with an art or science videodisc was minimal in contrast to what might have been possible if students had continual access to a videodisc player in their home rooms. Thus, large-group instruction helped to maximize the average amount of time each child might have with the videodisc materials.

Teachers recognized the value of small-group sessions where children had more direct control over the videodisc experience. Despite this perceived value, three of the four teachers expressed their difficulty with having some children work with the videodisc while the rest of the class was engaged in other work. While all four teachers regularly engaged students in small-group, hands-on work such as art projects and science experiments, students typically did the same type of work and fulfilled the same assignment. The coordination of different types of learning activities occurring simultaneously proved somewhat problematic. It should be noted that all four teachers made special arrangements to allow children to use the videodisc materials in small groups outside of regular class time—during lunch time or other periods.

With respect to small-group work during class time, teachers differed in their views and solutions to the challenges posed by small-group work with the disc. Anna, one of the art teachers, voiced some concern about coordinating children in her classroom:

> I like it to be a group experience, with everyone talking [together] about what's happening. I found it distracting and hard to keep people working that were working, and having some see parts of the disc.

She saw increased hardware resources housed in a computer lab as a somewhat better arrangement, but said that she also felt that children's work with an art disc would be best supervised by an art teacher rather than a computer lab teacher.

Susan, the other art teacher, anticipated the same problem of coordinating children engaged in both videodisc and nonvideodisc work, and elected to have small groups of students work with the videodisc in the library across from her room rather than in the art classroom. She felt that the library

> was a more studious and more conducive place. My art class doesn't lend itself to high tech equipment—I would have been very nervous about getting clay on it. It would have had to have its own separate space, requiring me to give up other space.

However, given the short distance between the library and her art room, Susan was able to "have her cake and eat it too": students had a quiet, separate spot to work in, and she was able to visit frequently to supervise and direct their work with the disc.

Interestingly, it was the difference in classroom patterns that contributed to the success of the videodisc in Elenore's eighth grade science class, which used the Space discs. This class was a more traditional learning environment than Janet's classroom, and emphasized teacher-led classes and highly structured science experiments. In this case, small groups left the classroom to work on disc projects related to the classroom lessons, but under the supervision of one of the researchers. Elenore felt that her students benefited from the exposure to something new that was a break in their daily routine:

> Everything is so regimented and disciplined here that just the format—the way they left the rest of the class to work on it, the fact that they didn't have to get it right all the time—made for a more relaxing way to learn, which I think was very good.

In sum, the various models of videodisc use provided teachers with multiple strategies of integrating videodisc technology into their classroom curricula and routines. As others have noted (Fuller, 1985; Glenn, 1983; Withrow & Roberts, 1984), videodiscs can serve as important audiovisual aids for large-group instruction in a way that is easily incorporated into the learning patterns in many classrooms while still offering superior visuals under user control. On the other hand, small-group or single-learning videodisc stations may challenge certain established classroom management strategies, yet have the potential to offer interesting, highly interactive learning opportunities for children.

Videodiscs as an Alternative to Traditional Media

As our other research has shown (Char, Hawkins, & Freeman, in preparation), elementary school classrooms make extensive use of information resources that are highly visual, such as book illustrations, films, magazines, maps, hands-on experiences, and field trips. In the present study, we found that videodiscs clearly addressed these visual information needs in classrooms. Furthermore, teachers and students recognized that videodiscs had the potential of offering them a learning resource that had distinct advantages over other media traditionally available in schools.

Teachers and students stated that one of the major advantages of the archival videodiscs used in the study was in providing a vehicle for presenting provocative, realistic, high-quality visual material rarely available in classrooms. For example, by definition archival discs contain images that have been deemed significant enough in a real-world context to merit being stored in an archive. Thus, the archival discs provided visuals that were important and relevant to teachers and students, and did not trivialize the knowledge gained from examining visual objects, actions, and phenomena.

Students who used the Space discs felt that the videodisc images were more interesting and motivating than their usual focus of class work, made certain space and science concepts "come alive," and that the visual motion sequences aided them in grasping certain ideas in physics:

> In class we have talk sessions, copy sessions...we discuss, we write a lot, and we memorize...but you forget, because you don't want to go back and read your notes. With the laser disc you see it, and it leaves an impression, and you want to go back and see it again so you understand it better.
>
> It's exciting because you see footage that's real. You don't just have to imagine what it's like to be in space or make believe that you're there [like you have to do with books].

It's easier to understand when you can see things, better than when you just talk about it. Like the hammer and feather [being dropped on the moon's surface]—I know why that works now.

Similarly, the teacher who used the *Bio Sci* disc felt that photographs and moving footage provided her students with powerful visual verification of scientific phenomena analogous to hands-on experiences:

There are two different kinds of concreteness which can verify something for you—there's the manipulative approach where you move things around and see what happens; and there's seeing that it's part of the real world, that things really work the way you've learned they do. And they're two different ways of verifying for yourself, instead of just reading it or hearing somebody talk about it. [The disc provided students with visuals that show important phenomena at the microscopic level.]

A second advantage of videodiscs over other media, which teachers and students commented on, stemmed from the medium's massive storage capacity and frame-accurate, random-access capability. Due to these technical features, teachers and students were impressed that videodiscs could provide them with a large array of visuals and control over the access and replaying of images:

Clearly, it would have been very costly, time consuming for a teacher to have been able to get a hold of all these slides....I could never have gotten the range; even with every Van Gogh book in the library, it wouldn't offer his complete works the way that disc did....[and with the videodisc keypad] it becomes a more individual thing, where children make choices and pick out where the computer should go, and [become more personally invested in the experience]. [Susan, *Van Gogh* teacher]

    *   *   *   *   *

I like it because you can go back and see it again, like a memory bank.... With a museum guide, even if you don't like him, you have to go with him. With a computer, you can jump around. [Van Gogh students]

A third major advantage of the videodiscs was that they allowed teachers and students to exercise control over the pacing and directionality of motion footage in ways not usually possible with television or films, thereby leading to greater focus and possibly new types of insights about physical phenomena:

What I liked best was that I could get right to what I wanted immediately, and sections that were film, like cell division, could go through in slow motion and retrace back. [Janet, *Bio Sci* teacher]

    *   *   *   *   *

You could really see the frog cells split up—it was amazing. And you could back up fast, make it all one again, then start it over....We got to control it ourselves. I liked that....You can move around more, and do more—like back it up, and go fast forward. [*Bio Sci* students]

Another advantage of videodiscs is their programmability, and the ability to create simulations and establish other problem-solving contexts to motivate and focus children's visual inquiry and thinking. The "Orbit Adventure" game created for the Space disc and the two art mystery games created for the *Van Gogh* disc were often cited as students' favorite videodisc experience, and the teachers acknowledged the importance of story premises for establishing problem contexts that are interesting and motivating to children:

> [With the "Orbit Adventure" game] you have to make choices and you get more involved....It's exciting—you feel like you're under pressure. You get into the problems because you don't want to die [in the game]....You really have to figure it out in order to make the right move—if you don't, you'll get burned up [in the earth's atmosphere]. [Various students using Space I discs]
>
> * * * * *
>
> The "Orbit Adventure" game really got them involved. It put kids at the center so they had to make choices. [It really encouraged them to think critically, which doesn't happen enough in school]. [Elenore, Space teacher]
>
> * * * * *
>
> [The art mysteries] made you smarter every minute. Like a detective. Like it had questions, and made you take out your brain and really react to it. [Student using *Van Gogh* disc]
>
> * * * * *
>
> [It was the mystery games where] they were the most animated, where the most discussion went on among themselves. They had the greatest stake, a vested interest, where the kids really had to think and were called upon to know detail. [Susan, *Van Gogh* teacher]

In sum, videodisc technology can offer an exciting alternative to the information resources traditionally available to schools. These potential strengths lie in the presentation of superior high-quality visuals of real-world phenomena, greater user control over the accessing and displaying of visual images, and the availability of interactive, problem-solving contexts for children's learning.

Accompanying this new medium, however, was the novelty of the hardware itself. All the teachers found it necessary to describe to their students some of the special features of the technology, such as how it worked and what a disc was like. Some teachers expressed some initial anxiety with the hardware, such as knowing how to work the buttons on the videodisc keypad, how to boot the disc, or how to deal with the system if it crashed. A few mentioned that a major issue to be considered was hardware cost, but were curious about the price of different systems and discs and remained enthusiastic about the possible advantages of the technology.

The Role of Teachers in Incorporating
Videodisc Technology into Schools

Findings from our study challenge two common, but diametrically opposed, assumptions held by professionals in the videodisc industry: that teachers are simply consumers of existing videodiscs; or that teachers are designers and programmers who possess the knowledge, time, and energy to redesign and retrofit videodiscs. We found that teachers could be valuable contributors to the videodisc design process, but could not (or should not) be expected to invest the sizable amounts of time required to reprogram videodiscs.

During initial teacher interviews and planning sessions, our field-test teachers were extremely helpful in discussing which aspects of the discs seemed most relevant and promising with respect to their curricula, and offered various ideas for disc design and accompanying print materials. For example, both art teachers had ideas for different portfolio groupings (i.e., a series of paintings programmed as a group, such as all the Van Gogh paintings that featured suns, moons, and stars), which led to the design of three new portfolios and pointed to the importance of offering the programmed options where teachers and students could "online" create their own portfolios. The two art teachers also discussed their ideas concerning what they hoped children would gain from looking at and creating portraits and from describing their art work; these ideas formed the pedagogical bases for the two art mystery games.

Similarly, Janet, the teacher who used the *Bio Sci* disc, helped create the supplementary cross-references for the archive's print index, which allowed children to select appropriate images from the disc. Using her knowledge of her subject area, the children's background in biology, the classroom organizational patterns, and the nature of the assignment, Janet was able to bridge the gap and create a good match between the massive, archival videodisc and her students' curriculum needs, interests, and abilities.

One of the most important findings of the field test was a realistic assessment of the significant amount of time, expertise, and energy needed to create high-quality materials, even when retrofitting excellent existing discs. Even our research team, who had had previous experience in software design and development, underestimated the work entailed in retrofitting discs.

When planning the field test, our research purposively made the decision to work collaboratively with teachers and assist them in the creation and adaptation of materials, rather than assuming that teachers would have the time, expertise, or inclination to take on such a task in addition to their regular teaching load. The teachers' role in disc design was primarily that of reviewing the contents of the disc and discussing their reactions and ideas with the researchers; it was the researchers' responsibility to implement the teachers' ideas, as well as to add ideas of their own.

Despite the more limited role played by the teachers, they devoted a considerable amount of time to the planning and design of the disc. For example, Elenore, the teacher who used the Space discs in the science class, spent approximately 18 hours reviewing the contents of the disc, meeting with the researchers to plan the disc design, and reviewing the final disc materials. Elenore described the design process in the following way:

> First you have to run through the disc and see what's available, then you make notations about exactly what footage you want, then there's your own mental planning of what you're going to do. If it's level 1 (i.e., videodisc player controlled by a keypad), you search out the frames in class; if it's level 3 (i.e., computer-controlled videodisc), you put it together and program it—that's where most of the work is.

Another key role played by the teachers during the actual use of the videodiscs in the classroom was helping to focus students' attention on particular aspects of the disc visuals. They extended and enhanced student discussion, probing children's understanding of what they were seeing, and getting them to articulate their reactions to the videodisc images.

Susan, one of the art teachers, assumed an active role in bringing certain aspects of the paintings to the children's attention, having students verbalize their ideas and feelings about a painting, and generating more general discussion about art composition and art history. When the children were working alone without Susan, they were still highly engaged with the disc and often discussed elements of the pictures. However, their comments tended to be along the lines of pointing out specific content features of the pictures, making free associations with other paintings they had seen, or aesthetic appreciation (e.g., "Look at the dog"; "That looks like George Washington"; "Oh, that's pretty"), with little follow through or elaboration. With Susan, the discussions were much more focused and extended. When a child commented that a certain impressionist painting did not resemble a Van Gogh work, Susan encouraged her to explain why and the child proceeded to discuss contrasts in the artist's use of color and brush stroke.

Janet also played a significant role in assisting children with the *Bio Sci* disc, helping them to locate appropriate pictures for their presentations. She encouraged them to make appropriate use of the references on the paper index, and often directed them toward those general sections of the disc that were most fruitfully explored. In Janet's absence, children tended to select pictures that could unequivocally be photographs of Central Park and reject those photos that clearly were not, even though they featured pictorial elements that were relevant to a student's presentation. For example, some children would see a picture of a green, grassy field as an example of the kind of terrain they would like to see in the park, but reject it on the grounds that it featured a mountain in the background (and thus could not be Central Park). With Janet's help, students began to see how they could incorporate such pictures into their presentations by verbally directing the audience to focus on the relevant aspects of the picture.

CONCLUSIONS

Our field test turned out to be far more involving than the usual classroom research situation in which teachers are given educational materials to try out. Our method was to work closely with teachers to find ways of integrating the technology into their classrooms. We did some of the leg work involved in reviewing the disc materials to find appropriate images, created software to be used in classroom presentations and small-group activities, and were even involved at times with supervising small groups of students. These activities, however, gave us a more realistic picture of the level of effort that is required to take advantage of the unique features of the videodisc. We were also able to see very clearly some of the excitement the medium can generate when used well.

Like other software materials, the videodisc can be effectively used in small-group settings where children can engage directly in problem-solving activities. However, taking full advantage of small-group learning may require additional resources not available in all classrooms. It is sometimes difficult for teachers to manage a class in which the children are not all working at the same task. One solution is to use videodisc materials in school libraries or other resource centers where the work is often individualized and additional teachers, such as the school librarian, can help to manage the diversity of activity. But moving the videodisc out of the classroom makes it difficult to integrate it with the regular subject matter and to utilize the classroom teacher's expertise. Videodisc programs designed for small-group activity may be more usable if they are accompanied by lesson plans that help the teacher move back and forth between large- and small-group activities.

The videodisc can work in a variety of settings because it can be an information archive, a filmstrip, a film, a simulation, or a game. At the heart of the medium is the capacity to store high-quality video images. At the simplest level, the videodisc can take the place of portfolios of photographs, filmstrips, educational films, and other traditional media. Placing these materials on videodiscs, however, can lead to a profound change in their educational value and use. First, collections of photos or slides can be far more extensive than is normally available in school libraries or in teachers' private collections. Second, greater flexibility of presentation is introduced. For example, a film can be slowed or stopped or played backwards, making possible careful analysis of movement or change. The teacher can use a film as an accompaniment to a lesson, where before it was only possible to play it through without stopping. Third, the random-access capability of the videodisc player allows the material to be under computer control. Thus, the images can be used in a wider variety of ways than just linear presentation: They can become parts of games or simulations, or become parts of a child's oral report.

While we should not underestimate the amount of effort involved in creating classroom activities out of the raw materials on the videodisc, we should also be aware of the high level of interest that the materials themselves generate. In the first place, the materials, considered as pictures or films, are familiar to teachers; they are simply more plentiful and flexible. Second, there is a quality of realism that appears to be the result of such factors as the quality of the image, and the archival nature of many videodiscs—the images are not just examples but the entire corpus (e.g., the works of Van Gogh). Also, many of the discs contain raw footage with minimal editing (e.g., the Apollo missions), thus giving a feeling of immediacy.

The attractiveness of the raw materials makes them amenable to classroom use. However, the vastness of the archives and the complexity of the options means that teachers need to structure the materials in order to use them effectively. One kind of general-purpose software tool that can be useful across a wide variety of archival discs is a database management system (DBM) that provides indexing and searching capacities with respect to the images on the disc and the textual or numerical data. Such a DBM goes well beyond the raw data on the disc because it makes the information readily accessible in a variety of modes. The DBM should be sufficiently flexible to allow teachers to create their own data fields; that is, to index the images according to their own categories, and to create "slide shows" with sequences of images. While teachers may not have the time to review and index an entire disc, it appears likely, based on the field test, that they could work with a DBM to create special-purpose image sequences and categorizations using the basic indexing provided by the software.

Bringing the disc images under computer control is the feature that most clearly distinguishes the videodisc from other media such as slides, films, and books. Unlike text- or graphics-based software, the videodisc provides a strong element of familiarity, and it is this familiarity of the disc content that may lead to teachers' willingness to work with computer-based DBMs to create customized classroom materials. Simulations and games in which the computer control is more complex may also be well accepted by teachers because of the use of familiar content. It may be possible to create authoring systems that allow teachers to customize this class of software because the basic building blocks—video images— are more familiar than the graphics images used in most microcomputer simulations.

The new videodisc medium radically restructures familiar content because the individual images can be accessed randomly and rapidly. The new medium is deceptively similar to the old medium of slides and films because often the content is quite literally transferred to the new medium. While it is true that the videodisc can be used simply as a replacement for portfolios of photographs or educational films, we are mainly interested in the transformations that occur when materials are designed to take advantage of the unique features of the new medium. These transformations include changes in the way instruction is organized, since the videodisc lends itself to small-group problem solving as well as whole-class lecture/demonstration. Even in whole-class lessons, the medium can integrate film presentation with class discussion because of its interactive nature. The interest shown by teachers and students during our field tests indicates that the videodisc medium could result in more lively and engaging classroom processes.

AUTHOR NOTES

Funding for the research reported here was provided by the Sony Corporation of America and CBS Educational and Professional Publishing.

CHAPTER 13

COMPUTERS AND GIRLS: RETHINKING THE ISSUES

Jan Hawkins

INTRODUCTION

Interviewer: What was the reaction from people when you became interested in math and then later computer science?

Nancy: Well, my math professor thought it was great, of course. My
parents didn't think it was such a great idea. As far as my
career was concerned, my father did not like the idea too
much. He did not think it was a good field for a woman to be
in.

Interviewer: Did he say why?

Nancy: Well he considered computer science to be very engineering-
like, I don't know why really. Maybe too hard, and maybe
because it wasn't English. And maybe also 'cause he thought
my chances of getting a job would not be too good. My
mother never understands what I'm doing. She doesn't
understand computers at all.

The issue of equity of access to and learning about computers has become an important topic in education. It is a common concern that all
children have equal opportunity and appropriate support for acquiring
competence with the technology. These concerns derive from (a) the
belief that because many careers will require competence with computers, knowledge of information technology will be a source of power
in the future, and (b) the fact that currently there are differences among
groups of people in their access to bodies of information which may be
exacerbated by unequal opportunities for learning about technology.
Two important dimensions of difference are social class and sex. With
respect to the latter—if current projections are accurate—girls are likely
to learn less about and have less ability to control this increasingly important cultural tool.

This chapter presents a perspective about sex differences in relation to learning about computers, and then attempts to analyze the ways in which technology is thought about that have implications for how it is incorporated into educational settings. It will be argued that in addition to the problem of equity of access to the hardware, girls and young women are often not given appropriate support and contexts for learning about the technology.

Three lines of converging arguments will be examined. First, we will consider the fact that computers are commonly identified with the domains of mathematics and science. This categorization has tacit implications for how they are incorporated into educational settings and, more broadly, into functions in our society.

Second, for a number of years there has been widespread concern about sex-related learning differences in science and mathematics, and it is not surprising to find these differences emerging in the area of computers. A large body of research investigating these problems for science and mathematics has taken into consideration attitudes, interest and achievement, career statistics, and analyses of the social processes of classrooms. A number of programs have been developed to ameliorate the problems. Our ways of understanding and addressing these problems will be considered as an analogue to our thinking about current technological issues.

Third, we have conducted a number of studies at the Center for Children and Technology concerning the processes of children's learning and the use of computers in education. These studies provide us with an interesting body of material about patterns of sex differences in learning with computers. Our findings, and those reported by others, will be reviewed in light of the perspective developed here.

COMPUTERS AS TOPICS AND AS TOOLS

Interest and achievement in the areas of science, mathematics, and technology have been repeatedly demonstrated to be linked to sex in educational and work environments. As computers—common exemplars of technology—continue to play an ever-expanding role in people's lives, their conceptual bonding with the topic areas of mathematics and science has important educational implications.

While computers are used for many other purposes, their computational properties as applied to science and engineering problems are especially salient. Interviews with 8- to 12-year-old children indicate that their understanding of computers emphasizes the role of these machines in science and math tasks (Mawby, Clement, Pea, & Hawkins, 1984). Additionally, computers are commonly thought of as "built" from mathematical elements and concepts. This leads to the inference that in order to work with computers, people must be mathematically inclined or have prior math skills—an inference that may not be accurate. The relationship among skills in these domains has been tested in a research program investigating the prerequisites and cognitive consequences of programming experience for children (Kurland, Pea, Clement & Mawby, in press).

The designation of computers as a curriculum topic, and their prominent membership in the mathematics/science category, leads to a particular kind of treatment in educational settings. As documented by Sheingold, Kane, and Endreweit (1983), schools often acquire hardware with very little idea of how it will be used. Because the larger cultural framework plays a major role in determining their placement, computers are initially incorporated into mathematics or science curricula (e.g., Saunders, 1978), and computer science is often taught in the mathematics department. On the other hand, some schools define computer literacy as a new curriculum area in which the teaching of programming skills is frequently dominant.

This treatment of computers as a topic subsumed under science/mathematics/technology has serious educational consequences for girls. Because they are most often linked with an area that has long been dominated by males, computers typically enter the classroom with an aura of sex-related inequities that has an impact on both learners and teachers.

Another way of thinking about how to incorporate computers into educational environments is to view them as tools that can be adapted to a wide variety of purposes in all subject areas—language, art, music, information gathering, and organizing—in addition to their time-honored use in mathematics, science, and technology (Sheingold, Hawkins, & Kurland, 1983). This conception of the computer as a universal, symbolic machine that can aid in the acquisition of knowledge in a number of areas can serve to broaden its category membership. The interpretation of the technology for educational settings is central to how women and girls assess its relevance to their own learning.

WOMEN IN MATHEMATICS AND SCIENCE

A number of studies now documenting sex differences in the use of computers find that boys tend to be more interested in and make more use of the equipment than girls (Hess & Miura, 1983; Lockheed, Nielsen, & Stone, 1983), particularly for functions such as programming (Becker, 1982). As has been the case with mathematics (G. Burton, 1979; Minuchin & Shapiro, 1983; Osen, 1974), parents tend to be more supportive of boys' learning in this area than girls' (Miura & Hess, 1983). Examination of the wealth of literature analyzing sex differences in the areas of science and mathematics offers a perspective on the assumptions that underlie these differences for computers. It is important to look at these differences in the context of societal beliefs and social conditions as well as the factors that appear to mediate their developmental course, particularly in educational settings.

History of Sex Differences in Mathematics and Science

There is a long history of reported differences between boys and girls in interest and achievement in mathematics, science, and related disciplines. A discussion written in 1965, for example, makes very similar points to two written in 1970 and 1983, respectively:

> Secretary of Labor Willard Wirtz has expressed concern. . . . ''It is essential that the nation adopt a more favorable attitude toward the presence of women in many traditionally male-dominated professions''. . . . The image, which dooms the woman [for example] engineer to a lonely and intellectual life, supposes her to be mannish, aggressive, frustrated and unpopular. It lives on, even though the field has changed. . . . It has been ''in'' for a girl to reject and suppress a talent for math. It isn't feminine. Her parents believe that, perhaps, and so do her friends. And so she believes it, too, unless she is something of an independent thinker. (Peden, 1975)

> * * * * *

> Various of my friends are, as I am, women in science. Although our professional lives have not run the straight course of our husbands', mostly scientists as well, our work has not suffered from any prolonged disruptions. Yet each time we meet, our men mostly talk science while we usually linger on the subject of ''women in science.'' What has gone wrong?...If success in science requires an almost straight life course from which few deviations can be permitted, the woman should be judged not after the damage has been done, from the point of view of the prejudiced male, but rather one should ask: How, if at all within our present social organization, can we create conditions under which numbers of women may make outstanding contributions to science? (Yevick, 1970)

> * * * * *

> In recent years, underrepresentation in enrollments in mathematics courses by females and minorities has started to receive considerable attention. For example, in 1979 NCTM established a task force on ''Problems in the Mathematics Education of Girls and Young Women''. . . . In view of the increasing importance of mathematics for keeping student options open for higher education and careers, this attention to equity issues is timely. (Taylor, 1983)

Thus, we can see a history of concern on the part of educators with the fact that girls are significantly less likely to be actively engaged with these topics, both in school and in later careers. This state of affairs rests on an assumption, largely shared by many children, parents, and teachers, that these areas are not "appropriate" for girls. Burton (1979), Brush (1980), and Taylor (1983) provide statistical evidence of differential enrollment and interest in mathematics courses by sex at high school and college levels. What is the reason for this?

Historically, careers in science and mathematics have been dominated by men (Burton, 1979; Fennema, 1980). While some women have chosen these careers, they often view themselves as unusual and are so perceived by others; they follow career paths that often require them to make difficult choices about their life goals (Peden, 1975; Yevick, 1970). Girls have limited contact with career models in these areas, both in their educational environment where science and mathematics teaching are often dominated by men (Minuchin & Shapiro, 1983), and in the general culture where relatively few women choose such careers (Brush, 1980; Kreinberg, 1981; Simpson, 1978). Young women are explicitly and implicitly told that the long and dedicated hours and intense competition associated with these professions may conflict with the traditional feminine goals of family and children. Thus, girls may be unmotivated to pursue these subjects in school because they are not understood to be relevant to their later lives (Brush, 1980). There is considerable evidence that sex differences are robust for reported interest in these areas and perceived appropriateness for men and women (e.g., Emmerich & Shepard, 1982; Entwisle & Baker, 1983; Stein & Smithells, 1969).

Development of Differential Interest and Achievement
In order to understand those experiences of children that support differential interest and achievement, a number of studies have been conducted. These studies have asked several questions, the first and most logical being: Is there a biological basis for reported differences in abilities? Research has indicated that there may be sex-linked differences in some types of mathematical ability, indexed by spatial reasoning tasks (Maccoby & Jacklin, 1974). In addition, in-utero levels of the male hormone, testerone, may influence the development of genius-level mathematical ability in a small percentage of the population, as evidenced by a study correlating high-level mathematics ability with characteristics known to be related to excess testerone during fetal life (Kolata, 1983). However, a biological explanation does not fully account for observed differences in mathematics interest and achievement in the general population of boys and girls (Hess & Miura, 1983).

A second and perhaps more important question is whether the nature of the tasks posed in mathematics learning supports the engagement of boys as opposed to girls. A number of studies indicate that particular characteristics of children's learning tasks may be an important factor in the development of sex differences. For example, Licht and Dweck (1982) suggest that achievement orientations may be different for the two sexes in various subject areas. Girls and boys interpret failure feedback differently; girls are more likely to attribute difficulty in solving problems to their own lack of ability, whereas boys are more likely to attribute failure to other situational facators. Mathematics tasks are commonly organized in such a way that the occurrence and salience of failure is greater than for verbal tasks (cf. Brush, 1980); that is, the solution of a mathematics problem is either correct or incorrect, and the correct solution of problems illustrating a new mathematics concept is often preceded by a series of failures. In contrast, many verbal tasks are interpretive (e.g., writing an essay) and therefore subject to more flexible evaluation which, in turn, may lead to further development of the ideas expressed. Frequent encounters with failure in mathematics tasks may thus be interpreted differently by girls and boys with respect to their self-assessed abilities.

Lenney (1977) offers considerable support for the argument that men and women react to achievement situations differently. Her analysis of adult performances indicates that women's self-confidence seems to be affected by specific task characteristics, the kind and quality of feedback offered, and the degree to which competition and evaluation play a part. For example, she presents evidence that women are more likely to express confidence in tasks that feature social as opposed to intellectual skills. Women also appear to be less confident than men in situations where there is little or ambiguous feedback. She concludes that, as a general attribute, women may be no less confident of their ability to achieve than are men, but they may be more sensitive to particular characteristics of an achievement situation in assessing their own competence.

Parsons, Kaczala, and Muce (1982) were interested in understanding what social processes in classrooms might give rise to differential feedback for boys and girls, and thus to differential expectations and self-confidence in mathematics. Classrooms were observed to determine the amount and kind of feedback given by teachers to high- and low-math-achieving boys and girls. They found that children have equivalent achievement expectations when praise and criticism are equally distributed across sex and teacher-expectancy groups. However, the social processes in classrooms can influence children's expectations for themselves: Girls have lower expectations for their own performance in classrooms where they are treated differently from boys.

A third question is whether particular aspects of the larger culture (media, parents, school authorities) give different messages to boys and girls about gender-appropriate interests. A brief examination of advertising in technological areas reveals that it is overwhelmingly male-oriented. For example, one magazine advertisement for office software depicts a group of men standing around a computer, engrossed in solving a problem. A woman sits polishing her fingernails in front of the machine, clearly uninvolved, while awaiting their conclusions. The majority of advertising for products and jobs in the area of computer technology is directed toward a male audience.

Starting with kindergarten, the process of schooling is one that sorts children according to the abilities considered to be important, and by interests which the educational experience helps to define. "Who am I in the criteria of this school system, and what is it appropriate for me to do?" This sorting happens in both obvious (tests, tracking systems) and subtle (instructional feedback, interaction with teachers and peers) ways. From a very early age, children are made aware that choices and performance are going to determine both the quality of their experience in school and their subsequent career choices (Minuchin & Shapiro, 1983). Such sorting processes undoubtedly give differential messages to boys and girls about the appropriateness of their participation in different areas. This process is documented by an ethnographic examination of the sorting that occurred over the course of one year in a junior high school:

> Two girls, Charlotte and Margot, were talking with Mrs. G, the art teacher. Charlotte said the math class was really hard for her. It worried her that she was having problems because she comes from a family of teachers and she really feels the pressure is on her to do well in school. . . . Then Charlotte remarked, "It will really hurt me to be a 'C' student in math because I want to go into architecture and the math will cut me right down." Mrs. G. responded by telling Charlotte that she has so many other talents and she should concentrate on using them to her advantage. She suggested the art field. Charlotte: "Yeah, maybe I ought to think about going into something like textile design." (Goldman, 1982, p. 13)

Thus, both the larger culture and the culture of the school are continually providing boys and girls with information about their abilities (by which they are sorted and re-sorted) and about the future they can expect based on the kinds of abilities they exhibit in the interpretive context constructed by adults.

In summary, it is likely that all of the above factors play some role in the differential interest and achievement of boys and girls in the area of mathematics. The complex nature of the environment supporting these differences makes this an intractable problem and one not easily addressed by a single type of program. A number of societal messages support the inference that interest in these areas is unusual for girls and may present life conflicts if selected as a career choice. The organization of tasks in schools and the social processes of classrooms appear to further support sex differences in "ownership" of and expectations about one's ability in science and mathematics.

Educational Programs

A variety of educational programs have been developed in recent years to address the inequities between boys and girls in mathematics and science achievement. Many of these programs focus on helping girls to consider mathematics/science as future career choices by presenting them with role models of women scientists and mathematicians (e.g., Simpson, 1978; Project EQUALS at the Lawrence Hall of Science, Berkeley, CA). The students are told about interesting careers in these fields and are shown how preparation in school can help them to realize these goals. Similarly, teachers in various curriculum areas are made aware of the relevance of mathematics and science to girls' future lives (e.g., Kreinberg, 1981). In this way, the programs present mathematics or science as general curriculum topics that are important for girls' futures, rather than as diverse and interesting tools for accomplishing goals in their present lives.

Those programs that emphasize changing the self-perceptions of girls with respect to science and mathematics as necessary skills for future careers have been recommended as the most promising (Brush, 1980), and have been demonstrated to be effective in certain school systems (e.g., Taylor, 1983). But since it is often hard for young children to think so far ahead, this approach alone would appear to be inadequate. It is important to recognize that mathematics and science are tools that children can use in their everyday lives. In many school settings, relatively little effort is made to adapt the learning environment to children's interests and orientations. Focusing attention on the possible continuities between present interests and future directions is a further step.

Brush (1980) suggests that mathematics teachers can make classes more enjoyable for students by developing mathematics tasks that emphasize creativity and interpretation rather than success or failure. She offers the example of a teacher who incorporates geometry skills into a project to design the layout of a room. By the same token, girls may benefit from and feel more involved with learning experiences that are relevant to their current interests and circumstances.

PATTERNS OF DIFFERENCE WITH COMPUTERS IN CLASSROOMS

As noted above, most of the work on sex inequities in science and mathematics discusses these issues holistically rather than focusing on the areas, skills, applications, and circumstances that may differentially engage individuals. If we view the computer as a subject, it is likely that differential interest and achievement will be similarly analyzed in global terms. We are already seeing studies that report significant overall differences between boys and girls. The reports tend to describe the computer as a unitary topic, rather than attending to the characteristics of the particular situations where differences are found. The studies noted above (e.g., Lenney, 1977; Licht & Dweck, 1982) indicate that aspects of the work context are very important in understanding the appearance of sex differences in achievement. An examination of the pattern of sex differences in the educational use of the computer as a tool is therefore important.

In order to answer questions about learning and the use of the technology in education, the Center for Children and Technology (CCT) has conducted studies examining the different uses of computers in classrooms. These studies demonstrate patterns of sex differences. Two situational factors appear to be major determinants of the engagement of boys and girls with the technology: the function for which the computer is used, and the organization of the setting in which the children work. Several of the studies are briefly discussed below.

Survey of Schools

Sheingold et al. (1983) conducted an in-depth survey of three geographically disparate school districts to determine how computers were being used in both elementary and secondary schools. Personnel at all levels were interviewed and classrooms were observed. At many of the locations there were clear trends indicating that boys were more likely than girls to make use of the machines. However, this pattern was related to the fact that computers were frequently used for teaching programming, mathematics, or data processing in business classes where boys were the dominant users. It was also the boys who found opportunities to use computers outside of regular class time. In contrast, the teachers in one school reported that girls' interest was aroused when they were presented with software in the form of graphics tools that allowed them to create pictures and designs. The study concluded that sex was the most obvious factor affecting differential use of the machines at all grade levels across sites. These differences tended to polarize in the higher grades, when students entered the departmental system where computers were concentrated in the mathematics and business subject areas.

Programming

An increasingly common use of microcomputers in schools at all levels is for programming. A series of studies was conducted by researchers at CCT over a period of two years to investigate children's learning of the programming language Logo. These studies addressed two issues: (a) the cognitive aspects of learning to program, and whether knowledge of programming concepts would be generalized to other problem-solving situations; and (b) the social and organizational aspects of incorporating microcomputers into classroom settings (Hawkins, Sheingold, Gearhart, & Berger, 1982). Two classrooms participated in the 2-year research project (8- and 9-year-olds, and 11- and 12-year-olds). Each classroom was equipped with six microcomputers, which were integrated into the learning environment. As part of the classroom schedule, all the children were assigned individual times to work at the computer; they also had the choice of using the machines before or after school and during lunch. Thus, boys and girls had equal opportunity to work with the machines over the course of the school year.

In-depth involvement with these classrooms over a protracted period allowed us to study the development of programming understanding and the various factors influencing the incorporation of computers into educational settings. Because the findings of this work are too extensive to discuss in detail here, we will only note the results that pertain to the emergence of sex differences.

First, in order to investigate how children learn to program in Logo and how expertise in programming develops, we developed a number of measures, including: case studies of four children—two boys and two girls (regular interviews with the children, tasks to document command and concept understanding, and monitoring of ongoing work); assessment instruments to determine level of knowledge of commands and program structures; program memory tasks to indicate level of program understanding; and problem-solving tasks accompanied by in-depth interviews with the most advanced students. In general, we saw a clear trend for boys to perform better than girls on all these tasks. For example, the two boys in the case-study component developed significant programming expertise over the course of the school year, as revealed by their knowledge of commands and the complexity of the programs they developed. The girls showed less interest than the boys and developed less facility with Logo.

At the end of the school year, all the children were given the programming knowledge assessment, which consisted of three parts: (a) knowledge of individual programming commands (definition and use); (b) ability to write a variety of short programs to execute specified goals; and (c) ability to debug programs containing different classes of errors. (For a detailed description of the tasks, scoring procedures, and findings, see Pea, Hawkins, Clement, & Mawby, 1984.) For both age groups, boys performed considerably better on all measures of programming expertise, and in general showed more enthusiasm for the work and spent more time programming (mean: 34 hours for boys, 22 for girls, $p < .01$).

With respect to knowledge of programming commands, the mean score for boys was 47.2, and 25.1 for girls ($p < .01$). There were also marked sex differences in program composition skills. In this part of the assessment, children were asked to write lines of code using increasingly sophisticated programming concepts. Older children were more skilled than younger children, and the boys in each age group displayed more skill than the girls. In this analysis, a child's efforts in each of seven subtasks were classified into one of three categories: (a) correct; (b) partially correct (i.e., lines of code were correct, but the child failed to organize them procedurally or to return the "object" which executed the program to its starting position); and (c) wrong or no attempted solution. The younger boys wrote correct or partially correct programs in 36% of the cases, younger girls only in 6%; older boys were correct or partially correct 70% of the time, older girls only 26% of the time.

Similarly, boys displayed more programming skill in the third component of the assessment—debugging faulty programs: The mean score for younger boys was 31.1, and 19.9 for younger girls; the mean score for older boys was 48.9, and 17.4 for older girls.

As part of the study, an ethnography of each classroom was developed, which included observations, regular interviews with the teachers (both males) and students, documentation of student work, and videotapes of activities. Analysis of the teacher interviews indicates that a frequently expressed concern was the noticeable sex differences in interest and accomplishment with the programming work. Both teachers were asked to indicate which children they judged to be "the best programmers, experts"; no number was specified. After the first year, four boys were selected by the teacher as the best programmers in the younger class. The teacher of the older children also selected four boys as the most skilled members of the class.

The teacher of the younger group felt that

> Girls' involvement was highly correlated with *my* interest in it. There seemed to be less clearcut benefits for girls—boys wanted to control it. They acted as if it were made for them. The teacher of the older children speculated:
> Mechanical? Math? I'm not sure. Something I did failed to connect them. The girls who didn't work at the computers were not necessarily worse in math, but school math is different from mathematical interest. They tended to be conscientious students, and take school seriously, so some did school math well but were not really interested in it.

At the end of the year, the children completed a questionnaire which, among other items, asked them to nominate two class members who were, in their judgment, "experts" in computers. Three boys were overwhelmingly selected by the older children; two boys were designated by the younger group (see Hawkins et al., 1982, for further discussion).

When the teachers assessed the first year's work of computer programming, they reported dissatisfaction with the progress of most children and expressed particular concern about the apparent sex differences. As preparation for the second year, the teachers reorganized their presentation of the material so as to better support children's learning (e.g., presenting a more structured sequence of concepts, development of project ideas). During both years, finding functional goals for their work as they learned Logo was a continuing problem for the children. Many did not have a clear understanding of how to adapt computer programming to projects in which they were interested. Over the course of the second year, the teachers tried to spend more time with the girls and to devise projects (such as programming word games) that might better accommodate their interests. At the outset, one teacher felt that girls would stay involved as long as he introduced them to and helped them to use new skills.

However, by the end of the second year, the teachers reported that they continued to see sex differences in the amount of interest in and commitment to programming tasks. They were again asked to designate which children in this second group were the "experts," and which were "good, proficient programmers" but less knowledgeable than the experts.

In contrast to the first year, the teacher of the younger children indicated that four girls (one "outstanding") and two boys were experts. However, of the eleven children in this class judged to be proficient, ten were boys. Sex differences were particularly striking among the older children (11s and 12s): The teacher judged six boys and one girl to be experts, and seven boys and three girls as proficient:

> It's really incredible, it's so clear and I'm sure I contribute some to that, but I feel a lot of it is just them. They're 12 years old and they, I think, have stereotypic views of themselves, very strong stereotypic views of themselves....So it's hard, and I think that a lot of it has to do with our culture. At any rate, it's also noticeable that the boys tended to be very interested in computers and machines, and I think this year more than ever before. Any discussion about hardware was among the boys last year, but this year the discussion has been overwhelming....Certainly, in terms of percentage of how much of [the boys'] talk is about computers, let's say—compared to girls—it's astronomically high.

It is important to note that these sex differences did not appear across the board: As noted above, four girls in the second year class developed considerable expertise. There were individual girls in each class who displayed a lot of interest, performed well, and were judged by both teachers and peers to be competent with computers. The expert girls tended to be competent in all school subjects. This overall competence was not always true of expert boys, some of whom had previously shown little interest or competence in school but who "blossomed" when they started working with computers.

Our studies examining the development of programming skill in the classrooms of relatively young children indicate robust differences between boys and girls in levels of interest and achievement. This is particularly striking in light of the teachers' sensitivity to the problem and their efforts to include girls in the work.

In a related study concerning the development of programming expertise (Kurland, Mawby, & Cahir, 1984), professional adult programmers were interviewed about their backgrounds, interests, and current work modes. Included in the sample were several young women, all of whom indicated that they were considered to be "deviant" in their career choices and found themselves to be a small minority of the students pursuing computer science.

Word Processing Tools
Another rapidly expanding use of computers in education is word processing—computers used as tools for writing. Studies were conducted at CCT to assess available word processors, and when none was found to be adequate for children, formative research helped to inform the development of such a tool. Observational studies were done in two classrooms (10-year-olds) over the course of a school year to determine how well the tool worked for both children and teachers. It was found that boys and girls were about equally involved in the use of the word processor (Pea & Kurland, in press). The teachers reported that the word processor seemed to invite more collaborative writing among children. There is some indication that collaboration may be a preferred work context for girls (Hawkins, Chapter 1, this volume; A. Rubin, personal communication, 1984). While it is unclear whether children wrote *differently* as a result of experience with the word processor, it was noted that many wrote *more*. Use of the software did not appear to be mediated by sex.

This pattern of interest in the word-processing aspect of computers was also observed at the Lawrence Hall of Science (M. Linn, personal communication, 1985). In programs to teach children (10 to 16 years of age) about computers, enrollments of boys and girls were approximately equal for word-processing courses, but a majority of boys selected programming.

Mathematics and Science Software
Another project has been concerned with the research and development of software for use in the science and mathematics curricula of fourth through sixth grade classrooms. Three pieces of software were developed and tested, both with individual children and in classrooms (Char, Hawkins, Wootten, Sheingold, & Roberts, 1983). The software was designed to make use of the unique and powerful features of computers, and to model ways in which the tools are actually used by adults in their work. This research is part of a larger effort—the Project in Science and Mathematics Education—to produce an integrated set of software and materials

for classrooms (as well as television and videodisc). One mandate of the project is to encourage girls to develop an interest in science and mathematics. The three pieces of software include: (a) a tool to gather data about physical phenomena (temperature, light, sound) and to display these measurements in various types of graphic formats; (b) a simulation to introduce principles of navigation and the geometry involved; and (c) a series of games designed to introduce children to programming concepts in Logo. Since these programs fit into the existing mathematics/ science curricula of elementary classrooms, the pattern of findings concerning girls' participation is especially interesting.

Each piece of software was tested for a month in four different elementary classrooms with both male and female teachers. The classrooms were selected to represent different geographical locations and socioeconomic groups. We were interested not only in determining individual children's conceputal understanding, but also the patterns of use in the complex learning setting of the classroom. The teachers were asked to incorporate the software into their ongoing work. During and following the month-long experiment, classrooms were observed, teachers and students were interviewed, and all participating students completed an assessment questionnaire that documented amount of use, degree of interest, and development of understanding of the major concepts and skills presented in the software.

The variations in the design of the software allowed us to see the importance of two factors in the emergence of such differences: the type of software as it fit into the mathematics/science environment (tool, simulation, game); and the way in which the work was organized and put into context by the teacher.

Differences between boys and girls were most notable for one of the three pieces of software—the tool used to gather and display data. Boys tended to make more use of this software than girls, often working in groups, with the girls either uninterested or watching from afar. Overall, boys reported a greater degree of interest in and used the software more frequently (52% reporting multiple uses vs. 36% for girls). Boys were also more apt to report that they liked the software a lot (58% vs. 40% of girls). However, reported appeal was also a function of what was done with the software. In one classroom where children used the software to do "experiments" of interest to them (e.g., personalized activities in which they measured their own body temperatures), 80% of both boys and girls reported that they liked the software. In other classrooms, the software was used to perform such experiments as recording the loss of heat from different volumes of water.

On the other hand, while the other two pieces of software were no less technical or mathematical, there were few apparent sex differences in their use or appeal. For example, the triangulation principles introduced in the simulation software were complex mathematical concepts. In the case of the programming games, girls were more likely to report that they liked the software (83%) than were boys (64%). The simulation program appealed equally to both sexes, and there were no appreciable differences in children's responses to the comprehension questions.

We can speculate about two features of the software that contributed to their appeal for girls. First, learning experiences with these two pieces of software tended to be collaborative enterprises. The simulation game was designed such that children were required to play cooperatively. Teachers also chose to organize the programming games as collaborative work between pairs of children. Second, the goals of the software were less explicitly scientific than was the case for the data-gathering tool. The latter was introduced as part of the science curriculum for conducting experiments using the scientific method. The experimental orientation was problematic both for the teachers, who had had little science training and were not at ease with tasks requiring scientific experimentation, and for the girls, who expressed little interest in this kind of task.

In contrast, the goals of the other two software pieces were less directly tied to the traditional mathematics/science curricula. Mathematics/science concepts were embedded as useful tools in achieving the goals of the games (rescuing a trapped whale, finding locations on a map). The teachers were less likely to incorporate these pieces of software directly into the mathematics/science lessons, but rather to use them as independent learning units.

Thus, the pattern of sex differences in these studies is interesting in that the differences appear to be related to the particular use of the computer, and the way this use is organized and supported in the classroom.

CONCLUSION

The extensive work that has been done on the emergence of sex differences in relation to learning and achievement indicates that this is a complex and deeply rooted problem that appears to be related to many factors: the impact of societal images on girls; the expectation of different life goals for boys and girls; the structure of learning tasks; the nature of the feedback in performance situations; and the organization of the classroom setting. Investigations of sex differences typically focus on a general domain, such as mathematics ability, where the inequalities are apparent. It is necessary, however, to look deeper—to examine the functional uses of the material in particular situations in order to understand the circumstances in which boys and girls express interest and achieve competence.

As the new technology is introduced into more and more educational settings, it is important to consider the computer as a universal symbolic machine that can be designed and used for a variety of purposes. However, in the absence of a broader perspective, computers tend to be subsumed under mathematics or science curricula, and thus take on the already existing stigma of sex differences.

In summary, since the computer can be seen as a flexible tool, attention must be paid to software design and to the organization of children's classrooms experiences. There are two promising avenues for realizing these goals. First, it is important that computers be used in classrooms as tools for achieving a variety of goals (e.g., word processors, music editors). There need to be opportunities for use that match the goals and interests of individual children, along with appropriate support for learning about the technology. Second, the careful design of software in the areas of mathematics and science may enable girls to view these subjects as personally useful to them. This, of course, will require taking into account both the design of the programs and the organization of learning in the classroom.

AUTHOR NOTES

The preparation of this manuscript and the research reported was supported by the Spencer Foundation, the Department of Education, and the National Institute of Education. I would like to thank Cathy Clement, Carla Freeman, Peggy Heide, Moni Homolsky, Midian Kurland, Ron Mawby, Roy Pea, and Karen Sheingold for their comments and suggestions about the perspective presented here.

CHAPTER 14

INFORMING THE DESIGN OF SOFTWARE THROUGH CONTEXT-BASED RESEARCH

Jan Hawkins and D. Midian Kurland

In recent years, formative evaluation has begun to emerge as a discipline with its own questions, methodologies, and interpretive structures (cf. Hendrick, 1984; Mielke, 1982). Formative evaluation is designed to inform the development of a product or program. As part of such development efforts, formative research is necessarily interpretive and is designed in accordance with the type of product under study. Just as products and their intended users vary greatly, so must formative evaluation methods vary; there is no research formula that applies across all products. Educational software and the use of computers in educational settings pose new problems, and methods to address these problems have been developing in recent years.

The main purpose of research evaluation for educational software is to determine whether the product is "working," and what modifications may be desirable to improve its functioning. "Working" can mean many things, among them:

- Do members of the target audience understand the purpose of the software?
- Can users manipulate its various parts?
- Do users enjoy interacting with it?
- Are the directions clear?
- Does the program run without errors (crashing)?
- Do users understand and learn what the product is intended to teach?

The research has two primary goals in improving how the product works: to determine whether the software is *usable,* and to determine whether it is *useful;* that is, whether a program or system effectively engages students in learning. While this latter goal sounds like summative evaluation, we believe that it is crucial to examine students' understanding and learning at the formative stage of software development so as not to produce an enjoyable but ineffective product that does not fulfill its intended pedagogical goals.

For some software development questions of usability, it is often enough to try out parts of the program with students in the target age group. For example, if a program is to use a joystick device, it is a relatively straightforward matter to isolate the joystick routines. With the controllers set at different sensitivity levels, children can go through these routines and researchers can determine the optimal sensitivity level for children's accurate use of the device.

There are several strategies for conducting formative research on the usefulness of the software under development.

1. Valuable information is gained by testing with students fragments of existing programs, or programs that embody some of the ideas or interface features of interest.
2. Aspects of the design can be tested with other media, such as storyboards or vocabulary lists.
3. As the software is developed, prototype versions can be examined with children.
4. Members of the target groups (students and teachers) can be interviewed about their needs and ideas.

While formative evaluation would appear to be a straightforward component of any software development effort, the actual conduct of the work is frequently hampered by constraints of time and money. Today, the time span for developing a new piece of educational software is often very short: Six months is not uncommon, while a year or 18 months is considered unusual. The development schedule may not allow for prototype testing, especially if the testing is to be completed and analyzed in time to influence the ongoing development of the software. Since continual testing with fast turn-around time is expensive, formative evaluation is often a casualty of budget cutbacks. Thus, it is important for software developers to be sensitive to other forms of research that can help to guide choices in the development of new educational programs.

In this chapter, we discuss two additional formative research strategies, both of which illustrate ways that other types of research data can be used formatively even if that was not their intended use. In the first case, research was conducted to illuminate the intended context of use, a strategy that goes beyond what is ordinarily thought of as needs assessment. We then go on to discuss the development of educational software that is based on prior cognitive research.

Thus, in addition to conducting formative evaluation on the program itself, the development team must know how to make creative use of other forms of research in order to guide the design and development process. For high-quality educational software, this process needs to be informed by more than formative studies testing versions of that particular product. In particular, we want to stress the importance of understanding and designing for the special context of the classroom. To illustrate this point, we first describe a research study in which we examined how one group of products fared in the context of science and social studies classrooms. This study demonstrated an important way in which the classroom context influences how software is used and interpreted by teachers and students.

STRATEGY ONE:
STUDY THE INTENDED USE

In one of our recent projects, we were concerned with analyzing tool software for use in classrooms. By "tool" we mean that category of software that is designed to help people do, and perhaps do better, the tasks that they already perform in particular settings. These software tools include, for example, word processors, database management systems, spreadsheet programs, and music and graphic editors. Like any well-designed tool, these pieces of software can fit seamlessly into a work setting and add to people's power and efficiency. Consequently, the tool designer must understand in depth the nature of the work being done, and the ways in which a tool might help to do that work better.

Classrooms present an interesting case: The complexity and unique qualities of these settings are typically given insufficient attention by tool designers. Schools are quite different from the business settings for which many of today's software tools have been designed. Since the work of classrooms is helping people to learn, teachers are faced with the complex task of assessing the understanding of students at different developmental levels, and then finding ways to improve or deepen that understanding. The task is made even more complicated by the fact that it is carried out in a classroom: an elaborate social system where one or two adults organize the activity of a large group of novices.

The task of understanding and managing information is pervasive in our society and takes many forms throughout school life. In the best of circumstances, children learn to ask and revise questions, where and how to find information about a topic or question, and how to organize information into their own framework. It is important to think carefully about the design of educational software, not only because children should learn about these systems for future careers, but because well-designed tools may support acquisition of the necessary skills with new levels of sophistication and flexibility that go beyond what is ordinarily achieved in school.

We wanted to discover what functions and features were desirable in the design of information-managing tools and how they could best be used for learning. Were current tools adaptable to the classroom, or was a fundamentally different approach to design necessary for learning these skills in this setting? Formative research for many kinds of educational tool software can take advantage of existing tools that were intended for use in other settings. Examining how related tools function in the learning setting makes it relatively easy to obtain valuable information for design decisions that goes beyond what can be gleaned from testing prototype versions of a tool during the development process and provides the bigger picture—the tasks and processes in existing complex settings that affect the interpretation, assimilation, and use of the software.

Information-managing software tools help to perform a variety of tasks: formulating questions and problems, organizing, recording, storing, retrieving, and querying bodies of information. Currently, the dominant types of information-managing tools are database management (DBM) systems, which range from large and complex systems for mainframe computers (e.g., management of governmental census data) to small and simple programs for microcomputers (e.g., filing systems for home records).

Accordingly, we began by asking: How do tools designed for a business environment adapt to the classroom setting, and what can we learn about the characteristics of this setting that might contribute to design? We conducted a series of studies to answer these questions. First, we selected samples of DBMs and analyzed them in terms of their features and functions. Each piece of software was critically examined from the perspective of its potential for educational use in classrooms. We were particularly interested in how such systems might be used to support the development of critical inquiry skills—those skills involved in asking and revising questions, finding and analyzing relevant information, organizing material into an informed perspective, or problem solution. Second, classrooms already making use of DBMs were located through a telephone survey and by examining educational publications. Students' work was observed and teachers and students were interviewed. Third, DBMs were introduced into classrooms that had not previously used them, and the assimilation process was observed over a period of months. Finally, interview studies were conducted with a range of teachers and students concerning the types of information-managing tasks that are done in classrooms and how these skills are learned with and without computer assistance.

Our findings can be summarized briefly as illustrative of the importance of carefully examining context as a component of the formative enterprise. First and most strikingly, our survey of schools indicated that very few were making use of DBMs in classrooms, and it was the rare teacher who made use of a system in ways that supported the acquisition of the critical inquiry skills we envisioned. When we looked carefully at the schools using the systems and at the software itself, we found that they were used predominantly for administrative tasks analogous to those commonly done in business environments (e.g., student record keeping, attendance, grades).

In the few schools that made use of DBMs with students, we found a range of tasks. The tools were most easily assimilated into tasks in which students kept files of their work, their interests (e.g., baseball scores), or information about members of the class. In classes where students were being taught *about* the computer, DBMs served as examples of software students might use in later jobs. In these cases, students were asked to do such tasks as design a system to keep track of credit card accounts. Teachers found it much more difficult to assimilate the tools into the text-based, creative, information-managing tasks that are often called "research." For example, one teacher asked students to design a database format to handle information they were gathering about legal cases. He felt that this kind of activity would give students valuable insights into what it means to organize and reorganize information for different purposes. This kind of use, however, required significant time and imagination on the part of the teacher.

As a second level of study, we introduced DBMs into new classrooms and encouraged teachers to use them in a variety of ways. We wanted to see how easily these tools, given considerable support, could be put to creative use. The teachers readily adopted the tools as record-keeping devices (student work files, keeping track of data from science experiments)—the use for which the systems had been designed. However, they found it difficult to see ways of using the tools more creatively; that is, to help children learn how to ask questions and organize information for their own purposes.

The teachers found no easy way to integrate the systems for critical inquiry purposes, due in part to the way the tools are documented and to particular features that make them difficult to interpret in novel ways for classroom use, and in part to the way such tasks are conceptualized and organized in classrooms. For example, with respect to tool features, DBMs require students to define their data organization prior to working with the computer. Once designed, the format is very difficult to change in most systems. This is a problem for novices who are just beginning to learn about organizational schemes and who need to be supported by the technology in their experimentation. In addition, students more commonly work on tasks where they generate a great deal of notes and texts in their "research" work. The limited labels and notes accepted by database systems left some students frustrated.

From our interview study, it was apparent that the teachers placed a high value on their students' critical inquiry skills, and most believed this to be an important goal of their work. While articulate about what they wanted to accomplish, many teachers were unclear about the processes involved and unsure about how best to support individual students. Most did not interpret DBMs as a useful tool to achieve their goals. Therefore, in light of our examination of the educational setting, it would appear necessary to design a new kind of tool for supporting the development of critical inquiry skills. Such a tool should be designed to fit into and extend the activities already being carried out in this domain.

STRATEGY TWO:
APPLY BASIC RESEARCH TO THE
PROBLEM OF PRODUCT DEVELOPMENT

Sensitivity to the ethnography of the classroom is important when developing a new piece of software. However, in addition to "fitting in," software should perform a function that is both educationally valid and for which there is not a simpler, cheaper, nonelectronic alternative. Much of the current educational software fails on one or more of these criteria. For instance, a lot of math drill-and-practice software fits in nicely with classroom organization, but offers little beyond what workbooks can provide in exchange for the added expense and inconvenience. On the other hand, as we have just seen, DBMs offer exciting new possibilities for teachers that older technologies cannot, but this software is a poor fit with teachers' understanding of the inquiry process as it is practiced in schools. Finally, programs like Logo do not fit in neatly with many teachers' ideas about what they should be teaching, nor are they easy to use once a teacher has decided to take the plunge (Hawkins, Chapter 1, this volume; Pea & Kurland, 1984a). The challenge for the designer of educational software is to create software that teachers will perceive as potentially useful (and therefore will use) and which, once introduced into the classroom, will adequately support students in their use of the program.

To meet the challenges of classrooms, educational software must proceed from a firm understanding of the content domain that the program addresses. Persuasive theoretical perspectives about development support the notion that skill development is specific to particular types of media and the learning interactions they afford (cf. Laboratory of Comparative Human Cognition, 1985; Vygotsky, 1978). Basic research can provide the software designer with detailed knowledge about the skills involved in a particular domain and their developmental course. The most powerful form of research is that which carefully examines the skills in the context of learning. Skills required by a particular piece of software can be analyzed on the basis of educational and cognitive research that has been done with children. For example, in order to develop a series of programs for teaching algebra, an understanding of the development of mathematical and hypothetical reasoning abilities is essential. But this research, gathered for other purposes, is often difficult to apply to the specific problems of software design. Because such research is time consuming and expensive, in-depth studies are rarely attempted within the common time frame and economic constraints of software development. Thus, current educational software usually reflects a superficial understanding of the content area and how the targeted skills are learned by most children.

While designers must generally use some combination of existing research knowledge, their own intuitions, and the results of formative testing, occasionally there are opportunities for more directly linking basic resarch with design. We have been fortunate in this regard. In one of our projects, we studied children learning the Logo programming language in middle-school classrooms. A 2-year program of classroom-based research was conducted to investigate the cognitive and social consequences of children's learning Logo. In a series of classroom- and laboratory-based studies, we examined the development of programming concepts in fourth and sixth graders (cf. Pea & Kurland, 1984a; Pea, Kurland, & Hawkins, Chapter 9, this volume).

Logo was designed to afford a unique environment for the development of general problem-solving skills through the learning and practice of programming. The designers' view of the cognitive/developmental potential of the language (cf. Papert, 1980) was but one way of viewing Logo. Only through watching students learn to program in the context of use was it possible to become familiar with how the language was perceived by teachers and students. Based on our observations and experiments, the problems of Logo as a classroom learning environment became apparent. It was possible to identify features of the programming environment and the learning context that directly affected the nature of the learning that occurred.

Our research also allowed us to identify certain key conceptual difficulties that the children encountered in learning Logo. This information about the development of programming skills in the classroom environment became central to the design of a series of games to support the development of children's understanding of programming. This software was developed as part of the Project in Science and Mathematics Education, which has produced a set of integrated materials, including a television series (*The Voyage of the Mimi*), four pieces of microcomputer software, and print materials for engaging fourth through sixth graders in science and mathematics learning.

In designing software to support learning, the goal is to incorporate features that will increase the probability that desirable behaviors will occur. In the "raw" Logo environment, we found that the probabilities of observing desirable programming behaviors were relatively low—the environment did not optimally support novices in acquiring programming skills. We therefore wanted to devise an environment where such behaviors were more likely and were better supported. The findings from our research convinced us that some systematic support is needed for students in their first encounter with the programming environment. Identification of a developmental course and common "conceptual bugs" were central to the design effort (e.g., Pea & Kurland, 1984b).

Observations of students informed us that, for design purposes, *early* development of programming skill can be seen as proceeding through three general phases. At the outset, students use commands that have a one-to-one mapping with screen effects; they are able to see at once the effects of a command they have entered. For example, when FORWARD 10 is typed, the Logo turtle immediately moves forward 10 units. In the second phase, students begin to string together commands that have a one-to-one command/action relationship, but the execution of each command is delayed until a sequence has been completely entered (e.g., FD 10 RT 90 FD 10). At this point, students are writing simple programs, but the structure is completely linear and transparent—for any one command, there is one screen action and the instructions follow each other sequentially. If an action is to be repeated, the instruction is simply rewritten.

In the third phase, students begin to create nonlinear programs. This involves *commands that operate on other commands*, rather than themselves causing specific screen effects. Students now make use of operations upon operations in the programming environment. For example, they write conditional statements which direct the computer to perform contingent actions. The programming is no longer strictly linear, but begins to make use of concepts involving flow of control; that is, the program refers and transfers control to other parts of itself.

Of the students we observed in all three phases of programming over the course of a school year, only a few entered this third phase. Yet the kind of mental activity required by phase three is widely believed to promote desirable general cognitive effects.

Our design problem then became how to help more students reach phase three programming understanding. In the next section, we briefly describe the software that was developed, and discuss how key features were derived from the research and incorporated into the design.

DESIGNING PROGRAMMING SOFTWARE

A series of seven games ("Whale Search 1 and 2"; "Turtle Steps 1, 2, and 3"; "Doodle Mode" and "Superdoodle Mode") was designed to introduce children to fundamental programming concepts through Logo-like turtle graphics. Programming concepts were introduced sequentially, one per game. The games were designed to build on each other so that earlier concepts would be incorporated into and assumed in later games. Three different formats were used. In the first two games, children learn the basics of moving around the screen by constructing simple movement commands for an object (in this case, a "boat"). In the first game, players learn to move their boat around on the screen in order to rescue a whale trapped in a fishing net. The second game is based on the scientific practice of identifying individual humpback whales by matching photographs of a whale's fluke markings (the unique black-and-white patterns on the underside of each whale's tail) with catalogues of photographs from previous sightings of whales. Here, more precise movements are required: Players must move their boats close enough to a whale to take a "snapshot" of its flukes in order to identify it from a roster of whale tails. These two games were designed to give students practice in the basic movement commands in order to begin to write procedures in Logo.

In the second set of games ("Turtle Steps 1, 2, and 3") students begin to write programs to define an object's movement. In this case, students are writing commands and programs to move a turtle in different "dance" patterns around the screen. Repetitive patterns of dots appear in different places on the screen and the player must write procedures that allow the turtle to land on each of the spots in the pattern. As a player proceeds through the three games, it is to her advantage to reuse portions of code by writing and saving procedures, as well as to learn to use iteration commands. Learning these programming practices to construct turtle movements enables the player to win in fewer moves.

The third format ("Doodle Mode") is an open-ended sketch mode in which students can use any of the commands and techniques they have learned in the previous games to make their own patterns and drawings.

RESEARCH FINDINGS AND SOFTWARE DESIGN

Each game in the sequence emphasizes a different phase of early programming learning. "Whale Search 1 and 2" focus on phase 1 of programming, in which students practice precision of movement by matching commands to screen effects. "Turtle Steps 1" emphasizes phase 2, in which students begin to acquire skill in generating sequences of commands prior to execution. "Turtle Steps 2 and 3" focus on phase 3, in which students learn about programs and reusing code, as well as about commands that operate on other commands. The games were designed to support students in three dimensions of learning programming through

Logo: (a) increased precision of measurement and movement within the microworld; (b) ability to write increasingly complex programs; and (c) increased emphasis on the elegance and efficiency of programs. Selected features that were incorporated to support children's learning in each phase are described below.

Phase 1

In this phase, the design incorporated features to help students in their first encounter with Logo. Our earlier research findings indicate that the following types of support might help students with specific difficulties:

Measurement tools. We found that students had great difficulty in achieving desired screen effects because they could not accurately relate the numbers they typed for movement commands with the turtle's action (e.g., how far the turtle moves when you type FD 100). Many students got stuck at the level of simply getting an object to move in predictable ways, and this prevented them from moving on in programming learning. In order to help students master basic movement commands, we included two measuring tools in the games that players could request at any point: Distance and Angle. These tools allowed students to try out various movements while a digital counter recorded the amount of movement or degrees of turn. In this way, students were able accurately to measure their moves before constructing commands.

Forward and rotating sounds. We observed that students often fused rotational and movement commands (e.g., when typing RT 90, students expected the turtle to turn *and* move forward; some students believed FD 20 to be an acceptable command). Without a clear idea of what degrees were, young students used these commands inappropriately and failed to dissociate the two kinds of movement. One way of emphasizing the distinction was to use the two measuring tools described above, and for this reason they were implemented as two discrete menu choices. In addition, the movement of the object was slowed down and accompanied by two different noises as it either rotated or moved. By slowing down the movement and drawing attention to it through sound, students could observe the subtle effects of rotate commands as the turtle turned.

Functional context. We observed that many students had great difficulty defining goals for themselves when working with Logo. Presented with a blank screen and a few simple commands, many students did not know how to go beyond a random walk around the screen in this microworld. The game formats provided a functional context for learning precision of movement and programming concepts. For example, in "Whale Search," students position their turtle (or boat, in the context of the game) over small whale icons. While there is no penalty for using a large number of turns to position the boat correctly, a prompt appears informing the player about how many commands he or she needs to reach the whale. In "Turtle Steps," economy and efficiency of movement is supported by severely limiting the number of turns allowed per game. Specifically, there are fewer turns allowed than there are targets to land on. Therefore, to be successful in the game, players must move precisely *and* use the iterative and procedural components supported by the game environment. These formats provide motivational support and discourage the typing of random commands.

Cooperative work. Our studies in classrooms indicated that students tended to collaborate as they worked on Logo problems (cf. Hawkins, Chapter 1, this volume). We wanted to increase the likelihood that students would discuss their commands and be reflective about their plans for locating the whales. In addition, we wanted to begin to encourage the programming practice of sharing code, a common way of working among programming professionals (cf. Kurland, Mawby, & Cahir, 1984). Thus, in "Whale Search 2," a cooperative game component is introduced. Rather than playing against each other, two students must work together for a common score. Each player controls his or her own boat, but they must decide together how to take snapshots of all the whales on the screen in the fewest possible moves.

In "Turtle Steps 1," two players can work together on the same screen to land on the targets. As in "Whale Search," each controls his or her own turtle. In "Turtle Steps 2 and 3," each player still controls his or her own turtle, but any procedures either player creates goes into a common workplace (LIBRARY), where either player can then make use of them. The notion of a common or shared library of procedures not only introduces many interesting cooperative possibilities, it also focuses players' attention on the concept of a work space where procedures are stored until they are called for by a program. In our previous research, we found that children had a great deal of trouble with this notion.

Phase 2

For phase 2 learning, the design incorporated features to help students make the transition from direct mode to writing reusable procedures. We knew from observing students in classrooms that they initially, and sometime chronically, made little use of procedures in their work. For an expert programmer, procedures that divide up a programming problem into steps are an indispensable way of reusing code within and across programs and greatly increase the efficiency of producing complex programs. However, we found that students in early phases of learning seldom had a reason to develop problem-decomposition practices. Procedures were nonfunctional for the types of problems that they chose or were given (e.g., drawing a house). Students' programs were often so simple and local that building programs from multiple procedures increased the effort to get the desired effect. In the context of the classroom, we found that structured programming did not have the function it had for expert programmers. It was therefore necessary to provide a framework that would give students a reason to collect individual commands as reusable and combinable units. "Turtle Steps 1," designed to support the development of the notion that programs are collections of commands, allowed players to reuse blocks of previously written commands as a single turn.

In addition, present implementations of Logo do not support students' understanding of how a string of commands relates to order of execution and screen effects. Our research suggested that students do not conceptualize procedures in terms of their component commands; they must make a large conceptual step between writing one command and seeing its immediate effect, and writing a program in edit mode and seeing it executed simply by calling its name. Students may understand the individual commands that make up the procedure BOX (e.g, FD 100, RT 90). However, typing in the word BOX calls the previously written procedure from "storage," but students do not see the individual commands as the program is executed. This introduces an element of magic that works against understanding the relationship between code and effects. "Turtle Steps 1" was designed to support the conceptual transition from individual, immediately executed commands to procedures by taking a smaller conceptual step. The design preserves the relationship between individual commands and their effects, even when the program is in control of screen execution. The design of the interface for "Turtle Steps" sought to address these problems in several ways:

1. The program code and its effects on turtle movement were juxtaposed on the screen at all times. The screen consisted of a "dance floor" where turtle movements were executed, and a "window" which displayed at all times the code that the student had written.
2. Students' understanding of programs as collections of commands was supported by providing students with the REUSE option. Students could select portions of code, originally written as individual commands, and use them again as a whole unit. That is, students were encouraged to write sequences of single line code (each line of which was immediately executed) and then to collect this code into a larger unit (procedure) that was executed all at once.
3. When students elected to REUSE a sequence of previously entered commands, the execution of that proto-procedure was carried out by having an arrow indicator point to each line of code as it was executed. In this way, we hoped to help students see the relationship between the ele-

ments of the procedure and the screen effects. Students could also control the execution by freezing the movement (pressing the space bar) and examining the relationship of the turtle to the program that was controlling it. We wanted to encourage students to monitor at all times the correspondence between the turtle and the code that was controlling it, and thus, to remove the mystery from "opaque" procedures.

Phase 3

For phase 3 learning, the design incorporated features to help students master flow of control and iteration. Our observations have shown that students generally define a new procedure to get a specific and isolated screen effect, instead of building up a library of often-used procedures within and across programs. Design objectives for "Turtle Steps 2 and 3" were to encourage, support, and reward students for creating reusable procedures. In addition, we wanted to introduce students to the critical but difficult programming concept that commands can operate on other commands. This notion is a precursor to understanding control structures, conditionals, branching instructions, and a general grasp of flow of control in a program. Therefore, these games introduced the following features:

1. A sensible context for reusing procedures: Patterns of spots were repeated in different places and orientations on the dance floor. By creating a procedure in one location, students could efficiently reuse this procedure in different places, rather than having to waste moves by retyping sequences of commands.
2. A straightforward, prompted, and intuitively reasonable method for creating procedures: Students were asked to indicate which section of code they wanted to REUSE, and to name that procedure. The program was then stored in a LIBRARY that could be consulted at any time. Each procedure name and the code that composed it were immediately available to players.
3. Players were given a simple means of keeping track of procedures, and all procedures created by either player were accessible to both. This was intended to increase the utility of the procedures and the likelihood that students would reflect on and discuss their work.
4. A new command, REPEAT, was introduced, which at the simplest level acquainted the student with the notion that commands can operate on commands—in this case, through iteration. Players could instruct the turtle to move in a repetitive pattern by defining a movement sequence and specifying the number of times that sequence was to be repeated. Students could monitor the execution of this iteration by observing a digital "counter" that indicated which round the turtle was executing.
5. When a player used a stored procedure, the name of the procedure was written in the command box. In order to help students monitor command execution, the procedure expanded into its individual lines of code. Each command was pointed to by the indicator as the turtle moved. The proce-

dure "closed up" again to its name when its execution was completed. This was designed to focus students' attention on the fact that procedures are composed of individual commands *and* that the rules for execution within a procedure are identical to the rules for a sequence of individual commands. Thus, we intended to fortify the bridge between the behavior of a very simple command and the way that a sophisticated procedure with embedding is executed. This shifts the focus from a notion of the computer "knowing how" to do a procedure to demonstrating that the computer mechanically follows straightforward rules of program execution.

6. The scoring component of the game was closely linked to the efficient use of REUSE, REPEAT, and procedures stored in the LIBRARY. Students were encouraged to write component procedures and efficiently use them in order to complete all the dance steps in the minimum number of moves.

Programming Practices

Finally, in designing these games we were interested in encouraging students to develop good overall programming practices. Our research had shown that many students tended to do two things that impeded their learning to program effectively. First, they tended to string out long sequences of commands on a single line before having the commands executed. Procedures written in this style are frequently buggy and difficult to parse or read. Students would often erase a whole procedure and rewrite it rather than trying to discover where they went wrong. The second tendency, related to the first, was that students paid very little attention to error messages, primarily, it would seem, because they did not know how to interpret them (e.g., I DON'T KNOW HOW TO STOP AT LEVEL 2 OF BOX). Even the TRACE function in Logo was of little use, since students did not have a clear notion of Logo flow of control or the sequence in which commands and procedures should be executed. We sought to address both of these problems in our design of the programming interface.

Detailed error messages. We wished to create more detailed error messages that would be more helpful to students' present level of knowledge. Therefore, we designed messages that pinpointed the problem in the program as closely as possible, and coached students about what to do (e.g., "Put a space between command and number"). In addition, we wanted students to see that it made more sense (i.e., was more efficient) to fix bugs than to begin again. Thus, when a student received an error message, the cursor was automatically placed where the error occurred, and prompts at the top of the screen explained how to edit the command.

One command per line. Since few students were concerned with reusing code in their programs, they paid little attention to techniques that would make their programs more readable and comprehensible. Their

tendency to write "paragraphs" of code—continuous screens of commands that were difficult to decipher—decreased the probability of code
sharing between students. The editor developed for "Turtle Steps"
limited students to one command per line. Even when entering a series
of commands (e.g., following the REPEAT command), the editor automatically placed each command on its own line. When executed, the
code was automatically formatted and indented to make it maximally
readable.

Finally, our research suggested that there is a more general problem
for novice programming students. There are too many new things to
learn and keep track of in an open-ended programming environment:
editor commands, commands in the language, commands for filing and
retrieving work spaces or programs, relationships between commands,
rules for flow of control, and so on. Since our goal in these activities was
to focus students on the learning of programming *concepts*, we felt it was
important to minimize the cognitive load that was required to manipulate
the interface in writing programs. Thus, we relied heavily on explicit,
context-dependent screen prompts, on an elegant 3-command (type,
move, delete) editor, and on a very limited number of basic commands
and control structures.

CONCLUSION

Formative studies are important sources of information for design decisions. However, our work leads us to believe that the formative process
for the development of educational software needs to be informed by
more than strictly formative studies that assess student response and
understanding at various stages of implementation of design ideas.
First, understanding of the goals, tasks, and activities of participants in
the context of use for the software is essential. The perspective provided
by this sort of research about classrooms goes beyond what is ordinarily
meant by "needs assessment." Second, understanding the thinking processes involved in a particular domain such as programming provides
essential guidance for design of a software environment to support such
learning.

AUTHOR NOTES

The research reported here was supported by a grant from the Carnegie
Corporation and a contract from the U.S. Department of Education
(Contract No. 300-81-0375). The work of many people contributed to the
development of the ideas presented here. We would especially like to
thank Cynthia Char, Glen Clancy, Carla Freeman, Bernard Goodman,
Roy Pea, Doug Wedel, and the teachers and students in the classrooms
where we worked.

CHAPTER 15

PRACTICES OF NOVICES AND EXPERTS IN CRITICAL INQUIRY

Jan Hawkins, Ronald Mawby, and
Jane Marie Ghitman

THE CONTEXT OF CRITICAL INQUIRY

The availability of computer technology has begun to change the ways in which information is stored and used by people for many different purposes. More change is promised. In this chapter, we are concerned with the initial steps of a problem: How do we take advantage of features of the technology by designing software that will help students better to learn and practice inquiry into a problem, question, or body of information? We are concerned with supporting those processes that help people not only to find information, but to use it well. Designing supports for the complex processes involved in inquiry work must be influenced by deep understanding of the tasks themselves and how both experienced and inexperienced inquirers work.

In the first section, we briefly discuss the overall notion of an "information age" and the role of cognitive tools. In the next two sections, we describe two studies done prior to developing software, which give us information about (a) how individuals skilled in inquiry go about their work, and (b) how students (fifth-sixth, and eighth graders) carry out an inquiry task. The information helps us better to understand, and thus design, computer-based supports for good inquiry practices.

The Information Age

There has been much recent discussion about the massive and rapid increases in the quantity of information over the last century. For example, in 1865 there were only two journals for the recording of scientific information; today there are over 100,000. It may be easier to rediscover a fact than to find out if it has been described before in the vast array of scientific literature (Waddington, 1977).

There is increasing recognition that it is not simply the quantity of information that is changing, but also the ways in which information is made available and used (cf. Kochen, 1975; Office of Technology Assessment, 1982). The rapid expansion of new technologies based on computers is often cited as an engine for this information explosion. In addition, increasing recognition of the enormous complexity and interdependence of the world's problems (population, hunger, energy, nuclear proliferation) leads to the conclusion that new tools and new ways of thinking are necessary to grasp the relationships among the vast fields of information needed for even partial understanding in pursuit of reasonable actions (Hamburg, 1984).

> Modern society is undergoing profound technological and social changes brought about by what has been called the information revolution. This revolution is characterized by the explosive development in electronic information technologies and by their integration into complex information systems that span the globe. The impacts of this revolution affect individuals, institutions and governments—altering what they do, how they do it, and how they relate to one another. (Office of Technology Assessment, 1982)

Emphasis on information quantity as symptomatic of an information age has implications for associated revisions in the educational system. Such a concern tends to direct us to information access as a central educational goal. But appeal to massive changes in the quantity of information is not the only, nor perhaps the most intriguing, dimension for thinking about information technology in relation to development and education. The technology may make it possible to progress toward educational goals that have long been valued but difficult to achieve, such as skills of critical inquiry (cf. Duschl, 1985 and Cornbleth, 1985 on problems of practicing inquiry in science and social studies).

Cognitive Tools

By common assumption, tools are devices that amplify the powers of people. Grounded in the image of inventions that extend or enable physical skills, such as hammers and rakes (Morris, 1969), the concept of tool has also been applied to the arena of the mind. Some psychologists have selected this metaphor as a vehicle for describing the interaction between mind and world that characterizes developmental processes (e.g., Bruner, 1966b; Olson, 1974; Vygotsky, 1978). The symbol system of natural language is often cited as the first-encountered and most powerful cognitive tool. With it the possibilities for communication and representation of reality greatly expand. Language is particularly well suited to such cognitive accomplishments as the representation of past and present events, and the ability to reflect hypothetically about action. Likewise, mathematics and formal logic (Davis & Hersh, 1980; Kneale & Kneale, 1962), iconic representation (Olson, 1974; Salomon, 1974), and heuristics for problem solving (Polya, 1957) can be described as tools for the amplification of cognitive capacities.

Emphasis on particular symbol systems and accompanying technologies varies over time and cultures (Cole & Scribner, 1978; Luria, 1976). For example, there has been considerable attention given to the effect of written language on cognitive abilities. It has been argued that codifying spoken language in a written symbol system relieves the burden on memory and can change the possibilities for discourse in a culture (cf. Goody, 1977; Olson, 1977; Ong, 1982; Pea & Kurland, in press). The written system supports a new way of using the symbols of language, leading to increased explicitness. With these tools, people can construct fundamentally different forms of communication than they can in oral cultures.

Invention of the printing press also had a profound impact (Eisenstein, 1979), expanding the audience for written language and further supporting the tendency toward autonomous, explicit rendering of meaning in text. There has been increasing interest lately in the effects of computerized word processing on writing skill (Bereiter & Scardamalia, 1984; Kurland, 1984; Pea & Kurland, in press). The development of writing technologies illustrates how historical changes in the ability to manipulate verbal symbols changed the relationship between internal and external sources of information, the cognitive tasks that are common practices for various cultures, and the ways in which different kinds of mental skills are emphasized (Scribner & Cole, 1981). The values and practices of the culture determine the definition of literacy—what one has to know to be considered literate at particular locations and times (Resnick & Resnick, 1977)—and, concomitantly, the goals and practices of education. The forms of knowing elicited by written text are often considered the dominant mode of learning in school. Text-based knowledge and those skills required to extract meaning from or construct texts and other written symbolic forms have become central goals of our educational system (Olson, 1977).

Similar arguments have been made about the relationship among symbol systems of formal logic and mathematics, the technologies that have been developed to manipulate them (e.g., the abacus, the slide rule, the calculator, symbol manipulation programs such as muMath), and mental abilities:

> The principal functions of a symbol in mathematics are to designate with precision and clarity and to abbreviate. The reward is that, as Alfred North Whitehead put it, ''by relieving the brain of all unnecessary work, a good notation sets it free to concentrate on more advanced problems, and, in effect, increases the mental powers of the race.'' (Davis & Hersh, 1980, p. 124)

Computers as Cognitive Tools

Computers can be described as universal symbolic machines. Software provides ways of manipulating basic symbol systems (mathematics, programming languages, written language) and representational forms (graphics, color, music). People can manipulate relationships among elements in symbol systems in ways that are orders of magnitude both faster and qualitatively different from what was possible before. For example, research chemists can use an intelligent simulation program to explore the properties of new molecules. Through the 3-dimensional representation available in the program, scientists can rotate the molecules and "see" relationships in new ways. A music composition tool allows children and adults—even nonmusicians—to compose pieces in order to study the structural properties of music. Computers are not simply machines that store and organize information; they are tools for amplifying capacities to create and explore the relationships in a body of information.

To be effective, such tools must be adapted to the particular work environment and to the capacities of the users to understand and make use of their power. Thus far, business and the communications industry have taken the lead in shaping the symbolic powers of computers to their work and making these tools available to aid noncomputer specialists. Such a process integrates the desirable features of the tools with the functional requirements of the setting. The incorporation of effective software can, reciprocally, have the impact of changing and expanding the ways in which people conceptualize a variety of tasks (Pea, 1985). Writing tools, for example, can free writers to compose in nonlinear ways (J.S. Brown, 1984a) as well as to place much greater emphasis on editing.

Critical Inquiry as Problem Solving

Critical inquiry, as we define it, is active development of a question or problem, and exploration of information in order to find an answer or develop a connected, meaningful perspective. It involves information management, since the material must be located and selected from various sources, but it goes beyond mere retrieval to refinement of questions and organization and evaluation of information for a purpose. Previous assumptions are critically examined in this process. Appropriately designed computer technology may well be an effective means of supporting the very development of these skills.

Skill in critical inquiry has long been a concern of educators and scholars (cf. Dewey, 1933; Whitehead, 1929). These skills are recognized as essential to philosophical studies (Russell, 1959) and scientific thought (Toulmin, 1972, 1982). In an information age they are especially important for all citizens—for making thoughtful and informed decisions about everyday aspects of their lives, and about the issues that confront them as members of a complex society (e.g., whom to vote for, issues of nuclear proliferation, depletion of resources). As analysts of the current educational situation point out:

> Literacy means more than simply decoding words. It means the ability to comprehend and understand ideas and arguments to a degree that allows an individual to use them. Literacy implies clear thought; that is, one must read easily and sensitively enough to comprehend at least the basic arguments presented by contemporary political and social life; without that ability and the correlative ability to present such arguments oneself orally and in clear writing, a citizen cannot fully participate in a democracy. Any community that expects collective, affirmative government requires a literate citizenry. (Sizer, 1984)
>
> * * * * *
>
> Competency in reading, for example, may well include not only the ability to literally decipher a simple written passage, but other skills as well: the ability to analyze and summarize...and the ability to interpret passages inferentially as well as literally....Competency in writing may well comprise not just the ability to write a sentence or paragraph, but the ability to gather and organize information coherently. (Task Force on Education for Economic Growth, 1983)

Critical inquiry skills are close kin to what has been described as reflective thinking—the ability to stand back from a topic or problem and reflect on it from a variety of perspectives. Students need to learn how to organize and evaluate information critically from a position that allows them to question the ways in which the issue has been seen before.

While most school tasks are well defined, many of the most pervasive problems encountered outside of school are ill defined (Simon, 1977a). Ill-defined problems are those whose exact nature must be identified as part of the problem-solving process. For example, in researching and writing a report on "The Middle East," students become aware that there are many political and economic factors at work. To develop a coherent report, they must clearly identify what some of the problems are. Critical inquiry involves even more than finding, evaluating, and piecing together information; it requires clarifying the question or problem. As one writer says about reflective inquiry:

> Reflection...is a purposeful movement whose end is understanding. And to understand something means to place it in the context of a system. If one is confronted with a general topic, then the first thing to do is to resolve it into a question, or perhaps a series of questions. The reason is that answering questions is what thought *is* in its very essence; it springs from them; it is guided by them; unless they light the way, it is lost in the dark....If one is to think to the point, one must usually specify the problem into something far more definite than its first form. A question is an attempt by a system of ideas to mend a hole in its own fabric. (Blanshard, 1939)

Process of Inquiry

There is a long tradition of research and practice which demonstrates that skills of inquiry are complex to learn, and are commonly not well taught in classrooms (cf. Cornbleth, 1985; Resnick, 1985). A number of programs have been developed to teach critical thinking (e.g., Philosophy for Children; CORT), but thus far evaluation of their effectiveness has been meager (Bransford, Stein, Arbitman-Smith, & Vye, 1985). One of the most promising research projects focusing on the development of critical reading skills (a component of effective inquiry) has involved students in a process of reciprocal teaching. Critical reading skills are modelled for students, and students are encouraged to question the text effectively (Palincsar & Brown, 1984). Likewise, Bransford et al. (1985) demonstrate that critical questioning and active inference-making differentiate skilled from unskilled readers. Providing support for making inferences from texts improves the performance of poor students.

A variety of cognitive and developmental studies, while not directly concerned with critical inquiry performance as a goal, provide information about the development of component processes and offer possibilities for designing supports for novices. From a Vygotskian perspective, such supports might "scaffold" students in appropriate places to enable them to carry out the whole task. Inquiry tasks are complex (e.g., Rowe, 1973; Suchman, 1962), requiring the ability to identify problems; parse problems and develop plans; comprehend, select, and organize qualitative and quantitative information; and develop methods for testing ideas. A variety of research efforts suggests that particular attention be paid to at least three areas of support needed for the complex activity of critical inquiry: (a) finding and representing problems effectively; (b) managing the parts of inquiry tasks; and (c) selecting and organizing appropriate information. Each of these areas will be illustrated briefly by a small selection of studies.

Problem definition. Studies have shown that novices have difficulty in representing problems effectively; that is, understanding how to identify a problem and how to parse it so that progress can be made. A variety of investigators have examined the features of efficient problem solving in science and mathematics (e.g., Greeno, 1980; Greeno, Glaser, & Newell, 1983; Simon, 1982; Tuma & Reif, 1980). It appears that an important part of the problem-solving process for skilled individuals is the representation of the problem in a way that allows efficient application of prior knowledge and strategies. For instance, skilled individuals will often divide a problem into subcomponents to be approached separately (Larkin, McDermott, Simon, & Simon, 1980; Smith & Bruce, 1981); ill-structured problems can be handled by dividing them into smaller, well-structured ones (Simon, 1973). Experts may also proceed by successive refinement of the problem, planning at various levels.

Skilled individuals also appear to make use of their prior framework of knowledge for establishing a problem representation (see Voss, Greene, Post, & Penner, 1983), and for evaluation of the relevance and utility of new information. Bransford et al. (1985) report that successful students realize that they need new information through clarifying a problem situation. Markman (1977) finds that children can locate required information in a text if they are alerted to its necessity at the outset. Skilled readers may represent a problem by setting up a hierarchy of information to guide them as they read. Rieger (1977), for example, hypothesizes cognitive "watchers"—indicators that are mentally instantiated at the outset of a problem-solving episode and are "checked off" when the appropriate information is encountered.

Managing inquiry. Students ordinarily cannot manage all the parts of inquiry work without support. It has been repeatedly demonstrated for a range of problems that novices have trouble organizing their work on the subcomponents of a problem, keeping track of information and intermediate results (generated during their work), and remembering when to apply strategies or use information (e.g., Gick & Holyoak, 1980; Paris, Scardamalia, & Bereiter, 1984; Smith & Bruce, 1981). Limits on processing capacity can lead to accumulation of errors over the course of a problem-solving episode (Resnick, 1981). In previous research (Hawkins, Char, & Freeman, 1984), we found that students knew little about the parts of an inquiry task or how to coordinate information from one part of the task with another. A variety of studies have shown that certain types of external cues or supports can help students to accomplish tasks.

Schoenfeld (1983), working with geometry problems, has shown that students have difficulty knowing where they are when working on a problem; explicit structures for monitoring location in a problem-solving episode enable students better to stay on task. Likewise, research on writing processes and the learning of study skills demonstrates that temporary external supports, such as prompts or sequenced questions, help to sustain complex executive processes (Dansereau et al., 1979; Scardamalia & Bereiter, 1984).

Information manipulation. Studies have shown that experts know how to select and manipulate information for the problem at hand: selecting useful material, making appropriate inferences, and organizing relationships for a problem (e.g., Voss et al., 1983). Novices have difficulty with each of these inquiry subtasks (e.g., Collins, Gentner, & Rubin,

1982). Research has demonstrated that students have difficulty in identifying structure in texts and remembering relationships (e.g., A.L. Brown, 1982; Scardamalia & Bereiter, 1984). A number of intervention studies argue that students require techniques for helping them to make explicit the relationships among pieces of information (e.g., Bereiter & Scardamalia, 1984; Collins, Gentner, & Rubin, 1981; Pressley & Forrest-Pressley, 1985).

Limitations. These studies inform us about general issues to attend to as students attempt to solve complex problems. The conclusions are drawn from evidence about a range of problems, but most commonly well-formed problems in mathematics or science, or studies of reading that use single texts. Design of support for the complex processes of inquiry, however, must be informed by further investigation of inquiry tasks themselves and how experts and novices go about this work. We were particularly interested in how people develop problems and how multiple information sources are used. We therefore conducted two preliminary studies to better inform us about the way these tasks can be carried out.

OVERVIEW OF STUDIES

We set out to understand more about inquiry practices. Two studies, one with expert adults and one with young novice student inquirers, were conducted to examine how inquiry is conceived and carried out by experts, and about what fifth-sixth and eighth grade students do when confronted with an inquiry task. The studies were intended to be the basis for further research, and to provide information that would contribute to the development of software and other cognitive tools for supporting the processes and development of inquiry skills.

We wanted first to know how experts in inquiry think about and report their work: What processes do they use? What are their tools and their training? At this early point in the work, we set out to find a range of experts, to sample professions that require their practitioners to carry out problem definition, information gathering, and organization/synthesis of information. We identified individuals in a number of professions where inquiry is a key component, and conducted in-depth clinical interviews.

STUDY 1: INTERVIEWS WITH EXPERT INQUIRERS

In this study, we set out to explore the procedures that experts use to develop questions and problems, and to find, organize, and synthesize information. We also wanted to explore their perspectives on this type of work as part of their professional lives: their definition and analyses of components; salient features of practice; their training. We were interested in how this activity is characterized by people of considerable experience, as a long-term goal for student development, and in the variability across individuals. Research on writing, for example, makes clear that expert writers differ significantly from novices and from each other in how they organize their writing activity (see Pea & Kurland, in press), yet there are commonalities in the procedures that make up their craft. Similarly, we assume that when experts conduct inquiry, different individuals prefer different techniques and strategies.

Method

Ten experts representing several professions were selected to participate. A search was conducted for individuals who represented different content areas and problem types, including social science, history and economics, policy research, science, research psychology, college teaching, journalism, and archaeology.

An interview guideline was developed to probe experts' perceptions and definitions of tasks, the specific procedures and tools they used, and how they reported the development of their inquiry skills. We found that one of the most effective means for eliciting the information was to ask people to describe and analyze a particular, recent project they had done. John-Steiner (1985) also found that asking people to respond to specific characterizations of creative work was the best means for eliciting their reflections about their creative processes—her object of study.

Since this was designed to be an exploratory investigation, the material was analyzed qualitatively for important themes, for the range of procedures used, and for information relevant to choosing alternatives in the design of a computer-based tool. The results of these interviews are summarized here in terms of eight pervasive themes.

Orienting Perspective and Motivation

Many of the experts discussed distinctions between problems that engaged their interest, and problems that they were required by circumstance to work on but felt little personal motivation to address (e.g., dissertations, assigned professional work). For example, one individual described his dissertation as a rigid exercise in methodology that allowed no flexibility for redefinition of the problem: "So I got lost in the mountain of data, and I was very happy when I lost half of it on a train." Where there was little personal motivation, people reported either avoiding work on the problem ("That one sat around for years because nobody knew what to do with it"), or figuring out ways to transform the problem into something interesting. For example, one person reported that he could usually get himself interested by thinking about his role as one of clarifying the alternative arguments for other people (Congress) who would have to make use of the information.

In contrast, when people spoke about work on problems of personal interest, the dialogue had energy and eloquence. One woman spoke about her current work on the political situation in Nicaragua as framed by larger historical questions of the effects of American foreign policy: For her, the "small" questions she was addressing fit clearly into issues that were passionately engaging. A theme that ran through the discussion of motivating problems was the notion that work on these problems began with one's "own thinking"—that the work started with one's own ideas and then progressed outward to the literature and to experts in the area. The motivation to build one's own framework of understanding (which was expected to be structured and restructured with learning) in the attempt to build a comprehensive picture was apparent for all of these experts: "It's getting hold of it, and seeing it evolve, putting the pieces of fruit in a basket, and suddenly realizing that you've got something, something that has integrity."

For some, the enterprise had to do with a sense of ownership—not simply of the work, but of the issues addressed in the problem:

> If you don't have a reason to do it, there's not motivation. That's one of my biggest problems with schools. I've felt that so much of my life I've been pushed around. That's my point for wanting motivation, it makes me feel that I'm a part of something, and that's terribly important for feeling good about myself.

The Development of Questions and Problems

People described the finding and development of questions or problems as a major and intense part of the research process; this was talked about in both analytic and intense emotional terms. Analytically, all the experts described question development as a recursive process, a finding that coincides with theoretical accounts of the logic of the natural history of questions (Rescher, 1982) and problem posing (Collingwood, 1939). One may begin with a specific question or a vague idea of a topic or an area, but inevitably this original idea will be modified—often severely— as the research proceeds. The revisionary process was described as both anticipated and exciting:

> Questions have to be continually reformulated on the basis of results that you're getting from your research so that you can look differently and more closely at what you're getting. You begin to pose questions to the material in front of you.

> * * * * *

> So you shift, you can't just tack it on. It requires a reorganization of everything. This is not like stringing beads.

Most people spoke about the struggle with and the anxiety of the initial question-posing phase of the research. While reporting that embarking on a new adventure with a new research problem could be exciting and invigorating, many also found that the uncertainty and lack of control of a topic brought anxiety, which disappeared only gradually as the problem was mastered:

> It's the worst and best part of the research, long term, that you end up with the questions you wish you started with. It's the hardest part, formulating the beginning questions, right at the start.
>
> *   *   *   *   *
>
> When I start, all I have is an inkling that something is interesting, and that my judgment then is perfectly awful. But there's no other way.
>
> *   *   *   *   *
>
> The less well stated a problem is at the start, the easier it is to rethink. But at the beginning I'm scared, anxious. I focus on the details to make sure I don't miss anything.

There was a variety of means available to people to help them with the initial problems of formulation. Some experts, particularly those whose jobs required them to investigate areas different from their content expertise, brought a general framework to guide them at the outset. For example, one person assigned to investigate industrial use of energy resources was particularly concerned with problems of the use of human resources. This perspective provided a way into the research area for him. Another reported that his overall values about the organization of society helped him at the start of an inquiry:

> If the values of society shifted in an irreversible way, I'd like to understand that before they shift rather than afterwards say, ''Too bad about that.'' So that guides what I take a look at—values, those things I see as genuinely lost if we don't first understand; but money as the guiding concern—no.

Initial structuring of an inquiry field was also reported to be guided by social factors, such as the needs of the audience for the research, or the kinds of investigations that others in the area were doing; for example: ''People are always looking for holes, little gaps, but framing the question is different, is really the hardest. That so much research is *just* built on other research is an indication of this.'' This issue of social factors in inquiry work is discussed in a subsequent section.

Experts reported that they began by putting together an initial map, grid, outline, bits and pieces of a structure, major actors so they could make a judgment from a thought platform about where to begin, all the while knowing that in the end it wouldn't be the best one for their purpose. There is a tension, made explicit by a few, between leaving options open and uncertain, and making selections about how to direct the investigation. Some described the anxiety-provoking necessity of allowing new connections to form, using metaphors, borrowing ideas or strategies from other fields:

> You have to find something else that would relate, that would make this investigation possible, that allows you to see this in a new way.
>
> *   *   *   *   *
>
> You need to overcome the rigidity of how it's been seen before by assuming there are new connections among things. There is pressure to go out and get the data quickly, and this operates as an inhibitor on creative activity. It's important to extend ideas to new domains, without any assurance that one is correct, since that is not the issue.

Process, Tools, Procedures

Experts' discussion of the processes by which they conducted inquiry included the overall characteristics of the process, the tools they used for organizing, and the techniques by which they extended their thinking.

Overall process. To experts the overall inquiry process was most frequently discussed as consisting of parts or stages. The framework of parts appeared to provide benchmarks about where they were in the work. Following the initial question-development phase, people intensively collect information into some structural "body," perhaps writing a rough draft of the ideas—the "so-what?" phase, as someone called it. Then there is the critique or "throwing out" phase.

The discussion of parts or phases of the process was permeated by perceptions of its cyclical quality. Information collection always helps to redefine questions; critiques of organizing ideas by self or others often lead to collection of new information. One expert described notetaking as cyclical, consisting of several passes:

> At the beginning, you read through stuff and take fuller notes because you don't know what you're going to use. Then, when you know what you're doing, you get more efficient. You take notes seriously, you have insights into where you're going, why this paper is important. You reread something in light of something else you've seen. You also take signpost notes—what's fact, what's opinion, what's your idea, what's their idea.

Some experts find it difficult to decide on the final organization of an inquiry; there may be two or more ways in which it makes sense to organize the information, and difficult-to-conceptualize tradeoffs may be involved. Each must be experimented with, and sometimes a hard choice made. For instance, one historian reported that he had to decide whether to present an argument by ordering the evidence chronologically or by region; each had different consequences for the argument.

> You write something down and look at it yourself and try to convince yourself that you have some essence. And usually you don't the first time, and so you end up going out to get some more information and getting criticism.

Tools for organizing. People reported that they used a variety of tools to help them in organizing inquiry. Several said that note cards were central to their process of information collection—each source or idea written on a separate card and cross referenced. The cards could then be sorted or laid out in spatial arrays in the organizing phase. Others reported that outlines were their preferred framework: "I want to see an outline developing in my head as I go along." Still others used lists for information that were one dimensional, and charts to represent relationships in two or more dimensions. Finally, some reported that diagrams using different shapes, colors, directional arrows, and hierarchical relationships most easily allowed them to organize their information.

Several expert inquirers pointed to the need to collect and order different types of information as they worked (e.g., bibliographic information must be collected in a separate file). Two who frequently worked with numerical data reported that they collected them on a single page and then looked at the numbers. Their goal was twofold: to find meaningful patterns, and to find ways to simplify the data so that others would be able to understand.

Other individuals reported that they began by putting down all their ideas as they occurred, and then found the order afterwards:

> What I have to do, and maybe everybody's different, is put everything down at once, and I know it's going to be all wrong, but it's just that I need to talk about it. Then I start putting it in order.

This person drew lines between ideas, but "the hardest part is figuring out what is the subset of what—the underwhat."

Several experts found that word processors had become important tools in their work. One described this software as useful for "unburdening" his ideas, which could then be readily examined and edited. Word processors appeared to be most useful at the stage of inquiry when people were ready to write down ideas about the organization of information and initial passes at solution in a free-form and unedited way.

Techniques for extending thinking. Several experts reported that they used dialectical techniques to develop their arguments, to find holes in their information and thinking. Some exaggerated a developing argument and pushed it to the extreme to see how far it would hold: "It comes from my math background. I test propositions by hyperbole, see if they are true in the far state." Collins and Stevens (1982) have reported that similar rhetorical moves are used by inquiry teachers in a variety of disciplines. Others constructed an argument or solution, and then switched roles to argue against it or for an alternative. Another technique was to apply decision-making procedures: "I list every known factor that might influence a situation, and I require myself to weigh the factors. Then I need to decide whether or not I have nerve enough to bet on a conclusion.'' One man reported that he posed himself the challenge of constructing rules for his data; attempts to articulate the rules helped him to see what he didn't understand.

Respect for Resources

People described the need to immerse themselves in the resources or data that provided facts and alternative viewpoints about the area they were investigating. Resources were viewed by different individuals in the following terms: levels, from the broadest to narrowest; primary versus secondary or raw versus interpreted; critical assessment. With respect to levels, a few experts pointed out the importance of recognizing the kind of information that was relevant to answering different categories of questions. Taking economics as an example, someone might want to understand a general theoretical proposition—why capital needs to expand. At a second level, someone might want to know what world factors affected a particular foreign policy decision, like entering World War II. At a still lower level, one might want to know the specific local and psychological factors affecting the decision of a president to veto a specific bill. Different kinds of resources and arguments are necessary for questions at each of these levels, and in order to build arguments one needs to learn how to use information from the various levels.

All experts mentioned distinctions between primary and secondary sources, or raw and interpreted data. They preferred to have access to both types: peoples' interpretations and the source materials that were used to construct the interpretations. It is important to understand how others have argued and drawn conclusions about a problem, but it is also essential to respect and preserve the ''raw'' information. In the case of a social scientist, this might be the numerical results of an experiment or a full bibliography: ''I look at their bibliography to see their sources, to see what their world view is''; in the case of an archaeologist, this might be careful recording of the inscription on an artifact. All felt that it was essential to have access to the information from which other workers had derived their conclusions in order to draw their own, and to examine the assumptions underlying another's analysis.

The respect for raw sources went hand in hand with a discussion about the nature of the critical activity involved in examining information. Information search involves not just accumulating information, but evaluating it:

> It is not a bad idea to make your criteria explicit about what is good information and what is shoddy. You examine the information that way, and make your own biases explicit. You might also realize a detour you need to make because you don't know enough to evaluate something.

Critical examination of information allowed inquirers not only to question previous conclusions, but to move in new directions:

> Consulting literature can be done with a lack of intelligence that is beyond belief, if you don't know how to pursue. You need to learn that you may not know where the hell something leads, but you need to follow up that lead.

While engaged in the process of developing their own interpretations, some experts acknowledged that careful probing of the literature often revealed that an idea had been developed by previous scholars:

> You read as much as you can—get general perspectives. Because one thing you find out is that generally there's nothing new under the sun. I've found with every aspect of my research that whatever neat thing we find out now, at least the suggestion of it was made before 1906. It's truly great!

This individual described himself as a great respecter of careful scholarship, wide reading, and painstaking development of comprehensive bibliographies.

Some experts also recognized the burden placed on them as interpreters of information for others. Critically aware of how necessary it is to question assumptions and massage data, they felt it necessary to present data to their audience as simply and accurately as possible and to consider carefully the presentation of their own conclusions:

> We are living in a time of enormous respect for numbers. What I realize I am trying to do in my work is explain uncertainty, and we can never be certain. I often see a lack of understanding of what numbers mean, and an intense desire to use them, to use them against uncertainty.

Social Aspects

Frequently embedded in the talk of experts about their inquiry was their awareness of its social aspects. "It's an interactive process, that's for sure." The social nature of the work took several forms. Some experts began their problem-development phase of work by identifying major figures in an area and consulting with them: "People are collections of wisdom." This was generally done by those inquirers who were working in a new area, one outside their personal content expertise. Some working within their own domain reported that one efficient way of thinking about a new problem was to identify those individuals who had points of view about the issue, and build a conceptual map of the area based on this knowledge: "Experts know not just all the research, but all the names and faces to associate with it. This way gives you more rich access points to the information, makes it easier to grasp." Thus, one useful way of conceptually organizing an area is through the complex "chunks" associated with the points of view of different people working in the area. In addition, talking to another person involved in a similar problem was often reported to yield a fresh perspective much more quickly and effectively than would solo pursuit of the print literature: "Another person can convince you that they see the problem in a different way—it's the old light bulb."

Experts reported that inquiry work often involved expanding their own problem-solving capacities by putting together a collaborative group. Some reported that they "networked experts" who helped to define questions and problems, served as information resources, and offered critical maps of existing literature. Others reported that they selected individuals with different kinds of expertise to help with the inquiry (e.g., scientists, economists, educators). These diverse individuals efficiently brought different bodies of knowledge and strategies to an inquiry situation: "I like mixing it up with people of all sorts, bouncing off their speciality. It helps me to arrive at the big picture."

For some experts, other people also served as representatives for different stages of the problem-solving process. For example, one noted that he always tried to have a content expert and a journalist on his research team. The content specialist pressed to keep the problem open, to accumulate more information, whereas the journalist brought the opposite pressure—to organize the information and arrive at closure. Another believed that inquiry work required the interplay of creativity and analysis, alternatively opening up a problem to the imagination and constraining what was there. This expert believed himself to be good at the analytic part, but felt he needed a colleague to carry out the creative aspect of the work. In his projects, he always sought to include someone who could play what he perceived to be the creative role.

Audience

Inquiry experts keep a constant eye on audience considerations. Interest in organizing the work for effective communication was discussed in two distinct ways. The professional lives of some of the inquirers were oriented toward understanding a problem area and presenting information to an audience who could use it as a basis for action: "I need to make the work analytically sound, to back conclusions with solid information. I need to ask whether it is important to the nation." The inquiry process of these experts was thus influenced by the need of this audience for particular types of information, and for clear direct presentation and effective argument: "As I develop the questions, I am always thinking about the needs of my audience."

Other experts believed that it was important to conduct and present their work in a way that also made it accessible to such people as students and lay audiences. The issue of making information available was a background feature of their work process: "I refuse to accept that just a few people should be able to think about these questions." One expert pointed out that the nature of the inquiry work was implicitly communicative: "Except in math, everything involves argument because the premises are always in dispute. You are trying to get people to understand and adhere to your theses." One of the experts believed that an essential feature of his work was to communicate with the public about the findings of his science—both his own research and that of others— Because without that "it becomes an intellectual back-scratching affair that doesn't help anybody."

Finishing

When is an inquiry project finished? People talked about the problem of closure in their work. Most indicated that they never reached a point when they felt that the work was done; they simply had to decide that it was over, or that for the present they could do nothing more productive on the problem. As noted above, one expert reported that he liked to include a "closer" in his working group—an individual who would press for conclusion. Others talked about externally imposed deadlines such as publication schedules. These were seen as artificial but effective markers for ending the inquiry process.

Some poeple, while not concluding that they had fully solved the problem, reported that they had gotten as far as they could at the closure point, but might pick up the problem again in the future. Others believed they were heading for closure when the "big picture" began to solidify: "You get to the point when you can write things and have them come out in order without really struggling because it's already organized in your head." For some people, reaching this point with a problem could take years; others reported that they had to decide that no more could be added, that they had to come to terms with finishing: "If you're going to finish, you have to figure out what sort of questions you will find unsolvable and leave it at that."

Teaching Inquiry

Different people emphasized different things when asked what they saw as essential to inquiry training for students in schools. One highlighted the problem of uncertainty: Students should work with problems and issues, make judgments about things that have no certain solution. He believed that students should be trained to "calibrate their judgments" early in their education by dealing with problems that don't have certain/single answers: "I can give you a probably right answer, but I can't give you a certain answer. And the real problems of the world are never certain."

Other people highlighted the importance of teaching skills of finding information and evaluating it: "That's the main thing education should do, not teach them facts, but where to find them." Students should also be taught that they can be critical of information, and to examine what they uncover from various ponts of view. Skill in role-playing arguments was emphasized. Students need to be taught to be advocates, to practice arguing on one side and then the other in order to fully understand different perspectives on a problem. One expert noted the lack of training in how to develop "chains of evidence" in school. Students need to be explicit about the components of their inquiry: "How do you support something, what are your arguments, what are your sources, and how do you know if you are right or not?" The indiscriminate use of sources was noted as a major problem among both adults and children: "There is, somehow, the myth that if it's published it's true."

One expert pointed out the importance of failure, particularly when beginning work in a new area. Students should be encouraged to explore new territory: "Teach a kid not to be embarrassed, because they are going to make some stupendous mistakes. Great! Kids only see information in textbooks, not why something matters." And finally, one person pointed to the need to recognize one's connection to and place in the history of knowledge:

> Then you sit back and realize that if you're lucky, 80% of what you devote your career to will be okay, because it would be supreme arrogance to think that this generation, of all generations that ever lived, will be found to be right.

This interview material helped us to conduct the second study, in which we were concerned with how inexperienced individuals do inquiry work.

STUDY 2: CHILDREN'S STRATEGIES
IN AN INQUIRY TASK

In a second study, we designed a text-based inquiry task, using multiple information sources, to analyze the skills and strategies of fifth-sixth and eighth grade students as they solved the problems we posed. We conclude with a discussion of the implications of this exploratory work for the design of computer-based tools for supporting critical inquiry.

Students were posed a task in which they were presented with a problem, and four different short texts containing information useful for finding a solution to the problem. The problem had more than one possible outcome, and the information in the texts could be used to support alternative arguments. We were interested in how students used the information from the different types of documents: their strategies for notetaking, relating and organizing the information, and what information was selected.

Method

Participants. Students from two eighth grade classrooms and two mixed fifth-sixth grade classrooms took part in the study. The school is ethnically mixed and draws most of its students from the families of middle- and upper-middle-class professionals. There were 40 fifth-sixth grade students (20 boys; 20 girls), and 27 eighth grade students (14 boys; 13 girls).

Materials. Students were given, as source materials for their work, four documents which described the situation of a fictitious island nation called Tallyland. The task was introduced by telling students that they had been sailing around the world and had landed on Tallyland to repair storm-damaged sails. They were told that Tallyland was peopled by members of a traditional society that did not have enough food for its expanding population. The leader had recently died and the people were hungry, confused, and divided about whether to change some of their traditional ways of doing things. The task of each student was to provide counsel about how to solve the food shortage and overpopulation problems.

In order for them to offer informed advice, students were given four documents relating to the situation in Tallyland: (a) a speech by a village elder advocating and arguing for traditional practices; (b) a letter written by a young mother in response to the elder's speech recommending new techniques such as those used with great success by a neighboring island; (c) a fictitious report to the United Nations on farming methods and population control in different types of traditional societies; and (d) an invented encyclopedia article describing the history, people, land, climate, and agriculture of Tallyland. The texts of documents (c) and (d) were accompanied by graphs.

The documents were designed to be of different formats (report-like presentation of "facts," and persuasive) and to include information both relevant and irrelevant to the problem at hand. For example, the encyclopedia article included information about farming methods and foreign trade, which was relevant, as well as information about the land forms in the mountains, which was not. Documents also contained some mutually supporting information, as well as conflicting information (depending on the point of view of the writer). Students were given a set of pages that were blank except for the label "Notes" at the top, and a page labelled "Organization" on which to organize the information in support of a solution.

Procedures. Students were told that they were participating in a study of the inquiry process—what they do when they write research reports. The usual steps in the process were described as finding information, reading, taking notes, organizing the information, and writing an essay. Students were told that they did not have to write the essay, but to do all the other steps and decide what advice to give the Tallylanders. Pilot testing had shown that students were very product-oriented, and had difficulty in grasping our interest in only the intermediate products that lead up to an essay; their tendency was simply to write the essay. Our final instructions avoided this difficulty. Students were given an hour to do the task, and all were able to finish within this time.

Results

Students' written productions were analyzed for the procedures they used in taking notes and organizing the information. We also examined the content of the material they chose to record. We first identified the range of strategies exhibited by examining and comparing each student's notes. The resulting list of procedures provided a basis for coding the work. The notes of each student were then reexamined and coded accordingly. Strategies used on the organizing page were likewise identified and coded.

For the content analysis of the information selected by the students, each document was first parsed into individual information "units." The units constituted a list of each new item of information as it was accrued in sentences or parts of sentences in each document. For example, in the village elder's speech, four units are used to describe his view of the importance of families: (a) children are our strength; (b) families are large; (c) the spirit of families is strong; and (d) families are key to survival. The list of information units presented in each document was used to analyze the content of each student's notes. Their productions were coded for the presence or absence of each unit.

Notetaking evidence. Nine different strategies could be distinguished in the students' work. However, 80% used one of three alternatives: (a) a list of points, clearly separated by source document; (b) a list of points mixed up by source; and (c) a mixture of information from documents and students' own ideas.[1]

Older students favored procedures (a) and (c), while younger students more frequently made use of (b). The children in one fifth-sixth grade favored (b) (47.4%) or (c) (36.8%). No children in this class used

---

[1] The other six infrequently used strategies included: (a) outline of dilemma; (b) list of own ideas; (c) essay; (d) questions directed to authors of documents; (e) notes copied directly from documents; and (f) categorization with topical headings.

(a). The children in the other fifth-sixth grade class looked more like the eighth graders: 28.6% of these students used (a), as compared with 30.8% and 35.7% in the older classes. Relatively few students overall distinguished among documents in their notes (26.9%); the source of the information seemed less important for later interpretation than the facts in and of themselves. Attention to the importance of source or context may be a necessary emphasis in teaching inquiry skills.

However, even if students did not themselves distinguish among documents in their notes, we could determine the source of the recorded information by its substance. We examined how many students took notes on each of the four documents. Overall, the encyclopedia received the most attention: 83.6% of all students recorded information from this article. The UN report was second (74.6%), followed by the speech (70.1%) and the letter (65.7%). These differences can be largely accounted for by the differential pattern of the younger students. The older students consistently took notes on each of the four documents (77.9% of the eighth graders took notes on each document), producing a larger volume of notes than the younger students. The younger students could be distinguished by the fact that they were more variable in their attention. These students were more likely to attend to the encyclopedia article than to any other document. It appeared that many in this younger group found the encyclopedia more important, salient, reliable, or easier to extract information from than they did the other texts.

We need also to consider the effect of order of document presentation. Two split-half orders were presented for comparison. Some students were handed the documents in order 1 (UN report, encyclopedia, speech, letter), whereas others received them in order 2 (speech, letter, UN report, encyclopedia). Order of presentation affected attention to all documents except the encyclopedia article; students receiving the personal, persuasive documents first were more likely to take notes on them (speech, 87%; letter, 84%) than those receiving them last (speech, 54%; letter, 48%). By contrast, the encyclopedia appeared to be treated as an essential information source regardless of order.

What type of information were students most likely to record? The content analysis of the notes showed us what information children chose to record. We identified a total of 164 information units in the four documents, of which 57 were either information in topic sentences or paragraph summaries. To get an idea of what information seemed to be most important to students, we discuss here those pieces of information that were recorded by 30% or more of the students. We were interested both in the salience of the information within the document itself (topic sentences of paragraphs and document-summary sentences were identified), and in the relevance of the information to the problem.

We found that six information units, all of which were from the topic sentences of paragraphs, were recorded by 30% or more of the eighth grade students, thus suggesting that the document items most frequently noted were also the most salient parts of the individual documents. It should be noted that all six units were from two of the documents—the encyclopedia article and the UN report. For example, one unit recorded by 37% of the eighth grade students was a topic sentence in the UN report advocating better farming methods for a particular society. The six pieces of information most frequently recorded by the eighth graders were also plausibly problem relevant: Three of the information units were solutions offered for three different types of societies in the UN report (e.g., the best solution is population control); the remaining three were descriptions of some condition of the current Tallyland situation (e.g., people cultivate land the way their ancestors did).

Seven information units were recorded by at least one-third of the younger students, who were more variable with respect to the salience and relevance of information they recorded. Three units were from topic sentences or paragraph summaries; four were not. As was the case with the eighth graders, the encyclopedia article was favored: Six of the seven units were from this article. Four of the information units most frequently recorded by the fifth-sixth graders were not relevant to the problem, namely, units of information from the encyclopedia article that described land forms on the island (e.g., average elevation). Occasionally, a student drew the inference that land elevation could be related to farming conditions, but most students simply recorded the facts. The remaining three pieces of information, which described the traditional situation of the culture (e.g., they are just beginning to be modern), were relevant.

Organizing strategies. Students were asked to design, on a separate page, an organization for the information that would help them to write an essay in support of their solution to the problem. Six different organizing strategies were identified: (a) topics or categories; (b) a list of points; (c) an essay; (d) a dichotomous list; (e) an outline; or (f) nothing, relying only on notes.

Overall, outline formats (26%) and lists (31.3%) were the most frequently used, followed by categories (19%). A few students wrote an essay despite instructions (6%), or divided the information dichotomously into new versus old ways (8%), or did nothing (13%).

There were interesting differences by age in the type of strategy adopted. Older students were more likely than younger students to make outlines (55%) or to do nothing (19%), whereas younger students were more likely than the older group to make lists (40%) or to use categories (28%). None of the younger students made an outline and, interestingly, few did nothing. There was no apparent difference by teacher in strategy used within age groups. It appeared that the older students had begun to learn about hierarchical organization of information and some made use of this technique, whereas the younger students tended to collate items or organize information into groups.

In examining the content of these outlines, groupings, or lists, it was apparent that the information selected from notes for this organization and the way in which it was structured was, in most cases, only tangentially related to the problem that was posed to students. For example, one student organized his notes into categories: food, climate, people, and methods; the information tended not to be organized in a way that would support advice offered to Tallylanders, but seemed to take on a life of its own. There was little monitoring of the appropriateness of the information selected to the problem-solving task. The structure was generated from a body of notes that was excerpted from texts, but was not regrouped in a way that made it clearly useful as support for a solution to a problem.

With respect to solutions proposed, only 60% of the students offered a solution on their organizing page; most of the remaining students identified some sort of solution in their notes. The solutions offered on the organizing page generally did not clearly relate to the organization of information that preceded or followed them.

DISCUSSION

This preliminary study of students' inquiry practices in a constrained problem context demonstrates that most of the students in the classes we investigated possessed some notion of the requirements of information extraction from text documents. Most demonstrated that they had some procedures at their disposal for taking notes and for organizing the information they recorded when asked to do so in preparation for writing an essay. Thus, these students knew something about the form of this type of inquiry activity. This information is useful to us in thinking about the design of a technological tool that will support and extend students' inquiry abilities.

Two findings in the performances of these students are especially noteworthy for thinking about the development of such a system:

1. The encyclopedia article had a special status as an information source, especially among the younger students: Either the familiarity of the format or the type of information presented appeared to draw students to the encyclopedia as a source worthy of attention. There is a need to help stu-

dents recognize how to make use of information from different sources, and the value of attending to the context and reasoning of documents in which information is presented.

2. Students tended to perform the information-gathering and organizing activities as though they were quasi-independent of the problem they were asked to resolve. This is consistent with findings from previous studies with other types of problems: Students have difficulty coordinating phases of problem solving and monitoring their place in a problem-solving episode (e.g., Schoenfeld, 1983). It appears that the documents delivered to the students were "attacked," to be stripped of their information in a more or less systematic way with little evidence of attention or critical evaluation of the sources or, especially among younger students, whether or not information was problem relevant. While the subsequent information-organization might have been sophisticated, it was seldom built into a structure that directly supported an argument or solution to the problem. Thus, for most students the information-gathering processes seemed in part to be separated from the problem they were presumably attempting to solve.

IMPLICATIONS

The juxtaposition of experts' reflections on their practices with the performances of novices in an inquiry task suggests some ways in which well-designed tools in an inquiry-oriented curriculum might guide students to construct inquiry knowledge and skills. The task posed to the students had constraints different from the interview situation of the experts: It was an artificial setting in which a particular formulation of a problem was given to students. However, when their performances were examined against the backdrop of experts, the descriptions yielded some clues about what such a tool might emphasize.

Experts emphasized the importance of question development and refinement as a central part of the inquiry process. Although we posed a particular problem to students, there was no indication that they used the information to recast, resee, or develop the problem they began with. We see a need to help students engage in this aspect of inquiry in the recursive manner of experts.

Experts were also characterized by selection, annotation, and evaluation of information from a variety of sources. Many were careful to record and evaluate the sources of the information, seeking to understand biases and relate the material to their developing conceptual framework. There were often multiple passes through the information as they worked more deeply on the problem. There was recognition of the importance of consulting multiple perspectives or of composing teams that would bring these perspectives to the work. In contrast, few students indicated the source of their excerpted material; facts were commonly listed without regard to their context. Sources also received differential attention. The encyclopedia was most highly regarded, especially by the younger students. With the exception of the encyclopedia (an indication of its dominance), the documents were subject to order effects; persuasive texts received least attention if they were encountered last. It would be valuable to draw students' attention to the utility of source and context information, to enlarge their vision of the types of information that are useful, and to help them evaluate material for its qualities and in relation to the framework they are developing for understanding a problem. Perhaps it is even more important for them to see that they have and are developing a framework.

Experts in inquiry recognized the necessity to consider their solutions/conceptualizations/syntheses of information from multiple perspectives. They had tools for rigorously examining the strengths and problems of their tentative formulations. This critical process led them to develop their ideas and to recognize where more information was needed. While students demonstrated that they had some basic tools available for ordering information (e.g., outlines and lists), it was the rare student who gave evidence of trying out alternative hypotheses, critically juxtaposing their ideas with evidence. Thus, inquiry supports should help students to see and carry out this important phase of inquiry practice, and provide them with the means for critically considering their ideas.

Finally, experts discussed inquiry as a fundamentally social process. The constraints on the task we posed to students allowed us to see little about students' ideas in this regard; the one indirect piece of evidence was the differential status accorded the factual documents and the persuasive documents. The latter provided information about the social dimensions of the problem and the audience for proposed solutions. Students paid little attention to these aspects of the material. To support inquiry, the social dimension should be integrated into the work of students, perhaps by structuring some inquiry as group problem solving and by emphasizing the importance of people and their perspectives in finding and understanding the context of information.

We are currently building computer-based tools to help students develop inquiry practices. A series of studies is helping us to determine the most likely ways to design this inquiry support system, which, when completed, will be used to better understand how students gain expertise in this arena.

The system being built focuses primarily on inquiry practices in science. The interviews with experts illuminate, however, that effective inquiry is a central part of work in a wide variety of domains. Hence, we believe that it is necessary to emphasize the need for a cross-curriculum approach to inquiry skills. They are important processes to apply in mathematics, language and literary work, history and social studies, as well as science. In addition to deepening command of the contents and structural relationships within subject matter domains (e.g., fluency in algebraic formulas, facts about historical periods), students need to gain skills in critically understanding this information and in making use of it for purposes that go beyond recall for tests or answers to teacher-generated questions. They must come to respect their own power to generate and pursue issues or questions of personal interest to them.

AUTHOR NOTES

We are grateful to the Carnegie Corporation for the grant that supported this work. Roy Pea and Karen Sheingold provided many useful ideas and suggestions. We are also indebted to the "inquiry experts" and students who gave generously of their time and thought.

REFERENCES

Abelson, R.P., & diSessa, A. (1981). *Turtle geometry: The computer as a medium for exploring mathematics*. Cambridge, MA: MIT Press.

Adams, M.J. (1980). Failure to comprehend and levels of processing in reading. In R.J. Spiro, B.C. Bruce, & W.F. Brewer (Eds.), *Theoretical issues in reading comprehension: Perspectives in cognitive psychology, linguistics, artificial intelligence and education*. Hillsdale, NJ: Erlbaum.

Adelson, B. (1981). Problem solving and the development of abstract categories in programming languages. *Memory and Cognition, 9*, 422–433.

Adler, M.J. (Chair). (1983, November). The Paideia proposal: A symposium. *Harvard Educational Review, 53*(4).

Anderson, J.R., Greeno, J.G., Kline, P.J., & Neves, D.M. (1981). Acquisition of problem solving skill. In J.R. Anderson (Ed.), *Cognitive skills and their acquisition*. Hillsdale, NJ: Erlbaum.

Anderson, R.E. National computer literacy, 1980. (1982). In R.J. Seidel, R.E. Anderson, & B. Hunter (Eds.), *Computer literacy: Issues and directions for 1985*. New York: Academic Press.

Arons, A.B. (1984). Computer-based instructional dialogs in science courses. *Science, 224*, 1051–1056.

Atwood, M.E., Jeffries, R., & Polson, P.G. (1980). *Studies in plan construction. I: Analysis of an extended protocol* (Tech. Rep. No. SAI-80-028-DEN). Englewood, CO: Science Applications.

Atwood, M.E., & Ramsey, H.R. (1978). *Cognitive structures in the comprehension and memory of computer programs: An investigation of computer debugging* (Tech. Rep. No. TR-78A21). Alexandria, VA: U.S. Army Research Institute for the Behavioral and Social Sciences.

Au, K.H., & Jordan, C. (1981). Teaching reading to Hawaiian children: Finding a culturally appropriate solution. In H.T. Trueba, G.P. Guthrie, & K.H. Au (Eds.), *Culture in the bilingual classroom: Studies in classroom ethnography*. Rowley, MA: Newbury House.

Bamberger, J. (1983, April). The computer as sandcastle. In K. Sheingold (Chair), *Chameleon in the classroom: Developing roles for computers*. Symposium conducted at the American Educational Research Association, Montreal, Canada.

Bamberger, J., & Schon, D.A. (1982). *Learning as reflective conversation with materials: Notes from work in progress* (Working paper No. 17). Cambridge, MA: Massachusetts Institute of Technology, Division for Study and Research in Education.

Bank Street College. (1981). *Development of a television series on science and mathematics education which incorporates interactive television and microcomputers*. Proposal to the U.S. Department of Education. New York: Bank Street College of Education.

Barnhardt, C. (1985). *Creating communities with computer communication.* Paper prepared for Council on Anthropology and Education, at the meeting of the American Anthropological Association.

Barr, A., Bennett, J., & Clancey, W. (1979). *Transfer of expertise: A theme for AI research* (Working paper HPP-79-11). Stanford, CA: Stanford University, Heuristic Programming Project.

Barr, A., & Feigenbaum, E.A. (Eds.). (1982). *The handbook of artificial intelligence* (Vol. 2). Los Altos, CA: William Kaufmann.

Barstow, D.R. (1979). *Knowledge-based program construction.* Amsterdam: North-Holland.

Bastian, A., Fruchter, N., Gittell, M., Greer, C., & Haskins, M. (1985). *Choosing equality.* New York: The New World Foundation.

Becker, H.J. (1982). *Microcomputers in the classroom: Dreams and realities* (Report No. 319). Baltimore, MD: Johns Hopkins University, Center for Social Organization of Schools.

Bereiter, C., & Scardamalia, M. (1982). From conversation to composition: Instruction in a developmental process. In R. Glaser (Ed.), *Advances in instructional psychology* (Vol. 2). Hillsdale, NJ: Erlbaum.

Bereiter, C., & Scardamalia, M. (1984). Levels of inquiry in writing research. In P. Rosenthal, S. Walmsley, & L. Tamor (Eds.), *Research in writing: Principles and methods.* New York: Longman International.

Berliner, D. (1984, November). Presentation at Conference on Planning the School of the Future, Vanderbilt University, Nashville, TN.

Berman, P., & McLaughlin, M.W. (1978). *Federal programs supporting educational change. Vol. III: Implementing and sustaining innovations* (R-1589/8-HEW). Prepared for the U.S. Office of Education. Santa Monica, CA: Rand Corp.

Bernstein, A., Therrien, L., Engardio, P., Wise, D.C., & Pollock, M.A. (1985, September 2). The forgotten Americans. *Business Week,* pp. 50–55.

Black, S.D., Levin, J.A., Mehan, H., & Quinn, C.N. (1983). Real and non-real time interaction: Unraveling multiple threads of discourse. *Discourse Processes.*

Blanshard, B. (1939). *The nature of thought* (2 vols.). London: George Allen & Unwin.

Boden, M.A. (1979). *Piaget.* Glasgow: Fontana.

Bonar, J. (1982, August 4–6). Natural problem solving strategies and programming language constructs. *Proceedings of the Fourth Annual Conference of the Cognitive Science Society,* Ann Arbor, Michigan.

Bonar, J., & Soloway, E. (1982, November). *Uncovering principles of novice programming* (Research Report No. 240). New Haven, CT: Yale University, Department of Computer Science.

Botkin, J., Dimancescu, D., & Stata, R. (1984). *The innovators: Rediscovering America's creative energy.* New York: Harper & Row.

Boyle, C.F., & Anderson, J.R. (1984, April). *Acquisition and automated instruction of geometry proof skills.* Paper presented at the meeting of the American Educational Research Association, New Orleans, LA.

Bransford, J.D., Barclay, J.R., & Franks, J.J. (1972). Sentence memory: A constructive versus terpretive approach. *Cognitive Psychology, 3,* 193–209.

Bransford, J.D., Stein, B.S., Arbitman-Smith, R., & Vye, N.J. (1985). Three approaches to improving thinking and learning skills. In S.F. Chipman, J.W. Segal, & R. Glaser (Eds.), *Thinking and learning skills* (Vol. 1). Hillsdale, NJ: Erlbaum.

Brooks, F.P., Jr. (1982). *The mythical man-month: Essays of software engineering.* Reading, MA: Addison-Wesley.

Brooks, R.E. (1977). Towards a theory of the cognitive processes in computer programming. *International Journal of Man-Machine Studies, 9,* 737–751.

Brooks, R.E. (1980). Studying programmer behavior experimentally: The problems of proper methodology. *Communications of the ACM, 23*(4), 207–213.

Brown, A.L. (1982). Learning and development: The problems of compatibility, access, and induction. *Human Development, 25,* 89–115.

Brown, A.L. (1983). Learning to learn how to read. In J. Langer & T. Smith-Burke (Eds.), *Reader meets author, bridging the gap: A psycholinguistic and social linguistic perspective.* Newark, NJ: Dell.

Brown, A.L. (1984, April). *Learner characteristics and scientific texts.* Paper presented at the meeting of the American Educational Research Association, New Orleans, LA.

Brown, A.L. (in press). Metacognition, executive control, self-regulation and other even more mysterious mechanisms. In R.H. Kluwe & F.E. Weinert (Eds.), *Metacognition, motivation and learning.* West Germany: Luhlhammer.

Brown, A.L., Bransford, J.D., Ferrara, R.A., & Campione, J.C. (1983). Learning, remembering, and understanding. In J.H. Flavell & E.M. Markman (Eds.), *Cognitive development* (Vol. III), of P.H. Mussen (Ed.), *Handbook of child psychology* (4th ed.). New York: Wiley.

Brown, A.L., & Smiley, S.S. (1978). The development of strategies for studying texts. *Child Development, 49,* 1076–1088.

Brown, J.F. (1983, June). *The mathematics and science teacher shortage.* Paper written in preparation for the first and second conference of the Commission on Teacher Credentialing, Sacramento, CA.

Brown, J.S. (1984a, March). *Idea amplifiers—New kinds of electronic learning environments.* Paper presented at the Claremont Reading Conference, Claremont Graduate School of Education, Claremont, CA.

Brown, J.S. (1984b). Process versus product: A perspective on tools for communal and informal electronic learning. In *Report from the Learning Lab: Education in the electronic age.* New York: Educational Broadcasting Corporation.

Brown, J.S., & Burton, R.B. (1978). Diagnostic models for procedural bugs in basic mathematical skills. *Cognitive Science, 2,* 155–192.

Brown, J.S., Burton, R., & de Kleer, J. (1982). Pedagogical, natural language and knowledge engineering techniques in SOPHIE I, II, and III. In D. Sleeman & J.S. Brown (Eds.), *Intelligent tutoring systems.* New York: Academic Press.

Brown, J.S., & VanLehn, K. (1980). Repair theory: A generative theory of bugs in procedural skills. *Cognitive Science, 4,* 379–426.

Brown, R.D., & Newman, D.L. (1980, July). *A formative field test evaluation of tumbling and Spanish videodisc* (Project paper No. 2). Lincoln: Videodisc Design/Production Group, University of Nebraska-Lincoln.

Bruner, J.S. (1960). *The process of education.* Cambridge: MA: Harvard University Press.

Bruner, J.S. (1966a). On cognitive growth. In J.S. Bruner, R.R. Olver, & P.M. Greenfield (Eds.), *Studies in cognitive growth.* New York: Wiley.

Bruner, J.S. (1966b). *Toward a theory of instruction.* New York: Norton.

Brush, L.E. (1980). *Encouraging girls in mathematics.* Cambridge, MA: Abt Books.

Bunderson, C.B., Olsen, J., & Baillio, J. (1981). *Proof-of-concept demonstration and comparative evaluation of a prototype intelligent videodisc system.* Final report to the National Science Foundation. Orem, UT: WICAT, Inc., Learning Design Laboratories.

Burns, G., Cook, M., & Dubitsky, B. (1982, June). *The Logo project at Bank Street: A perspective on children, teachers and computers.* Paper presented at the National Educational Computing Conference, Kansas City, MO.

Burton, G. (1979). Regardless of sex. *The Mathematics Teacher, 72,* 261–270.

Burton, R.R. (1981). DEBUGGY: Diagnosis of errors in basic mathematical skills. In D.H. Sleeman & J.S. Brown (Eds.), *Intelligent tutoring systems.* New York: Academic Press.

Burton, R. (1982). Diagnosing bugs in a simple procedural skill. In D. Sleeman & J.S. Brown (Eds.), *Intelligent tutoring systems*. New York: Academic Press.

Byte. (August 1982). Special issue on Logo.

California Basic Education Data System. (1982–83). *Student enrollment by course*. Sacramento: CA: Department of Education.

California State Department of Public Instruction. (1985, March). *Mathematics framework for California, kindergarten-12*, Sacramento, CA.

Carey, S. (1984). Cognitive development: The descriptive problem. In M.S. Gazzaniga (Ed.), *Handbook of cognitive neuroscience*. New York: Plenum.

Carry, L.R., Lewis, C., & Bernard, J.E. (1979). *Psychology of equation solving: An information processing study*. Austin, TX: University of Texas at Austin, Department of Curriculum and Instruction.

Case, R. (1985). *Intellectual development: From birth to adulthood*. New York: Academic Press.

Case, R., & Kurland, D.M. (1980). A new measure for determining children's subjective organization of speech. *Journal of Experimental Child Psychology, 30*, 206–222.

Case, R., Kurland, D.M., & Goldberg, J. (1982). Operational efficiency and the growth of short-term memory span. *Journal of Experimental Child Psychology, 33*, 386–404.

Center for the Social Organization of Schools. (1983–1984). *School uses of microcomputers: Reports from a national survey* (issues 1–6). Baltimore, MD: Johns Hopkins University.

Chall, J.S. (1983). *Stages of reading development*. New York: McGraw-Hill.

Char, C. (1983, April). Research and design issues concerning the development of educational software for children. In K. Sheingold (Chair), *Chameleon in the classroom: Developing roles for computers*. Symposium conducted at the meeting of the American Educational Research Association, Montreal, Canada. (Also available as Technical Report No. 14, Center for Children and Technology, Bank Street College of Education, New York, NY.

Char, C. (1985, April). *Formative research in the design of television and educational software on science for children*. Paper presented at symposium, "The Voyage of the Mimi: Perspectives on Teacher Education in the Science Curriculum," at the meeting of the American Educational Research Association, Chicago, IL.

Char, C., Hawkins, J., & Freeman, C. (in preparation). *Information and research inquiry in schools: A case study of teachers' conceptions of, and current practices in, information gathering*. New York: Bank Street College of Education, Center for Children and Technology.

Char, C., Hawkins, J., & Freeman, C. (1985). *Incorporating database software into the classroom context: An ethnographic study*. Paper presented at the meeting of the American Educational Research Association, Chicago, IL.

Char, C., Hawkins, J., Wootten, J., Sheingold, K., & Roberts, T. (1983). *"The Voyage of the Mimi": Classroom case studies of software, video, and print materials*. Report to the U.S. Department of Education (Contract No. 300-81-0375). New York: Bank Street College of Education, Center for Children and Technology.

Char, C., & Newman, D. (1985). *Design options for interactive videodisc: A review and analysis*. New York: Bank Street College of Education, Center for Children and Technology.

Char, C., & Tally, W. (1985). *Using interactive videodisc technology in schools: Four classroom case studies*. New York: Bank Street College of Education, Center for Children and Technology.

Chase, W.G., & Simon, H.A. (1973). Perception in chess. *Cognitive Psychology, 4*, 55–81.

Chi, M.T.H., Feltovich, P.J., & Glaser, R. (1981). Categorization and representation of physics problems by experts and novices. *Cognitive Science, 5*, 121–152.

Chion-Kenney, L. (1984). Computer, school, family in Houston: A "total commitment." *Education Week, IV*(10), 1.

Chipman, S.F., Segal, J.W., & Glaser, R. (Eds.). *Thinking and learning skills* (2 vols.). Hillsdale, NJ: Erlbaum.

Clement, J., Lochhead, J., & Monk, G. (1979). *Translation difficulties in learning mathematics* (Tech. Rep.). Amherst, MA: University of Massachusetts, Cognitive Development Project, Department of Physics and Astronomy.

Coburn, P., Kelman, P., Roberts, N., Snyder, T.F.F., Watt, D.H., & Weiner, C. (1982). *Practical guide to computers in education.* Reading, MA: Addison-Wesley.

Cole, M., & Griffin, P. (1980). Cultural amplifiers reconsidered. In D.R. Olson (Ed.), *The social foundations of language and thought: Essays in honor of Jerome S. Bruner.* New York: Norton.

Cole, M., & Scribner, S. (1978). Introduction. In M. Cole, V. John-Steiner, S. Scribner, & E. Souberman (Eds.), *Mind in society: The development of higher psychological processes.* Cambridge, MA: Harvard University Press.

The College Board. (1985a). *Equality and excellence: The educational status of black-Americans.* New York: Author.

The College Board. (1985b). *National college-bound seniors, 1985.* New York: Author.

Collingwood, R.G. (1939). *Autobiography.* London: Oxford University Press.

Collins, A., & Gentner, D. (1982, August). Constructing runnable mental models. *Proceedings of the Fourth Annual Conference of the Cognitive Science Society,* Ann Arbor, MI.

Collins, A., Gentner, D., & Rubin, A. (1981, October). *Teaching study strategies* (Report No. 4794). Cambridge, MA: Bolt Beranek & Newman.

Collins, A., & Stevens, A.L. (1982). Goals and strategies of inquiry teachers. In R. Glaser (Ed.), *Advances in instructional psychology* (Vol. 2, pp. 65–119). Hillsdale, NJ: Erlbaum.

Confrey, J. (1984, April). *An examination of the conceptions of mathematics of young women in high school.* Paper presented at the annual meeting of the American Educational Research Association, New Orleans, LA.

Confrey, J., Rommney, P., & Mundy, J. (1984, April). *Mathematics anxiety: A person-context-adaptation model.* Paper presented at the annual meeting of the American Educational Research Association, New Orleans, LA.

Cornbleth, C. (1985). *Socioecology of critical thinking.* Paper presented at the meeting of the American Educational Research Association, Chicago, IL.

Cromer, R.F. (1974). The development of language and cognition: The cognition hypothesis. In B. Foss (Ed.), *New perspectives in child development* (pp. 184–252). London, England: Penguin.

Crystal, D. (1980). *A first dictionary of linguistics and phonetics.* New York: Cambridge University Press.

Curtis, B., Sheppard, S.B., Milliman, P., Borst, M.A., & Love, T. (1979). Measuring the psychological complexity of software maintenance tasks with the Halstead and McCabe metrics. *IEEE Transactions on Software Engineering, SE-5*(2), 96–104.

Dansereau, D.F., Collins, K.W., McDonald, B.A., Holley, C.D., Garland, J., Diekhoff, G., & Evans, S.H. (1979). Development and evaluation of a learning strategy training program. *Journal of Educational Psychology, 71*(1), 64–73.

Davis, P.J., & Hersh, R. (1980). *The mathematical experience.* Boston, Birkhauser.

Davis, R., & Lenat, D.B. (1981). *Knowledge-based systems in artificial intelligence.* New York: McGraw-Hill.

Dede, C. (1983, September). The likely evolution of computer use in schools. *Educational Leadership,* 22–24.

de Kleer, J., & Brown, J.S. (1981). Mental models of physical mechanisms and their acquisition. In J.R. Anderson (Ed.), *Cognitive skills and their acquisition.* Hillsdale, NJ: Erlbaum.

Dennett, D.C. (1978). *Brainstorms.* Montgomery, VT: Bradford.

Dewey, J. (1900). *The school and society*. Chicago: University of Chicago Press.

Dewey, J. (1902). *The child and the curriculum*. Chicago: University of Chicago Press.

Dewey, J. (1933). *How we think*. Boston: Heath.

Dewey, J. (1938). *Experience and education*. New York: Collier Books.

Dewey, J., & Bentley, A.F. (1960). *Knowing and the known*. Boston: Beacon Press. (Original work published 1949)

Diaz, S. (1984, November). *Bilingual-bicultural computer experts: Traditional literacy through computer literacy*. Paper presented at the American Anthropological Association Conference, Denver, CO.

DiPersio, T., Isbister, D., & Shneiderman, B. (1980). An experiment using memorization/reconstruction as a measure of programmer ability. *International Journal of Man-Machine Studies, 13*, 339–354.

diSessa, A.A. (1982). Unlearning Aristotelian physics: A study of knowledge-based learning. *Cognitive Science, 6*, 37–75.

diSessa, A. (1983). Phenomenology and the evolution of intuition. In D. Gentner & A.L. Stevens (Eds.), *Mental models*. Hillsdale, NJ: Erlbaum.

Donaldson, M. (1978). *Children's minds*. Cambridge, MA: Harvard University Press.

duBoulay, J.B.H., & O'Shea, T. (1976). *How to work the Logo machine: A primer for ELOGO* (D.A.I. Occasional paper No. 4). Edinburgh: University of Edinburgh, Department of Artificial Intelligence.

duBoulay, J.B.H., O'Shea, T., & Monk, J. (1981). The black box inside the glass box: Presenting computer concepts to novices. *International Journal of Man-Machine Studies, 14*, 237–249.

Duschl, R.A. (1985). Science education and philosophy of science: Twenty-five years of mutually exclusive development. *School Science and Mathematics, 85*(7), 541–555.

Dwyer, T.A. (1975). Soloworks: Computer based laboratories for high school mathematics. *Science and Mathematics*, 93–99.

Education Commission of the States. (1985). *Reconnecting youth: The next stage of reform*. Report of the Business Advisory Commission to the Education Commission of the States. Washington, DC: Author.

Ehrlich, K., & Soloway, E. (1983). An empirical investigation of the tacit plan knowledge in programming. In J. Thomas & M. Schneider (Eds.), *Human factors in computer systems*. Norwood, NJ: Ablex.

Eisenstadt, M., Laubsch, J.H., & Kahney, J.H. (1981, August). *Creating pleasant programming environments for cognitive science students*. Paper presented at the meeting of the Cognitive Science Society, Berkeley, CA.

Eisenstein, E.L. (1979). *The printing press as an agent of change*. New York: Cambridge University Press.

Emmerich, W., & Shepard, K. (1982). Development of sex-differentiated preferences during late childhood and adolescence. *Developmental Psychology, 18*, 406–417.

Entwisle, D., & Baker, D. (1983). Gender and young children's expectations for performance in arithmetic. *Developmental Psychology, 19*, 200–209.

Eric Clearinghouse on Urban Education. (1984, January). Microcomputers: Equity and quality in education for urban disadvantaged students. *ERIC/CUE Digest, 19*. New York: Teachers College.

Feigenbaum, E.A., & McCorduck, P. (1983). *The fifth generation: Artificial intelligence and Japan's computer challenge to the world*. Reading, MA: Addison-Wesley.

Feldman, D.H. (1980). *Beyond universals in cognitive development*. Norwood, NJ: Ablex.

Feldman, D.H. (1982). A developmental framework for research with gifted children. In D.H. Feldman (Ed.), *Developmental approaches to giftedness and creativity*. San Francisco: Jossey-Bass.

Fennema, E. (1980). Teachers and sex bias in mathematics. *The Mathematics Teacher, 73,* 169–173.

Ferralli, A., & Ferralli, K. (1985, June). Interactive video in education: A new approach. *The Videodisc Monitor,* 14–15.

Feurzeig, W., Horwitz, P., & Nickerson, R.S. (1981, October). *Microcomputers in education* (Report No. 4798). Prepared for: Department of Health, Education, and Welfare, National Institute of Education; and Ministry for the Development of Human Intelligence, Republic of Venezuela. Cambridge, MA: Bolt Beranek & Newman.

Feurzeig, W., Papert, S., Bloom, M., Grant, R., & Solomon, C. (1969). *Programming languages as a framework for teaching methematics* (Report No. 1899). Cambridge, MA: Bolt Beranek & Newman.

Fey, J.T. (Ed.), with Atchison, W.F., Good, R.A., Heid, M.K., Johnson, J., Kantowski, M.G., & Rosen, L.P. (1984). *Computing and mathematics: The impact on secondary school curricula.* College Park, MD: National Council of Teachers of Mathematics.

Fischer, K.W. (1980). A theory of cognitive development: The control and construction of hierarchies of skills. *Psychological Review, 87,* 477–531.

Flavell, J., & Draguns, J. (1957). A microgenetic approach to perception and thought. *Psychological Bulletin, 54,* 197–217.

Floyd, R.W. (1979). The paradigms of programming. *Communications of the ACM, 22*(8), 455–460.

Frederiksen, N. (1984). The real test bias: Influences of testing in teaching and learning. *American Psychologist, 39*(3), 193–202.

Freeman, C., Hawkins, J., & Char, C. (1984). *Information management tools for classrooms: Exploring database management systems* (Tech. Rep. No. 28). New York: Bank Street College of Education, Center for Children and Technology.

Friedland, P.E. (1979). *Knowledge-based experiment design in molecular genetics* (Report No. 79-711). Standord, CA: Stanford University, Computer Science Department.

Friedman, W.J. (Ed.). (1982). *The developmental psychology of time.* New York: Academic Press.

Fuller, R. (1985). From the dragon's lair to the Tacoma Bridge. *Videodisc and Optical Disc 5*(1), 37–51.

Galanter, E. (1983). *Kids and computers: The parents' microcomputer handbook.* New York: Putnam.

Gardner, H. (1983). *Frames of mind: The theory of multiple intelligences.* New York: Basic Books.

Gardner, H., & Wolf, D. (Eds.). (1979). *New directions for child development: Early symbolization.* San Francisco: Jossey-Bass.

Gates, A.J. (1947). *The improvement of reading.* New York: Macmillan.

Gelman, R. (1978). Cognitive development. *Annual Review of Psychology, 29,* 297–332.

Gelman, R., & Baillargeon, R. (1983). A review of some Piagetian concepts. In J.H. Flavell & E.M. Markman (Eds.), *Cognitive development* (Vol. III, pp. 167–230), of P.H. Mussen (Ed.), *Handbook of child psychology* (4th ed.). New York: Wiley.

Gentner, D., & Stevens, A.L. (Eds.). (1983). *Mental models.* Hillsdale, NJ: Erlbaum.

Gick, M.L., & Holyoak, K.J. (1980). Analogical problem solving. *Cognitive Psychology, 12,* 306–335.

Gick, M.L., & Holyoak, K.J. (1982). Schema induction and analogical transfer. *Cognitive Psychology, 15,* 1–39.

Glenn, A. (1983, May). Videodiscs and the social studies classroom. *Social Education,* 328–330.

Goldin, S.E., & Hayes-Roth, B. (1980). *Individual differences in planning processes* (Note N-1488-ONR). Santa Monica, CA: Rand Corp.

Goldman, S. (1982). Dissertation, Teacher's College, Columbia University.

Goldstein, I., & Papert, S. (1977). Artificial intelligence, language, and the study of knowledge. *Cognitive Science, 1,* 84–123.

Goodlad, J.I. (1984). *A place called school: Prospects for the future.* New York: McGraw-Hill.

Goody, J. (1977). *The domestication of the savage mind.* New York: Cambridge University Press.

Gould, J.D. (1977). Some psychological evidence on how people debug computer programs. *International Journal of Man-Machine Studies, 7,* 151–182.

Gould, J.D., & Drongowski, P. (1974). An exploratory investigation of computer program debugging. *Human Factors, 16,* 258–277.

Green, C.C., & Barstow, D. (1978). On program synthesis knowledge. *Artificial Intelligence, 10*(3), 241–279.

Greenfield, P.M. (1984). *Mind and media.* Cambridge, MA: Harvard University Press.

Greeno, J.G. (1980). Trends in the theory of knowledge for problem solving. In D.T. Tuma & F. Reif (Eds.), *Problem solving and education: Issues in teaching and research.* Hillsdale, NJ: Erlbaum.

Greeno, J., Glaser, R., & Newell, A. (1983, March). *Research on cognition and behavior relevant to education in mathematics, science, and technology.* Report submitted to the National Science Board Commission on Precollege Education in Mathematics, Science, and Technology by the Federation of Behavioral, Psychological, and Cognitive Sciences.

Gregg, L.W., & Steinberg, E.R. (Eds.). (1980). *Cognitive processes in writing.* Hillsdale, NJ: Erlbaum.

Guskey, T.R. (1986, May). Staff development and the process of teacher change. *Educational Researcher, 15*(5), 5–12.

Hamburg, D.A. (1984, June). Science and technology in a world transferred. *Science,* 943–946.

Havelock, E.A. (1976). *Origins of Western literacy.* Toronto, Ontario: Ontario Institute for Studies in Education.

Hawkins, J. (1983). *Learning Logo together: The social context* (Tech. Rep. No. 13). New York: Bank Street College of Education, Center for Children and Technology.

Hawkins, J., Char, C., & Freeman, C. (1984). *Software tools in the classroom.* Report to the Carnegie Corporation. New York: Bank Street College of Education, Center for Children and Technology.

Hawkins, J., & Kurland, D.M. (1984). *Analysis of software tools.* New York: Bank Street College of Education, Center for Children and Technology.

Hawkins, J., & Sheingold, K. (1985). *The beginning of a story: Computers and the organization of learning in classrooms* (Tech. Rep. No. 35). New York: Bank Street College of Education, Center for Children and Technology.

Hawkins, J., Sheingold, K., Gearhart, M., & Berger, C. (1982). Microcomputers in schools: Impact on the social life of elementary classrooms. *Journal of Applied Developmental Psychology, 3,* 361–373.

Hayes, J.R., & Simon, H.A. (1977). Psychological differences among problem isomorphs. In N.J. Castellan, Jr., D.B. Pisoni, & G.R. Potts (Eds.), *Cognitive theory* (Vol. 2). Hillsdale, NJ: Erlbaum.

Hayes-Roth, B. (1980, November). *Estimation of time requirements during planning: The interactions between motivation and cognition* (N-1581-ONR: A Rand Note). Santa Monica, CA: Rand Corp.

Hayes-Roth, B., & Hayes-Roth, F. (1979). A cognitive model of planning. *Cognitive Science, 3,* 275–310.

Hayes-Roth, F., Waterman, D., & Lenat, D. (Eds.). (1984). *Building expert systems.* Reading, MA: Addison-Wesley.

Heath, S.B. (1981). Toward an ethnohistory of writing in American education. In M.F. Whiteman (Ed.), *Writing: The nature, development, and teaching of written communication* (Vol. 1). Hillsdale, NJ: Erlbaum.

Heath, S.B. (1983). *Ways with words: Language, life, and work in communities and classrooms.* Cambridge: Cambridge University Press.

Heller, J.I., & Greeno, J.G. (1979). Information processing analyses of mathematical problem solving. In R. Tyler & S. White (Eds.), *Testing, teaching, and learning.* Washington, DC: National Institute of Education.

Hendrick, R. (1984). *From test to tube: Formative research in children's television.* Unpublished manuscript, Harvard University, Cambridge, MA.

Hess, R., & Miura, I. (1983). *Gender and socioeconomic differences in enrollment in computer camps and classes.* Unpublished manuscript, Stanford University, Stanford, CA.

Hess, R.D., & Miura, I.T. (1984, February). *Issues in training teachers to use microcomputers in the classroom: Example from the United States* (Report No. 84–C2). Palo Alto, CA: Stanford University, Institute for Research on Educational Finance and Governance.

Hoffmeister, A., Engelmann, S., & Carnine, D. (1985). *Designing videodisc-based courseware for the high school.* Paper presented at the meeting of the American Educational Research Association, Chicago, IL.

Hord, S.M., & Loucks, S.F. (1980). *A concerns-based model for the delivery of inservice.* Austin, TX: Research and Development Center for Teacher Education.

Howe, J.A.M. (1980). Developmental stages in learning to program. In F. Klix & J. Hoffman (Eds.), *Cognition and memory: Interdisciplinary research of human memory activities.* Amsterdam: North-Holland.

Howe, J.A.M. (1981). *Learning mathematics through Logo programming* (Research paper No. 153). Edinburgh: University of Edinburgh, Department of Artificial Intelligence.

Howe, J.A.M., O'Shea, T., & Plane, F. (1979). Teaching mathematics through Logo programming: An evaluation study. In R. Lewis & E.D. Tagg (Eds.), *Computer-assisted learning—scope, progress and limits.* Amsterdam: North-Holland.

Hunt, E. (1978). Mechanics of verbal ability. *Psychological Review, 85,* 109–130.

Inhelder, B., Sinclair, H., & Bovet, M. (1974). *Learning and the development of cognition.* Cambridge, MA: Harvard University Press.

Jeffries, R. (1982, March). *A comparison of the debugging behavior of expert and novice programmers.* Paper presented at the meeting of the American Educational Research Association, New York City.

Johnson, J.P. (1982). Can computers close the educational equity gap? *Perspectives: The Civil Rights Quarterly, 14*(3).

Johnson, W.L., Draper, S., & Soloway, E. (1983). An effective bug classification scheme must take the programmer into account. *Proceedings of the Workshop on High-Level Debugging,* Palo Alto, CA.

John-Steiner, V. (1985). *Notebooks of the mind.* Albuquerque: University of New Mexico Press.

Kahnemann, D., Slovic, P., & Tversky, A. (Eds.). (1982). *Judgement under uncertainty: Heuristics and biases.* New York: Cambridge University Press.

Kahney, H., & Eisenstadt, M. (1982, August 4–6). Programmers' mental models of their programming tasks: The interaction of real-world knowledge and programming knowledge. *Proceedings of the Fourth Annual Conference of the Cognitive Science Society,* Ann Arbor, MI.

Kehrberg, K., & Pollak, R. (1982, January). Videodisc in the classroom: An interactive economics course. *Creative Computing, 8*(1), 99–101.

Kelly, H., & Gardner, H. (1981). Editor's notes: Tackling television on its own terms. In H. Kelly & H. Gardner (Eds.), *Viewing children through television: New directions for child development.* San Francisco: Jossey-Bass.

Kneale, W., & Kneale, M. (1962). *The development of logic.* Oxford: Clarendon Press.

Kochen, M. (Ed.). (1975). *Information for action: From knowledge to wisdom.* New York: Academic Press.

Kolata, G. (1983). Math genius may have a hormonal basis. *Science, 222,* 1312.

Kreinberg, N. (1981). 1000 teachers later: Women, mathematics and the components of change. *Public Affairs Report, 22,* 1–7.

Kurland, D.M. (1985). *Software tools for the classroom computer.* New York: Bank Street College of Education, Center for Children and Technology.

Kurland, D.M. (1985). *The Bank Street interface: Design principles for the development of user-friendly software.* New York: Bank Street College of Education, Center for Children and Technology.

Kurland, D.M., Mawby, R., & Cahir, N. (1984, April). *The development of programming expertise.* Paper presented at the meeting of the American Educational Research Association, New Orleans, LA.

Kurland, D.M., Pea, R.D., Clement, C., & Mawby, R. (in press). A study of the development of programming and thinking skills. *Journal of Educational Computing Research, 3.*

Kurland, D.M., & Pea, R.D. (1985). Children's mental models of recursive Logo programs. *Journal of Educational Computing Research, 1,* 235–243.

Laboratory of Comparative Human Cognition. (1982, April). Microcomputer communication networks for education. *The Quarterly Newsletter of the Laboratory of Comparative Human Cognition, 4.*

Laboratory of Comparative Human Cognition. (1983). Culture and cognitive development. In W. Kessen (Ed.), *History, theory, and methods* (Vol. I), of P.H. Mussen (Ed.), *Handbook of child psychology* (4th ed.). New York: Wiley.

Laboratory of Comparative Human Cognition. (1985). *Non-cognitive factors in education.* Subcommittee report to the National Research Council Commission on Behavioral and Social Sciences Education. La Jolla, CA: University of California, San Diego.

Langley, P., Ohlsson, S., & Sage, S. (1984). *A machine learning approach to student modelling* (Tech. Rep. No. CMU-RI-TR-84-7). Pittsburgh, PA: Carnegie-Mellon University, Robotics Institute.

Larkin, J.H., McDermott, J., Simon, D.P., & Simon, H.A. (1980). Expert and novice performance in solving physics problems. *Science, 208,* 1335–1342.

Lawler, R.W. (1980, July). *Extending a powerful idea* (Logo Memo No. 58). Cambridge, MA: Massachusetts Institute of Technology, Artificial Intelligence Laboratory.

Lempers, J.D., Flavell, E.R., & Flavell, J.H. (1977). The development in very young children of tacit knowledge concerning visual perception. *Genetic Psychology Monographs, 95,* 3–53.

Lenney, E. (1977). Women's self-confidence in achievement settings. *Psychological Bulletin, 84,* 1–13.

Leont'ev, A.N. (1981). *Problems in the development of the mind.* Moscow: Progress Publishers.

Lesgold, A.M. (1983). A rationale for computer-based reading instruction. In A.C. Wilkinson (Ed.), *Classroom computers and cognitive science.* New York: Academic Press.

Lesgold, A.M., & Reif, F. (1983, June). *Computers in education: Realizing the potential.* Chairman's report of a research conference, Pittsburgh, PA.

Levin, H.M., & Rumberger, R.W. (1983). *The educational implications of high technology* (Project Report No. 83-A4). Palo Alto, CA: Stanford University, NIE Institute for Research on Educational Finance and Governance.

Levin, J.A. (1982). Microcomputers as interactive communication media: An interactive text interpreter. *Quarterly Newsletter of the Laboratory of Comparative Human Cognition, 4,* 34–36.

Levin, J.A., & Boruta, M.J. (1983). Writing with computers in classrooms: "You get EXACTLY the right amount of space!" *Theory Into Practice, 22,* 291–295.

Levin, J.A., & Kareev, Y. (1980). *Personal computers and education: The challenge to schools* (CHIP Report No. 98). La Jolla, CA: University of California, San Diego, Center for Human Information Processing.

Lewis, C. (1981). Skill in algebra. In J.R. Anderson (Ed.), *Cognitive skills and their acquisition*. Hillsdale, NJ: Erlbaum.

Lewis, M.V., Fraser, J.L., & Unger, P.V. (1984). *Anticipating future influences on vocational education*. Columbus: Ohio State University, National Center for Research in Vocational Education.

Licht, B., & Dweck, C. (1982). *Sex differences in achievement orientations: Consequences for academic choices and attainments*. Unpublished manuscript.

Lieberman, A. (1984). Quoted in *Computer education*. Ridgewood Public Schools, Ridgewood, NJ.

Lindsay, R., Buchanan, B.G., Feigenbaum, E.A., & Lederberg, J. (1980). *DENDRAL*. New York: McGraw-Hill.

Lockheed, M., Nielsen, A., & Stone, M. (1983). *Sex differences in microcomputer literacy*. Paper presented at the National Educational Computer Conference, Baltimore, MD.

Loucks, S.F., & Zacchei, D.A. (1983, November). Applying our findings to today's innovations. *Educational Leadership*, 28–31.

Luehrmann, A. (1981). Computer literacy: What should it be? *Mathematics Teacher*, 74.

Luria, A.R. (1976). *Cognitive development: Its cultural and social foundations*. Cambridge, MA: Harvard University Press.

Maccoby, E., & Jacklin, C. (1974). *The psychology of sex differences*. Stanford, CA: Stanford University Press.

Mann, W.C. (1975, March). Why things are so bad for the computer-naive user. *Information Sciences Institute*.

Markman, E.M. (1977). Realizing that you don't understand: A preliminary investigation. *Child Development, 48*, 986–992.

Markman, E.M. (1985). Comprehension monitoring: Developmental and educational issues. In S.F. Chipman, J.W. Segal, & R. Glaser (Eds.), *Thinking and learning skills* (Vol. 2). Hillsdale, NJ: Erlbaum.

Massachusetts Educational Television. (1981). *Videodisc field test report*. Cambridge, MA: Author.

Matz, M. (1981). Towards a process model of high school algebra errors. In D.H. Sleeman & J.S. Brown (Eds.), *Intelligent tutoring systems*. London: Academic Press.

Mawby, R. (1984, April). *Determining students' understanding of programming concepts*. Paper presented at the meeting of the American Educational Research Association, New Orleans, LA.

Mawby, R., Clement, C.A., Pea, R.D., & Hawkins, J. (1984, February). *Structured interviews on children's conceptions of computers* (Tech. Rep. No. 19). New York: Bank Street College of Education, Center for Children and Technology.

Mayer, R.E. (1976). Some conditions of meaningful learning for computer programming: Advance organizers and subject control of frame order. *Journal of Educational Psychology, 68*, 143–150.

Mayer, R.E. (1975). Different problem solving competencies established in learning computer programming with and without meaningful models. *Journal of Educational Psychology, 67*, 725–734.

Mayer, R.E. (1979). A psychology of learning BASIC. *Communications of the ACM, 22*, 589–593.

Mayer, R.E. (1981). The psychology of learning computer programming by novices. *Computing Surveys, 13*, 121–141.

Mayer, R.E., & Bayman, P. (1981, August). Psychology of calculator languages: A framework for describing differences in users' knowledge. *Communications of the ACM, 24*(8), 511–520.

McKeithen, K.B., Reitman, J.S., Rueter, H.H., & Hirtle, S.C. (1981). Knowledge organization and skill differences in computer programmers. *Cognitive Psychology, 13,* 307–325.

McKernon, P.E. (1979). The development of first songs in young children. In H. Gardner & D. Wolf (Eds.), *New directions for child development: Early symbolization.* San Francisco: Jossey-Bass.

McLaughlin, D. (1984). *Teachers' use of technology: Experiences of the videodisc/microcomputer network.* Paper presented at the meeting of the American Educational Research Association, New Orleans, LA.

McLuhan, M. (1964). *Understanding media: The extensions of man.* New York: McGraw-Hill.

McNett, I. (1983, June). *Demographic imperatives: Implications for educational policy.* Report of forum on "The Demographics of Changing Ethnic Populations and Their Implications for Elementary, Secondary and Postsecondary Educational Policy." Washington, DC: American Council on Education.

Mehan, H. (1984a). Institutional decision-making. In B. Rogoff & J. Lave (Eds.), *Everyday cognition: Its development in social context.* Cambridge, MA: Harvard University Press.

Mehan, H. (1984b). Exploiting the interactive capabilities of microcomputers. In H. Mehan & R. Souviney (Eds.), *The write help: A handbook for computers in classrooms.* La Jolla: CA: University of California, San Diego, Center for Human Information Processing.

Mehan, H. (1985). Microcomputers and classroom organization: Some mutual influences. In *Computers in classrooms: A quasi-experiment in guided change.* Final Report to the National Institute of Education. La Jolla, CA: University of California, San Diego, Center for Human Information Processing.

Mehan, H. (1985, December). *Microcomputers and classroom organization: The more things change the more they change each other.* Paper presented at the meeting of the American Anthropological Association, Washington, DC.

Mehan, H., & Souviney, R. (Eds.). (1984). *The write help: A handbook for computers in classrooms.* La Jolla, CA: University of California, San Diego, Center for Human Information Processing.

Michaels, S. (1985). Classroom processes and the learning of text editing commands. *The Quarterly Newsletter of the Laboratory of Comparative Human Cognition, 7*(3), 69–79.

Michalski, R.S., Carbonell, J.G., & Mitchell, T.M. (Eds.). (1983). *Machine learning: An artificial intelligence approach.* Palo Alto, CA: Tioga.

Mielke, K.W. (1981). The educational use of production variables in formative research in programming. In *Television as teacher.* Bethesda, MD: National Institute of Mental Health.

Mikulecky, L. (1982). Job literacy: The relationship between school preparation and workplace actuality. *Reading Research Quarterly, 12,* 400–419.

Miller, L.A. (1974). Programming by non-programmers. *International Journal of Man-Machine Studies, 6,* 237–260.

Minksy, M. (1970). Form and content in computer science. *Communications of the ACM, 17*(2), 197–215.

Minksy, M. (1983). Why people think computers can't. *Technology Review, 86*(6), 65–81.

Minuchin, P., & Shapiro, E.K. (1983). The school as a context for social development. In E.M. Hetherington (Ed.), *Socialization, Personality, and Social Development* (Vol. IV), of P.H. Mussen (Ed.), *Handbook of child psychology* (4th ed.). New York: Wiley.

Miura, I., & Hess, R. (1983). *Sex differences in computer access, interest, and usage.* Paper presented at the meeting of the American Psychological Association, Anaheim, CA.

Moll, L. (1985). *Promoting Hispanic student achievement: Microcomputer applications.* Paper presented at the meeting of the American Educational Research Association, Chicago, IL.

Morris, W. (Ed.). (1969). *The American heritage dictionary of the English language.* Boston: American Heritage & Houghton Mifflin.

Nathan, J. (1984, March). A computer specialist at work. *Learning,* 41–44.

National Academy of Sciences. (1984). *Research briefings 2984*. Report of the Briefing Panel on Information Technology in Precollege Education.

National Academy of Sciences, National Academy of Engineering, & Institute of Medicine. (1984). *High schools and the changing workplace: The employers' view*. Washington, DC: National Academy Press.

National Assessment of Educational Progress. (1980). *Procedural handbook: 1977–78 mathematics assessment*. Denver: CO: Education Commission of the States.

National Assessment of Educational Progress. (1985). *The reading report card: Progress toward excellence in our schools*. Princeton, NJ: Educational Testing Service.

National Center for Education Statistics. (1980). *Digest of education statistics 1980*. Washington, DC: United States Government Printing Office.

National Center for Education Statistics. (1984). *The condition of education*. Washington, DC: U.S. Government Printing Office.

National Commission on Excellence in Education. (1983). *A nation at risk: The imperative for educational reform*. Washington: DC: U.S. Government Printing Office.

National Council of Teachers of Mathematics. (1980). *An agenda for action*. Palo Alto, CA: Dale Seymour.

National Science Teachers Association. (1982). *Science-technology-society: Science education for the 1980s*. Washington, DC: National Science Teachers Association.

Newell, A. (1980). One final word. In D.T. Tuma & F. Reif (Eds.), *Problem solving and education*. New York: Halsted Press.

Newell, A., & Simon, H. (1972). *Human problem solving*. Englewood Cliffs, NJ: Prentice-Hall.

Newman, D., Riel, M.R., & Martin, L. (1983). Cultural practices and Piaget's theory: The impact of a cross-cultural research program. In D. Kuhn & J.A. Meacham (Eds.), *On the development of developmental psychology*. Basel: Karger.

Newman, W.M., & Sproull, R.F. (1979). *Principles of interactive computer graphics* (2nd ed.). New York: McGraw-Hill.

Nickerson, R.S. (1981). Why interactive computer systems are sometimes not used by people who might benefit from them. *International Journal of Man-Machine Studies*, 14, 469–481.

Nickerson, R.S. (1982). Computer programming as a vehicle for teaching thinking skills. *Thinking: The Journal of Philosophy for Children*, 4, 42–48.

Nisbett, R.E., & Ross, L. (1980). *Human inference: Strategies and shortcomings of social judgement*. Englewood Cliffs, NJ: Prentice-Hall.

Norman, D.A. (Ed.). (1981). *Perspectives on cognitive science*. Hillsdale, NJ: Erlbaum.

Norman, D.A., & Draper, S.W. (Eds.). (1986). *User centered system design: New perspectives on human-computer interaction*. Hillsdale, NJ: Erlbaum.

Noyelle, T. (1984a, August). *Conceptualizing the impact of the new computer technology on industries, firms and human resources with a special emphasis on white collar work and service industries*. New York: Columbia University, Conservation of Human Resources.

Noyelle, T. (1984b, October). *Employment discrimination in the service economy*. Paper presented at the conference on "Women, Clerical Work and Office Automation: Issues for Research" organized by the Women's Bureau, U.S. Department of Labor, and the panel on technology and women's employment, National Research Council, Washington, DC.

Noyelle, T., & Stanback, T., Jr. (1984, February). *Technological change and employment: A "first pass" at conceptualization*. Interim report to the Ford Foundation. New York: Columbia University, Conservation of Human Resources.

Nystrand, M. (Ed.). (1981). *What writers know: The language, process, and structure of written discourse*. New York: Academic Press.

Oakes, J., & Schneider, M. (1984). Computers and schools: Another case of " . . . the more they stay the same"? *Educational Leadership*, 42(3), 73–79.

Office of Technology Assessment. (1982). *Informational technology and its impact on American education*. Washington, DC: U.S. Government Printing Office.

Olson, D.R. (Ed.). (1974). *Media and symbols: The forms of expression, communication, and education*. Chicago: University of Chicago Press.

Olson, D.R. (1976). Culture, technology and intellect. In L.B. Resnick (Ed.), *The nature of intelligence*. Hillsdale, NJ: Erlbaum.

Olson, D.R. (1977). From utterance to text: The bias of language in speech and writing. *Harvard Educational Review, 47,* 257–281.

Olson, D.R., & Bruner, J.S. (1974). Learning through experience and learning through media. In D.R. Olson (Ed.), *Media and symbols: The forms of expression, communication, and education*. Chicago: University of Chicago Press.

Olson, J.K. (1984, April). *Microcomputers and the classroom order*. Paper presented at the meeting of the American Educational Research Association, New Orleans, LA.

Ong, W.J. (1982). *Orality and literacy: The technologizing of the word*. New York: Methuen.

Osen, L. (1974). *Women in mathematics*. Cambridge, MA: MIT Press.

Palincsar, A.S., & Brown, A.L. (1984). Reciprocal teaching of comprehension-fostering and comprehension-monitoring activities. *Cognition and Instruction, 1,* 117–175.

Papert, S. (1972a). Teaching children thinking. *Programmed Learning and Educational Technology, 9,* 245–255.

Papert, S. (1972b). Teaching children to be mathematicians versus teaching about mathematics. *International Journal for Mathematical Education, Science and Technology, 3,* 249–262.

Papert, S. (1980). *Mindstorms: Children, computers, and powerful ideas*. New York: Basic Books.

Papert, S., Watt, D., diSessa, A., & Weir, S. (1979). *An assessment and documentation of a children's computer laboratory*. Final Report of the Brookline LOGO Project: Cambridge, MA: Massachusetts Institute of Technology, Department of Artificial Intelligence.

Paris, P., Scardamalia, M., & Bereiter, C. (1984, April). *Construction and use of goal hierarchies in writing*. Paper presented at the meeting of the American Educational Research Association, New Orleans, LA.

Parsons, J., Kaczala, C., & Muce, J. (1982). Socialization of achievement attitudes and beliefs: Classroom influences. *Child Development, 53,* 322–339.

Pea, R.D. (1982). What is planning development the development of? In D. Forbes & M. Greenberg (Eds.), *New directions in child development: Children's planning strategies* (pp. 5–27). San Francisco: Jossey-Bass.

Pea, R.D. (1983, April). Logo programming and problem solving. In K. Sheingold (Chair), *Chameleon in the classroom: Developing roles for computers*. Symposium conducted at dren and Technology, April 1983).

Pea, R.D. (1984). Symbol systems and thinking skills: Logo in context. *Preproceedings of the 1984 National Logo Conference*, Massachusetts Institute of Technology, Cambridge, MA.

Pea, R.D., & Hawkins, J. (1984). Children's planning processes in a chore-scheduling task. In S.L. Friedman, E.K. Scholnick, & R.R. Cocking (Eds.), *Blueprints for thinking: The development of social and cognitive planning skills*. New York: Cambridge University Press.

Pea, R.D., Hawkins, J., Clement, C.A., & Mawby, R. (1984). *The development of expertise in Logo by children*. New York: Bank Street College of Education, Center for Children and Technology.

Pea, R.D., & Kurland, D.M. (1984a). *Logo programming and the development of planning skills* (Tech. Rep. No. 16). New York: Bank Street College of Education, Center for Children and Technology.

Pea, R.D., & Kurland, D.M. (1984b). On the cognitive effects of learning computer programming. *New Ideas in Psychology, 2*(2), 137–168.

Pea, R.D., & Kurland, D.M. (in press). Cognitive technologies for writing. *Review of Research in Education, 13.*

Peden, I. (1975, January). The missing half of our technical potential: Can we motivate the girls? *The Mathematics Teacher,* 2–12.

Perfetti, C.A. (1983). Reading, vocabulary, and writing: Implications for computer-based instruction. In A.C. Wilkinson (Ed.), *Classroom computers and cognitive science.* New York: Academic Press.

Piaget, J. (1960). *The psychology of intelligence.* Totowa, NJ: Littlefield & Adams.

Piaget, J. (1962). *Play, dreams and imitation in childhood.* New York: Norton.

Piaget, J. (1965). *The moral judgement of the child.* New York: Free Press.

Piaget, J. (1969). *The child's conception of time* (A.J. Pomerans, Trans.). New York: Ballantine.

Piaget, J. (1970). Piaget's theory. In P.H. Mussen (Ed.), *Carmichael's manual of child psychology.* New York: Wiley.

Piaget, J. (1971). *Biology and knowledge.* London: Routledge & Kegan Paul.

Piaget, J. (1972). Intellectual evolution from adolescence to adulthood. *Human Development, 15,* 1–12.

Piaget, J. (1973a). *The child and reality: Problems of genetic psychology.* New York: Grossman.

Piaget, J. (1973b). *To understand is to invent.* New York: Grossman.

Piaget, J. (1976). *The grasp of consciousness.* London: Routledge & Kegan Paul.

Piaget, J. (1983). Piaget's theory. In W. Kessen (Ed.), *History, theory, and methods* (Vol. I), of P.H. Mussen (Ed.), *Handbook of child psychology* (4th ed.). New York: Wiley.

Piaget, J., & Inhelder, B. (1969). *The psychology of the child.* New York: Basic Books.

Podemski, R.S. (1984, May). Implications of electronic learning technology: The future is now! *T.H.E. Journal,* 118–121.

Pogrow, S. (1985, December). *An evaluation of the effectiveness of the HOTS Program.* Paper prepared for review by the JDRP Committee of the National Diffusion Network. Washington, DC: National Diffusion Network.

Polya, G. (1957). *How to solve it: A new aspect of mathematical method* (2nd ed.). Garden City, NY: Doubleday-Anchor.

Pressley, M., & Forrest-Pressley, D. (1985). Questions and children's cognitive processing. In A.C. Graesser & J.B. Black (Eds.), *The psychology of questions.* Hillsdale, NJ: Erlbaum.

Price-Williams, D., Gordon, W., & Ramirez, M. (1969). Skill and conservation: A study of pottery-making children. *Developmental Psychology, 1,* 769.

Quality Education Data. (1984, January) [Microcomputer data]. Unpublished raw data presented to the Naval Materials Council, Dallas, TX.

Quinsaat, M.G., Levin, J.A., Boruta, M., & Newman, D. (1983, April). *The effects of microcomputer word processing on elementary school writing.* Paper presented at the meeting of the American Educational Research Association, Montreal, Canada.

Rampy, L.M. (1984, April). *The problem solving style of fifth graders using Logo.* Paper presented at the meeting of the American Educational Research Association, New Orleans, LA.

Rescher, N. (1982). *Empirical inquiry.* Totowa, NJ: Rowman & Littlefield.

Resnick, L.B. (1981). Instructional psychology. *Annual Review of Psychology, 32,* 659–704.

Resnick, L.B. (1984). Toward a cognitive theory of instruction. In S. Paris, G. Olson, & H. Stevenson (Eds.), *Learning and motivation in the classroom.* Hillsdale, NJ: Erlbaum.

Resnick, L.B. (1985). *Cognition and the curriculum.* Invited address at the meeting of the American Educational Research Association, Chicago, IL.

Resnick, D.P., & Resnick, L.B. (1977). The nature of literacy: An historical exploration. *Harvard Educational Review, 47*(3), 370–385.

Rich, C., & Shrobe, H.E. (1978). Initial report on a Lisp programmer's apprentice. *IEEE Transactions on Software Engineering, SE-4,* 456–467.

Riche, R.W., Heckler, D.E., & Burgan, J.U. (1983). High technology today and tomorrow:

A small slice of the employment pie. *Monthly Labor Review,* 106(11), 50–58.

Rieger, C. (1977). Spontaneous computation in cognitive models. *Cognitive Science, 1,* 315–354.

Riel, M. (1983, February). Education and ecstasy: Computer chronicles of students' writing together. *The Quarterly Newsletter of the Laboratory of Comparative Human Cognition, 5*(3), 59–67.

Riel, M. (1984). The introduction of computers and the possibility of change. In H. Mehan & R. Souviney (Eds.), *The write help: A handbook for computers in classrooms.* La Jolla: CA: University of California, San Diego, Center for Human Information Processing.

Riel, M., Levin, J.A., & Miller-Souviney, B. (1984). *Dynamic support: Interactive software development.* Paper presented at the meeting of the American Educational Research Association, New Orleans, LA.

Roberts, T., & Char, C. (1982). *In-house memos: Teacher panel reports* (Nos. 1–3). New York: Bank Street College of Education, Center for Children and Technology.

Rogoff, B., & Lave, J. (Eds.). (1984). *Everyday cognition: Its development in social context.* Cambridge, MA: Harvard University Press.

Rogoff, B., & Wertsch, J.V. (Eds.). (1984). *Children's learning in the "zone of proximal development".* San Francisco: Jossey-Bass.

Ross, P., & Howe, J. (1981). Teaching mathematics through programming: Ten years on. In R. Lewis & D. Tagg (Eds.), *Computers in education.* Amsterdam: North-Holland.

Rowe, M.B. (1973). *Teaching science as continuous inquiry.* New York: McGraw-Hill.

Rubin, A., & Bruce, B. (in press). QUILL: Reading and writing with a microcomputer. In B.A. Jutson (Ed.), *Advances in reading/language research* (Vol. III). Greenwich, CT: JAI Press.

Russell, B. (1959). *The problem of philosophy.* London: Oxford University Press.

Salomon, G. (1974). What is learned and how it is taught: The interaction between media, message, task and learner. In D.E. Olson (Ed.), *Media and symbols: The forms of expression, communication, and education.* Chicago: University of Chicago Press.

Saunders, J. (1978, May). What are the real problems involved in getting computers into the high school? *The Mathematics Teacher,* 443–447.

Scardamalia, M., & Bereiter, C. (1983). The development of evaluative, diagnostic, and remedial capabilities in children's composing. In M. Martlew (Ed.), *The psychology of written language: A developmental approach.* London: Wiley.

Scardamalia, M., & Bereiter, C. (1984). *Development of strategies in text processing* (occasional paper No. 3). Ontario: Ontario Institute for Studies in Education, Centre for Applied Cognitive Science.

Schank, R. (1982). *Dynamic memory.* New York: Cambridge University Press.

Schank, R.C., & Abelson, R.P. (1977). *Scripts, plans, goals and understanding.* Hillsdale, NJ: Erlbaum.

Schoenfeld, A.H. (1983). Episodes and executive decisions in mathematical problem solving. In R. Lesh & M. Landau (Eds.), *Acquisition of mathematics concepts and processes.* New York: Academic Press.

Scribner, S. (1977). Modes of thinking and ways of speaking: Culture and logic reconsidered. In P.N. Johnson-Laird & P.C. Wason (Eds.), *Thinking: Readings in cognitive science.* New York: Cambridge University Press.

Scribner, S., & Cole, M. (1981). *The psychology of literacy.* Cambridge, MA: Harvard University Press.

Shavelson, R.J., Winkler, J.D., Stasz, C., Feibel, W., Robyn, A.E., & Shaha, S. (1984, March). *"Successful teachers' patterns of microcomputer-based mathematics and science instruction* (N-2170-NIE/RC). Report to the National Institute of Education. Santa Monica: CA: Rand Corp.

Sheil, B.A. (1980). Teaching procedural literacy. *Proceedings of ACM Annual Conference*, 125–126.

Sheil, B.A. (1981, March). Coping with complexity. *Xerox Cognitive and Instructional Sciences Series, CIS-15*.

Sheingold, K., Hawkins, J., & Char, C. (1984). "I'm the thinkist, you're the typist": The interaction of technology and the social life of classrooms. *Journal of Social Issues, 40*(3), 49–61.

Sheingold, K., Hawkins, J., & Kurland, D.M. (1983). *Software for the information age*. Manuscript submitted for publication.

Sheingold, K., Kane, J., & Endreweit, M. (1983). Microcomputer use in schools: Developing a research agenda. *Harvard Educational Review, 53*(4), 412–432.

Sheingold, K., Kane, J., Endreweit, M., & Billings, K. (1981). *Study of issues related to implementation of computer technology in schools* (Tech. Rep. No. 2). New York: Bank Street College of Education, Center for Children and Technology.

Sheppard, S.B., Curtis, B., Milliman, P., & Love, T. (1979). Modern coding practices and programmer performance. *IEEE Computer, 5*(2), 41–49.

Shif, Z.I. (1969). Development of children in schools for mentally retarded. In M. Cole & I. Maltzman (Eds.), *A handbook of contemporary Soviet psychology*. New York: Basic Books.

Shneiderman, B. (1977). Measuring computer program quality and comprehension. *International Journal of Man-Machine Studies, 9*, 465–478.

Shortliffe, E.H. (1976). *Computer-based clinical therapeutics: MYCIN*. New York: American Elsevier.

Shrobe, H.E., Waters, R., & Sussman, G. (1979). *A hypothetical monologue illustrating the knowledge of underlying program analysis* (Memo No. 507). Cambridge, MA: MIT Artificial Intelligence Laboratory.

Shweder, R.S. (Ed.). (1980). *Fallible judgment in behavioral research*. San Franscico: Jossey-Bass.

Siegel, L.S., & Brainerd, C.J. (Eds.). (1978). *Alternatives to Piaget*. New York: Academic Press.

Siegler, R.S. (1981). Developmental sequences within and between concepts. *Monographs of the Society for Research in Child Development, 46*(2, Serial No. 189).

Siegler, R.S. (1983). Information-processing approaches to development. In W. Kessen (Ed.), *History, theory, and methods* (Vol. I), of P.H. Mussen (Ed.), *Handbook of child psychology* (4th ed.). New York: Wiley.

Sime, M.E., Arblaster, A.T., & Green, T.R.G. (1977). Reducing programming errors in nested conditionals by prescribing a writing procedure. *International Journal of Man-Machine Studies, 9*, 119–126.

Simon, H.A. (1973). Does scientific discovery have a logic? *Philosophy of Science, 40*, 471–480.

Simon, H.A. (1977a). *Models of discovery*. Dordrecht, Holland: Reidel.

Simon, H.A. (1977b). What computers mean for man and society. *Science, 195*, 1186–1191.

Simon, H.A. (1980). Problem solving and education. In D.T. Tuma & F. Reif (Eds.), *Problem solving and education: Issues in teaching and research*. New York: Halsted Press.

Simon, H.A. (1982, June). *Cognitive processes of experts and novices*. Talk given at Cahiers de la Foundation Archives Jean Piaget, No. 2–3, Geneva, Switzerland.

Simon, H.A., & Hayes, J.R. (1976). The understanding process: Problem isomorphs. *Cognitive Psychology, 8*, 165–190.

Simmons, W. (1985). Social class and ethnic differences in cognition: A cultural practice perspective. In S.F. Chipman, J.W. Segal, & R. Glaser (Eds.), *Thinking and learning skills* (Vol. 2). Hillsdale, NJ: Erlbaum.

Simpson, L. (1978). Girls and science careers: A program for change. *Tabs, 1,* 3–4.

Sizer, T.R. (1984). *Horace's compromise: The dilemma of the American high school.* Boston: Houghton Mifflin.

Sleeman, D., & Brown, J.S. (Eds.). (1982). *Intelligent tutoring systems.* New York: Academic Press.

Smith, E.E., & Bruce, B.C. (1981). *An outline of a conceptual framework for the teaching of thinking skills* (Report No. 4844). Prepared for National Institute of Education. Cambridge, MA: Bolt Beranek & Newman.

Snyder, T. (1984, June). Tom Snyder: Interview. *inCider,* pp. 42–48.

Soloway, E., Bonar, J., & Ehrlich, K. (1983). Cognitive strategies and looping constructs: An empirical study. *Communications of the ACM, 26,* 853–860.

Soloway, E., & Ehrlich, K. (1982, August 4–6). Tacit programming knowledge. *Proceedings of the Fourth Annual Conference of the Cognitive Science Society,* Ann Arbor, MI.

Soloway, E., Ehrlich, K., Bonar, J., & Greenspan, J. (1982). What do novices know about programming? In B. Shneiderman & A. Badre (Eds.), *Directions in human-computer interactions.* Norwood, NJ: Ablex.

Soloway, E., Lochhead, J., & Clement, J. (1982). Does computer programming enhance problem solving ability? Some positive evidence on algebra word problems. In R. Seidel, R. Anderson, & B. Hunter (Eds.), *Computer literacy: Issues and directions for 1985.* New York: Academic Press.

Soloway, E., Rubin, E., Woolf, B., Bonar, J., & Johnson, W.L. (1982, December). *MENO-II: An AI-based programming tutor* (Research Report No. 258). New Haven: Yale University, Department of Computer Science.

Souviney, R., Martin, L., & Black, S. (1984, July). Final Report of the Mathematics Project, University of California, San Diego.

Spiro, R.J. (1980). Constructive processes in prose recall. In R.J. Spiro, B.C. Bruce, & W.F. Brewer (Eds.), *Theoretical issues in reading comprehension: Perspectives in cognitive psychology, linguistics, artificial intelligence and education.* Hillsdale, NJ: Erlbaum.

Sprio, R.J., Bruce, B.C., & Brewer, W.F. (Eds.). (1980). *Theoretical issues in reading comprehension: Perspectives in cognitive psychology, linguistics, artificial intelligence and education.* Hillsdale, NJ: Erlbaum.

Statz, J. (1973). *Problem solving and Logo.* Final report of Syracuse University Logo Project, Syracuse University, New York.

Stefik, M.J., & de Kleer, J. (1983, April). Prospects for expert systems in CAD. *Computer Design,* 65–76.

Stein, A., & Smithells, J. (1969). Age and sex differences in children's sex-role standards about achievement. *Developmental Psychology, 1,* 252–259.

Sternberg, R.J., & Rifkin, B. (1979). The development of analogical reasoning processes. *Journal of Experimental Child Psychology, 27,* 195–232.

Stevens, A.L., Collins, A., & Goldin, S. (1979). Misconceptions in students' understanding. *International Journal of Man-Machine Studies, 11,* 145–156.

Suchman, J.R. (1962, June). *The elementary school training program in scientific inquiry* (Project No. 216). National Defense Education Act of 1958, University of Illinois.

Sutton-Smith, B. (1972). *The folkgames of children.* Austin: University of Texas Press.

Tally, W., & Char, C. (1985). *Children's understanding of the unique features of interactive videodiscs.* New York: Bank Street College of Education, Center for Children and Technology.

Task Force on Education for Economic Growth. (1983, June). *Action for excellence: A comprehensive plan to improve our nation's schools.* Washington, DC: Author.

Taylor, R. (1983). Equity in mathematics: A case study. *The Mathematics Teacher, 76,* 12–17.

Tharp, R.G. (1982). The effective instruction of comprehension: Results and description of the Kamehameha early education program. *Reading Research Quarterly, 17*(4), 501–527.

Thayer, R.H., Pyster, A.B., & Wood, R.C. (1981). Major issues in software engineering project management. *IEEE Transactions on Software Engineering, SE-7,* 333–342.

Tikhomirov, O.K. (1981). The psychological consequences of computerization. In J.V. Wertsch (Ed.), *The concept of activity in Soviet psychology.* New York: Sharpe.

Toulmin. S.E. (1972). *Human understanding* (Vol. I). Princeton, NJ: Princeton University Press.

Toulmin, S.E. (1982). The construal of reality: Criticism in modern and postmodern science. *Critical Inquiry, 9,* 93–111.

Tuma, D.T., & Reif, F. (Eds.). (1980). *Problem solving and education: Issues in teaching and research.* Hillsdale, NJ: Erlbaum.

Turing, A.M. (1950). Computing machinery and intelligence. *Mind, 59,* 433–460.

United States Department of Commerce. (1982–83). *Statistical abstract of the United States (1982–1983).* Washington, DC.

VanLehn, K. (1981, March). Bugs are not enough: Empirical studies of bugs, impasses and repairs in procedural skills. *Xerox Cognitive and Instructional Sciences Series, CIS-111.*

Videodisc Design/Production Group. (1979). *A summary of research on potential educational markets for videodisc.* Lincoln: University of Nebraska.

Voss, S.F., Greene, T.R., Post, T.A., & Penner, B.C. (1983). Problem-solving skill in the social sciences. In G. Bower (Ed.), *The psychology of learning and motivation* (Vol. 17). New York: Academic Press.

Vygotsky, L.S. (1978). *Mind in society: The development of higher psychological processes* (M. Cole, V. John-Steiner, S. Scribner, & E. Souberman, Eds.). Cambridge, MA: Harvard University Press.

Waddington, C.H. (1977). *Tools for thought: How to understand and apply the latest scientific techniques of problem solving.* New York: Basic Books.

Walberg, H.J. (1984). Improving the productivity of America's schools. *Educational Leadership, 41*(3), 19–26.

Waldrop, M.M. (1984). The necessity of knowledge. *Science, 223,* 1279–1282.

Wason, P.C., & Johnson-Laird, P.N. (1972). *Psychology of reasoning: Structure and content.* Cambridge, MA: Harvard University Press.

Waters, R.C. (1982). The programmer's apprentice: Knowledge based program editing. *IEEE Transactions on Software Engineering, SE-8*(1).

Watt, D. (1982, August). Logo in the schools. *Byte, 7*(8), 116–134.

Weir, S. (1981, May). *Logo as an information prosthetic for the handicapped* (Working paper No. WP-9). Cambridge, MA: Massachusetts Institute of Technology, Division for Studies and Research in Education.

Weir, S., & Watt, D. (1981). Logo: A computer environment for learning-disabled students. *The Computer Teacher, 8*(5), 11–17.

Werner, H. (1937). Process and achievement. *Harvard Educational Review, 7,* 353–368.

Werner, H. (1957). The concept of development from a comparative and organismic point of view. In D.R. Harris (Ed.), *The concept of development.* Minneapolis: University of Minnesota Press.

Whitehead, A.N. (1929). *The aims of education and other essays.* New York: Macmillan.

Wilkinson, A.C. (Ed.). (1983). *Classroom computers and cognitive science.* New York: Academic Press.

Wilson, K., Newman, D., & Char, C. (1985). *"The Voyage of the Mimi" disc: Development of an exploratory learning environment for children.* Paper presented at the meeting of the Society for Applied Learning Technology, Washington, DC.

Withrow, F., & Roberts, L. (1984). Educational perspectives. In R. Daynes & B Butler

(Eds.), *The videodisc book* (pp. 97–99). New York: Wiley.

Yevick, M. (1970). Some thoughts on women in science. *Technology Review, 72*.

Young, R.M. (1981). The machine inside the machine: Users' models of pocket calculators. *International Journal of Man-Machine Studies, 15*, 51–85.

Youngs, E.A. (1974). Human errors in programming. *International Journal of Man-Machine Studies, 6*, 361–376.

SOFTWARE REFERENCES

Apollo Space Disc. Space Archives Series, Video Vision Associates, Ltd., 39 East 21st Street, New York, NY 10010.

AppleWriter. Apple Computer, 20525 Mariani Avenue, Cupertino, CA 95014.

Bank Street Writer. Broderbund Software, 1938 Fourth Street, San Rafael, CA 94901.

Bio Sci Disc. Videodiscovery, Inc., P.O. Box 85878, Seattle, WA 98145.

EasyWriter. Information Unlimited Software, Inc., 2401 Marinship Way, Sausalito, CA 94965.

Ecosystems, Bank Street College Project in Science and Mathematics. Holt, Rinehart & Winston, 393 Madison Avenue, New York, NY 10017.

EMACS. Digital Equipment Corporation, 200 Baker Avenue, West Concord, MA 01742.

Framework. Ashton-Tate, 10150 West Jefferson Boulevard, Culver City, CA 90230.

ICE. University of Illinois, Champaign, IL.

Interactive Text Interpreter. Interlearn, Inc., P.O. Box 342, Cardiff By The Sea, CA 92007.

Introduction to Computing, Bank Street College Project in Science and Mathematics. Holt, Rinehart & Winston, 393 Madison Avenue, New York: NY 10017.

Maps and Navigation, Bank Street College Project in Science and Mathematics. Holt, Rinehart & Winston, 393 Madison Avenue, New York, NY 10017.

National Gallery of Art Disc. Videodisc Publishing, Inc., 381 Park Avenue South, Suite 1601, New York, NY 10016.

Planner. Bolt Beranek and Newman, Inc., 10 Moulton Street, Cambridge, MA 02238.

Quill. Bolt Beranek and Newman, Inc., 10 Moulton Street, Cambridge, MA 02238.

The Random House Thesaurus. Dictronics Publishing, Inc., 362 5th Avenue, New York, NY 10001.

Scripsit. Tandy/Radio Shack, One Tandy Center, Fort Worth, TX 76102.

Space Shuttle. Space Archives Series, Video Vision Associates, Ltd., 39 East 21st Street, New York, NY 10010.

Story Maker. Bolt Beranek and Newman, Inc., 10 Moulton Street, Cambridge, MA 02238.

TECO. Digital Equipment Corporation, 200 Baker Avenue, West Concord, MA 01742.

Thinktank. Living Videotext, Inc., 450 San Antonio Road, Suite 56, Palo Alto, CA 94306.

UNIX. AT&T Bell Laboratories, 6 Corporate Place, Piscataway, NJ 08854.

Vincent Van Gogh Disc. Philips International/North American Philips Corp., 100 East 42nd Street, New York, NY 10017.

VisiWord. VisiCorp, 2895 Zanker Road, San Jose, CA 95134.

Whales and Their Environment, Bank Street College Project in Science and Mathematics. Holt, Rinehart & Winston, 393 Madison Avenue, New York, NY 10017.

The Word Plus. Oasis Systems, 2765 Reynard Way, San Diego, CA 92103.

WordStar. MicroPro International Corporation, 33 San Palo Avenue, San Rafael, CA 94903.

Writer's Workbench. AT&T Bell Laboratories, 6 Corporate Place, Piscataway, NJ 08854.

AUTHOR INDEX

A

Abelson, R.P., 93, 156, 278, *299, 314*
Adams, M.J., 92, *299*
Adelson, B., 163, *299*
Adler, M.J., 73, *299*
Anderson, J.R., 130, 136, 161, *299, 300*
Anderson, R.E., 159, *299*
Arbitman-Smith, R., 278–279, *300*
Arblaster, A.T., 157, *315*
Arons, R.B., 146, *299*
Atwood, M.E., 162–163, 170, 182, *299*

B

Baillargeon, R., 200, *305*
Baillio, J., 226, *301*
Baker, D., 246, *304*
Bamberger, J., 185, 204, *299*
Barclay, J.R., 93, *300*
Barnhardt, C , 99, *299*
Barr, A., 129, *300*
Barstow, D.R., 162, *300, 306*
Bastian, A., 87, *300*
Bayman, P., 165, *309*
Becker, H.J., 244, *300*
Bennett, J., 129, *300*
Bentley, A.F., 205, *304*
Bereiter, C., 158, 161, 275, 279–280, *300, 312, 314*
Berger, C., 171, 204, 251–252, *306*
Berliner, D., 74, *300*
Berman, P., 36–37, 48, 79, *300*
Bernard, J.E., 173, *302*
Bernstein, A., 67, *300*
Billings, K., 72–73, 75, 171, *315*
Black, J., 45
Black, S.D., 77, 161, *300, 316*
Blanshard, B., 277, *300*

Bloom, M., 152, 171–172, 180, *305*
Bobyn, A.E., 56, 89, 99, *314*
Boden, M.A., 139, *300*
Bonar, J., 157, 162, 175, 182, *300, 316*
Borst, M.A., 163, *303*
Boruta, M., 65, 204, *308, 313*
Boktin, J., 70, *300*
Bovet, M., 168, *307*
Boyle, C.F., 130, 136, *300*
Brainerd, C., 200, *315*
Bransford, J.D., 93, 139, 155, 157, 159, 176, 278–279, *300, 301*
Brewer, W.F., 163, *316*
Brooks, F.P., Jr., *300*
Brooks, R.E., 162, 170, 176, 181, *300*
Brown, A.L., 135–136, 139, 155, 157, 159–160, 163, 169, 176, 278, 280, *301, 312*
Brown, J.F., 77, *301*
Brown, J.S., 130, 135–136, 138–139, 162, 173, 276, *301, 303, 316*
Brown, R.D., 226, *301*
Bruce, B., 97, 163, 176, 278–279, *314, 316*
Bruner, J.S., 133, 142, 148, 274, *301, 312*
Brush, L.E., 246, 249, *301*
Buchanan, B.G., 128, *309*
Bunderson, C.B., 226, *301*
Burgan, J.U., 69–70, *313*
Burns, G., 74, *301*
Burton, G., 244, 246, *301*
Burton, R.R., 75, 130, 173, *301–302*
Byte, 178, *302*

C

Carbonell, J.G., 144, *310*
Cahir, N., 103–104, 203, 254, 268, *308*
Campione, J.C., 139, 155, 157, 159, 176, *301*

319

SUBJECT INDEX

A
Advance organizer, 160
AlgebraLand, 139
Artificial intelligence, 128–131, 134–135,
  136–137, 140–141, 142–143, 145

B
Bank Street College Projects
  Information Managing Tools Project,
    260–263, 273–298
  Interactive Video Project, 223–241
  Logo learning, 3–34, 60–62, 178–196
  MASTTE, 39–56
  science and mathematics education,
    35–56
Bank Street Filer, 96
Bank Street Speller, 98
Bank Street StoryBook, 96–97
Bank Street Writer, 97–98
Basic skills, *see Competency-based programs*
Behaviorism, 148
"Buggy" understanding, 135–136,
  138–139, 173

C
Cognitive science, 134–135, 144–145, 146
Cognitive trace systems, 137–138–139
Collaboration-cooperation, *see Peer
  collaboration, cooperation*
Competency-based programs, 88, 89–90,
  93–94
Computer Chronicles, 97
Computer literacy, 90, 96–98, 164–165, 172
Constructivism, 131–132, 152
Curriculum
  change in information age, 67–69, 73,
    75–76, 128–131

Curriculum (cont.)
  computer programming in, 103–104,
    109–110, 147–149, 160–161, 163–164
  integration of computers in, 73

D
Database management tools (DBMs),
    79–80, 96–97, 260–263
  Bank Street Filer, 96–97
  QUILL Library, 96–97
Decentering, 108, 112–113
Decomposition, analytic-synthetic,
    119–122
Developmental cognitive science, 147–152
Developmental theory, 135–145, 149–152
  accelerated learning, 142–143
  constructivism, 131–132, 152
  decalage, 134
  developmental technologies, 134–135
  and human-computer intelligent
    systems, 135–145
  information processing limits, 139–141
  sociocultural factors, 132–133
  stage theory, 131–132
  zone of proximal development, 133,
    135, 136–137, 143
    defined, 133
    use of computer tools in, 136–137
Discovery learning, 60–62, 107, 110,
    125–127, 132–133, 135, 137–138, 152,
    159–160, 178–179, 193, 195, 196

E
Elementary school, 198–208
  uses of microcomputers in, 202–206
  software as cognitive support during,
    203–204

325